Economic Cooperation
in the Middle East

Economic Cooperation in the Middle East

EDITED BY
Gideon Fishelson

Westview Press
BOULDER, SAN FRANCISCO, & LONDON

Westview Special Studies on the Middle East

Copyright © 1989 by Westview Press, Inc.

Published in 1989 in the United States of America by Westview Press, Inc., 5500 Central Avenue, Boulder, Colorado 80301, and in the United Kingdom by Westview Press, Inc., 13 Brunswick Centre, London WC1N 1AF, England

Library of Congress Cataloging-in-Publication Data
Economic cooperation in the Middle East.
  1. Middle East—Economic conditions. 2. Middle
East—Economic integration. 3. Jewish-Arab relations—
Economic aspects. 4. Economic development projects—
Middle East. I. Fishelson, Gideon.
HC15.15.E28 1989 337.1'5   88-26138
ISBN 0-8133-7535-5

Printed and bound in the United States of America

The paper used in this publication meets the requirements of the American National Standard for Permanence of Paper for Printed Library Materials Z39.48-1984

10   9   8   7   6   5   4   3   2   1

Contents

Preface, *Haim Ben-Shahar*   vii

Editor's Remarks, *Gideon Fishelson*   ix

Contributors and Their Affiliations   xi

Introduction, *Haim Ben-Shahar*   1

I.   THE PRE-PEACE ERA
        (ECONOMIC CONSIDERATIONS)   13

        1.   The Economic Burden of the Arms Race in
             the Middle East, *Eliezer Sheffer*   15
        2.   The Economic Aspects of Peace in the Middle
             East: Oil and the Arms Race, *Eliyahu Kanovsky*   31
        3.   Open Borders and Labor Mobility: Israel, the
             West Bank, and Gaza, *Ephraim Kleiman*   55
        4.   The Economics of Occupation in Palestine
             Since 1948 and the Costs of Noncooperation,
             Elias H. Tuma   79

II.   SOLUTIONS TO CONFLICTS
        AND THE RISKS OF COOPERATION   103

        5.   Arms Races and Arms Control in the Middle East,
             Michael D. Intriligator and *Dagobert L. Brito*   105
        6.   Economic Sanctions and the Middle East,
             Jeffrey J. Schott   123
        7.   Factor Migration, Trade, and Welfare Under
             Threat of Commercial Disruption, *Martin C. McGuire*   141

III.   REGIONAL COOPERATION: INTERNATIONAL
        EXPERIENCES AND OPTIONS AND THEIR
        IMPLICATIONS FOR THE MIDDLE EAST   161

        8.   A Marshall Plan for the Middle East: The U.S.
             Response, *Joyce R. Starr*   163
        9.   The Middle East Development Fund, *Amon Gafny*   167

v

10. Regional Integration in Latin America:
    The Experience and the Outlook
    for Further Cooperation, *Mario I. Blejer*   181
11. Technology: Development, International Trade
    and Cooperation, *Antonio Alonso-Concheiro*   209
12. The Effect of Science and Technology in Regional
    and Global Development, *Sam Nilsson*   237
13. Liberalization of Service Transactions, *Brian Hindley*   253

IV.   SUGGESTIONS FOR AND ANALYSIS OF SPECIFIC
    PROJECTS IN THE MIDDLE EAST   267

14. Trade Regimes in the Middle East, *Seev Hirsch*   269
15. The Economic Relations Between Israel and Egypt:
    Tourism, 1979–1984, *Yoram Meital*   283
16. The Potential for Cooperation in Water Projects
    in the Middle East at Peace, *Elisha Kally*   303
17. A Proposal for a Cooperative Water Project:
    The Aqaba-Eilat Canal/Port, *Baruch Raz*   327
18. The Multinational Business Development Fund:
    A Framework for Economic Cooperation
    and Peace in the Middle East, *Riad Ajami*   335
19. Key Findings of the Middle East Economic
    Cooperation Projects, *Gideon Fishelson*   347

Index   367

vi

Preface

This book contains the proceedings of the Armand Hammer Conference on Economic Cooperation in the Middle East that was held at Tel Aviv University on June 1–3, 1986. The conference was held under the auspices of the Armand Hammer Fund for Economic Cooperation in the Middle East Under Peace.

The objective of the Hammer Fund is to foster economic cooperation between Israel and her neighbors. Multinational economic relations can offer effective leverage in the political negotiations towards peace and — once it is attained — they can reinforce the countries concerned to become partners in prosperity. To this end the Fund seeks to identify areas of mutual economic interest and recommend specific joint economic projects.

The success of the conference was due first and foremost to the contribution made by all participants, and to the valuable cooperation and advice of the members of the academic committee: Professors Seev Hirsch, Baruch Raz, Gideon Fishelson, and the academic coordinator Dr. Leonardo Leiderman; the advisors, Professors Itamar Rabinowitz and Assaf Razin; and to the administrative staff, Yoram Shamir, Gerda Kessler, Esther Landau, Lionel Pyetan and particularly to Ruth Kimmel.

Professor Haim Ben-Shahar
Head, Steering Committee

Editor's Remarks

The editorial board of the Proceedings of the Armand Hammer Conference on Economic Cooperation in the Middle East is proud to present this collection of studies presented at the conference.

This conference was the first in which politicians, academicians, policymakers and business entrepreneurs discussed the opportunities as well as the risks, benefits, and economic costs that peace offers and involves.

Although the framework for the conference was the Middle East, contributors also consider experience from other tense parts of the world, which face similar problems. Such experience can provide examples and guidelines for possible benefits that peace in the Middle East might open up.

The conference took place at Tel Aviv University, which provided an academic atmosphere and helped attract top quality lectures and interested participants.

In light of the diverse economic aspects of the peace process, the conference was divided into 7 sessions, each dealing with a fairly homogeneous topic. This volume contains revised versions of the papers presented at the conference sessions and reflects discussions of each study and its ramifications as well as additional ideas that came forth.

The editorial board would like to thank all those that contributed to the success of the conference. Their effort was rewarded and will be further recognized and appreciated in the future.

The volume opens with an overview of the research effort encouraged and financed by the Armand Hammer Fund for Economic Cooperation in the Middle East. The overview is written by Professor Ben Shahar, who initiated the research at Tel Aviv University.

The following collection of studies is divided into four sections:

The first section deals with the pre-peace era, which is typified by the military buildup and its corresponding heavy economic costs (Sheffer, Kanovsky) and by occupier-occupied relations (Kleiman, Tuma).

The second section focuses on solutions to conflicts (Intriligator and Brito), methods to achieve their resolution such as sanctions (Schott), and risks of cooperation (McGuire).

The third section examines economic integration in the Middle East, its implications and possible costs. It also explores means of financing economic integration projects and the experience of other regions (Starr, Gafny, Blejer, Concheiro, Nilsson, Hindley).

The fourth section analyzes the consequences of peace and economic cooperation in the Middle East (Hirsch, Meital, Kally, Raz, Ajami, Fishelson).

This division is meant to help guide the reader through the studies without implying anything about the relative significance of any specific section. The collection is a unified self-contained package, in which each study supports and is supported by the others. The editors feel it is the most comprehensive representation of current economic thinking on the issue of peacemaking that is now available.

The main idea that continually surfaced and that sums up the findings of the conference is that political and economic relations and agreements are strongly interrelated and must move forward simultaneously. One strengthens and reinforces the other and it is unlikely that either can stand alone.

Professor Gideon Fishelson
Scientific Coordinator of the "Economic
Cooperation in the Middle East
Under Peace" Research Project

Contributors and Their Affiliations

Riad Ajami, Director, Interdisciplinary Center for Technological Analysis and Forecasting at Tel Aviv University

Antonio Alonso-Concheiro, Foundacion Javier Barros Sierra, Mexico

Mario I. Blejer, International Monetary Fund, Washington, D.C.

Dagobert L. Brito, Department of Economics, Rice University

Gideon Fishelson, Professor, Department of Economics, Tel Aviv University, and Head, Economics Section, Interdisciplinary Center for Technological Analysis and Forecasting

Arnon Gafny, Chairman of the Board, Koor Industries, and former director, Bank of Israel

Brian Hindley, The World Bank, Washington, D.C.

Seev Hirsch, Jaffee Professor of International Trade, School of Business Administration, Tel Aviv University, and Visiting Research Fellow, Trade Policy Research Center, London

Michael D. Intriligator, Center for International and Strategic Studies, Departments of Economics and Political Science, UCLA

Elisha Kally, Interdisciplinary Center for Technological Analysis and Forecasting

Eliyahu Kanovsky, Professor of Economics, Bar Ilan University, Ramat Gan

Ephraim Kleiman, Professor of Economics, Hebrew University, Jerusalem

Martin C. McGuire, Department of Economics, University of Maryland

Yoram Meital, Department of Middle East History, University of Haifa

Sam Nilsson, International Federation of Institutes for Advanced Study (IFIAS), Sweden

Baruch Raz, Director, Interdisciplinary Center for Technological Analysis and Forecasting at Tel Aviv University

Jeffrey J. Schott, Institute for International Economics, Washington, D.C.

Eliezer Sheffer, Visiting Professor, Department of Economics, Hebrew University, Jerusalem

Joyce R. Starr, CSIS, Georgetown University, Washington, D.C.

Elias H. Tuma, Department of Economics, University of California at Davis

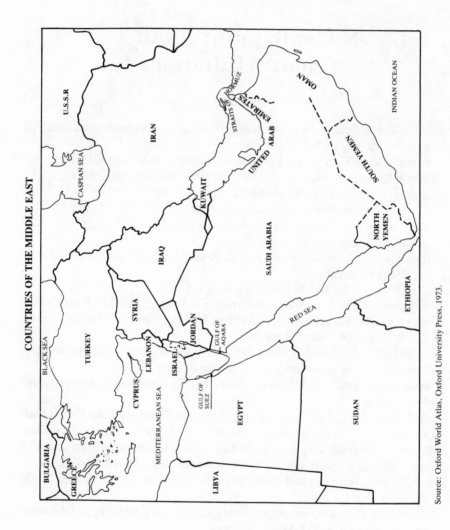

COUNTRIES OF THE MIDDLE EAST

Source: Oxford World Atlas, Oxford University Press, 1973.

Introduction

Economic Cooperation in the Middle East: From Dream to Reality

Opening Address*

Professor Haim Ben-Shahar

Lasting peace among nations is characterized by a broadly based network of relations among them, of which economic relations are a most important and definitive dimension. This is particularly true among neighboring countries. After the signing of the peace agreements by the nations of Europe at the end of the Second World War, economic relations began to develop, and within 12 years these led to the establishment, in 1957, of the European Economic Community, which included such previously long-term enemies as France and West Germany. Today the notion of an economically divided Europe is unthinkable. We believe that this example is applicable to the Middle East, once there is a breakthrough in negotiations towards peace.

---

*Delivered in the presence of His Excellency, the President of the State of Israel, Mr. Chaim Herzog; the Minister for Economic Affairs, Mr. Gad Ya'acobi; the Chairman of the Board of Governors of Tel Aviv University, Sir Leslie Porter; the President of Tel Aviv University, Professor Moshe Many and many other honored guests.

The purpose of this address is to present the Hammer Project on Economic Cooperation in the Middle East under peace, its roots, its history, its development, and the main findings of the research activities carried out within its framework.

■ The Background

The question may well be asked—why research the economics of peacemaking?

Until the visit of President Sadat to Jerusalem in 1977, the Israeli public did not believe in the reality of peace in our time. The main items on the national agenda, as expressed in both government policy and public opinion, were ensuring the very survival of the State, economic growth and accelerated population growth through immigration. There were other priorities, too, such as raising the educational level, cultural enrichment, and social and ethnic integration, and indeed, important advances were made in these areas.

However, one subject, planning and preparation for peace, was excluded from the agenda of priorities. There was, of course, a genuine desire for peace, but a belief in the possibility of its ever coming about in our time was lacking. The immediate needs of survival exhausted all existing resources, economic and social, as well as intellectual and psychological, leaving no room for contemplating and planning for the seemingly unrealistic notion of peace.

As long ago as the mid-1970s, we at Tel Aviv University believed it to be our national duty as scholars whose institution was supported by the public, to contribute to vital national concerns, which were within the realm of our competence in research, analysis and planning. Among the many and varied areas of our activities were, for example, the establishment of the Jaffee Center for Strategic Studies, which is concerned with strategic issues impinging upon the very existence of the State, and the Sapir Center for Development, which deals with issues of internal policy, particularly its economic and social dimensions.

Along with these, we decided to establish a framework for planning for peace. It was clear that the subject of peace was not receiving the attention it deserved, not, as already noted, for lack of a desire for peace, but because there were always more apparently urgent and immediately relevant needs. We felt we were well equipped to contribute to the advancement of this neglected, seemingly "abstract" process of thinking about and planning for peace. These efforts and activities require little in the way of money but much in the way of strongly motivated, dedicated and experienced researchers.

In 1976, while serving as President of Tel Aviv University, I broached the subject with several international personalities, requesting their help. Among those responding positively were David Rockefeller, the Chairman of the Board of Chase Manhattan, and William Simon, then U.S. Secretary of the Treasury. Together we drew up plans for the establishment of a center for research on international economic cooperation, the central concern of which was to be the Middle East. Then, in November, 1977, President Sadat made his historic peacemaking initiative.

The very real prospects for achieving a peace agreement with Egypt proved to us that we had been right in our insistence on the immediate necessity of planning for peace, and it was only a pity that we had not started even earlier.

Following President Sadat's visit to Jerusalem, we worked, together with David Rockefeller, on modifying our previous proposals, this time for joint economic research with an Egyptian university. David Rockefeller presented the proposals to President Sadat early in 1978, but by then the peace negotiations between the Egyptian and Israeli governments had already reached the state of crisis that was to continue until the Camp David meeting of September 1978, and the issue of joint research was left pending.

In view of the circumstances, we made a decision in the early months of 1978 that, whatever the Egyptian stand on joint research, we would go ahead independently, offering to join up with them at any time they saw fit. It was this decision that led us to Dr. Armand Hammer, Chairman of Occidental Petroleum.

Dr. Hammer has always seen the development of economic relations as an instrument for promoting peace. In 1978, we presented our plans to him and requested his support. This was two months prior to the signing of the Camp David accords, a time of crisis in the negotiations with Egypt. Without hesitation, Dr. Hammer agreed to lend us his support, even though the prospects for peace at that time appeared slim indeed. He gave generously of his own resources, recruited additional resources from among his friends, and gave the prestige of his name to the project. It may be safely said that without Dr. Hammer, his personality and drive, the project would never have come about.

In 1981 we embarked systematically upon our research projects, the main findings of which will be presented at this conference.

■ Principles Underlying Our Research

Economic factors play a decisive role in international relations, serving very often as a pretext for going to war and as a reason for peaceful alliances.

In the last decade the importance of oil and its crucial effect upon international relations have been only too well demonstrated. While the Israeli-Arab conflict is not over economic issues, they are expected, nevertheless, to play an important role, in the following respects.

1. Economic factors are likely to constitute an obstacle in political relations. For instance, the shortage of water in Israel, the Gaza Strip and the West Bank may well further aggravate the political conflict.

2. Economic factors may serve as compensation for political concessions, as, for instance, in the negotiations on the territory of Taba.

3. Most importantly, any peace agreement remains merely a piece of paper until it is reinforced by the development of a substantial and broad-ranging system of relations between the signatories. Cultural relations and joint sporting activities are both important but economic relations create a lasting interest in peace and therefore are still more important.

It is essential, furthermore, to plan the economic relations in a way which will bring about the desired results and avoid the undesirable, while taking into account a complex range of considerations:

a. The economic benefits must be shared equally between the sides. Moreover, for each side there must be a substantial level of benefit that justifies cooperation. Costs of dissociation, which increase the interest of all sides in peace, are also involved.

b. Care must be taken not to create one-way dependence in areas of vital interests. This will only deter the potentially dependent side from entering into the relationship and tempt the other side to exert pressure to obtain undue benefits.

c. The areas of cooperation must be chosen from among those which will cause a minimum of friction between the parties. This means that the projects must be of a type which benefit both sides equally rather than helping one side at the expense of the other.

d. The psychological aspect, too, must not be ignored. The subjects chosen must be such that each side feels its contribution is positive and made without loss of dignity. For instance, plans based on the Israeli brain and Arab brawn, though they may be economically worthwhile for all concerned, must be approached with hesitation, because they are psychologically problematic. Therefore, planning must be very cautious. Not all subjects that meet the economic criteria should be recommended.

Another guiding principle which directed our work was that the scope of research topics should be fundamental, thorough and long-term, and not subject to the vagaries of the political pendulum, of which there have been many.

We have gone ahead steadily with our work, without letting it be affected by the highly variable political situation, and are now prepared to place our proposals at the disposal of policymakers in Israel, in other countries of the

Middle East, and in friendly nations seeking to help in mediating the peace process in our region. Our work contains no classified material pertaining to security and is available to the public at large.

It is our aim to be prepared for the eventual arrival of suitable conditions for the implementation of one or another of our programs. Each of these could be implemented at the appropriate time, like contingency plans at a military headquarters.

■ The Potential for Economic Development in the Middle East

Peace may provide the momentum for economic development in the Middle East. The potential for such development lies in the area's natural resources and plentiful manpower. Manpower is not confined to Israel — one and a half million Egyptian teachers, engineers, scientists and managers are presently employed in the Gulf states, and numerous Palestinians are studying at universities in neighboring Arab countries. Potential markets exist and both foreign and local capital are available.

International corporations perceive the potential of the Middle East for large-scale economic and commercial growth and development. At present, however, they are deterred from embarking upon concrete ventures by political uncertainty and military risks.

We have investigated the potential for growth and development under conditions of peace and cooperation and have made a number of interesting estimates of growth which would be possible if there was peace. Within ten years of peace, the GNP of Israel could be about 22 percent higher than in the absence of peace. Had the peace process begun in 1982 with accelerated economic growth accompanying it, by 1992 Israel's GNP could have been $8.4 billion larger than is forecast with the continuation of existing conditions. Similar developments could have taken place in the Arab states bordering upon Israel: Egypt, Syria, Jordan and Lebanon. Had peaceful relations been established in 1982, the total GNP of these four countries could have been 24 percent, or $20 billion, higher after ten years. The standard of living and per capita consumption, and, of course, levels of investment would also have risen by similar percentages. (See Table 1.)

Accelerated growth under conditions of peace is due to the following factors:

*Defense expenditures would be lower, releasing more resources for investment and growth. Manpower employed by the military establishment, too, would be released for productive employment. This latter factor is particularly important for Israel, where military reserves duty obligations are particularly heavy.

Table 1
Supplemental Economic Growth Under Conditions of Peace

	Israel $billion	%	Neighboring Arab Countries $billion	%
GNP	8.4	22	20.0	24
Private consumption	3.5	18	9.2	15
Investments	4.3	55	11.7	52

* Under conditions of peace, more foreign capital for investment would be attracted to the region so the cost of capital would be reduced.
* Development of intraregional trade would increase economic efficiency and create additional sources of employment and opportunities for growth.
* Cooperation in economic projects, particularly in the development of the region's infrastructure, would also contribute to economic growth.

All these factors would contribute to an improvement in education levels achieved, in professional expertise, and in productivity.

■ Economic Development Plans

The work of the research program is conducted within the framework of the Interdisciplinary Center for Technological Analysis and Forecasting at Tel Aviv University by a team of researchers in the areas of economics, engineering, geography, statistics and other relevant disciplines.[1]

The following is a brief survey of the main research projects and their findings.

Water

The region suffers from an imbalance of water resources, shortages being particularly acute in the Gaza Strip and the West Bank, as well as in Israel. The water resources of the Gaza Strip and the West Bank today are only 250 million cubic meters per year, while demand is expected to increase to 600 million cubic meters within the next 15 years. At the same time, water surpluses from the Nile in Egypt and the Litani River in Lebanon flow unused into the Mediterranean and most of the winter floods of the Yarmouk River in Jordan are lost by evaporation after they flow into the Dead Sea. Jordan's agriculture is being retarded by the inadequacy of her water supplies.

Israel already utilizes all her available resources of surface and subterranean water, including the share of the Jordan River's headwaters allocated to her under the Johnston Plan of the 1950s. Israel, therefore, has no water resources available for diversion to the West Bank and Gaza Strip, and is, in fact, herself in need of additional water for which she is prepared to pay a high price, in view of the economic benefits associated with it. A regional water plan need not await the achievement of peace. To the contrary, its preparation, before a comprehensive peace settlement is attained, could help to clarify objectives to be aimed for in achieving peace.

Egypt has drawn up plans to convey one billion cubic meters of Nile water per year by canal to the Sinai Peninsula. This project could be extended to make it possible to purchase 350 million cubic meters for use in the Gaza Strip and the West Bank and 250 million cubic meters for use in Israel.

A regional water plan would provide the possibility for a water exchange scheme. It would be cheaper to supply Israel's Negev with Nile water than to pump water from the Sea of Galilee, as is presently being done. The water now supplying the Negev could be pumped from the Sea of Galilee to closer destinations on the West Bank.

Cooperation between Jordan and Israel would permit storing the Yarmouk's winter floodwater in the Sea of Galilee, for use by Jordan and the West Bank when needed. The cost of conveying Yarmouk water to the Sea of Galilee would be only $30 million, which is far less than from any other source, and the project would make it possible to utilize an additional 200 million cubic meters of water per year.

The project would support the peace process in that it would enable Jordan to expand the agricultural development of its main irrigated area, the Ghor Valley, and would offer some relief for Jordan's severe urban water shortages, as well as increasing water supplies to the West Bank.

The Litani waters are already fully utilized or earmarked for future Lebanese development projects. Nevertheless, marginal quantities (some 100 million cubic meters per year) might be allocated for a diversion into the Jordan River drainage basin, for supply to the West Bank, Jordan and — political circumstances permitting — also to Israel.

Energy

In the Middle East the imbalance in the distribution of energy resources is particularly acute. Israel and the four Arab countries directly bordering her lie outside or on the margin of the oil belt that stretches from Iran and Iraq to the Persian Gulf. Only Egypt and Syria have their own petroleum reserves, and these are not large enough to allow for long-term exports. Lebanon, Jordan and Israel have virtually no oil. However, an optimal utilization of energy resources which are available could be facilitated by cooperation. One potential type of cooperation could be overall integration of the electric power transmission grids of Israel, Egypt, Jordan and Lebanon. By taking advantage of the differences in peak demand periods, power supply shortages in one country might be made up from surpluses in the other, leading to a better utilization of power generation capacity and thereby reducing the overall cost of electric power.

Another area of potential cooperation is the generation of hydroelectric power. One such hydroelectric project would involve diverting water from the southern section of the Litani River to the Jordan basin, to take advantage of the greater descent to the Sea of Galilee (to 200 meters below sea level) than to the Mediterranean coast. The southern Litani waters thus diverted might then be used to supply the West Bank, Jordan or Israel. A second project which has been proposed is the joint Jordanian-Israeli production of hydroelectric power through exploiting the 400 meter elevation difference between the Mediterranean or the Red Sea and the Dead Sea.

Gas Pipeline

In Egypt, as elsewhere in the world, natural gas is found either associated with oil (in which case it must be separated from it) or in independent subterranean pockets. Liquefaction of natural gas for shipping, which is very capital-intensive, decreases the profitability of natural gas exploitation by adding substantially to its final sales price.

Our proposal calls for the construction of a natural gas pipeline from the Nile Delta to the Beer Sheva and Zohar regions, to supply industrial enterprises (mainly chemical) in the south of Israel, to the Ashdod power station, and to the Gaza Strip. The amount of gas transported annually would be 2 million tons of fuel oil equivalent (FOE), to be conveyed by a 28" pipeline, 290 km long. At $15 per barrel of FOE, the project would provide Egypt with an income of over $200 million per year and provide Israel with clean and relatively inexpensive fuel.

An Israel Terminal for the TAPLINE
(Trans-Arabian Pipeline)

The existing TAPLINE was constructed in the 1940s by Standard Oil of California and the Texas Oil Company for the export of Saudi Arabian oil to the West. With the outbreak of hostilities in Palestine in 1947, the entrepreneurs decided to divert the pipeline from Haifa to Sidon in Lebanon. The unrest that subsequently overtook Lebanon made the line inoperative.

Our proposal to reactivate the TAPLINE would involve its extension by a 150 km pipeline from Mafraq in Jordan to Haifa in Israel. This would reduce the cost of transporting oil to Israel, the West Bank and the Gaza Strip.

The main economic benefit of the proposed extension of the TAPLINE to Haifa, whose capacity will considerably exceed Israel's own oil requirements, would be as an outlet for exports of crude oil to Europe and to the U.S. The cost of tanker transport from the Persian Gulf to Europe via the Suez Canal is 40% higher than the potential cost of transporting it through the TAPLINE to Haifa and from there by tanker to Europe.

Agriculture

The high degree of complementarity between the agriculture of Egypt and of Israel affords considerable opportunities for mutually beneficial cooperation. Cooperation in agriculture, however, has more far-reaching political implications than economic relations in other areas. Firstly, agriculture in Egypt, as in many other countries, is inseparably intertwined with the country's social structure and culture. Secondly, the disparities in the main characteristics of the agricultural sectors of the two countries would make cooperation less symmetrical than in other areas of economic cooperation.

If Egypt were to reach a political decision to encourage agricultural cooperation with Israel, three areas would seem to be the most promising: bilateral trade in complementary farm products; the transfer of Israeli know-how, particularly in irrigation methods and development of desert crops; and joint ventures in setting up of farm and associated agro-industries in Egypt's "new lands," outside the traditional areas of the Nile Valley and Delta. Preliminary initiatives have already been made in some of these areas. Specific plans have been outlined by our research team.

The Fertilizer Industry

The fertilizer industries in Egypt and Israel exhibit numerous complementarities. Therefore, cooperation between them might yield substantial dividends in the form of a stronger competitive position for both of them in existing and new markets.

The three primary fertilizer ingredients are nitrogen (N), phosphorus (P) and potassium (K), and more advanced fertilizers are based upon PK, NP and NPK combinations. We propose construction of an industrial complex which would produce NPK fertilizers from an ammonia production unit of some 500,000 tons a year, which would be located in Egypt, and draw its potash requirements from Israel and its phosphates from both Israel and Egypt. The ammonia unit could offer about 20 per cent of its output to Israel in exchange for potash and phosphates. A third-country corporate partner could provide additional capital, expertise, marketing networks and mediation services, as well as security of supply in case of political or technical difficulties. The project might be expanded substantially if the parties decided to produce NPK products jointly for export.

Textiles

The Israeli clothing industry has established a strong market position in the Western European markets and, to a lesser degree, in the United States. An agreement with the European Economic Community guarantees most Israeli manufactures access on terms equal to those of E.E.C. producers. The Free Trade Area agreement signed with the U.S. in 1984 is expected to substantially improve Israel's position in that market as well.

The textiles and clothing industries of Egypt and Israel exhibit complementarities which might be used for creating a mutually beneficial division of labor. Israel could import the high value, long-staple cotton, for which Egypt is famous, to produce fine textile goods. Egypt could substitute the medium-staple cotton grown in Israel for Egyptian-grown cotton in the production of inexpensive clothing.

The most interesting potential for cooperation is to be found in the clothing industry. Both countries could learn from the example of the Western European clothing industry. It manages to survive despite fierce competition from both within and outside Europe, by breaking down the production process into several stages and carrying out each stage wherever there are competitive advantages vis-a-vis the rest of the world. Egypt has an obvious advantage in labor-intensive operations such as sewing. Israeli and Egyptian firms could therefore cooperate either by sub-contracting arrangements or through establishment of joint ventures. Egyptian firms could take advantage of Israel's capabilities in design, printing, dyeing and finishing.

Trade Relations

Four decades of hostility have precluded the possibility of any trade between Israel and her neighbors. The introduction of such trade relations may take two forms. The first is diversion of existing trade with other countries, and the second is creation of new trade when it is worthwhile for each side to replace existing production with purchases from the other. Conditions of peace, furthermore, may enable increases in output through joint ventures, to produce goods for joint export which were not hitherto manufactured by these countries.

Because of the importance of transportation and other transfer costs, and economies of scale, the benefits of bilateral trade can be substantial. In many countries, especially the smaller ones, so-called "border trade" makes up a large share of total commerce. A high proportion of international trade in perishable goods takes place between neighboring countries.

Our studies show that the potential trade diversion between Israel, Egypt, Jordan and Lebanon may amount to as much as $1 billion per year, excluding oil, which is already sold by Egypt to Israel. We estimate that $760 million of trade by Israel's neighbors may be diverted to Israel and some $240 million of Israeli trade might be diverted to Israel's neighbors, excluding oil. Two-thirds of the forecasted $1 billion of trade is expected to be conducted with Egypt and another one-sixth each with Jordan and Lebanon. In light of the peace with Egypt, suitable conditions already exist for the development of trade. Israel could sell electrical and metal goods to Egypt and purchase from Egypt cotton and cotton goods, nonferrous metals, cement, ammonia and sugar cane.

Other Projects

Other areas of potential cooperation being studied include infrastructure projects, such as development of regional transportation and communications systems and tourism. One of the proposed infrastructure projects is the establishment of a port at Gaza. The port would provide for the transport of 4–8 million tons, destined for Gaza, the West Bank, Jordan and Iraq. The cost of shipping via Gaza is estimated at $13/ton, compared with $36/ton via Aqaba. A 4 million ton and an 8 million ton port would provide employment for 1000 to 1500 workers, respectively.

A Regional Fund for Economic Development

In 1986, then Prime Minister Shimon Peres presented a plan for the establishment of a Regional Development Fund that would reach $25 billion within 10 years. The plan was based upon a proposal made in 1978, after President Sadat's visit to Jerusalem, by Mr. Arnon Gafny, then Governor of the Bank of Israel, and subsequently developed by Mr. Gafny in cooperation with Dr. Joyce Starr of the Center for Strategic and International Studies at Georgetown University. The financing for the fund proposed by Mr. Peres, which was conceived of as a sort of Middle East "Marshall Plan," was to come from the U.S.A., Canada, Europe and Japan, through the banking system, sale of government bonds, and government aid. The response abroad has been very positive, no doubt because the project is seen as promoting peace. The fund would be directed to specific investments in development projects, particularly projects based on regional cooperation, such as those being studied within the framework of the Hammer Project. If this fund is established it will give great momentum to the economic development of the region, in addition to accelerating the peace process.

■ Concluding Remarks

Immediately after the signing of the Camp David accords, David Rockefeller met with President Sadat in Washington. According to David Rockefeller, President Sadat confided in him his feeling that the path of peace with Israel which he had chosen was probably the most important and dangerous decision in his life. President Sadat felt that his future depended upon his success in demonstrating to his people the advantages of peace for the economic development of Egypt. The urgent and earnest appeal he made to David Rockefeller to help him in bringing American industry to Egypt was designed to help achieve this goal.

Following the 1986 fall in oil prices, Egypt is facing serious economic difficulties. The country has decreased income from oil exports and from Egyptians who formerly worked in the oil-producing states of the Persian Gulf. President Mubarak must contend with these problems. Through economic cooperation with Israel within the framework of an international fund for Middle East development and economic projects of the kind presented here, Egypt may be able to avert an economic crisis and embark upon the road to economic prosperity. Israel, too, will gain economic benefits, so both sides have nothing to lose, and everything to gain from peace.

Such economic interactions will also demonstrate the tangible benefits to be derived from cooperation and development and thus contribute to the peace process and the drive towards economic prosperity in the region as a whole.

I hope that these thoughts and plans will not remain within the realm of abstract yearning, but will become reality soon.

■ Notes

1. The team included, in alphabetical order, Dr. Ephraim Ahiram, Dr. Simha Bahiri, Professor Gideon Fishelson, Ms. Shelly Hecht, Professor Seev Hirsch, Mr. Elisha Kally, Mr. Yoel Raban, Professor Baruch Raz, Mr. Abraham Tal, Ms. Hilary Wolpert, researchers and assistants.

Section I

The Pre-Peace Era

This section contains four studies, two of which discuss the military build-up in the Middle East and its implications for the countries involved. The other two studies analyze the occupier-occupied relationship from an economic point of view.

Sheffer looks at the economic burden of the arms race. The burden is particularly heavy due to the economic constraints on the countries involved and their limited resources. Sheffer provides the data on the share of military expenditures in GNP, total resources and consumption. Syria tops the list, followed by Israel.

In addition, Sheffer identifies trends in defense expenditures in the countries of the region. Egypt is the only country that has not increased its defense expenditures in real terms since 1972. Sheffer concludes that the arms race has aggravated negative economic conditions (in Syria and Israel) and has clearly affected productivity and resource allocation.

Kanovsky studies the link between the oil boom and military spending in the Middle East. Without massive oil revenues, he argues, military spending would have been far smaller. Kanovsky examines economic, military and labor market developments in Saudi Arabia, Egypt, Syria, Jordan and Israel between 1973 and 1984. He predicts that the military outlays and all other public expenditures of oil-dependent economies (Egypt, Jordan, Syria) will be cut substantially as a result of lower oil prices. Whether these developments will bring the Middle East closer to peace is doubtful, but the end of the oil boom provides hope for continuing the reduction in military expenditures.

Kleiman analyzes the effects of the 1967 opening of borders between Israel, the West Bank, and the Gaza Strip (WBG) on the labor markets in these three areas. Removing the impediments to labor flows had important social and economic implications. The flows decreased the huge disparity in wages between Israel and WBG and provided the only possible solution to the severe scarcity of jobs in the WBG. The shortage of jobs has continued, and there has been an almost continuous upward trend in the number of WBG residents employed in Israel. One interesting conclusion of the analysis is that there is no relationship between the relative wages in various sectors received by the two populations and the share of WBG residents in total employment in these sectors.

Tuma's study tests the hypothesis that the military occupations of parts of Palestine, regardless of who the occupier was during the 1948-1985 period, benefitted the occupier economically. If this hypothesis is not rejected one can assume that the current occupation will not be terminated because of economic factors. While Tuma leaves untested the issue of economic benefits to the indigenous population, he concludes that Israel has paid little attention to the economic welfare of the territories. Tuma points towards minimal facilitation of investment in industry and manufacturing and towards bureaucratic obstacles. Thus, he argues, the economy of the territories stayed underdeveloped and not in a position of harmonious relations with Israel. To prove these claims, Tuma presents a careful analysis of socioeconomic changes in the West Bank and the Gaza Strip since 1948.

1

The Economic Burden of the Arms Race in the Middle East

Eliezer Sheffer

■ Introduction

This paper updates an earlier study that discussed trends in the years 1954 to 1979,[1] and attempts to examine developments in military expenditures in four countries in the region from 1979 to 1984, under conditions of growing economic constraints. Unfortunately, deficient data and unrealistic official exchange rates undermine the accuracy of comparisons and of some of the results. Nevertheless, it is our hope that despite these shortcomings some light can be shed on the broader aspects of the arms race in the Middle East.

The rapid process of armament that has taken place in recent years has turned the Middle East into one of the largest arsenals of conventional modern weapons on earth. The armies in the area from Libya to the Persian Gulf are equipped with some 20,000 battle tanks, 3,000 combat aircraft, 15,000 armored fighting vehicles and personnel carriers, 12,000 units of field artillery and large quantities of various missiles and other modern weapons. A recent study estimates the ratio of military capital stock to GNP in 1984 as high as 1.78 in Israel, 1.37 in Syria, 1.30 in Jordan and 0.76 in Egypt.[2] These very high ratios clearly reflect a continuous large-scale military build-up requiring enormous domestic and foreign currency resources.

Most nations of the region are poor (excluding the rich oil exporters) and their economies are tiny. A military buildup of such an order could not have taken place without massive external military and economic aid. The arms race in the area has been pushed up to its present high level, far beyond the limited economic capacity of the confrontation states, due to the growing involvement of the superpowers in the Middle East. There is no example, in modern times, anywhere else in the world of so intensive a defense effort continuing over three decades as that being conducted by certain nations of the Middle East.[3]

Not all rearmament in the region is a direct outcome of the Arab-Israeli conflict. At least part of it is designated for other purposes, such as inter-Arab rivalries, the Gulf War, and Libya's expansionist intentions in Africa. Nevertheless, Israel must consider the growing military potential in the whole region in her assessment of the balance of power and the planning of her defense strategy.

This discussion of the economic burden of the arms race does not embrace the entire region, but is confined rather to Israel and the confrontation states. The Arab states bordering Israel have been involved since 1948 in armed conflict with Israel far more than any other Arab states. Human and material resources have been wasted in this ongoing conflict, instead of being diverted to alternative productive uses. It is quite impossible to express in precise quantitative terms the economic cost of the conflict and the military buildup, but some indicators and estimates may be presented to give an idea of its dimensions.

■ The Size of the Economies and Their Military Expenditures

Table 1.1 illustrates the limited magnitude of the economies of Israel and three of her neighbors. It may be seen that, with the exception of Israel, levels of per capita incomes are very low. International comparisons of this type raise serious difficulties, particularly when quality of data is poor and official exchange rates diverge significantly from their real value. The source of the data in Table 1.1 is the World Bank Atlas 1985. The World Bank attempts to emend comparison procedures by adjusting in exceptional cases the conversion factor of domestic currencies to U.S. dollars and also by smoothing the impact of fluctuations in domestic prices and exchange rates in single years by using a three-year base period.[4] It seems, nevertheless, that GNP figures in Table 1.1 for Syria and Egypt are overvalued in dollar terms, due to inappropriate conversion factors, a point that will be elaborated upon below, though the official exchange rate of the Syrian lira was adjusted somewhat in the World Atlas figures.

These tiny and poor economies allocate very high proportions of their resources to military purposes. Syria, for which the proportion is highest, in 1984 allocated some 29 percent of GDP and 22 percent of total available resources, while in Israel the ratios were 23 and 20 percent, respectively.[5] The populations of Jordan and Israel are the smallest and their armed forces

Table 1.1 Gross national product and population

	GNP at Market Prices (millions of U.S. $)		Population (thousands)		GNP per Capita (U.S. $)	
	1982	1983[a]	1982	1983[a]	1982	1983[a]
Egypt	29,550	31,880	44,315	45,364	670	700
Syria	15,870	16,510	9,458	9,810	1,680	1,680
Jordan	4,400	4,200	2,485	2,573	1,690	1,710
Israel	21,440	21,990	4,027	4,101	5,320	5,360

[a]Preliminary estimates

Source: World Bank Atlas 1985

absorb large shares of their limited manpower resources. Even in Syria, with its population of 10 million, the labor force amounts to only 25 percent, and of this close to 10 percent makes up the country's armed forces of some 250,000. Similar low rates of participation in the labor force characterize other Arab nations in the region, the reasons including the very high ratios of the age groups up to 15 years old and the very low rates of participation of women in the labor force. In Israel, the share of the labor force in total population is close to 33 percent, as compared to 45 percent or even more in industrial countries. In Jordan the armed forces account for 13 percent of the labor force.

Jordan and Syria export labor to neighboring oil states and a shortage of labor has become a serious constraint in recent years to economic growth. Upward pressure on wages, moreover, has accelerated inflationary developments in both countries. In order to alleviate these pressures, Jordan has been obliged to import workers, mostly from Egypt. In view of the threats it faces, Israel has to maintain a relatively large army. Though based largely upon reserve duty, 13 to 15 percent of the labor force is permanently mobilized.

Reported military expenditures in the confrontation states are incomplete and understate significantly the real economic burden. Though numerous and largely reliable publications on military equipment, and size and composition of armed forces are put out, no similar comprehensive data on defense expenditures is generally available. The three Arab confrontation states omit from their official defense budgets arms purchases from abroad, as well as domestic military capital expenditures. At best their reported defense outlays include local currency operating expenditures. Military imports are also excluded from the balance of payments statistics, and from data on final uses in national accounts. The data on financing and servicing of accumulated external military debts are also not disclosed. Only Israel reports comprehensive data on defense expenditures and their financing.[6]

Since the import component of total military expenditures in the Middle East is very high, its exclusion makes any published figures on military expenditure meaningless.

In 1984, 36 percent of Israel's total defense consumption was spent abroad. It is safe to assume that domestic production of military equipment in the less developed neighboring countries is smaller and that the import component of defense outlays is larger. Even using a rule of thumb and adding a rough estimate for military imports of 40 percent of total defense outlays will undoubtedly make the estimate for actual military expenditures more realistic. Such an estimate must be treated with all necessary reservations and should be regarded as an order of magnitude only, rather than an accurate figure. Nevertheless, it seems preferable to the deficient reported data. Some distinguished international institutions that publish estimates on military expenditures sometimes prefer to quote official reported data accompanied by a note that "estimates are with a high degree of uncertainty."[7]

In Table 1.2 total defense expenditure ratios are presented after adjusting the reported official data by an assumed 40 percent import component. The same adjustment is also applied to total resources and public consumption.

The most striking feature of these ratios is their extremely high levels, in Syria and Israel in particular. The ratio of military expenditure to GDP in the United States was 6.9 percent in 1984, and in the larger states of Western Europe it ranged from 3 to 5 percent. In Egypt, the ratio has declined dramatically during the last decade, following the disengagement and peace agreements with Israel.

In all three Arab states, GNP exceeds GDP significantly owing to their net exports of labor services and relatively large receipts of workers' remittances. Israel is a net importer of labor from the administered territories, which explains why the figure for military expenditures as a percentage of GNP is higher than for GDP. All four countries are net capital importers, largely in the form of grants, which enables them to finance a large civilian import surplus as well as their large military imports. Specific military grants reduce the economic burden of the proportionally huge defense outlays of these small economies, which otherwise could not have been sustained for any length of time. Total resources are defined as GNP plus the civilian and the estimated military import surpluses. Table 1.3 also illustrates the fact that in all four countries the bulk of public consumption is for military purposes, leaving relatively small shares for social and economic services.

Even if we omit the uncertain estimate of military imports and present a ratio of domestic military expenditures only to reported public consumption (excluding also military imports), the downward-biased ratios are still very

Table 1.2 Total military expenditure in 1984

	Percent of GDP	Percent of GNP	Percent of total resources	Percent of public consumption
Egypt	11.5	10.2	9.1	57
Syria	28.9	27.6	21.9	84
Jordan	18.3	16.2[a]	12.8[a]	77
Israel	22.8	23.9	19.6	66

[a]A higher estimate of net factor income from abroad, composed largely of workers' remittances from abroad, reduces the defense/GNP ratio to 14.9 percent and the defense/total resources ratio to 11.9 percent.

Source: Table 1.4 and Appendices 2 and 3 below.

Table 1.3 Reported defense and public consumption, 1984 (in local currencies)

	Reported defense expenditure	Reported public consumption	(1) as percentage of (2)
	(1)	(2)	(3)
Egypt (m LE)	2,397	5,430	44.1
Syria (m LS)	12,997	17,200	75.6
Jordan (m JD)	168	254	66.1
Israel (bn IS)	1,022	1,802	56.7[a]

[a]Local defense consumption as percentage of total domestic public consumption (Bank of Israel Annual Report for 1984).

Source: IMF country surveys, citing data provided by the Ministries of Finance of the respective countries.

high. Few countries in the world allocate such high proportions of their public consumption to defense.

■ Comparisons of Absolute Figures

Any attempt to compare military outlays in U.S. dollar terms encounters another serious obstacle: the selection of an appropriate conversion factor. This problem is particularly difficult in the cases of Egypt and Syria, where multiple exchange rates prevail. In both these countries the official exchange rate diverges by a large margin from other recognized exchange rates, according to which a large share of transactions is officially conducted. IMF experts, as well as other observers, have recommended devaluing and unifying the exchange rates in Egypt and Syria. While the authorities in both countries recognize the need for a currency reform, they hesitate to carry it out for fear of negative repercussions on prices under the prevailing fiscal conditions.

In Jordan and Israel, the problem of selecting conversion factors is less serious, since official exchange rates were quite adequate in 1984.

The conversion factors applied in the following tables for Egypt and Syria for the 1984 figures are LE 1.17 and LS 5.425 per U.S.$, respectively. In Egypt four exchange rates prevailed in 1984: a Central Bank rate, a commercial bank official rate, a commercial bank premium rate, and a free market rate. A growing share of transactions is being authorized at the latter two rates. The premium rate was maintained throughout 1984 in the range of LE 1.12 to LE 1.20 per U.S.$. On January 5, 1985, the premium rate depreciated to LE 1.245 and the free market rate to LE 1.38 per U.S.$.[8] In our opinion, a rate of LE 1.17 per U.S.$ would serve more appropriately as a conversion factor for the 1984 figures than any other authorized exchange rate.

In Syria, an official exchange rate of LS 3.925 per U.S.$ has been retained unchanged since April 1976. This rate has long been overvalued, and in fact since August 1981 a parallel market rate of LS 5.425 per U.S.$ has been in effect. A growing share of exports is being exchanged at this parallel rate, which diverges by 38 percent from the official rate. Private imports are required at present to advance a 50 percent deposit. In February 1985, a tourist exchange rate was established at LS 8.55 per U.S.$.[9] The official rate was already significantly overvalued in 1984 and was therefore inappropriate to serve as a conversion factor. The parallel market exchange rate of LS 5.425 is probably more appropriate for the 1984 figures.[10]

As may be seen from the estimates of Table 1.4, Israel's defense outlays of $5.4 billion are the largest, equalling some 70 percent of the combined military expenditures of the three neighboring states. The gap between Israel and the other three states increased during the years 1979 to 1984, following a prolonged trend of a declining gap, as is illustrated in Table 1.5. In 1984, Israel spent U.S. $1,940 million out of its total public defense consumption in foreign currency. Some U.S. $1,490 million of this amount are reported in balance of payments statistics as direct military imports, largely financed by U.S. military aid, the residue being spent abroad on unspecified items. It should be reiterated that Israel's data is much more reliable than the rough estimates produced for the other three states.

Table 1.4 Total military expenditure estimates, 1984 (converted to U.S. $ m)

	Officially reported	Conversion factor	(1) in U.S. $ m	Estimate of military imports	Total
	(1)	(2)	(3)	(4)	(5)
Egypt	LE m 2,121	1.17	1,800	1,200	3,000
Syria	LS m 13,000	5,425	2,400	1,600	4,000
Jordan	JD m 168	0.379[a]	450	300	750
Sub-total			4,650	3,100	7,750
Israel	IS bn 1,022[b]	293.21[a]	3,485	1,940	5,425

[a]Official exchange rates
[b]Domestic public defense consumption

Source: Appendix 3

Table 1.5 Indices of military expenditures, 1954-1984 (Israel = 100)

	1954	1963	1972	1979	1984
Egypt	235	150	90	55	55
Syria	40	35	30	55	74
Jordan	50	20	10	10	14
All three states	320	210	125	120	143
Israel	100	100	100	100	100

Source: For the years 1954-1979, see Eliezer Sheffer, "The Economic Burden of the Arms Race Between the Confrontation States and Israel," in Zvi Lanir (ed.) *Israeli Security Planning in the 1980s* (A JCSS Book, Praeger, 1984), pp. 147, 160-2. For the year 1984 indices are derived from Table 1.4 above.

■ The Pace of the Arms Race

An important trend is evident from the figures in Table 1.5. Until 1972, Israel was closing rapidly the gap between her defense expenditures and those of the neighboring states. Between 1972 and 1979 this trend actually leveled off and from 1979, because of the accelerated pace of rearmament in Jordan and Syria, the gap began to grow.

The period from 1955 to 1972 was characterized by a very rapid process of rearmament and a steep rise in the ratio of defense to national product in all countries, with the exception of Jordan (see Appendix 1). This ratio rose from 6.4 percent of GNP in the three Arab states in 1954 to 17.4 percent in 1972, while in Israel it increased from 6.3 percent to 20.8 percent. Defense expenditures increased between 1954 and 1972 in real terms by 10 percent per year in the three Arab states and by some 15 percent per year in Israel, as shown in Table 1.6. During that period, Israel experienced a very rapid pace of economic growth of 9.5 percent annually, as compared to 4.4 percent per year in the three Arab states. Thus, Israel succeeded in reducing substantially the gaps in both economic and military expenditures.

After 1973, these trends took a sharp turn. In Israel accelerated inflation and recurrent balance of payments crises were manifested in a sharp decline in the growth rates of the economy. These mounting economic difficulties forced Israel to slow down the rate of growth of its military expenditures, which even dropped slightly in real terms between 1979 and 1984. The growth rates of the economy fell sharply from their high pre-1973 levels, averaging 9.5 percent, to only 2.5 percent per year over the last decade.

In contrast to Israel, the period between 1973 and the early 1980s was one of economic prosperity in the neighboring states. These countries benefited directly and indirectly from the steep rise in oil prices and the growing wealth of the Arab oil-exporting states. Egypt and Syria are both small net exporters of oil and have benefited directly from the improvement in their terms of trade. They and Jordan have furthermore exported large numbers

Table 1.6 Annual real rates of growth in defense expenditure, 1954-1984[a] (percentages)

	1955-72	1973-79	1980-84
Egypt	10.2	0.3	-1.1
Syria	14.1	18.2	4.5
Jordan	4.9	11.1	6.5[b]
All three states	10.3	6.8	2.3
Israel	15.6	7.5	-1.3

[a]Calculated from defense expenditures in current U.S. dollars deflated by the inflationary rate in the United States.
[b]The rate of growth is probably overvalued, since the base year 1979 has not been adjusted by an estimate for the unrecorded military imports.

Source: For the period 1955-79, see Eliezer Sheffer, *op. cit.*, pp. 160-3. Growth rates for 1980-84 are derived similarly by deflating figures for 1984 in Table 1.4 above at United States 1979 prices.

of workers to the booming, rich Arab oil states, which have also provided them with financial assistance (see Appendix 4).[11] All these favorable economic developments have been reflected in an upward turn in rates of economic growth.

Egypt is the only country in the region that has not increased its defense expenditures at all in real terms since 1972. Since terminating the conflict with Israel, Egypt's defense burden has declined sharply from 18 percent of GNP in 1972 to only 10 percent in 1984, following the freeze in military expenditures and the sharp rise in rates of economic growth. In the past, Egypt held a dominant position among the confrontation states, accounting for 70 percent of the composite military outlay of the whole group. Her share declined to 46 percent in 1979 and further to only 38 percent in 1984 (see Table 1.5).

In contrast to Egypt and Israel, Syria and Jordan have accelerated their rearmament pace since 1973, with financial aid from the rich Arab oil states. The flow of aid funds to the confrontation states increased sharply in 1979, after Egypt made peace with Israel.[12] Syria's total military outlays, which had been rising at extremely high rates, caught up with Egypt's in 1979 and by 1984 had exceeded them by one-third. In 1972, Syria's defense outlays amounted to only one-third of Egypt's. Thus a far-reaching shift in the balance of military power has taken place in the region, with the increase of Syria's and Jordan's share in total military expenditures of the four states under discussion. The combined military budgets of Syria and Jordan reached close to 90 percent of Israel's in 1984, as compared to only 40 percent in 1972. A most rapid military buildup in Syria and Jordan coupled with high rates of economic expansion became feasible from 1973 to the early 1980s, because of exceptionally favorable economic conditions and massive external financial aid.

After surging ahead for almost a decade, the rate of growth of defense expenditures began to decline in Syria and Jordan, as a result of deteriorating economic conditions. The contraction of oil production in neighboring oil states combined with a fall in oil prices was reflected in a sharp decline in their oil incomes and a slowdown in economic activity. These developments, whose impact began to be felt in 1982, have affected adversely the economies of all Arab states in the region. Reduced workers' remittances and financial aid to Syria and Jordan have put the economies of these countries under considerable strain. The reduction in the availability of foreign exchange forced restraint upon public current and capital spending, including defense. In Syria, output actually declined in the period 1983-84 and probably remained unchanged in 1985. It seems likely that Syria's GDP in 1985 has not exceeded that of 1981 at constant prices.

In Jordan, very little economic growth has taken place since 1982, following a decade of very high rates of economic expansion, as shown in Table 1.7. Egypt, too, despite a substantially lower defense burden, has faced strong domestic and external imbalances in recent years, as a result of reduced external resources. Economic conditions in Egypt have been adversely affected by the changing conditions in world oil markets as well as weaker economic activity in the rich oil states of the Middle East.

Certain interesting conclusions regarding the arms race in the region may be drawn on the basis of the estimates presented in this section and in Appendix 1.

a) It looks as though Egypt has quit not only the path of war but the arms race, too. As its defense expenditures have not actually risen since 1972, their ratio to the rapidly-growing GNP has declined sharply.

b) Because of mounting economic difficulties in the early 1980s, the pace of armament slowed down significantly everywhere. Nevertheless, the ratio of defense to GNP continued to grow in Syria and in Jordan, notwithstanding the decline in the rate of growth of military expenditures, because of the marked economic slowdown in these countries. Only in Egypt and Israel did the defense/GNP ratio decline.

c) A sharp turn in economic trends is most striking in Syria and in Jordan, where growth rates have fallen dramatically since 1982. In Egypt, too, economic performance has deteriorated in recent years. While Israel has been experiencing an economic slowdown from as far back as 1973, economic conditions have been deteriorating since the early 1980s.

Table 1.7 Annual real rates of growth, 1972-85 (percentages)

	1972-82 GNP[a]	Gross Domestic Product[b]			
		1982	1983	1984	1985
Egypt	9.4	8.6	9.0	7.6	n.a.
Syria	8.6	3.2	-0.4	-2.1	0.0[c]
Jordan	11.5	5.8	4.0	1.6	n.a.
Israel	2.5	0.8	2.0	1.1	1.0

[a]World Bank Atlas 1985.
[b]Data reported by official agencies, cited in IMF country surveys.
[c]Preliminary, based on trends in the first 10 months of the year.

■ The Defense Burden

How much of the worsening economic performance in the four states should be attributed to their heavy and, in some cases, growing defense burdens, and how much of it results from other factors, such as the sharp decline in foreign grants and other foreign exchange resources, remains an open question. Indisputably, in some countries of the Middle East, military expenditures have reached exceptionally high levels. An arms race proceeding at growth rates averaging 18 percent or even 11 percent per annum, as was actually evident in Syria and in Jordan between 1973 and the beginning of the 1980s, is not sustainable for any length of time. Only exceptionally favorable economic and financial circumstances enabled it to continue for as long as it did. Countries with narrow economic bases are of necessity limited in the defense expenditures they can support, and galloping rearmament must inevitably threaten to swallow up intolerable shares of available resources. External aid permitting defense budgets exceeding 28 percent of GDP cannot be regarded as necessarily stable for any length of time.[13]

The arms race in the Middle East has undoubtedly aggravated economic conditions in some countries. It has intensified strains on human resources, and is reflected in huge budgetary deficits, as well as increased rates of taxation in some countries, which adversely affect productivity and resource allocation. In all four countries balance of payments problems have arisen, as well as strong domestic inflationary pressures. Policy measures aimed at reducing growing imbalances, such as increased import restrictions, higher rates of taxation, and reduced development budgets, inevitably slow down economic growth and thereby preclude persistently high rates of growth of military expenditures. The accumulation of large military-related external and domestic debts undermines the efficiency of monetary and fiscal policies.

As noted earlier, it is impossible to isolate and estimate quantitatively the economic effects of arms races. Nevertheless, the dimensions are so great that it is quite safe to assume that the deceleration of economic growth in Syria and in Israel, and the growing imbalances in their economies, are at least partly due to a prolonged, intensive defense effort. Exorbitant defense expenditure ratios as are evident in both states, eventually crowd out investments and retard economic growth. This, of course, limits the ability to perpetuate a rapid process of armament, unless massive external aid is forthcoming. Various observers of economic developments in Syria relate the present weak position of the economy to the country's huge defense expenditures. In Jordan, too, rapidly-growing defense budgets, accompanied by a reduction in foreign aid and other foreign exchange resources, have aggravated economic performance in recent years.

In Israel, the defense burden has also reached intolerable proportions. It is not surprising therefore that a substantial reduction of defense expenditures plays a central role in the present economic stabilization program. Both Israel and Syria receive large amounts of foreign aid, which helps them to finance their military imports and part of their civilian external deficit. Nevertheless, the intensive defense effort requires, at the same time, large domestic resources. Only exceptionally high levels of external aid, or other unpredicted developments, such as the discovery of substantial oil deposits, will enable the resumption and sustaining of an armament process at its previous exorbitant pace.

■ Notes

1. Eliezer Sheffer, "The Economic Burden of the Arms Race Between the Confrontation States and Israel," in Zvi Lanir (ed.) *Israel Security Planning in the 1980s* (A JCSS Book, Praeger, 1984).

2. Ariel Halperin, "The Development of Military Capital Stocks in Israel and the Confrontation States" (Hebrew), Discussion Paper 86.01, The Maurice Falk Institute for Economic Research in Israel, Jerusalem, January 1986.

3. See Table 1.6 and Appendix 1.

4. See "Technical Notes," World Bank Atlas 1985, p. 28.

5. See Table 1.2.

6. Some observers argue that even regarding Israel's defense data reported figures have a downward bias, because of inadequate definitions and classifications. See Eitan Berglas, "Defense and the Economy: The Israeli Experience," Discussion Paper No. 83.01, Section III, The Maurice Falk Institute, Jerusalem, January 1983.

7. See *Sipri Yearbook 1985*, Tables of World Military Expenditure (London: Taylor and Francis, 1985).

8. At the end of November 1985, the various rates per U.S.$ were as follows: Central Bank rate LE 0.70 (unchanged since January 1, 1979), commercial bank official rate LE 1.35, and premium rate LE 1.81.

9. In September 1985, a fourth authorized exchange rate for travel abroad of LS 11.25 per U.S.$ was introduced.

10. In the World Bank Atlas 1985, an implicit conversion factor of about LS 4.5 per U.S.$ is applied for the year 1983.

11. Arab aid to Egypt terminated in 1979 after the signing of the peace treaty with Israel and has been substituted by U.S. aid.

12. See Appendix 4.

13. See Appendix 4.

APPENDIX 1

DEFENSE EXPENDITURES AS A PERCENTAGE OF GNP, 1954 TO 1984

	1954	1963	1972	1979	1984
Egypt	6.1	10.0	18.1	11.5	10.2
Syria	4.2	9.6	15.8	24.7	27.6
Jordan	20.0	15.8	16.4	14.8	16.2
All three states	6.4	10.3	17.4	15.7	16.0
Israel	6.3	10.8	20.8	25.0	23.9

Sources: For the years 1954 to 1979, see Eliezer Sheffer, *op cit.*, pp. 150, 158-61. For 1984, see Table 1.4 and Appendices 3 and 4.

APPENDIX 2

NATIONAL PRODUCT AND TOTAL RESOURCES, 1984
(in millions of dollars at current prices)

	Conversion Factor	GDP	GNP	Civilian Import Surplus	Estimate of Military Imports	Total Available Resources
Egypt	1.17	26,100	29,400[b]	2,440[b]	1,200	33,040
Syria	5.425	13,850	14,500[c]	2,200	1,600	18,300
Jordan	0.379[a]	4,100	4,620	960	300	5,880
Israel	293.21[a]	23,750	22,690	2,950	1,940	27,580

[a]Official exchange rates
[b]Includes workers' remittances of $3,300 million, which constitutes an average for the reported years, 1983/84 and 1984/85.
[c]An estimate of $600 million of workers' remittances is included.

Source: For the three Arab states, official agencies (ministries of finance and central banks), cited in IMF country surveys. For Israel, Bank of Israel Annual Report, 1984.

APPENDIX 3

RECORDED[a] MILITARY EXPENDITURES, 1979-1984
(in millions of domestic currency units at current prices)

	Syria (LS m)			
	Current Prices	Constant 1980 Prices[b]	Jordan (JD m)	Egypt[c] (LE m)
1979	6,190	7,527	114.9	772
1980	8,804	8,804	118.2	1,065
1981	9,484	8,150	138.0	1,475
1982	10,703	8,816	156.7	1,683
1983	11,309	8,926	168.0	2,121
1984	12,997	9,757	168.0[d]	2,397
1985[d]	13,000	--	186.0	--

[a]Official recorded data is assumed in this study to represent local currency expenditures only.
[b]Deflated by implicit GDP price deflator.
[c]In Egypt, from 1980 onward data refer to years starting in July and terminating in June of the next calendar year.
[d]Preliminary budget estimates.

Source: Finance ministries and central banks, quoted in IMF country surveys.

APPENDIX 4

PUBLIC SECTOR FOREIGN GRANT RECEIPTS

	Jordan (SDRs millions)	Syria (U.S. $ millions)
1978	171	782
1979	773	1,629
1980	955	1,510
1981	1,019	1,711
1982	866	1,292
1983	666	1,219
1984	588	1,119

Sources: For Syria, Central Bank of Syria, *Quarterly Bulletin* (various issues), quoted in IMF country surveys. The rates which are applied in this table to convert Syrian pounds into U.S. dollars are as follows: 1978-80, LS 3.952; 1981, LS 4.173; 1982, LS 4.190; 1983, LS 4.115; and 1984, LS 4.214.

For Jordan, Central Bank of Jordan, converted at JD1 = SDR 2.579 (quoted in IMF country surveys).

2

The Economic Aspects of Peace in the Middle East: Oil and the Arms Race

Eliyahu Kanovsky

Shortly after Sadat's visit to Jerusalem in 1977, I wrote an essay on the possible economic implications of peace between Israel and its Arab neighbors. I noted the possible gains from trade, tourism, joint projects, technical cooperation, and so on, but I emphasized that *by far* the most important economic benefit would stem from a major reduction in the military burden. This analysis was extended in a subsequent essay written shortly after the conclusion of the Israel-Egypt agreement in 1979.[1] All that has occurred since that time has strengthened this conclusion.

Wars, the threat of war, and the arms race have afflicted the Middle East at least since the 1950s, but the oil boom of the 1970s and early 1980s gave a powerful boost to the dimensions of military spending in the region. I am not suggesting that the quantum leap in oil revenues was the cause of the arms race.

There are many sources of tension in the region going far beyond and often totally unrelated to the Arab-Israeli conflict. But, in the absence of massive oil revenues, military spending would, of necessity, have been far smaller. According to estimates of the U.S. Arms Control and Disarmament Agency (ACDA) the seven Arab members of OPEC (Saudi Arabia, Kuwait, The United Arab Emirates, Qatar, Iraq, Libya and Algeria) increased their share of total world arms imports from 4 percent in 1972 to 30 percent in 1983. But these figures do not tell the whole story. These newly rich Arab countries

The author wishes to express his sincere gratitude to the Littauer Foundation and to the president of the foundation, Mr. William Frost, for the grant which made this research possible.

31

provided large-scale financial aid to the poorer Arab states (though the latter complained that the rich were niggardly), both for economic and military
purposes. Data regarding economic aid are published, often incomplete,
but data with respect to military aid, though widely-reported, are not included in the published statistics of the donor or recipient countries. These
include the payment by the rich Arab states to Western or Soviet-bloc arms
suppliers for deliveries to Egypt (until 1979) to Syria, Jordan, Oman and
others. If we add these four to the seven Arab members of OPEC, the Arab
share of world arms imports rose from 12 percent in 1972 to 43 percent in
1983. If we add the other Arab states (Bahrain, Lebanon, Sudan, North
Yemen, South Yemen, Morocco and Tunisia) the Arab share of world arms
imports rose to over one half in 1983 (Tables 2.1 and 2.2).[2]

In absolute terms the rise in Arab arms purchases (Arab OPEC plus
Egypt, Syria and Jordan) was from $1.3 billion in 1972 to $15.5 billion in 1983.
Measured in real terms arms imports in 1983 were almost five times their
1972 level (Table 2.2, note 2). But arms imports, though a good indicator,
constitute only part of military outlays. Local expenditures for the construction of military bases, maintenance, the support of the armed forces, etc.,
often exceed or greatly exceed the cost of imported military equipment.
Moreover, an increase in military equipment necessarily entails more local
expenditures for bases, maintenance, manpower, and so on. Thus, for example, Saudi military budgets averaged $19 billion per annum in 1981-83 ac-
cording to Saudi sources, or almost $24 billion per annum according to
ACDA estimates, while its arms imports were $3.1 billion per annum during
that period (Table 2.3). The ratio of local military expenditures to military
imports varies from country and over time. The Saudi ratio is unusually high,
five to six and one half dollars of local spending to one dollar of arms imports. In Israel the ratio was about two to one in 1981-84.[3] In other words,
even if one assumes that Israel, Egypt, Jordan and Syria had their arms imports financed by others, the burden of *local* military expenditures falls on
their own economies.

While the military budget (assuming it is reasonably accurate) is the best
single indicator there are indirect costs as well. The military budget takes
no account of the foregone civilian production of those in the armed forces.
While in countries such as Egypt and Syria with high levels of unemployment, mainly disguised unemployment, it may be argued that many of those
in the armed forces might otherwise swell the ranks of the unemployed, the
same is not true of Israel, Jordan and Saudi Arabia. The latter two import
labor on a large-scale, though Jordan's labor *exports* are about twice their
labor *imports*. For Israel, which has maintained close to full employment,
the absorption of manpower by the armed forces, including reserve duty,
reduces civilian production. But even in those countries like Syria and

Table 2.1 Oil Export Revenues (millions of dollars)

Year	1972	1973	1974	1975	1976	1977	1978	1979	1980	1981	1982	1983	1984
Saudi Arabia	4,545	7,802	31,166	27,880	36,309	41,125	37,390	58,623	101,422	111,545	73,263	42,807	34,261
Kuwait	2,370	3,525	10,394	8,425	8,593	8,778	9,424	16,779	17,676	13,793	8,828	9,948	10,394
United Arab Emirates (UAE)	1,035	1,740	6,306	6,817	8,379	9,259	8,661	12,862	19,390	18,761	15,965	13,016	12,412
Iraq	1,022	1,836	6,506	8,176	9,114	9,505	10,850	21,289	26,136	10,388	10,100	9,650	11,241
Libya	2,472	3,456	7,126	6,036	8,298	9,748	9,296	14,912	20,452	15,003	13,944	11,387	11,131
Qatar	382	601	1,979	1,758	2,137	1,987	2,295	3,509	5,387	5,316	3,988	3,039	4,195
Algeria	1,029	1,523	4,267	4,295	4,791	5,562	5,856	8,746	12,647	12,985	10,770	9,467	9,189
Arab Members of OPEC - Total	12,855	20,483	67,744	63,387	77,981	85,964	83,772	136,720	203,110	187,791	136,858	99,314	92,824
Other Larger Middle East Oil Exporters													
Iran	3,636	5,617	20,904	19,634	22,923	23,599	21,684	19,186	13,286	12,053	19,233	19,924	12,945
Oman	230	327	1,136	1,439	1,562	1,569	1,503	2,152	3,281	4,403	4,099	4,033	4,150

Source: International Monetary Fund International Financial Statistics (various issues)

Notes: 1. For Saudi Arabia, Kuwait, Algeria, and Iran, the figures include exports both of crude and refined oil. For the others the data refer to crude oil exports, only. Other than Algeria, the exports of the first group are mainly crude oil.
2. The 1983 and 1984 figures may have an upward bias. Much larger quantities were sold at discounted prices sometimes disguised under barter deals.
3. The figure for Oman in 1984 is my own estimate.

Table 2.2 Middle East Arms Imports (millions of dollars, unless otherwise stated)

Year	1972	1973	1974	1975	1976	1977	1978	1979	1980	1981	1982	1983
Saudi Arabia	100	80	340	250	440	875	1300	1200	1800	2900	3100	3300
Kuwait	5	–	–	50	80	310	300	60	40	120	130	100
United Arab Emirates (UAE)	10	10	50	30	100	130	50	150	170	230	30	40
Iraq	140	625	625	675	1000	1500	1600	2300	1900	3700	4300	5100
Libya	160	180	330	550	1000	1200	2000	2500	2200	2500	2900	1900
Qatar	–	–	–	10	–	40	20	20	90	150	270	230
Algeria	10	40	20	90	320	480	725	450	525	1200	1100	350
Total Arab members of OPEC	425	935	1365	1655	2940	4535	5995	6680	6725	10,800	11,830	11,020
Share of world arms imports (%)	4.1	6.8	11.1	13.0	17.6	23.1	25.8	24.2	22.7	29.7	30.8	30.1
Other Arab Oil Exporters												
Egypt	550	850	230	350	150	250	400	625	550	575	2100	1700
Syria	280	1300	825	380	625	650	900	2100	2700	2100	1900	1700
Oman	5	10	10	40	10	50	270	30	100	60	90	290
Jordan	30	50	80	80	140	120	170	100	260	1100	850	1100
Total Arab countries arms imports	1290	3145	2510	2505	3865	5605	7735	9535	10,335	14,635	16,770	15,810
Share of world (%)	12.4	23.0	20.5	19.7	23.1	28.5	33.3	34.6	34.9	40.2	43.6	43.2

35

Other

Iran	525	525	1000	1200	2000	2500	2200	1600	400	1000	1500	750
Israel	300	230	975	725	975	1100	900	490	800	1200	950	370

Source: U.S. Arms Control and Disarmament Agency *World Military Expenditures and Arms Transfers 1985*, and earlier issues.

Notes:

1. I have not taken into account within the listing of Arab countries the following: Bahrain, Lebanon, Sudan, North Yemen, South Yemen, Morocco, and Tunisia. Their inclusion would not alter the trends or conclusions in any significant manner. I have included Kuwait, Qatar, and the United Arab Emirates, despite the fact that they are relatively small buyers of arms. However, they have, according to many reports, provided financing, along with Saudi Arabia, for the arms purchases of Egypt (until 1979), Jordan, and Syria, as well as others.

2. The U.S. Arms Control and Disarmament Agency also publishes estimates in constant dollars. U.S. prices in 1983 were about two and one-half times those prevailing in 1972.

Table 2.3 Saudi Arabia -- Selected Data (billions of dollars -- unless otherwise stated)

Year	1972	1973	1974	1975	1976	1977	1978	1979	1980	1981	1982	1983	1984	1985
Oil export revenues	4.6	7.8	31.2	27.9	36.3	41.1	37.4	58.6	101.4	111.5	73.3	42.8	34.3	27.0
Military expenditures (ACDA estimates)	0.8	1.2	2.6	6.4	9.3	9.3	10.6	13.6	16.4	20.2	24.2	27.2	NA	NA
Military imports (ACDA)	0.1	0.08	0.3	0.3	0.4	0.9	1.3	1.2	1.8	2.9	3.1	3.3	NA	NA
Ratio of military exp. to GNP (ACDA) (%)	11.1	13.2	10.9	17.4	19.1	15.3	15.9	18.1	14.4	12.9	15.7	24.3	NA	NA
Foreign aid (balance of payments)	0.2	0.5	1.0	3.1	3.3	3.9	3.9	3.5	5.5	5.7	NA	NA	NA	NA

Fiscal Year	1972/3	1973/4	1974/5	1975/6	1976/7	1977/8	1978/9	1979/80	1980/1	1981/2	1982/3	1983/4	Projections 1984/5	1985/6
Total government revenues	3.9	11.4	28.4	29.3	38.5	37.9	39.3	63.0	104.8	108.2	71.8	59.5	47.9	54.8
Of which oil revenues	3.4	11.1	26.8	26.5	34.3	32.7	34.4	56.5	96.2	96.6	54.4	41.8	33.6	32.2
Total government expenditures	3.0	5.8	9.6	18.2	29.6	41.6	43.9	53.3	69.2	78.6	73.6	69.1	60.9	54.8
Of which military expenditures	0.9	1.5	2.5	6.7	9.0	9.1	10.6	16.9	16.5	19.3	19.4	18.4	19.6	17.6
Foreign aid	0.2	0.2	0.8	1.2	2.4	3.2	1.9	2.9	7.4	7.1	4.0	3.7	2.9	2.7

| Gross domestic product (GDP) | 10.3 | 26.0 | 39.7 | 46.6 | 58.1 | 64.6 | 74.5 | 115.2 | 156.8 | 154.3 | 121.1 | 110.0 | 101.0 | NA |
| Ratio of military exp. to GDP (%) | 8.7 | 5.3 | 6.3 | 14.4 | 15.5 | 14.1 | 14.2 | 14.7 | 10.5 | 12.5 | 16.1 | 16.7 | 19.4 | NA |

Sources:

Saudi Arabian Monetary Agency *Annual Reports*

Ministry of Planning, Kingdom of Saudi Arabia, *Achievements of the Development Plans 1390-1403 (1970-1983)*

International Monetary Fund *International Financial Statistics*, various issues

U.S. Arms Control and Disarmament Agency (ACDA) *World Military Expenditures and Arms Transfers 1985*, and earlier issues

Notes:

1. In the official national accounts, foreign trade and balance of payments figures are in accordance with the common calendar. Budgets and other national accounts are in accordance with the Muslim calendar, which is about eleven days shorter than the common calendar.

2. The official balance of payments estimates omit foreign aid (official transfers) since 1982.

3. Oil export revenues for 1985 are the author's estimate.

4. 1984 figures are provisional estimates of actual revenues and expenditures.

5. 1985-86 figures, for the fiscal year ending in March 1986, are budgetary projections, not actuals. Revenues were surely far lower, and there was, without doubt, a large budgetary deficit. No official estimates are available at this writing (May 1986), nor have the Saudis published their projections for fiscal 1986/87.

Egypt, when the armed forces absorb those with technical and professional skills in short supply in the civilian economy, this has an adverse effect, and there is evidence that this occurs.

Labor force data are particularly poor in the less developed countries and most Middle Eastern countries are in that category. None publish the size of their armed forces, and we must therefore rely on outside estimates. One of the problems with these estimates is that the distinction common in western countries between the armed forces and internal security forces or police is blurred. Not infrequently the armed forces are called upon to protect the regime from internal subversion. If we accept the ACDA estimates of the armed forces and the national estimates of employment we find that the ratio of manpower in the armed forces to total employment (civilian plus military) rose very sharply in Syria from 6.6 percent in 1972 to 9.5 percent in 1983; in Egypt there was a slight decline (in relative terms) from 4.3 percent to 3.6 percent; in Jordan a sharp drop from 22.3 percent to 12.4 percent; while in Israel there was a slight increase from 11.0 percent to 11.8 percent. But the figures for Egypt are somewhat misleading. As one Middle East journal phrased it "over the past 10 to 15 years a second army has been created in Egypt . . . the Central Security Forces" which numbered 282,000 before they rioted in February 1986 according to the minister of the Interior.[4] These forces are in addition to the regular police, but apparently are excluded from the ACDA estimates of the Egyptian armed forces— 447,000 in 1983. One can also assume that the official military budget excludes allocations to this "second army." The ACDA estimate for Israel does not take account of reserve duty, and is, therefore, also an underestimate of diversion of manpower.

The oil boom of the 1970s and early 1980s had pervasive economic, social and political effects on the whole region. The massive public expenditures of the oil-rich countries drew millions of foreign workers from Arab, Asian and other countries. The remittances transferred by the workers to their families back home had an enormous impact. There was also a major rise in tourist spending on the part of the newly-rich visiting the poorer Arab countries. There was some private Arab investment in the poorer countries, especially in real estate, banking, and hotels. Trade opportunities were opened up or expanded. All this was in addition to financial aid for economic and military purposes. In booming economies the burden of military expenditures — measured as a ratio of GNP — may well decline, even if allocations are rising rapidly in absolute terms. With the end of the oil boom, the military burden is becoming particularly onerous. Both the major Middle Eastern oil exporting countries and the others in the region, Egypt, Syria and Jordan, are in the throes of a serious recession. My own projections are that oil prices will remain depressed over the long run, and that the impact of this drastic change will similarly be long-term.[5] However, there are also important differences and we shall therefore examine developments in Middle Eastern countries most affected by the oil boom.

▪ Saudi Arabia

In my various studies of Saudi Arabia, and of the Middle Eastern oil-exporting states, I have presented the thesis that governments tend to increase spending proportionately when revenues rise—with a relatively short time lag—but that there is a strong downward inflexibility with respect to public expenditures, both civilian and military. This implies that when revenues decline, and especially if they decline sharply, budgetary deficits are almost inevitable. Thus when Saudi budgetary revenues rose very sharply from less than $4 billion in fiscal 1972-73 to over $28 billion two years later, expenditures tripled, but lagged far behind the escalation in revenues, and huge budgetary and balance of payments (current account) surpluses emerged. But in subsequent years, while revenues continued to climb, the momentum of spending was so strong that budgetary and balance of payments deficits emerged in fiscal 1977-78 and again in fiscal 1978-79. The oil shock of 1979-80 was instrumental in bringing about an even sharper escalation in revenues, and again *initially* huge financial surpluses emerged. But public spending continued to rise sharply and deficits have been the norm in every year since 1982-83. Military expenditures, measured in current dollars, rose most sharply from less than $1 billion in 1972-73 to $9 billion in 1977-78, and then more than doubled to $19 billion four years later, according to official accounts, and were significantly higher according to ACDA estimates. What is particularly noteworthy is that despite increasingly severe budgetary and balance of payments problems since 1982, the military budget was not cut. The budgetary announcement for 1985-86 (ending March 1986) called for a 10 percent cutback in the military budget, but no data are available at this time with respect to actual revenues and expenditures in 1985-86. Even if it was implemented the cutback is very mild as compared with the 60 percent decline in revenues between 1981-82 and 1985-86. The areas of more significant cutbacks have been in construction and in foreign aid.

Since 1982 the published balance of payments figures omit foreign aid disbursements. From the reports of the major recipients it is clear that foreign aid from the rich Arab states, as a whole, have been cut back sharply. Financial aid for military purposes has been off-budgetary, both in the accounts of the Arab donors and recipients, but I have no doubt that it, too, has been curbed (Table 2.3).

■ **Egypt**

Between the mid-1970s and the early 1980s Egypt enjoyed a booming economy, in relative terms. This followed a decade of economic stagnancy. The underlying cause was mainly oil. In 1975 Egypt became a net oil exporter, i.e., oil exports exceeded oil imports, including refined oil products. Export revenues expanded as output rose, but the major boost came with the second oil shock of 1979-80, which pushed oil exports to over $3 billion per annum. These sums may be puny in comparison with Saudi oil exports of over $100 billion per annum in the early 1980s, but, for the Egyptian economy it provided a major boost. All other commodity exports, including cotton, averaged about $1.25 billion per annum in the first half of the 1980s. The reopening of the Suez Canal in 1975 and the completion of its expansion in 1980 to accommodate large oil tankers, raised transit dues to close to $1 billion per annum. The huge imports of the rich oil countries in the Gulf from Europe and America contributed to increased traffic through the canal.

During the 1970s and until the conclusion of the Egyptian-Israeli agreement in 1979, Egypt was the major beneficiary of Arab financial aid both for civilian and military purposes. According to Egyptian reports grants from the Arab states reached a peak of almost $1 billion in 1974 and again in 1975, dropping thereafter to about $300 million in 1978. However, there were also large-scale loans, which, in fact, have never been repaid. The rich Arab states also financed, at least in part, arms imports to Egypt. Since 1979 the U.S. has replaced Arab aid, both for economic and military purposes.

The oil boom in the neighboring states also had spill-over effects in terms of tourism, and some private Arab investment, especially in real estate, banking, and hotels. But, by far, of greatest importance was the mass migration of Egyptians to the oil states responding to the lucrative job opportunities in those booming economies. Estimates vary, but it appears that in 1982-83 there were some 2-1/2 to 3 million Egyptians working in other Arab countries, equivalent to between one sixth and one fifth of its labor force.[6] According to official Egyptian estimates, remittances sent home by these workers reached a peak of $3.9 billion in 1983-84 (Table 2.4). But it is believed that billions of dollars reach Egyptian families through unofficial channels. In any case, the total effect of these developments was a rapid growth in the economy during the latter half of the 1970s and early 1980s.

The system of multiple exchange rates and the widening gap between them, not to mention the much higher black market rate, makes an examination of military budgets in dollar terms an exercise in futility. This is espe-

Table 2.4 Egypt -- Selected Data (millions of dollars -- unless otherwise stated)

Year	1972	1973	1974	1975	1976	1977	1978	1979	1980/1	1981/2	1982/3	1983/4	1984/5
Total commodity exports	813	1000	1672	1567	1609	1974	1939	2424	3985	4144	3555	4033	4059
Of which Oil exports	41	62	187	305	622	696	915	1879	2857	3032	2468	2640	2659
Remittances received	81	85	310	455	842	988	1824	2269	2855	2082	3166	3930	2800
Grants received	290	579	994	986	624	386	296	36	--	130	500	700	900
Balance on current account	-174	20	-327	-1397	-807	-813	-924	-1507	-1605	-2164	-1284	-1415	-1856
Military expenditures (Budget)	506	710	777	774	1158	876	866	1131	1521	2107	2404	3030	3424
Military expenditures as % of GNP (Official accounts)	6.0	7.6	7.5	5.9	6.9	4.4	3.9	6.5	5.9	6.9	7.3	8.0	NA
Years									1980	1981	1982	1983	
Military expenditures (ACDA)	1245	2253	2697	2843	2561	2906	2288	2006	2241	--	2325	2679	
Arms imports (ACDA)	550	850	230	350	150	250	400	625	550	575	2100	1700	
Military expenditures as % of GNP (ACDA)	19.2	32.7	35.0	30.9	22.1	21.0	13.9	11.0	10.2	--	8.2	8.3	

Table 2.4 (continued)

Sources: International Monetary Fund *International Financial Statistics*, various issues

National Bank of Egypt *Economic Bulletin and Annual Reports*

Central Bank of Egypt *Economic Review and Annual Reports*

Middle East Economic Digest, London, various issues

Economic Intelligence Unit *Quarterly Economic Review and Annual Supplement*, various issues

U.S. Arms Control and Disarmament Agency *World Military Expenditures and Arms Transfers 1985*, and earlier issues

Notes:

1. As of 1980, the Egyptian official accounts were changed to fiscal years beginning July 1.

2. Conversion into dollars presents a major problem because of the system of multiple exchange rates. There are a number of widely varying official exchange rates, aside from the black market rate. In the table, the conversion was made at the rate of one dollar equals 0.70 Egyptian pounds. But this rate applies only to certain exports and imports. The rate for remittances, tourists, and others is far higher. Thus, towards the end of 1985 the official rate for remittances was one dollar equals 1.35 Egyptian pounds, and the black market rate, where much or most of the remittances are exchanged was one dollar equals 1.85 Egyptian pounds. Similarly, most of the tourist dollars find their way into the black market. Ideally, a weighted exchange rate would be used, but none is available, and it would, in any case, vary from year to year. The figures for oil exports are reasonably accurate.

3. The figures for grants received are also originally in dollars. Until 1979, they were primarily Arab grants, and since then, from the U.S. For both periods, these figures greatly understate the magnitude of foreign economic aid, even aside from military aid, which is not officially reported.

4. The official figures for military expenditures greatly understate their magnitude. Even the ACDA figures for more recent years appear to exclude, in whole or in part, the value of arms imports. Thus, if ACDA estimates of Egyptian arms imports in 1982-83 are reasonably accurate, it would imply that local military expenditures had dropped sharply--hardly plausible.

cially the case since foreign observers believe that in addition to the published military budget there are off-budgetary allocations. As noted earlier a "second army," the Central Security Forces, was established in the early 1970s numbering close to 300,000 before they rioted in February 1986. Allocations to this force are not included in the military budget. The ratio of the (published) military budget to GNP dropped from 7.6 percent in 1973 to about 4 percent in 1978, and then rose sharply to 6.5 percent in 1979 and 8 percent in 1983-84. These ratios most probably understate the military burden, but the trends require explanation, especially the doubling of the military burden between 1978 and 1983-84. The large-scale arms shipments in recent years, especially from the U.S., apparently called for large Egyptian allocations for local military expenditures (Table 2.4).

The ACDA estimates are *far* higher for the 1970s, but are close to Egyptian estimates (the ratio of military spending to GNP) in 1982-83. The ACDA estimates quite obviously ignore the cost of military imports at least for recent years.[7] Reports of continued large-scale arms imports in 1984 and 1985 imply that Egypt's military burden will become more onerous at a time when it is undergoing a worsening recession as a consequence of the oil crash.

■ Syria

Like Egypt, Syria enjoyed a period of prosperity following the Yom Kippur War until the early 1980s, mainly as a consequence of the regional oil boom. Oil production peaked in 1976 at 200,000 barrels per day declining to 170,000 barrels per day in 1984. However, the sharp rise in prices in 1979-81 raised oil export revenues sharply, accounting for 70-75 percent of total commodity exports. Until the mid-1970s Syria also benefited from transit dues arising from Iraqi exports via the Syrian pipeline. In 1979 there was a resumption of oil transit until the spring of 1982 when Iran persuaded Syria to close the pipeline in return for large oil shipments from Iran, partly gratis, and the balance at discounted prices and concessionary credit terms. In effect the Iranians were providing the Syrians with better quality oil to be refined for domestic consumption, enabling Syria to export most of its own oil.

Reported grants from the rich Arab states rose to a peak of $1.8 billion in 1981, the equivalent of over one-half of Syria's export earnings (goods and services). Subsequently there was a steady decline to $1.2 billion in 1984, *including* the value of the oil grant from Iran. There were also payments made by the rich Arab oil states for arms shipments to Syria, mainly from the Soviet Union. ACDA estimates of arms imports to Syria show a very strong rise in the late 1970s and early 1980s, probably reflecting the plethora of Arab oil revenues during this period, and hence the willingness and ability of the major Arab oil states to finance Syrian arms supplies (Table 2.5).

According to unofficial estimates there were 400,000 Syrians working in the Arab oil states in the early 1980s. At their peak (1979), recorded remittances were $900 million, the equivalent of 55 percent of commodity exports, including oil. Thereafter there was a steady decline to $327 million in 1984. The decline stemmed mainly from the increasing attractiveness of the black market (mainly in Beirut) as the gap between the official and free market exchange rate continued to widen. In any case, the huge inflow of remittances, including those transferred through unofficial channels, had a powerful stimulating effect on the economy.

The booming economy, and the abundance of foreign aid, enabled the authorities to allocate larger sums to the military. Official data show that the ratio of military expenditures, as reported in the budget, to gross domestic product, which had averaged 9.4 percent between 1968 and 1972 rose to the 14-16 percent range in 1976-84 (with the exception of 1980 when it reached 17 percent). This is a significant rise especially in view of the rapid growth of the economy until 1981. ACDA estimates for 1975-82 are quite similar and are apparently also based on official Syrian budgets. However, it is abundantly clear from an examination of the data that the budgets exclude, completely or largely, the value of imported military equipment. For a number of years (1979-81) ACDA estimates of Syrian arms imports exceed their estimates of military budgets (Table 2.5). In other words, Syrian military budgets refer wholly or largely to local expenditures. So long as the economy was booming and foreign aid was plentiful the Syrians could more readily bear the burden. The attempt to raise or even maintain a high level of military expenditures in the face of a stagnant or declining economy since 1982 can only make a bad situation worse.

■ Jordan

During the 1970s Jordan became, in effect, an "oil state" despite the fact that no oil had been discovered. Recent discoveries of small quantities of oil do not alter this conclusion. At their peak, grants from the rich Arab oil states reached $1.2 billion (in 1980 and in 1981) the equivalent of almost 30 percent of its GNP, or 63 percent of its exports of goods and services, excluding remittances. In addition there were concessionary loans, as well as the financing of military imports from western suppliers. No official data are available with respect to the latter. Remittances from Jordanians working abroad, mainly in the oil states, passed the $1 billion a year level in 1981,

Table 2.5 Syria - Selected Data (millions of dollars--unless otherwise stated)

Year	1972	1973	1974	1975	1976	1977	1978	1979	1980	1981	1982	1983	1984
Total commodity exports	299	356	783	930	1066	1070	1061	1648	2112	2230	2032	1928	1859
Of which oil	53	76	431	654	671	621	665	1187	1662	1661	1513	1369	NA
Remittances received	39	37	44	52	53	92	636	901	774	582	446	461	327
Grants received	45	364	416	654	402	1143	783	1627	1520	1819	1379	1278	1201
Balance on current account	28	339	167	93	-772	-233	4	959	251	-275	-251	-815	-852
Military expenditure (budgets)	208	388	451	886	938	996	1210	1577	2243	2416	2727	2881	3294
Military expenditure as a % of gross domestic product	8.5	14.9	10.5	15.8	14.5	14.3	14.5	15.7	17.0	14.3	15.2	15.5	15.0[a]
Military expenditure (ACDA)	398	472	547	933	982	996	1181	1462	1858	2068	2371	2138	NA
Military expenditure as % of GNP (ACDA)	10.5	14.6	12.3	15.7	14.5	14.2	14.4	15.7	16.5	15.6	15.8	13.0	NA
Arms imports (ACDA)	280	1300	825	380	625	650	900	2100	2700	2100	1900	1700	NA

[a]Estimated

46

Table 2.5 (continued)

Sources:

International Monetary Fund *International Financial Statistics*, various issues

Central Bank of Syria *Quarterly Bulletin*, various issues

Central Bureau of Statistics *Statistical Abstract*, various issues

U.S. Arms Control and Disarmament Agency *World Military Expenditures and Arms Transfers 1985*, and earlier issues

Middle East Economic Digest, London, various issues

Economic Intelligence Unit *Quarterly Economic Review*, various issues

Notes:

1. The system of multiple exchange rates makes a presentation of GNP in dollars meaningless. In 1985, the black market rate was about three times the official rate, and also higher than the rate offered to tourists and to Syrian workers abroad transferring their remittances.

2. Oil exports and oil imports are recorded at the official rate, and hence the dollar figures are more meaningful. I have not listed oil imports since at various times the Syrians received oil from the Iraqis in the 1970s and from the Iranians since 1982, at far lower than international prices. Iranian oil shipments to Syria since 1982 have been partly a grant and the balance at concessional prices under long-term, interest-free loan agreements.

3. Military expenditures from the budgetary accounts are given in dollar terms based on the official exchange rate which greatly overstates the value of the Syrian pound, especially in more recent years. The more meaningful figures are for the ratio to gross domestic product, or to gross national product as presented in the estimates of the U.S. Arms Control and Disarmament Agency.

4. It is obvious from the figures that arms imports are excluded, at least for the most part, from the military budgets. They are also excluded from the balance of payments.

5. The figures for grants understate the magnitude of foreign aid. They exclude Arab financing of Syrian arms imports, as well as concessional loans for civilian projects. In more recent years, the Iranians have provided what amounts to foreign aid through their oil shipments as noted above.

6. Remittances received grossly understate their real magnitude since most enter the country through unofficial channels, financing large-scale smuggling mainly from Lebanon, and are, therefore, unrecorded in the official national accounts.

plus another $.5–$1 billion entering Jordan through unofficial channels. These were massive sums in relation to the size of the economy with a GNP of $4.5–$5 billion in 1981-84. Jordan's geographic location near the booming economies in the Gulf enabled it to take advantage of enhanced trade opportunities, including transit trade. Tourists from the rich oil states, and private investment on the part of the newly-rich in those countries (mainly in real estate) gave further stimuli to the Jordan economy. In short, the rapid growth of the economy in 1972-82 was largely due to the indirect effects of the oil boom.

Official estimates of military spending show an up-trend, but at a much slower rate than the growth of the economy. According to these estimates, the ratio of military expenditures – as reported in the budget – to GNP, dropped sharply from 17-18 percent in 1972-73 to 9-10 percent in 1980-84. ACDA estimates are far higher, but the downtrend is similar – from 35 percent in 1972-74 to 21 percent in 1982 and 15 percent in 1983. The ACDA estimate for 1983 appears to be implausible, probably based on provisional figures. Jordanian data show no decline in 1983 (Table 2.6). What is also clear is that both Jordanian data, and even the far higher estimates of ACDA exclude all or most military imports. ACDA estimates of arms imports in 1981-83 exceed their estimates of Jordanian military spending. These imports were financed by the rich Arab states and the U.S.

Since 1982, Jordan, like the oil states, or those which became highly oil-dependent, has been suffering from a recession. Real GNP has grown by 2-3 percent per annum, i.e., less than the population growth rate. This may well restrain military spending in the future.

■ Israel

With respect to Israel's economy the effect of the oil shocks was precisely the opposite of that which occurred in the neighboring countries. The oil shock of 1973-74 and even more so the shock of 1979-80, had a powerful negative impact on Israel's economy. Until recently Israel's energy supply was almost exclusively based on oil. More recently one of the electric power plants utilizes imported coal. Oil imports rose precipitously from $97 million in 1972 to $775 million in 1978. Following the conclusion of the Egypt-Israel agreement Israel withdrew from the Sinai Peninsula including the oil field which had provided about one-fourth of Israel's consumption. Moreover, the withdrawal was concurrent with the second oil shock which raised prices from $12-13 to $30-40 per barrel. Israel's oil import bill shot up to over $2 billion in 1980 and again in 1981. Oil imports exceeded the importation of military equipment, or, if you will, they greatly exceeded all U.S.

48

Table 2.6 Jordan -- Selected Data (millions of dollars -- unless otherwise stated)

Year	1972	1973	1974	1975	1976	1977	1978	1979	1980	1981	1982	1983	1984
Gross National Product	619	736	869	1180	1694	2005	2599	3068	3976	4496	4758	4904	4903
Remittances received	20	46	75	166	410	471	522	601	784	1033	1084	1110	1237
Remittances paid	--	--	--	--	21	46	65	80	154	158	177	201	228
Grants received (total)	185	186	251	409	353	500	337	1057	1313	1260	1034	795	676
Of which													
From Arab States	65	72	145	331	234	402	216	989	1243	1196	953	712	593
Military expend. (from budgets)	109	128	137	151	280	252	291	383	396	418	446	463	437
Military expenditures as % of GNP (official figures)	17.6	17.4	15.8	12.8	16.5	12.6	11.2	12.5	10.0	9.3	9.4	9.4	8.9
Military expenditures (ACDA)	349	304	307	311	587	524	586	776	791	846	823	645	NA
Arms imports (ACDA)	30	50	80	80	140	120	170	100	260	1100	850	1100	NA
Military expenditures as % of GNP (ACDA)	35.8	36.5	34.1	28.7	41.8	31.1	27.4	31.1	27.3	24.7	21.0	14.9	NA

Sources: Central Bank of Jordan *Monthly Statistical Bulletin* and *Annual Report*, various issues
International Monetary Fund *International Financial Statistics*, various issues
U.S. Arms Control and Disarmament Agency *World Military Expenditures and Arms Transfers 1985*, and earlier issues (ACDA)

Notes:

1. Remittances received, i.e., transfers to Jordan from Jordanian workers abroad, include only transfers through official channels. Estimates of unofficial transfers range from 50 to 100% of the officially recorded figures.

2. Remittances paid represent transfers out of the country by foreigners working in Jordan. Various estimates for the nearly 1980s place their number at about 150 thousand, mainly Egyptians, about one half the number of Jordanians working abroad in the Arab oil states.

3. Military expenditures as shown in the budgets are greatly understated. Even the ACDA estimates appear to be too low. For more recent years, at least, ACDA estimates of Jordan's military expenditures are less than their estimates of arms imports. Apparently, they represent only local military spending.

4. Aside from grants--mainly from the rich Arab countries--Jordan received concessionary long-term loans, mainly from Western countries, as well as from Arab countries. Reported foreign aid, grants and loans, appear to exclude payments by the rich Arab states to Western arms suppliers on behalf of shipments to Jordan. The Jordanian budgets and balance of payments appear to exclude both arms imports and their financing.

grants, both for civilian and military purposes. The consequence was both an acceleration of inflationary pressures and a deterioration in the balance of payments. Furthermore, the arms buildup in the neighboring countries made it all the more difficult for Israel to reduce its outlays on the military.

In 1973 military expenditures were the equivalent of about one-third of GNP, dropping thereafter to 20-25 percent according to Israeli accounts or 25-30 percent according to ACDA estimates (Table 2.7). However, this tends to overstate the burden. If we assume that directly, or indirectly, U.S. aid *for all purposes* financed military imports from abroad (almost all from the U.S.), our conclusion would be modified. In the twelve-year period, 1973 to 1984 U.S. grants (military plus economic) were $15.3 billion; loans (net of repayments), $4.9 billion, while *direct* military imports were $17.5 billion (Table 2.7). No figures are published regarding indirect military imports, i.e., components, raw materials, equipment, spare parts, etc. for Israel's military industries. But there is strong reason to believe that in 1973-84 *total* U.S. aid approximated Israel's military imports. In other words, local military expenditures were borne by the Israeli economy, and are therefore a better measure of Israel's military burden. The ratio of local military expenditures to GNP reached a peak of 17 percent in 1973-75, and declined to the 14-15 percent level in subsequent years. This is a very heavy burden when compared with the large majority of other countries.

▪ Conclusions

In my recently-completed study "Saudi Arabia's Dismal Economic Future: Regional and Global Implications," I projected that oil prices will remain low—possibly in their current range of about $15 per barrel—into the foreseeable future, at least when measured in real terms. I also projected that the Saudi economy will remain depressed. There are, of course, important differences, but with few exceptions this also applies to other major oil-exporting countries in the region. This also implies growing problems for those economies, such as Egypt, Jordan, and Syria, which had become highly oil-dependent. I also noted that there is a strong downward inflexibility with respect to public expenditures, including military outlays. However, eventually, economic pressures mount and these may well compel the authorities to curb military spending in order to reallocate resources towards economic development. The announced 10 percent cut in the Saudi military budget for 1985-86 is at least a declaration of intent absent in earlier years when oil revenues had reached flood levels. Israel's current cutback in military spending is also a consequence of serious economic problems. I surmise that other countries will follow a similar policy in the

Table 2.7 Israel - Selected Data (millions of dollars--unless otherwise stated)

Year	1972	1973	1974	1975	1976	1977	1978	1979	1980	1981	1982	1983	1984
Exports - goods and services	2,128	2,683	3,525	3,594	4,270	5,883	7,065	8,312	10,091	10,770	10,452	10,268	10,858
Imports - goods and services	3,261	5,338	6,991	7,705	7,608	8,414	10,347	11,969	13,866	15,158	15,255	15,445	15,751
Of which													
Direct military imports	490	1,253	1,225	1,846	1,555	1,084	1,548	1,162	1,655	2,165	1,476	1,025	1,464
Fuel imports	97	211	596	638	685	738	775	1,406	2,116	2,043	1,914	1,607	1,593
Grants from the U.S. Government	71	820	672	973	1,344	966	1,046	1,453	1,556	1,424	1,258	1,619	2,213
Balance on current account (deficit)	55	335	1,470	2,114	626	310	894	870	814	1,456	2,187	2,325	1,543
U.S. Government loans (gross)	330	369	301	839	954	988	925	1,202	1,368	1,111	1,083	1,092	898
U.S. Government loans (net)	173	199	72	605	640	580	501	702	805	445	314	162	-140
Military expenditures as % of GNP	22	32	32	32	26	26	26	21	24	26	23	20	24
Local military expenditures as % of GNP	13	17	17	17	14	14	14	14	14	14	15	15	16
Military expend. GNP (ACDA) (%)	17.6	33.9	26.1	29.2	29.8	27.9	23.2	29.2	30.6	24.5	23.9	29.0	

Table 2.7 (continued)

Arms imports (ACDA)	300	230	975	725	975	1,100	900	490	800	1,200	950	370

Sources:

Bank of Israel *Annual Report*, various issues

International Monetary Fund *International Financial Statistics*, various issues

U.S. Arms Control and Disarmament Agency *World Military Expenditures and Arms Transfers 1985*, and earlier issues

Notes:

1. Fuel imports refer to oil only until recent years when Israel began to import coal for a new electric power station. The bulk of fuel imports continues to be oil.

2. Grants from the U.S. government includes both those designated as civilian and military.

3. The figures for U.S. government loans also include those for civilian and military purposes. The net figure is after the repayment of principal and interest due each year. In recent years the bulk of repayment has been on account of interest, arising mainly from long-term high-interest loans received by Israel from the U.S. government following the 1979 Camp David agreement. Thus in 1984 Israel paid $1,038 million to the U.S. government, $914 million on account of interest and only $124 million on account of principal.

4. The balance on current account refers to the import surplus minus all transfers, both private and governmental.

5. The ratio of military expenditures to GNP, as well as local military expenditures to GNP for 1972, refers to the average for 1971-72; the 1973-75 figures are averages for the three-year period and the same is true for 1976-78.

6. The estimates of arms imports of ACDA are significantly lower than "direct defense imports" as they are designated in the Bank of Israel reports. The discrepancy may be due to the latter's inclusion of all imports by the military forces, as well as imported services. The term direct defense imports in the Bank of Israel reports implies that imports of Israeli military industries--machinery, spare parts, raw materials, etc. are excluded.

not too distant future. If extra-regional powers curb their arms shipments to the region this would give further stimulus to what I believe will be a deceleration or an absolute decline in the regional arms race. It might be noted in this regard that the decline in oil and gas prices has had an adverse effect on the Soviet economy. Some 60 percent of its hard currency earnings comes from the sale of oil and gas to Western Europe. With the Middle East oil exporting countries less able to finance arms imports for themselves and others in the region, maintaining the same level of arms imports implies more financial aid from the arms suppliers. I am fully aware of the fact that the Soviet Union may, for political reasons, accept a greater share of financing arms shipments, but I would suggest that its own economic problems may add an element of restraint. I'm not sure whether these developments will bring us closer to peace in the Middle East. The recession in the oil exporting and oil-dependent countries may bring about political upheavals and strengthen revolutionary forces in the region. It is also possible that the leadership of the major Middle Eastern countries will come to the realization that they must grapple with their economic problems and that reducing military expenditures to the far lower levels common in other parts of the world will not only reduce the possibility of armed conflict, but also improve the economic welfare of their citizens. The end of the oil boom at least provides some basis for our hopes that the leaders of the Middle Eastern countries will alter their policies and reduce their massive and onerous allocations to the military in favor of economic and social betterment of their people.

■ Notes

1. E. Kanovsky, "The Economic Aspects of Peace" in A. Hareven ed. *If Peace Comes: Risks and Prospects,* 1978, and "The Economic Dimension of Peace" in A. Hareven ed. *A Chance for Peace: Risks and Hopes*, 1980, the Van Leer Jerusalem Foundation, Jerusalem.

2. The latest report of the U.S. Arms Control and Disarmament Agency, August 1985, provides data until 1983.

3. Bank of Israel *Annual Report 1984*, p. 47.

4. *The Middle East*, London, April 1986, p. 12; *Middle East Economic Digest*, 8 March 1986, p. 4.

5. E. Kanovsky, "Saudi Arabia's Dismal Economic Future: Regional and Global Implications" Occasional Paper, the Dayan Center for Middle Eastern Studies, April 1986.

6. E. Kanovsky, "Migration from the Poor to the Rich Arab Countries," The Dayan Center for Middle Eastern Studies, May 1984, and the abridged and updated version of this study in *Middle East Review*, Spring 1986, New York, pp. 28-36.

7. If we deduct arms imports from their estimates of Egyptian military budgets we are left with absurdly low estimates of local military spending. Apparently their estimates of Egypt's military spending refer to local expenditures, at least for recent years.

3

Open Borders and Labor Mobility: Israel, the West Bank, and Gaza*

Ephraim Kleiman

■ Introduction

The Arab-Israeli War, which accompanied the establishment of Israel in 1948, resulted in the partitioning of the formerly British-administered Palestine, west of the Jordan River, into three separate entities: the state of Israel, occupying most of the coastal plain of the country, as well as the northern and southern parts of it; the main area of both the Judean and the Samarian hills, occupying the eastern part of the country, annexed by the Hashemite Kingdom of Jordan, and known since then as the West Bank (of that kingdom); and a narrow coastal strip in the south of the country, the Gaza Strip, administered, one could say by default, by Egypt. Given the circumstances under which this division came into being, and the long unabated hostility of the adjoining Arab states towards Israel, it resulted in the complete isolation of these three entities one from the other. No movement of goods, services, or factors of production was allowed between the West Bank and the Gaza Strip on the one hand, and Israel on the other hand. And because Israel was wedged between them, no such movements could virtually take place between the other two regions. Insofar as economic relationships between them were concerned, the heirs to Mandate Palestine could have been situated on different planets. In the following two decades they developed independently of one another. In particular, they took no notice whatsoever of the comparative advantages that they may have possessed with respect to one another.

All this changed dramatically when, in the wake of the 1967 Six Days War, all these areas found themselves under one rule. Many of the previously valid restrictions on the free movement of goods or factors of production were thereby suddenly removed, whether by design or simply because they could no longer be effectively enforced. This resulted in major readjustments in the patterns of certain economic activities. For reasons that are in themselves worth investigating and that will be discussed here only *en-passant*, the removal of barriers on economic flows between the three regions was more complete in the case of labor than in those of capital or of agriculture produce or of manufactured goods. Consequently, the greatest adjustments to take place were those in the patterns of employment.

This paper chronicles and analyzes some of the changes that occurred in the labor markets of the three regions as a result of the removal of the impediments to labor flows across at least some of the former borders, and points out some of their social and economic implications.

■ The Background: On the Eve of Barrier Removal

As separate entities, the three areas considered here differed considerably in both the size and the characteristics of their labor markets. In terms of labor potential, by far the largest was Israel. At the time their integration process was just starting, it accounted, as can be seen from Table 3.1, for four-fifths of the total working age population in the three areas taken together. The smallest of the three was the Gaza Strip, with less than one-tenth of the total. In the economically active population the differences were even greater, Israel accounting for nearly 87 percent of the total, while Gaza accounted for less than one-twentieth. This ascending disparity between Israel and the other two areas was an expression of differences in their respective stages of economic growth and of social development. As shown in Table 3.2, the two smaller regions were characterized by a relatively high proportion of children in their populations on the one hand, and a low overall labor participation rate on the other hand, the latter amounting to no more than 0.6 of Israel's.[1] The fact that the crude participation rate of males in the West Bank and in Gaza was nearly double the overall rate indicates the nearly absolute failure of women there to seek employment outside their own households. The dissimilarity in the overall male participation rate itself is considerably reduced when the specific rates are standardized by Israel's age structure. As a comparison of the ratios in the last row of the table indicates, differences in the age structure of the working-age population and in the work patterns of women accounted, in almost equal shares, for nearly all the difference in the overall participation rate. The remainder was due to transitory effects of the 1967 war, discussed below, and to the income support and free schooling facilities that international agencies provided to the refugees of the 1948 Arab-Israeli conflict and to their descendants. The effect of the latter was especially pronounced in the Gaza Strip, where refugees constituted more than one-half of the total population (as against less than one-fifth in the West Bank), and where unemployment before 1967 tended to be higher and the going wage lower than in the more highly developed West Bank.[2]

The picture emerging from these data is consistent with that provided by the industry structure of employment. At the time considered here, Israel

Table 3.1 Distribution of population, labor force, and employment among the three areas, 1968[a] (percents)

	Israel	West Bank	Gaza Strip[b]	Total
Total population	74.9	15.6	9.5	100.0
Working-age population[c]	79.7	12.8	7.5	100.0
Civilian labor force	86.8	8.4	4.8	100.0
Persons employed	87.7	8.0	4.3	100.0

[a]Annual average for Israel; August-December average for West Bank and Gaza Strip.
[b]Inclusive of Northern Sinai.
[c]Population aged 14 +.

Sources: C.B.S., *Statistical Abstract of Israel*, 1969.

Table 3.2 Age-structure and labor participation rate indicators, 1968[a] (percents)

	Share of children in population[b]	Participation rates			Unemployment rate (males)
		Overall	Male Crude	Standard-ized[c]	
(1) Israel	32	50	72	72	5
(2) West Bank and Gaza[d]	48	30	57	67	13
(3) (2)/(1)	1.50	0.60	0.79	0.93	2.6

[a]Annual average for Israel; August-December average for West Bank and Gaza.
[b]Under age 14.
[c]By age-structure of Israel working age population.
[d]Inclusive of Northern Sinai.

Sources: C.B.S., *Statistical Abstract of Israel*, 1969.

was a semi-industrial, or industrializing country, where the share of agriculture in employment, which has been continuously declining in the preceding decade, amounted to about 10 percent by the end of the 1960s. In the two other regions traditional agriculture was dominant. With the return to normalcy and before the process of their economic integration started to leave its mark, it provided nearly half of all employment in the West Bank in 1969 and one third of it in the Gaza Strip, where lack of land effectively limited its size. Such high shares of agriculture, combined with the other characteristics described here, are suggestive of disguised unemployment and, more generally, of an excess supply of labor. And in fact, the nearly two decades of Jordanian rule in the West Bank were characterized by a nearly constant outflow of population towards the other, in that period more rapidly developing East Bank, as well as to the oil-rich countries of the Persian Gulf that lacked skilled workers. It has been estimated that about 400,000 persons, averaging annually 2.5 percent of the population, emigrated from the West Bank between 1948 and 1967.[3] The population policy of the Egyptian administration in the Gaza Strip, which restricted the freedom of movement of its inhabitants (Egypt itself being a surplus labor country), prevented similar developments from occurring there.

Israel, on the other hand, has been a country of immigration since its establishment. Though the initial great flood of immigrants had trickled down to a rivulet by the 1960s, there was not a single year after 1953 in which the immigration balance was negative. A short-lived but sharp recession pushed up the unemployment rate to over 12 percent in early 1967. On the whole, however, the Israeli government was unfailing in its commitment to full employment, and to the provision of permanent employment opportunities by maintaining a high level of capital investment.

The military and political developments, which made possible the dismantling of the barriers existing at that time and separating these three regions from one another, at first had diametrically opposed effects on the labor markets. Like most military conflicts, the Six Days War generated a refugee movement that continued after the cessation of hostilities and took the form of massive emigration from the territories occupied by Israel as economic conditions there deteriorated. It has been estimated that as much as 20 and 8 percent of the population of the West Bank and the Gaza Strip respectively migrated out of those areas by the end of 1968.[4] The resultant decline in domestic demand might just imaginably have been offset by the simultaneous shrinkage of the labor supply. But by severing these two regions from their former metropolis, the War also deprived them of the traditional markets for their products. At the same time, the shock of defeat and of military occupation, and the uncertainty fostered by the new situation, brought private investment to a standstill. The unavoidably depressing effects of these developments on the labor market were further aggravated by the circumstances of the members of the erstwhile civil service, many of whom felt themselves barred from employment lest they be accused of collaboration with the enemy. In the 1968 data presented earlier, these immediate post-war conditions were still reflected both in the low participation rates, which fell considerably short of their pre-war level, and in the high rates of reported unemployment, which averaged 11 and 17 percent in the West Bank and the Gaza Strip, respectively, in the second half of the year.[5]

Almost the exact opposite was true of Israel. There, success in the war and the rise in public expenditure engendered by it reversed the existing trend. By mid-1968 unemployment was reduced to 6 percent, less than half its rate a year earlier, and the country was embarking on a route of rapid economic expansion that was to continue until 1973. Thus, at the moment when economic intercourse between them was being renewed, the economies of Israel and of the former non-Israeli parts of Palestine found themselves in a complementary position, insofar as their labor markets were concerned.

■ Labor Flow Developments, 1967-1982[6]

The Israeli government seemed, at first, to have had no clear concept of the nature and even the desirability of the economic contacts to be established with the two areas brought so suddenly under its control. In fact, there was little precedent for such contacts. The three had been completely isolated from one another since the partitioning of the country twenty years earlier. But even before that, it had been split into two semi-autarkic economies, the forerunners of Israel on the one hand and the West Bank and Gaza on the other hand. In particular, the Arab sector used to boycott goods originating in the Jewish one, while the latter excluded Arabs from employment, in an attempt to preserve jobs for Jewish immigrants. It has been estimated that, exclusive of government and of public concessions, less than 15 percent of all wage earners (and less than 10 percent of all persons employed) in the Jewish sector before the 1936 inter-communal disturbances came from the much larger Arab sector, where they accounted for only 5 percent of the total labor force.[7] Not surprisingly, therefore, Israel's initial policy in 1967 was to maintain the West Bank and Gaza as separate economic entities until a political settlement was reached with the countries from which they were taken.

But as what was originally envisaged as a brief transition period began to stretch itself indefinitely, economic realities came to the forefront. The most pressing of these was the depressed economic state of the occupied areas, described in the preceding section. By September 1967, every ninth male in the labor force of the West Bank, and every fifth one in the Gaza Strip, were reported to be unemployed. As participation rates dropped sharply compared to the pre-war situation, effective unemployment was probably much greater than that, amount to about 30-33 percent in the West Bank and possibly as much as 40 percent in Gaza.[8] Obviously, such a state of affairs could not be tolerated for long, for both humanitarian and political expediency reasons. As both these areas were severely hit by the loss of the export markets for their agricultural produce, the provision of alternative outlets could alleviate much of the hardship. The main perishable agricultural crops, fresh fruit and vegetables, may easily have found a ready market in Israel itself. But their high prices there were maintained through a system of marketing boards and of production quotas designed to support the income level of the domestic agricultural producer. Given the powerful farming lobby in Israel, the government could hardly consider opening these markets to competing agricultural imports. Ultimately the problem was solved when, with the connivance, or at least acquiescence, of the Jordanian government, the traffic of goods was resumed across the Jordan River bridges (of which now, unlike in the past, the Gaza Strip could avail itself).

This "open bridges" policy also helped directly to reduce some of the negative pressures on the labor markets of the West Bank. As Jordanian citizens, West Bank residents could leave the area for Jordan, in search of employment there or further abroad, usually in the oil principalities of the Persian Gulf which lacked skilled workers. As described in the previous section, such permanent or transitory emigration took on quite significant proportions in the immediate post-war period and was to continue, albeit on a much smaller scale, also in latter years. However, until the dramatic rise in oil revenues in 1973, the demand for such expatriate workers was not unlimited and was restricted on the main, to skilled, educated personnel only. As in the case of European "guest-workers," it also could not be exploited without at least temporarily breaking up the family unit. And no such option was available to the residents of the Gaza Strip who, lacking Jordanian citizenship, were not admitted into the Hashemite Kingdom and were thus effectively barred from emigrating. Thus, though the open bridges arrangement provided some relief, high unemployment rates and relatively low wage levels continued to persist, as can be seen from Table 3.3, well into the following year.

In view of the depressed economic conditions prevailing in Israel in the immediate period preceding the 1967 War, residents of the West Bank and Gaza were, at first, prohibited from seeking employment there. But the length of the border separating these regions from Israel made strict enforcement difficult, especially as the war also shifted the military frontier further out, so that the old, so called "green line" of the 1949 armistice agreements became to a great extent a purely notional one. The pressure

Table 3.3 Monthly wage levels, in absolute terms and relative to Israel, and male unemployment rates, 1967-1969 (in IL and in percents)

	Monthly wages[a,b]		Male Unemployment Rate[c]		
	West Bank	Gaza Strip	West Bank	Gaza Strip	Israel
1967, pre-war	207.5[d,e]	146[d,f]	7.7	..	10.3
	37.2	26.0			
1967, September	..	..	29.8[g]	35.8[g]	9.9
	..	..			
1968, Aug.-Dec.	143	85	14.1[g]	17.8[g]	5.6
	24.0	14.2			
1969, Average	162	126	6.4	3.4	4.5
	26.3	20.5			

[a]Monthly wage figures for the West Bank and the Gaza Strip in the post-June 1967 period obtained by multiplying daily wages by average number of workdays per month.
[b]Italicized figures express the IL wage rates as percent of the average Israeli wage.
[c]Data for nearest quarter.
[d]As reported after the 1967 war.
[e]Calculated using an exchange rate of 8.4 IL per Jordanian Dinar (this was the official rate as of July 1967, the original official rate of 7.5 being unrealistically low).
[f]Calculated at an exchange rate of 6 IL per Egyptian Pound. See note (e) above.
[g]Unemployment rates inclusive of 'discouraged workers.' See also Lifschitz, *op. cit.*

Sources: Pre-war wages (as reported after the war), from C.B.S., "Labour Force - Part I," *Publication No. 4 of the Census of Population 1967* (Jerusalem, 1968), corrected for consistency in the definition of working-age population as those aged 14+ (see also Lifschitz, below); for later dates--C.B.S. Household Surveys. Exchange rates--from Y. Lifschitz, *Economics Development in the Administered Areas, 1967-1969*, Ministry of Defense, Tel-Aviv, 1970 (in Hebrew), pp. 51, 196-197.

exerted by the huge wage disparities proved too strong to resist, and as economic conditions in Israel started to change some less restrictive arrangements had to be worked out before long.

Jerusalem, which at the time constituted a special case, provided a model of the general developments soon to follow. With the formal annexation of its Eastern, formerly Jordanian sector to Israel, its residents were automatically exempted from the employment restrictions imposed on the West Bank population. At the same time, the reunification of the city gave rise to large scale construction activity in its Western, mainly Jewish sector, which was enhanced by the government's policy of enlarging its population, in an attempt to change the demographic balance of the capital. In the Eastern sector, on the other hand, construction came to a standstill. With intersectoral distances within the city often smaller than intra-sectoral ones, the resultant flow of construction workers from East to West rapidly assumed large proportions.[9] This movement was not recorded in the official statistics, which were now treating the labor force of the city's two parts as one.

By mid-1968, this pattern started to repeat itself in the rest of the country. The huge disparity in wages, and the scarcity of employment in the West Bank and in Gaza, made both Israeli employers and workers from these areas risk transgressing the prohibition on their employment in Israel. Encouraging this process was the low unionization rate among hired farm labor in Israel and the tendency of construction workers who were laid off during the preceding recession there to leave the industry for good in favor of less volatile employment.[10] With the decline in unemployment in Israel itself, the government decided later in the year to regularize the situation and to allow a certain number of workers from the West Bank and Gaza to be employed in Israel. To minimize any adverse effects on the labor scene in the latter, the original intent was to have the overall volume of this inflow closely regulated, diverting it mainly to manpower bottlenecked industries through labor exchanges established in these territories. For this same purpose, as well as to avoid charges of exploiting a captive labor force, it was decided to equalize the costs to employers of employing Israeli and imported labor. As Israeli social insurance legislation did not apply to nonresidents, the equivalent of the normal social insurance contributions was imposed on both employers and employees, the collection of which, as well as the distribution of the corresponding benefits, was administered by a special agency set up for this purpose in the Labor Ministry. This agency was also supposed to ensure that though non-unionized, workers from the territories were paid the same wage tariffs as Israeli ones.[11]

The overall trends in the employment of West Bank and Gaza workers in Israel are illustrated in Figure 3.1. Though the issue of official work-permits was at first strictly controlled, the number of workers employed under them grew very rapidly until 1972, since which time it has stabilized at an annual

Figure 3.1. Workers from the West Bank and Gaza employed in Israel: Total number, and number employed under work permits, 1968–1982

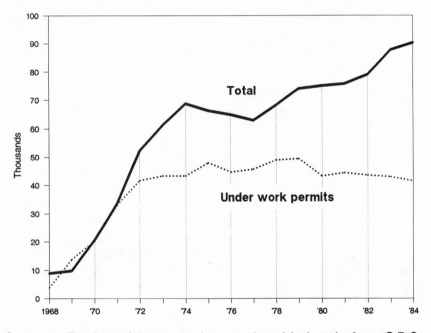

Sources: Total number reported as employed in Israel—from C.B.S., Household Surveys for the West Bank and Gaza. Figure for 1968 adjusted for underreporting—see Lifschitz (1970), p. 60. Employed under permits, C.B.S., Statistical Abstract, various years.

level of 40 to 50 thousand. The comparison of this figure with the continually growing one of the total reported to be employed in Israel shows unauthorized employment there to have increased steadily from the early 1970s onward. This should be ascribed not to the restriction of the number of permits granted, which seems no longer effective, but, on the contrary, to the growing ease with which employment can be found and maintained without them.[12] With social insurance levies amounting, on the average, to 30 percent of the basic wage tariff, employing such "unauthorized" workers considerably reduces labor costs to the Israeli employer, even if the wage he pays exceeds the official one. The workers, on the other hand, save themselves the corresponding, albeit much smaller, deductions from their earnings. As their ability to realize the future social benefits thereby forfeited is subject to political uncertainty relating to the status of the Territories, they may regard themselves better off by evading these deductions, even if paid below the official tariff. Furthermore, permits are not easily granted to casual laborers and cannot be obtained by youths under 17 years of age. With the reservations that the data on the total numbers employed in Israel and those working under permit are derived from two completely different sources, the difference between them shows "unauthorized" workers from the Territories to have exceeded 30 thousand by 1980-82.

The response to the employment opportunities provided by access to the Israel labor market varied somewhat between the two other regions. This is illustrated in Figure 3.2 by the two upmost curves, which show the proportion employed in Israel out of the total number of gainfully employed residents. Given the many contact points along the very extended border with the West Bank as well as (possibly) the initially more relaxed general atmosphere there, its residents tended or were allowed to avail themselves to a much greater extent at first of this opportunity than those of the Gaza Strip. With the restrictions on their employment in Israel effectively lifted by 1972 as implied above, the inflow from Gaza increased very steeply and as a share of all resident labor force there, equalled that of the West Bank. The behavior of this share in latter years reflects two different sets of factors. One, common to both regions, is that of the demand for labor in Israel; the other, which also affects its response to the former, is that of demand stemming from other outside sources. In both regions, this ratio peaked in 1974, as did the total number of their residents employed in Israel; when the continuing mobilization of military reserves in the aftermath of the Yom Kippur war resulted in labor shortages there. In the following three years, however, the effects of the slowdown in the Israeli economy began to be felt, expressing themselves, as can be seen in Table 3.4, in a sharp decline in the growth of total employment there as compared to both the preceding and the subsequent periods. But at the same time, the dramatic rise in oil revenues and a building boom in Amman offered new employment opportunities in the

Figure 3.2. Residents of the West Bank and Gaza employed in Israel, as proportion of all employed labor force in the region of their residence, and of Israel (percent)

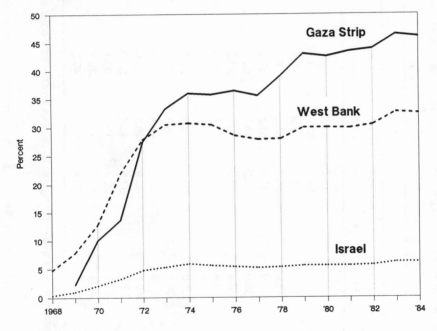

Sources: See Figure 3.1.

Table 3.4 Number of persons employed in the West Bank, Gaza, and Israel, by regions of residence and of employment, 1968-1984 (in thousands)a

	West Bank			Gaza Strip			Israel		
	Total	Of which employed Locally	In Israel	Total	Of which employed Locally	In Israel	Total	Of which resident Locally	Outside
1968b	82.9	78.9	4.0	44.5	44.5	..	914.9	910.9	4.0
1969	109.0	101.2	8.7	52.9	51.7	1.2	955.7	945.8	9.9
1970	114.6	99.8	14.7	58.7	52.9	5.9	983.8	963.2	20.6
1971	116.8	91.2	25.6	59.7	51.5	8.2	1030.9	997.1	33.8
1972	125.2	90.3	34.9	69.0	51.5	17.5	1099.8	1047.4	52.4
1973	126.4	87.8	38.6	68.2	46.6	22.7	1155.7	1094.4	61.3
1974	137.5	95.0	42.4	73.0	46.7	26.3	1165.2	1096.5	68.7
1975	132.3	91.9	40.4	72.6	46.7	25.9	1178.9	1112.6	66.3
1976	129.7	92.6	37.1	76.1	48.3	27.8	1192.1	1127.2	64.9
1977	127.3	91.9	35.5	77.2	49.5	27.5	1222.2	1159.2	63.0
1978	131.5	94.0	26.8	80.4	48.7	31.4	1281.2	1213.0	68.2
1979	132.8	92.5	39.8	79.6	45.5	34.3	1314.7	1240.6	74.1
1980	134.8	94.3	40.6	80.9	46.3	34.5	1329.6	1254.5	75.1
1981	133.4	93.5	39.9	82.5	46.6	35.9	1355.9	1280.1	75.8
1982	140.9	97.5	43.0	82.2	46.1	36.1	1377.4	1298.3	79.1
1983	147.2	99.1	48.1	85.3	45.6	39.7	1427.2	1339.4	87.8
1984	154.1	104.0	50.1	87.1	47.0	40.2	1449.7	1359.4	90.3

aThe minor discrepancies between sum of employment figures by regions and the total column occur in the original data sources.
bAugust-December.

Source: Israel, C.B.S., Household Surveys in Judea, Samaria and the Gaza Area, and idem., Statistical Abstract of Israel, various issues.

Gulf countries and in Jordan. The combined effect of these developments reflected itself in the total number of gainfully employed West Bank residents falling by nearly 7.5 percent in this short period without any rise in unemployment. As the decline in the number of West Bank residents employed in Israel was much more pronounced, both absolutely and relatively, than in that employed in the West Bank itself, the share of the former also declined. With foreign demand stabilized, and economic conditions in Israel again picking up, this trend reversed itself in later years, and both total employment and the share in it of employment in Israel can be seen to have regained their previous levels by the early 1980s.

As, for reasons discussed earlier, residents of the Gaza Strip had hardly any access to labor markets east of the Jordan River, they were affected by developments there only indirectly, insofar as they substituted for the West Bank labor withdrawn from the Israeli economy. The rising trend in the share of them employed in Israel, which was checked in the 1971-77 period, continued in later years until by 1982 this share was one and a half times as large there as in the West Bank.

Except for a brief period of decline in the mid-1970s, the total number of West Bank and Gaza residents employed in Israel, shown in the last column of Table 3.4, has been steadily increasing. However, it can be seen from Figure 3.2 that, despite slight year to year fluctuations, their share of all employment there stabilized around 1973-74 and never significantly exceeded the 6 percent level. As will be shown later, this figure by no means reflects their role in those industries in which they became concentrated. Nevertheless, it does indicate that the removal of barriers on labor movement between the West Bank, Gaza and Israel must have had much more portentous effects on the former, smaller, relatively labor-abundant two regions, than on the latter one.

■ Effects on Israel's Labor Market

From the point of view of the Israeli economy as a whole, the role played by "guest workers" from the West Bank and the Gaza Strip was quantitatively rather small. As can be seen from Table 3.5, in the decade from 1973 onward such workers accounted for between 5 and 6 percent of all persons employed in Israel's economy. However, as the other columns of the table illustrate, their share varied widely across industries from between one-quarter and one-third in construction to about one-eighth in agriculture and one-twentieth in manufacturing. The very low share registered for the rest of the economy is, in a sense, misleading, being the result of the statistical aggregation of widely differing sub-industries, which employ altogether over

60 percent of all workers in the economy. In some of these, e.g., sanitation, the share of "guest workers" may be expected to be very high; in others, e.g., financial services, it may be expected to be virtually nonexistent.

The employment of "guest workers" from without raises the question of its effect on the wage levels obtaining in the domestic market. To the extent that domestic and "guest" labor substitute for one another, the availability of the latter may be expected to lower the wage of domestic labor. (It was, in fact, to prevent or at least to mitigate such an effect, that the employment in Israel of West Bank and Gaza Strip residents was at first strictly regulated.) We hypothesized, therefore, that the depressing effect on wages would be greater the larger the size of the guest labor force relative to the domestic one. As real wages in Israel rose throughout most of the relevant period, we looked at the industry relatives and at their annual rates of change, rather than at absolute wage levels, and tried to relate them either to the share of guest workers employed in the corresponding industry group or to the annual rate of change in this share. However, no systematic relationship whatsoever was discernible, either across industries at given points of time or over time within industries, for observations on the main industry groupings of Table 3.5.[13]

The latter findings, or rather the lack of them, suggest that whatever competition may exist between domestic and guest labor, it does not fall along

Table 3.5 Share of residents of the West Bank and Gaza Strip in employment in Israel, by main industry group, 1970-1984 (percent)

	Total	Agriculture	Manufacturing	Construction	Other
1970	2.1	5.6	(0.1)	12.3	(0.4)
1971	3.3	8.2	2.0	16.7	(0.6)
1972	4.8	12.8	3.5	20.8	0.8
1973	5.3	12.5	3.9	24.9	1.0
1974	5.9	15.5	4.2	28.9	1.1
1975	5.6	11.8	4.3	28.6	1.2
1976	5.4	12.2	4.5	27.4	1.3
1977	5.1	12.3	4.6	25.0	1.5
1978	5.3	13.3	5.0	27.6	1.5
1979	5.6	13.2	5.4	29.4	1.5
1980	5.6	11.5	5.1	31.0	1.7
1981	5.6	11.1	4.4	33.0	1.6
1982	5.7	12.2	4.5	34.4	1.5
1983	6.2	12.7	5.1	33.9	1.8
1984	6.2	15.1	5.0	35.6	1.9

Source: C.B.S., *Household Surveys* and *Labor Force Surveys*, various years.

the lines of the main industry group classification used here. An alternative possible classification for this purpose is that used by occupation, and we hope to be able to repeat the investigation described above along occupational lines. Guest workers concentrated heavily in two occupational groups—unskilled and agricultural labor: They accounted for as much as two-fifths of all unskilled wage earners outside agriculture in the Israel economy in 1982. With the West Bank and the Gaza Strip supplying mainly the demand for unskilled labor in Israel, guest and domestic labor there may be largely complementary rather than competing. In particular, while about two-thirds of the residents of the West Bank and the Gaza Strip gainfully employed in 1982 had only eight years of schooling, the corresponding figure for Israel fell from 50 to only 25 percent between 1969 and 1982. Even when the growth of the labor force is taken into account, this means that the absolute number there of such relatively poorly educated and low-skilled workers fell by close to 240 thousand in this period—more than thrice the number provided by the guest labor force.

The evidence on hand suggests that guest labor *replaced* rather than *displaced* the local one. This was made possible by the very rapid growth of the Israel economy in the years immediately following the removal of the barriers on labor movements. Expansion on the one hand, and the gradual withdrawal or upgrading of less skilled domestic labor, on the other hand, created the potential for the large scale absorption of guest labor on a generally noncompeting basis. This development is reflected in Table 3.6, which compares the contribution of both domestic and guest labor in Israel to changes in employment there, by industry group. In the only industry in

Table 3.6 Changes in number of persons employed in Israel between 1970 and 1982, by main industry group and by source

	Change in number employed (thousands)			Guests as % of total
	Domestic labor	Guest labor	Total	
Agriculture	-10.8	5.1	-5.7	-89.5
Manufacturing	63.2	11.6	74.8	15.5
Construction	0.6	30.6	31.2	98.1
Other	282.1	11.2	293.3	3.8
Total	335.1	58.5	393.6	14.9

Source: Calculated from data on employment by main industry group, for Israel and for West Bank and Gaza Strip residents employed in Israel separately. C.B.S., *Statistical Abstract of Israel*, various years.

which the employment of domestic labor declined, agriculture, the increase in the number of guest workers accounted for only half of that decline. In the case óf construction, which accounts for about half of all guest workers, market integration was preceded by a period of contraction, described earlier, which resulted in a withdrawal of domestic labor force from the industry in advance of the appearance of guest labor on the market. As the industry expanded, domestic labor seem to have come, progressively, to be employed almost exclusively in supervisory capacities or in certain specific skills, so that the whole net growth of employment there is accounted for by guest workers. In the other industry groups, the whole guest workers' phenomenon was marginal when compared to the growth of employment in them.

The noncompeting labor absorption process hypothesized here is very similar to the one Israel's economy has experienced on two earlier occasions. The first was that resulting from the mass-immigration period of 1948-1951, in which the country's population doubled itself. It has been shown that since immigration was accompanied by the expansion both of general economic activity and of state bureaucracy, much of the veteran labor force was upgraded into more skilled, predominantly white-collar jobs, with the newcomers filling the slots further down the scale.[14] The second process was that of the entry, some years later, of an ethnic minority group, Israeli Arabs, into the main labor market. The Arab population that remained within Israel's frontiers after the 1948-49 war was overwhelmingly rural and was concentrated in the northern and north-central parts of the country. But the increasing pressure of a growing population on restricted land resources generated an ever-increasing pressure to search for alternative or supplemental employment.With the relaxation of the military administration to which the main centers of the Arab population were initially subjected, workers from these areas came to be employed in growing numbers outside their regional economy from the late 1950s onward. In their education levels, age structure, and rural background, the Israeli Arab workers of the early 1960s were very similar to the guest workers of the 1970s. They also teηded to find employment in the same industries and occupations: in agriculture, in the less skilled jobs in manufacturing and in services, and as construction workers.[15] In fact, the entry of labor from the West Bank and Gaza tends to repeat so closely the patterns demonstrated initially by Israeli Arabs, that it is probably the latter with whom, on the margin, they may have competed. In both cases, however, competition was probably much reduced by the longer established group vacating such jobs as a result both of better schooling and the increased demand for their skills, which the availability of even less skilled workers generated. In fact, whether ranked by the share of any given industry group in employment or by that of any given occupation, Israeli Arab labor almost always falls in between Israeli Jewish labor and that of guest workers from the West Bank and Gaza Strip. The one exception is that of skilled blue-collar workers other than in services,whose share of all male Israel Arab workers, 41 percent in 1982, exceeded the corresponding figures for both the Jewish and the guest labor force, which were 25 and 29 percent, respectively.[16] But this is also an intermediate position, in this case between the predominantly white-collar Jewish labor force, and the almost exclusively blue-collar guest one.[17]

In many respects the entry of workers from the West Bank and Gaza into the Israeli economy proceeded along lines similar to those of the entry of South European guest workers into West and North European economies. The phenomenon itself is by no means new; in fact, considerable movements of seasonal farm labor used to take place between East and West European countries before the First World War. Perhaps to an even greater extent than in the more recent European experience, Israel's guest labor, at the time of its absorption in the Israel economy, complemented rather than competed with domestic labor. However, this relationship may turn out to be asymmetric. In a severe economic contraction many workers could find downgrading to less skilled and less responsible occupations to be the only alternative to being laid off. What have been so far noncompeting labor groups may find themselves then set against one another in a highly competitive situation. Their occupational structure suggests that the potential object for the competition of Arab guest workers from the West Bank and the Gaza Strip is, first and foremost, the un- and semi-skilled Israel Arab worker.

■ The Effect of Integration on the Economies of the West Bank and the Gaza Strip

Unlike in the case of Israel, by far the most outstanding effect of the guest workers' phenomenon in the regions from which they originate is that of sheer size. With nearly one-third of all employed residents of the West Bank and close to one-half of those of the Gaza Strip working outside their community, the economic (not to mention the social and political) implications of employment in Israel are far from limited to labor markets only. We will consider here only some of the most outstanding of the latter.

One obvious result of the shift of labor from the West Bank and Gaza into Israel, is a change in the industry structure of employment in both these territories. As is the case in underdeveloped countries in general, both used to be characterized by heavy disguised unemployment in the traditional agricultural sector. The opening up of employment opportunities in Israel siphoned off this surplus labor. As can be seen from Table 3.7, the share of agriculture in employment in the West Bank declined from close to one-half

Table 3.7 Number of persons employed, by main industry group and by location of employment, the West Bank and the Gaza Strip, 1969 and 1982 (percent)

| | Employed | | | | | |
| | Locally | | In Israel | | Total | |
	1969	1982	1969	1982	1969	1982
	West Bank					
Agriculture	46.1	32.1	21.8	9.4	44.1	25.2
Manufacturing	15.5	15.9	11.5	17.9	15.2	16.5
Construction	8.9	10.6	50.6	54.1	12.2	23.9
Other	29.5	41.4	16.1	18.6	28.5	34.4
Total	*100.0*	*100.0*	*100.0*	*100.0*	*100.0*	*100.0*
	Gaza Strip[a]					
Agriculture	32.8	17.9	25.0	16.9	32.8	17.5
Manufacturing	13.9	14.8	8.3	17.4	13.9	15.9
Construction	10.0	8.5	50.0	51.2	10.0	27.2
Other	43.3	58.8	16.7	14.5	43.3	39.4
Total	*100.0*	*100.0*	*100.0*	*100.0*	*100.0*	*100.0*

[a]Total employment in Israel in 1969 was too small to affect the figures in the "total" column, which are identical with those for persons employed in the Gaza Strip itself.

Sources: C.B.S., *Statistical Abstract of Israel*, 1983, No. 34, Table XXVII/20, and unpublished C.B.S. figures.

of all persons employed in 1969 to less than one-third in 1982. The decline is even greater if we consider all workers resident in the West Bank irrespective of location of employment: By 1982 only one-quarter of them were employed in agriculture. Because of the severe scarcity of land in the Gaza Strip, the initial share of agriculture was lower there than in the West Bank. But it experienced a very similar development, with employment in this sector falling from one-third of all persons employed to less than one-fifth. Insofar as employment *within* both territories was concerned, the decline in the share of agriculture was accompanied by a rise in that of the "other industries" group, consisting mainly of services. This conforms, of course, to what international trade theory would lead us to expect – with more tradables exported or, as in the present case, with more goods-producing labor services exported, production for the domestic market will consist, to a greater degree, of nontradables, such as services. The present case differs, however, in that the good thus indirectly "exported" is, perhaps, the least tradable of all, viz., construction. There has been only a marginal increase in the share of construction in the West Bank, and none at all in the Gaza Strip. But because more than half of the residents of both the West Bank and the Gaza Strip employed in Israel are employed in construction, at least every fourth working resident of these regions is now a construction worker.

■ An International Perspective

Though the developments described in this paper may be unique to the political circumstances which brought them about, they are by no means unique in the actual phenomena they gave rise to. The extreme protectionist policies, and more generally, the vehement nationalism of the interwar period, brought to a stop the manpower flows that operated in Western economies until the First World War. Of these, those which made the most lasting impression, were the transatlantic flows of more or less permanent migrants from the Old World to the New. But though they left fewer records, similar flows also operated within the former, bringing East European workers to the farms and coal mines of northwestern Europe. Though many of them ultimately settled there, theirs was initially a temporary migration. In fact, some of it was even seasonal, the movement of hired agricultural labor migrating only for the time of the harvest. Such movements were quite large: Officially registered foreign labor amounted to 3 percent of the total labor force in Germany in the years immediately preceding World War I.[18]

The establishment of the European Economic Community removed many of the barriers to manpower movements between, as well as into, its member countries. And their rapid economic growth in the 1950s and 1960s provided an incentive for such movements on a scale greatly exceeding their earlier "border trade" magnitude. Because of the mainline political division of post-war Europe, the traditional labor exporting role of the East European countries was now taken over by those on its Mediterranean littoral, bringing Italian workers into Switzerland, Greek and Turkish ones into West Germany and Scandinavia, and Spaniards and Portuguese into France (besides those originating in its former North African possessions and the West and East Indians who migrated to the U.K.). By the early 1970s, foreign workers accounted for close to one-tenth of the labor force in Germany and for as much as 30 percent in Switzerland.[19] At the other end, work abroad absorbed more than one-tenth of the Yugoslav labor force by 1971 and has been estimated to have accounted for fully one-third of Portugal's labor force by the end of the decade.[20]

While the phenomenon of the Mediterranean "Gastarbeiter" in Western Europe has been widely commented upon, much less attention seems to have been paid to the development of similar phenomena in Third World countries. This started to assume considerable magnitudes following the increase in the revenues of the oil exporting countries after 1973. Unlike in the former case, some of the labor imported by the better off developing countries from other LDCs consisted of skilled workers and professionals to replace the more expensive and for political reasons no longer welcome Western expatriates. But it has been shown that in the case of the oil-exporters at least, the overwhelming majority of the guest workers was relatively unskilled and, as was also the case in Europe, came to be employed in menial jobs at the lower rungs of the occupational ladder.[21]

It is against this background that the developments described in this paper and their results have to be evaluated. In a "positive" as distinguished from a normative framework, we may wish to compare the pattern of labor distribution between Israel and the territories it has been administering since 1967 with that which would have evolved had the barriers on labor movement between them remained in place. As has been pointed out in section 2 above, economic stagnation there under Jordanian rule resulted in a large manpower outflow from the West Bank in the years before 1967. It may be expected that, were it not for the alternative offered by Israel's labor market, this outflow would have increased dramatically in the mid-1970s and, assuming some relaxation of Egyptian policy, that the same would also have been true of the Gaza Strip. Most plausibly, this manpower would have been attracted towards the same labor markets and employed in the same capacities as were migrants from the neighboring Arab countries.[22] It has been shown that in the seven oil-exporting Arab countries which attracted most of this migration, non-nationals constituted, on the whole, half of the labor force in 1975-76, the figures for the individual countries ranging from 33 percent in Libya to over 80 percent in the United Arab Emirates. In all these countries except for Bahrein, at least three-quarters of the migrants would have been employed in the construction industry, in which they would have accounted, in all seven oil exporters taken together, for two-fifths of all the labor engaged in this industry.[23]

What distinguishes the resort to the Israel labor market is the much lower physical costs of commuting to it, which made it possible for the overwhelming majority of the guest workers to continue living in their regular place of residence. It can be expected, therefore, that the proportion of the West Bank and Gaza Strip labor force employed outside these areas would have been much lower in the absence of this alternative. Their occupational structure, on the other hand, would have probably been much the same as that actually observed, with a very heavy concentration in construction. Unlike in Israel, they would have been working in the (perhaps to them) more congenial surroundings of Arab society and culture. To judge by their revealed preferences, these benefits were not considered sufficient to compensate them for prolonged absences from their domicile or for permanent emigration.

The share of guest workers in all employment in Israel (6 percent) is low not only when compared to the Arab oil exporters but even to many West European countries. Nor is their share in the construction industry there exceptional; indeed, it is almost identical with that observed in, say, Switzerland in 1974.[24] Historically, allowing labor inflow from the outside, other than in the form of Jewish immigration, went against the grain of Israel's social and economic policies. But we cannot altogether rule out the possibility that growing economic needs would have brought about a change in policy, even under less dramatic conditions than those generated by the 1967 war. However, because of the more distant supply sources then, the magnitude of the resultant labor imports into Israel would have been much smaller than they actually were. In both Israel on the one hand, and the West Bank and the Gaza Strip, on the other hand, the results of the integration between their labor markets was, most probably, quantitatively but not qualitatively different from those that would have obtained in its absence.

▪ Notes

*This paper is based on the chapter on "Integration in the Labor Market," in a larger study, conducted jointly with Michael Michaely, on "The Economic Integration of Israel, the West Bank and the Gaza Strip" (referred henceforth as Kleiman and Michaely, 1986), which was supported by a grant from the Ford Foundation, received through the Israel Foundation Trustees. I wish to acknowledge my debt to our research assistants, Emmanuel Avner and Idit Shkolnik, for their help, and to the Eckhardt Foundation of Ann Arbor for their financial support of the preliminary investigations which led to the present project. The assistance received from the personnel of the Israel Central Bureau of Statistics and from Mr. Shlomo Amir, special advisor at the Ministry of Labor, Jerusalem, is also gratefully acknowledged.

1. Since the various rates shown in Table 3.2 were almost identical in the West Bank and in Gaza, we present here only the aggregated data for the two regions.

2. On the whole, the participation rate of the refugees was somewhat lower than that of the nonrefugee population. *See*, e.g., Bregman, *Economic Growth in the Administered Areas* (Bank of Israel, Research Department, Jerusalem, 1974), Chapter III, where this issue is discussed in more detail.

The share of refugee population given here is that reported in the September 1967 Population Census, which shows the UNRWA figures to have grossly overestimated this population. See CBS, Census of Population 1967.

3. See M. Benvenisti, The West Bank Data Project: A Survey of Israel's Policies (American Enterprise Institute, Washington, 1984), p. 3.

4. Ibid., p. 4 and Table 3.3.

5. If the decrease, compared to pre-war levels, in participation rates is taken into account, the effective unemployment rate was much higher than that (see footnote 8 below). This, however, was a transitory phenomenon. The pre-war unemployment rate was close to 8 percent.

6. Overall surveys of economic developments in the West Bank and the Gaza Strip are provided by A. Bergman, op. cit., U. Litvin, The Economy of the Administered Areas, 1976-77 (Bank of Israel, Jerusalem, 1980), and R. Meron, The Economy of the Administered Areas, 1977-78 (Bank of Israel, Jerusalem, 1980). For non-Israeli sources, primarily on the West Bank, see V. A. Bull, The West Bank – Is It Viable? (Lexington Books, Lexington, 1975), and B. Van Arkadie, Benefits and Burdens: A Report on the West Bank and Gaza Strip Economies Since 1967 (Carnegie Endowment, New York, 1977). See also E. Kanovsky, Economic Development of Jordan (University Publishing, Tel Aviv, 1976).

7. See Z. Sussman, Wage Differentials and Equality Within the Histadrut, Massada, Ramat-Gan, 1974, (in Hebrew), p. 40, and J. Metzer and O. Kaplan, "Jointly but Separately: Arab-Jewish Dualism and Economic Growth in Mandatory Palestine," Journal of Economic History, 45, 2, June 1985, pp. 327-345.

8. The male participation rate for the West Bank in September 1967 was only 46.7 percent, as compared with 69.2 reported by the same population for the immediate pre-war period, adding another 22 percent to the registered unemployment figure. An alternative calculation, which regards as unemployed all males who responded that they did not seek employment because there was none to be found (i.e., discouraged workers), yields unemployment estimates of 30 and 36 percent for the West Bank and the Gaza Strip, respectively.

9. This was further enhanced by the fact that, unlike in the rest of Israel, Jerusalem's municipal ordinance required building in dressed stone, the traditional material of most West Bank construction, which requires special skills.

10. The entrance of workers from the West Bank and Gaza into these two industries was probably facilitated also by the fact that, already before 1967, a high proportion of workers there came from the Israel Arab Sector. For a further discussion, see below, in section 3.

11. To attain this, not only social insurance contributions, but also wage payments to workers from the territories are, in theory, made through the

Payments' Division of the Ministry. In practice, wage payments are made directly to workers in the form of advances against the sums due to them from the Division. Equal wage tariffs do not necessarily mean equal earnings.

12. The difference, between the total number reported as employed in Israel and that doing so under permit, exhibits a sudden jump in 1972, when the latter number was still growing. This suggests that, about this time, residents of the Territories became confident that reporting in household surveys as being employed in Israel would bring them no harm even if they did not possess work permits. This contrasts strongly with the situation in earlier years, when the numbers of those reported as employed in Israel fell short of that employed there under permit.

13. It should be mentioned, however, that, as pointed out by Zvi Sussman at the Conference, the overall proportion of workers from the Territories did appear with the "right," (i.e., negative) sign in a system of simultaneous equations estimating the determination of prices and wages for the economy as a whole, in a time series context, before 1974. *See* Y. Ertstein and Z. Sussman, "The Effectiveness of Price Controls and Wage Restraints in Israel, 1955-1974," *Studies in the Israel Economy, 1977*, N. Halevi and Y. Kopp eds. Jerusalem, 1978 (in Hebrew), pp. 15-29.

14. *See*, e.g., Halevy, N. and R. Klinov, *The Economic Development of Israel* (Praeger, New York, 1968), pp. 78-79, especially Table 21.

15. *See*, e.g., Makhoul, Najwa, "Changes in the Employment Structure of Arabs in Israel," *Journal of Palestinian Studies*, 11, 3, Spring 1982, pp. 77-102; Ben-Porath, Yoram, *The Arab Labor Force in Israel*, Jerusalem, 1966, and "Diversity in Population and in Labor Force," in *The Israel Economy: Maturing Through Crises*, Y. Ben-Porath ed., Cambridge, 1986, pp. 153-170.

16. Figures on Israeli labor force reconstructed from data in C.B.S. *Statistical Abstract of Israel*, No. 34, 1983, Table XII/9 and XII/18; figures on guest workers—*op cit.*, Table XXVII/20, and Table 3.7 above. Israeli statistics do not distinguish between the veteran Israel Arab population and that of the former Jordanian sector of Jerusalem annexed in the wake of the 1967 war.

17. The largely noncompeting position of the Israel Arab labor force relative to the guest one has been aptly characterized by Makhoul to the effect that "the *occupations* the Palestinian Arabs residing in Israel tend to perform rely more heavily on the use of other sources of *Arab* labor—specifically from the territories occupied in 1967"; Makhoul, N., *loc. cit.*, p. 78. The other half of Makhoul's statement (that "the *industries* they tend to enter rely rather more heavily . . . on the use of Jewish labor in response to macro-social and economic restructuring.") seems, however, to be less substantiated.

18. Based on figures of registered foreign workers as shown in K.J. Bade, "German Emigration . . . and Continental Migration to Germany . . .," *Central European History*, 12, 4, December 1980; estimates of German labor force

in 1910 derived from W.S. Woytinsky and E.S. Woytinsky, *World Population and Production*, New York, 1953. For a general analysis of the guest-worker phenomena, see Kindleberger, C.P., *Europe's Postwar Growth: The Role of Labor Supply* (Harvard University Press, Cambridge, 1967).

19. *See*, e.g., *Statistiches Jahrbuch fur die Bundesrepublik Deutschland*, and *Annuaire Statistique de la Suisse*, various issues.

20. For Yugoslavia, see W. R. Bohming, *Studies in International Labor Migration* (London 1984), Table 7.1.

21. For the best summary and analysis of the available information see, Birks, J. S., and L. A. Sinclair, *Arab Manpower: The Crisis of Development* (Croom-Helm, London, 1980); Shaw, R. P., *Mobilizing Human Resources in the Arab World* (Kegan Paul, London, 1983).

22. For an econometric model of the determinants of migration from the West Bank and the Gaza Strip, see Stuart K. Gabriel, and E. F. Sabatello, "Palestinian Migration from the West Bank: Economic and Demographic Analysis," *Economic Development and Cultural Change*, 34, 2, January 1986, pp. 245-262. Migration was found there, as may have been perhaps expected, to be a function of the differential between the unemployment rates in the external markets and in Israel. But as the model was based on annual observations and, more crucially, U.S. data were used as proxies of unemployment figures for the relevant external markets, we prefer to reserve judgment on these results despite their statistical significance.

23. *See* Shaw, R. P., *op. cit.*, Table 2.8.

24. *Ibid.*, p. 38. Compare also Bohming, *op. cit.*, Table 5.4, which shows the share of foreign workers in the German construction industry to have been twice as large as in the labor force as a whole.

4

The Economics of Occupation in Palestine Since 1948 and the Costs of Noncooperation

Elias H. Tuma

■ Introduction

The economic impact of occupation depends on the objectives, duration, form and degree of interaction, and levels of technology of the occupied and the occupier. Palestine was governed by Britain between 1918 and 1948 under a mandate by the League of Nations. In 1948 it was divided: One part became the state of Israel, including areas that were outside the Partition Plan of the United Nations which legitimized the creation of that state; these are the Western Galilee and the Triangle; another part, since then known as the West Bank, was occupied by Jordan and semi-integrated in the economy of that country; the third, the Gaza Strip, was occupied by Egypt and administered separately from the Egyptian economy. In 1967 Israel displaced both Jordan and Egypt and administered the West Bank and Gaza, first under military government and then under a mixture of military and civilian administration, on the assumption that the Israeli occupation is temporary, pending the establishment of peace between Israel and its Arab neighbors. This assumption has continued to prevail except with regard to East Jerusalem which has been annexed by Israel and united with the rest of Jerusalem as the capital of Israel, although the annexation has been largely political rather than economic in the sense of genuine integration.

Our concern is with Palestine since 1948, a period in which military occupation has been continuously exercised. The common impression is that military occupation has been detrimental to the economy of the occupied territories. However, this impression is usually applied to the Israeli occupation only, on the assumption that Egypt and Jordan were there to defend the territories against the Zionists. While this may be true of Egypt's role in Gaza, it is not true of Jordan's occupation of the West Bank, given that Jordan occupied the area and tried to integrate its economy with that of the East Bank without consulting the occupied people. Therefore, in assessing the impact of occupation, we shall compare the economic effects of occupation by Jordan and Egypt between 1948 and 1967 with those of occupation by Israel since 1967, and the economies of Jordan, Egypt, and Israel in the respective periods.

Our hypotheses are the following:

1) The military occupation of Gaza by Egypt was that of a caretaker and had little economic impact, especially because Gaza's level of economic development was probably higher than that of Egypt. Jordan's occupation of the West Bank, in contrast, was a way of saving Palestine from Israel with the hope of integrating it with Jordan. Therefore, Jordan's occupation was functional in promoting integration between the two sides of the Jordan. The impact on the West Bank could not have been significant since the levels of development on the two sides were not too far apart.

2) In contrast, Israel's occupation of the Galilee and the Triangle changed the character of those two districts, both by expanding Jewish settlement and by trying to transform the Arab economy to be in harmony with the Jewish economy, though the results have been far from ideal. However, the impact on the West Bank and Gaza was quite different: The occupation was considered temporary and the West Bank and Gaza were heavily populated by Arabs who would be hard to integrate in the Israeli economy. Therefore, Israel tried to minimize its costs of occupation and realize as many short run economic benefits as possible. However, as the military-political dynamics of the Arab Israeli conflict have changed in favor of Israel, the policy of occupation has become more inclined toward some degree of integration and long-term benefits. In both cases the material benefits to Israel have exceeded the material costs of occupation to Israel.

3) The people of Gaza and the West Bank, under the influence of a more advanced economy since 1967, have evidently benefited by means of technology transfer, higher levels of employment, and higher income levels. It is possible also that the economic costs to the residents of the occupied territories and to the aggregate economy, other than the expropriation of land as a political-military maneuver, were too small to affect the relative development of the economy. Put differently, it appears that the West Bank and Gaza have developed at least as much as they could have without the Israeli occupation, and certainly more so than they would have under Jordan and Egypt.

4) Finally, the costs of occupation may be extended to include the effects of noncooperation by the occupation forces or of lost opportunities to improve the economic structure of the occupied territories and reduce the costs of security at present and in the future.

In the next section I shall discuss the economic implications and possible effects of occupation in general. Then I shall discuss the conditions of occupation in Palestine by the various parties and try to measure the effects whenever possible. An attempt to assess the costs of lost opportunities will follow. The implications will form a summary of the findings and conclusions.

■ Meaning and Conditions of Occupation

Occupation means the physical presence of occupation forces in a given territory against the will of its residents and in opposition to the accepted international laws and institutions. [14, ch. 5 for a general discussion of occupation.] The occupation may be to enforce a policy on the occupied people, or to prevent them from exercising certain rights or behaviors. For example, the occupation forces may impose a policy of land expropriation and settlement, usurp water resource and raw material, or simply for territorial acquisition and domination. Alternatively, the occupation forces may aim only to prevent the occupied from conducting acts of war against the occupation forces outside the occupied territory. In other words, the occupation may be a defense measure to assure security of the occupying country. In this case, the occupation would shift the battlefield away from the home country into the occupied territory. Occupation for the purpose of settlement and resource exploitation tends to become long-term and to aim at integration of the economy of the occupied territory with that of the home country. We shall call this "Economic Occupation," e.g., Israel in the Galilee and the Triangle which fall outside the boundaries prescribed by the UN Partition Plan of 1947; Jordan in the West Bank. In contrast, occupation which is intended to last only as long as the security of the home country is believed to be threatened, may be called "Defensive Occupation," e.g., Israel in the West Bank and Gaza since 1967. It is possible to think of another kind of occupation, which may not be intended but which seems unavoidable when it happens; let us call this "Circumstantial Occupation," e.g., Gaza under Egypt. Another form is the "Strategic Occupation" which is any temporary military occupation intended only to secure a specific objective, such as the occupation of Lebanon by Israel in 1982. Finally, occupation may represent any combination of the above. These forms of occupation are summarized in Table 4.1.

Table 4.1 Forms of Military Occupation

1. Strategic Occupation

Objectives: Specific, other than occupation, against a third party, to secure certain benefits, etc.
Duration: Short — to accomplish a specific objective.
Process: Appease, help, cooperate with; OR subdue, humiliate, depress, usurp.
Economic Effects: Positive if former process, and negative if latter.

2. Defensive Occupation

Objectives: Enhance security; prevent threatening action; shift battleground to enemy territory.
Duration: As long as insecurity lasts.
Process: Disarm, disorganize, mobilize.
Economic Effects: Will range from extremely negative to extremely positive, depending on long-term targets.

3. Circumstantial Occupation

Objectives: Cope with an unexpected situation.
Duration: As short as possible, unless conditions change.
Process: Interfere as little as possible in occupied economy — act as caretaker.
Economic Effects: Positive or negative by default.

4. Economic Occupation

Objectives: Territorial or economic and business expansion; acquisition of resources; securement of markets, etc.
Duration: Long term.
Process: Depopulate and settle and develop; exploit; OR dominate and make dependent.
Economic Effects: Removal of technological gap and unification of the market, OR continuation and expansion of gap and creation of dependencies and dualities — economic imperialism.

5. Multipurpose Occupation

Any combination of the above, with variable characteristics, which are dynamic and may change during the process of occupation.

- Impact is a function of all three other characteristics, the technological gap, and response of the occupied to the occupation policies.

It should be useful to differentiate between occupation initially supported by international agencies, though it may be opposed by the residents of the occupied territory, and occupation which is opposed by both the international community and the residents. The area allocated to Israel by the United Nations in the 1947 Partition Plan illustrates the former, and the Galilee and the Triangle, whose occupation was opposed by the United Nations, illustrate the second. These various types of occupation often overlap in initial objectives so that the occupation may be both economic and defensive at the same time. The goals and policies may also change after occupation has taken place. For example, defensive occupation may seem promising as an economic enterprise, in which case it may be extended into economic occupation and its effects change accordingly.

Economic occupation must, by definition, be of net benefit to the occupier; otherwise, the occupation would not be undertaken or it would be terminated as soon as the negative net benefits become evident. Integration of the occupied people with the occupying power would be promoted as long as the benefits continue to prevail. Otherwise, depopulation of the occupied territory may be attempted to assure full control of the territory and the resources at the expense of the native people. If neither economic exploitation nor depopulation are possible the occupier will have no option but to withdraw. This form of occupation may be illustrated by the Israeli occupation of the Galilee from which large numbers of people were evacuated to make room for Jewish settlers. However, the Triangle could not be vacated of native people but the benefits were secured just the same. The impact of this form of occupation is to create a dual society with second class citizenship for the occupied people; this has been the case in Israel.

Occupation of the West Bank by Jordan in 1948 is another example of economic occupation, though Jordan would insist that its forces wanted only to defend Palestine against Israel. However, given that the West Bank was quickly turned to a civilian administration and that the people were given the equivalent of a Jordanian citizenship would indicate that Jordan had other intentions for the West Bank. In this case there was no need to remove the population but to take advantage of them as citizens and of the territory as an asset of Jordan. Integration was the obvious method. The net benefits would come from enlarging the market, exploiting the resources, mobilizing the labor force, and enhancing the viability of the Kingdom of Jordan. Since the West Bank economy probably was a little more advanced than that of the East Bank at the time of occupation by Jordan, the integration served to remove the gap by raising the level of development in the East Bank at the expense of the West Bank.

The occupation of Gaza by Egypt illustrates circumstantial occupation. Egypt came to the rescue of Palestine and was able to hold on to the Gaza Strip only. Egypt had virtually no option but to hold the territory, which it administered separately from the mainland. The interaction between the Gaza Strip and Egypt was limited and the impact was equally limited. It is possible that Egypt was waiting for a face-saving way of relieving itself of the responsibility of administering the Gaza Strip. It is possible also to think of Gaza as a buffer zone between Egypt and Israel, in which case the occupation of Gaza might have changed from circumstantial to defensive occupation, though against a third party, rather than against the occupied party. [The occupation by Israel of the Golan Heights from Syria and the Sinai from Egypt in 1967 would fit the concept of circumstantial occupation; these are not treated here because these territories were not parts of Palestine and the analysis would require a different emphasis from that placed on the occupation of Palestine.]

Occupation of the West Bank and Gaza Strip by Israel since 1967 has assumed a different character than their occupation by Jordan and Egypt. Though Israel might have had other plans for its own future, the occupation of these territories in 1967 was explained as forced on Israel by its defense needs. This position may be illustrated by Golda Meir's declaration that Israel would give up those territories for the signing of a peace agreement with the countries which had occupied them before 1967. Similarly the continuation of a separate administration in the West Bank and permission to maintain certain relations with Jordan, including the application of Jordanian law, tend to support Israel's claim that the occupation was defensive only. However, the policy of Israel has changed gradually, especially after the Begin Likud government came into office and speeded up Jewish settlement in the West Bank at relatively high economic costs. Subsequently there have been attempts to undermine the influence of Jordan on the West Bank and highlight the benefits of a closer relationship with Israel. The end result is that Israel, like Jordan, has been able to make the occupation a net economic benefit such that it has no economic reasons to withdraw. In fact the security argument may have become only an excuse to continue the occupation for economic objectives. This change suggests that long-term benefits became more important and short-term benefits less important than was the case in the early years of occupation. [4, esp. Ch. 6.] Therefore, the only reason for which Israel might end the occupation would have to be a political military reason, or a guarantee that any negotiated political peace agreement would assure that the long-term economic benefits would be sustained under the new arrangements.

■ Economic Costs and Benefits of Occupation

The costs and benefits may be divided into public and private. The latter relate mostly to economic activities in the micro sense, such as trade, capital investment, and labor earnings. The public economic costs and benefits relate to aggregate defense and administration budgets, as well as to indirect and invisible occupation effects on technology, economic structure, labor productivity, and the quality of life.

The occupation costs of defense are not easily determined because certain defense measures have to be undertaken in any case as long as there is a state of war, with or without occupation of enemy territory. Defense from within the occupied territory means that the defense boundaries have been pushed out. Whether the costs of defense would be raised or lowered as a result is uncertain. It is quite likely that occupation defense would be less costly than defense from within the national boundaries because any dislocation or destruction it might cause would be done in enemy territory, rather than in the home country. The difficulty of measuring the effects, however, is aggravated by the fact that occupation often follows a period of intensive war and costs of the war would no doubt overlap with those of occupation. Furthermore, it is possible that the costs of occupation may in part be borne by the occupied economy in the form of levies, indemnities, etc.

If we look at the military expenditures of Jordan, Egypt, and Israel as occupiers and as nonoccupiers, it appears that military expenditures have increased fairly steadily with some periodic fluctuations. The upward fluctuations usually seem to be more in response to defeat or the threat of defeat than as a result of occupation. According to the available data between 1963 and 1982 Egypt's military expenditure, as a percent of GNP, followed the same pattern as that of Israel and Jordan, regardless of who was an occupier and who was not. The jumps in expenditure came after the 1967 and 1973 wars, and were followed by declines, more so in Egypt than in Israel or Jordan, especially after the 1978 peace agreement with Israel. These patterns are shown in Figure 4.1. It should be noted that military expenditures by the three countries are highly correlated with each other, though the coefficient of variation is much higher for Egypt than for both Israel and Jordan, as Table 4.2.

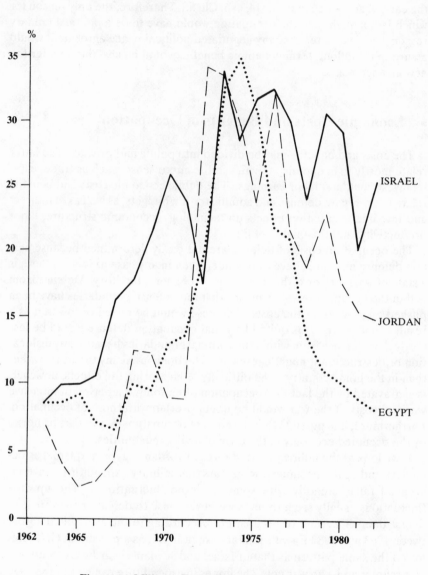

**Figure 4.1: Military Expenditure as Percent of GNP
Egypt, Israel and Jordan, 1963–1982**

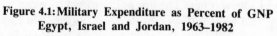

Source: U.S Arms Control and Disarmament Agency, WORLD MILITARY EXPENDITURES
AND ARMS TRADE, Washington, D.C., 1975 and 1984

Table 4.2 Military expenditure as percent of GNP, 1962-1982

Variable	Egypt	Israel	Jordan
Minimum	6.67	8.58	11.86
Maximum	35.00	34.10	35.80
Range	28.33	25.52	23.84
Median	10.70	24.03	21.50
Mean	14.99	22.46	22.41
Standard Error	1.99	1.85	1.76
Variance	78.89	68.57	62.10
Standard Deviation	8.88	8.28	7.88
Coefficient of Variation	59.26	36.86	35.17

Source of data: U.S. Arms Control and Disarmament Agency, *World Military Expenditures and Arms Trade,* 1963-1973 and 1972-1982. Washington, D.C. 1975, 1984.

It is possible, of course, to look at occupation as a reflection of the war situation, the alternative to which would be peace or a no-war situation. [20, Fig. 4.1] If we could assume a no-war settlement, we may predict a decline of the military expenditure by the warring parties at least by about half, as suggested by Egypt's example. According to some estimates, the defense expenditure of Israel in 1995 with the West Bank and Gaza still under occupation would be 24.1 percent of GNP; without them it would be 13 percent. [2, p. 58.] In another context I estimated the expenditure on a "hot war" to be as much as 10 times its level in the case of a "no-war" situation, and 4 or 5 times its level in a "cold war." [20, pp. 2-3.] Given these general impressions, it seems reasonable to conclude that the costs of defense with occupation, if separated from costs of the war leading to occupation, would be little different from the costs of defense without occupation. If so, the costs of defense from within the occupied territories cannot be considered a source of extra burden on the economy of the occupier.

The administration of occupied territories, military or civilian, often entails a separate administrative structure for the occupied territories. The costs would include all the extra expenses, including transfer payments necessary to administer the occupied areas over and above the defense requirements. Although it may be difficult to differentiate between the administrative and defense expenditures, the administrative costs may be estimated as the net transfers from the occupying country to the occupied territories, which may be positive or negative. It is quite likely that all three occupying countries were able to earn a revenue in the form of taxes, levies, fines and customs duties to offset the costs of administration. Furthermore given that the three occupiers have hardly invested in the building of an infrastructure in the territories, it is not unlikely that the net transfer would be negative. In other words, the administrative costs are most likely to be low enough to be offset by the revenues that are feasible under occupation.

The limited data available on administration may be used only as rough indicators. For instance, Jordan spent 11 million Jordanian Dinars (JD) in the West Bank in 1965, (probably including the military expenses), of which about JD 9 million were financed from tax revenues. The remainder was financed by unilateral transfers from the Ministry of Social Welfare and Employment. [25, p. 100.] Rough estimates indicate an annual expenditure by the military government of Israel of about IL 63 million in Gaza [and North Sinai] in current prices between 1968 and 1972, and about IL 41 million in the West Bank. [25, pp. 100, 101, 118 and 119.] Looked at from another standpoint, the costs of government services, including the military, in the occupied territories, may be estimated as equal to the unilateral transfers by the Israeli government to finance the trade deficit of the West Bank and Gaza with Israel, which amounted in 1975 to about 30 percent of the Israeli exports to the territories. [28, p. 37.] However, this expenditure was dispensed mostly to Jordanian and Israeli citizens employed by the occupation administration and therefore could not have been a burden to the occupier's national economy—unless we accept the argument that all military expenditure is a waste in any case. Finally, it is significant that the occupation administration in the West Bank and Gaza before and after 1967 spent very little on the infrastructure of the territories, thus keeping the economic burden to a minimum.

■ Economics Relations: Costs and Benefits

Trade. The occupied West Bank and Gaza were closely tied to Jordan and Egypt in trade relations between 1948 and 1967 and with Israel thereafter. Trade relations were determined mainly by market forces in the case of Jordan, and by administrative policy in the cases of Egypt and Israel. Were the occupied territories gainers or losers because of the occupation? Did they receive lower prices for their exports or pay higher prices for their imports than they would have without occupation? Did they pay high prices for their imports than did the citizens of the occupying country (given transportation cost differences), or did they receive lower prices for their exports than would the citizens of the occupying country have received for similar commodities?

To estimate the impact of trade as reflected in the terms of trade would assume the existence of an alternative to the status of occupied territories. However, the whole period covered has been a period of occupation. Therefore, it is not possible to estimate the terms of trade with no occupation from historical data. We may, however, examine the balance of payments, especially the current accounts, to see what light may be shed on the economic effects of occupation.

It is evident that some degree of dependence on the occupying economy has taken place, regardless who the occupier was. Before 1967 the West Bank had a deficit in the balance of trade with Jordan, and after 1967 it had a deficit with Israel. In both cases the deficit was financed by transfer payments from the occupying government or international agencies and from factor incomes earned abroad. Similarly, in both periods the occupied territories, especially the West Bank, exported more agricultural products than manufactured goods. It is interesting to note that after 1967 and the change of occupier, the West Bank continued to trade with Jordan, but in this case the deficit became a surplus in favor of the West Bank. An important feature of the trade with Israel has been the export to the latter of manufactured goods farmed out and financed by Israeli entrepreneurs who took advantage of the lower labor costs in the occupied territories. In other words, the trade benefits to the territories were embodied in job creation for the residents of the West Bank, and lower costs for the Israeli manufacturer, probably at the expense of the Israeli labor force.

But is it possible for the occupying country not to take advantage of the market potential of the occupied territories and enhance its own economy? The evidence shows that the occupiers took advantage of the occupation by facilitating trade between the two markets, and also by promoting protectionism in favor of the national economy. Protectionism has been instituted indirectly by restricting mobility, including trade, in the name of security and defense arguments. According to some observers, Israel has created a guaranteed market for its products, which has caused inefficiency in Israel, lowered the use of potential labor, and cost the economy large amounts of needed foreign exchange. It is estimated that exports to the occupied territories contained about 50 percent input value paid for in foreign currency, but they were exported and paid for in local currency. [28, I, p. 23.]

On the other hand, there is no evidence that had the occupied territories not traded with the occupier economy, they would have had a more favorable alternative. In one case at least, the end of occupation created economic hardships for the residents; this was after the Israeli withdrawal from Sinai. The farmers of Sinai were unable to dispose of their surplus agricultural products which they used to ship across the West Bank to Jordan. There is no evidence either that the residents of the occupied territories paid higher prices for their imports from Israel or Jordan than did the citizens of those countries. Therefore, given the available evidence, it is not possible to conclude that the trade relations with the territories were exploitive. It may, however, be possible to make a case that the private trade effects in both the occupied and the occupying economies were favorable, and the public aggregate effects were unfavorable. This means that the individual businesses were benefitting from trade at the expense of the aggregate economy, as has been the experience in most war situations.

An important item of trade between the occupied territories and the occupier economies has been labor services. The occupied territories have before and after 1967, had to depend on work in the occupying country to supplement their incomes and avoid unemployment. The benefits presumably accrue to both the employer and the employee, but not necessarily to the same degree. Our concern is with whether the worker from the occupied territory received more or less than the local average wage, and more or less than the average wage in the occupying country. This assumes that the workers would have found employment elsewhere, if not in the occupying country. However, should unemployment have been the alternative, the wage difference would no longer be the main criterion, and the total income of those who might be otherwise unemployed may be considered a net gain for the economy of the occupied territory.

Labor movement from the West Bank and Gaza before 1967 to Jordan, Egypt or the Gulf area gave the workers from the occupied territories an advantage presumably because they were better qualified technically than the average worker in those other markets. They were sought after because of their skills, rather than because of an overall shortage of labor. Therefore, it would seem logical that they would be compensated well enough to attract them to those countries. If so, there should be no question of exploitation unless it can be shown that they would have been otherwise unemployed and migration was their only alternative. On the other hand, given that the West Bank residents were treated like Jordanians, it would seem unlikely that they would have suffered from unemployment or unfair treatment compared with the Jordanians, given their skills and common culture. The situation in Gaza was different but there is little information to justify any generalizations.

Since 1967 both Gaza and the West Bank have been exporting labor services to Israel by daily commute. The numbers have grown large enough to finance 40 percent of the imports of the West Bank from Israel. The limiting factor on numbers has been the Israeli demand for labor, except when security measures interfered and caused distortions in the labor market. Certain points are agreed upon: The commuting workers receive lower wages and do more manual work than do the Jewish and Arab Israeli workers who are members of the Histadrut (General Federation of Labor); they receive fewer work benefits than do their Israeli counterparts, and have no work security compared with the secure position of Israeli workers. They are usually employed on a daily basis and the numbers can fluctuate frequently, depending on circumstances. The commuting workers have to comply with military rules and security requirements which often mean inconvenience, insult and humiliation, all of which may be considered a negative pay. Nevertheless these workers agree to commute to Israel rather than be unemployed or depend on the pay scale they would contract for at home. If so, they must be realizing benefits which make their commute worthwhile. However, this does not tell how much of a gap there is between what they receive and what they would have received if they did not commute.

The available data suggest that there was a big gap in the early years in favor of those commuting, compared with those staying in the territories. However, by commuting these workers made it possible for those remaining at home to enjoy a better market for their services than would have been possible, so that both the commuters and the noncommuters have enjoyed a relatively higher pay than before commuting. These comparisons are shown in Table 4.3.

In 1970 a worker staying in the West Bank received about 66 percent of what a commuter counterpart received in Israel. A worker staying in Gaza received 55 percent of the commuter counterpart. The situation has changed radically in the meantime so that in 1982 a West Bank worker received 93 percent of the commuter's pay and 97 percent if from Gaza. In

Table 4.3 Wages paid to workers from WBG in Israel and in WBG

	Israeli Shekels				Percent of Workers	
	In Isr. from		In WB	G	Empl. In Isr. from	
	WB	G			WB	G
Year	Col. 1	Col. 2	Col. 3	Col. 4	Col. 5	Col. 6
1970	11.8	11.7	7.9	6.5	14.7	5.9
1971	13.5	12.9	10.3	8.2	25.6	8.2
1972	17.0	17.6	13.7	12.8	34.9	17.5
1973	21.8	24.6	17.9	19.6	38.6	22.7
1974	28.7	30.4	25.3	27.2	42.4	26.3
1975	44.6	41.9	39.6	38.7	40.4	25.9
1976	53.4	53.5	50.0	49.6	37.1	27.8
1977	72.0	69.8	68.0	65.6	35.5	27.5
1978	112.1	109.2	105.5	102.9	36.8	31.4
1979	198.3	222.4	181.7	199.2	39.8	34.3
1980	394.0	420.0	364.0	392.0	40.6	34.5
1981	1121.0	1038.0	1040.0	1025.0	39.9	35.9
1982	2480.0	2470.0	2310.0	2420.0	43.0	36.1

Source: Fawzi A. Gharaibeh, *The Economies of the West Bank and Gaza Strip*, Boulder, Co.: Westview Special Studies on the Middle East, 1985 from Tables 3.14, 3.13 and 3.12 respectively.

both cases the difference hardly covered the transportation costs. The advantage of commuting, therefore, seems to center on the securement of employment at a relatively higher wage than would have been possible. Attempts to measure the impact of these foreign earnings on economic growth in the occupied territories suggest that these earnings were responsible for about half of the growth between 1968 and 1973, after allowing for the possible loss of income because of labor commuting. [25, pp. 121-2.] These estimates, however, tend to be optimistic regarding the availability of alternative employment in the absence of commuting.

The situation is different from the standpoint of Israel. Israel needs labor to replace those mobilized in the armed forces without resorting to mechanization which would cause a long-term reduction in demand for labor, and absorb foreign exchange resources which are in short supply. Furthermore, unemployment in the occupied territories could be a major source of political instability and could entail costs to reinforce security. Therefore, offering employment to workers from the occupied territories could serve as a measure of control as well as of pacification, while the work force could be a source of capital formation at a relatively low cost. Israel has benefited in all these respects by using Arab labor from within Israel as well as Arab commuters from the occupied territories. These workers, however, formed two classes of workers, both considered below the status of the Israeli Jewish worker and were paid on different scales. The Israeli Arabs who belonged to the Histadrut received equal pay for equal work with Jewish workers, if work was available, but the non-Histadrut members received lower wages. Rough estimates indicate that an Israeli Arab worker received an average gross annual income ranging from 66 percent to 93 percent of the average gross annual income of a Jewish counterpart between 1967 and 1976. Details are shown in Table 4.4.

The picture is different with regard to workers from the occupied territories. The average compensation per position occupied by one from the territories ranged from 30 percent to 46 percent of the compensation per position occupied by an Israeli worker (Jews and Arabs combined) between 1969 and 1981. The difference reflects both the inequality of compensation and the concentration of commuter workers in the lower paying jobs as Table 4.5 shows. In general, therefore, the Israeli employer benefited from employing workers from the occupied territories, not only by putting pressure on local wages, but also by assuring a supply of labor at lower than union wages, especially in time of war and general mobilization.

From a macro standpoint, however, the commute worker could be depriving the occupied territories of a strategically important source of labor and skills. Commuting could also develop into a form of dependency on the occupier economy to the detriment of the home economy. However, if labor had better alternatives, labor would not commute. Furthermore, depend-

Table 4.4   Gross annual incomes of Israeli Arab and Jewish urban employees (Israeli liras)

Year	Jews	Arabs	Ratio A/J
1967	9,400	7,000	74%
1968	9,600	7,000	73
1969	10,500	8,400	70
1970	11,900	8,100	67
1971	12,900	8,600	66
1972	15,500	11,200	72
1973	17,600	14,900	84
1974	26,600	23,200	87
1975	31,500	29,300	93
1976	49,100	42,400	86

Source: 1967-1973 from Zureik, Elia T., *The Palestinians in Israel*, London: Routledge & Kegan Paul, 1979; 1974-1976 from Lustick, Ian, *Arabs in the Jewish State*, Austin & London: University of Texas Press, 1980.

Table 4.5 Average wages per employee's post (Israeli shekels)

Year	Israeli Wages	Commuters' Wages	Ratio C/I
1969	63	22	.35
1970	69	25	.36
1971	80	24	.30
1972	91	38	.42
1973	116	46	.40
1974	158	69	.44
1975	221	98	.44
1976	292	135	.46
1977	434	175	.40
1978	669	276	.41
1979	1,273	553	.43
1980	2,872	1,229	.43
1981	6,871	2,916	.42

Based on *Statistical Abstracts of Israel*, 1982, Table XII/36; calculated by Abdullah Akyuz, using Van Arkadie's method, 25, p. 66.

ency is not a function of occupation but of the gap in technology between the interacting economies. With or without occupation, contact between two economies with unequal levels of technology is bound to give the edge to the more advanced economy. That edge could develop into a form of structural dependency, as has been the case in the relationship between the developed and the developing countries around the world. A more relevant question in this context is whether the labor commute has indirectly affected the structure of the economy of the occupied territories by influencing the technology, the supply of skills, and level of technological dependence.

Indirect and Invisible Effects. There have been arguments that the occupation has frustrated industrial development and growth in the occupied territories, discouraged investment, and robbed the occupied territories of qualified people. These effects may or may not be true, depending on the particular situation, technical qualification, available opportunities and so forth. We can only indirectly estimate the impact of these interactions by comparing aggregate results in the various territories before and during the various periods of occupation.

An overall picture of the impact may be seen by looking at the growth of incomes in the territories during the period of occupation. Whether under Jordan and Egypt or under Israel, the occupied territories have continued to increase their aggregate income at a favorable rate compared with the rates enjoyed by the respective occupiers. Between 1960 and 1966 the West Bank increased its GDP at an annual rate of 8.2 percent compared with 8.9 percent for the East Bank. Egypt and Israel increased their GDP between 1960 and 1970 at an annual rate of 4.3 and 8.1 respectively. Between 1970 and 1982 the occupied territories surpassed all three countries. The West Bank's GNP grew at an annual rate of 9.8 percent, and Gaza raised its GNP at a rate of 9.6, compared with 8.4 for Egypt's GDP, 3.1 for Israel's GDP and 9.3 for Jordan's GDP. [West Bank Figures are from 6, the rest are from 26, various pages.] These figures can only be indicative, given that the population changes would affect the quality of life associated with the increase in income, but the relatively favorable position of the occupied territories would not be affected.

Another indicator may be the change in the structure of the economy as represented by the size of the labor force engaged in industry. The position of the territories is less favorable than with respect to incomes, but more favorable than expected. The industrial labor force of the West Bank grew from 12.2 percent of the total labor force in 1961 to 16.5 percent in 1982. The percentages in Gaza changed from 3.2 to 15.9 which is the most dramatic change. Egypt's industrial labor force was 9.6 percent of the total in 1961 and 12.5 percent in 1982, compared with Israel's 23.8 percent which declined to 23.4 percent in the same years. Jordan's industrial labor force was 26 percent of the total in 1960 and 20 percent in 1980, as in Table 4.6, although

Table 4.6 Size of industrial labor force as percent of total

Country	1961	1968	1975	1982
West Bank	12.2	15.0	16.6	16.5
Gaza	3.2	16.2	14.2	15.9
Jordan	26(1960)			20(1980)
Egypt	9.6	11.1	12.3	12.5
Israel	23.8	24.0	24.8	23.4

Source: Computed from different references by Abdullah Akyuz; Jordan's data are from *World Development Report, 1984.* Other estimates suggest a lower rate of employment in industry in the occupied territories than shown above. The differences, however, are minor and the above figures are used because they are estimated in comparisons with those of the neighboring countries.

Jordan's figures are hard to verify. Looking at the details shows that Gaza was ahead of Egypt in 1961 and continued to be ahead. Israel and Jordan reduced the relative size of their industrial labor forces while both the West Bank and Gaza increased theirs relative to the total. In other words, the occupation did not form an obstacle in the way of enlarging the industrial sector. Actually Israel's economic behavior may have enhanced industry and manufacturing in the territories by farming out jobs to the territories, and by technology transfer and vocational training in both the West Bank and Gaza. [On vocational training *see* 6, pp. 51-2.] On the other hand, there has been little industrialization under occupation between 1968 and 1980. The "industrial" labor force was occupied in traditional manufacturing or in farmed out manufacturing for Israeli enterprises, so that little industrial capital formation in the territories was evident. On the contrary, it is generally agreed that industry stagnated, and so did the infrastructure which would have been necessary to promote industry. [25, p. 125; 13, pp. 12, 46-7, 88-89.]

The conditions of life may be assessed by looking at the health conditions and amenities of daily living. In spite of the fact that both the West Bank and Gaza have refugee camps, infant mortality has declined dramatically. In 1970-75 infant mortality in the West Bank was 34.8 per thousand; in 1976-80 it was 28.7 per thousand, compared with Jordan's 58 per thousand. The West Bank's rates are much higher than those of Israel's Jewish population but close to those of Israel's non-Jewish population, namely the Israeli Arabs whose rate of infant mortality in 1976-80 was 27.6 per thousand, compared with 14.1 per thousand for the Israeli Jews. Gaza's infant mortality rates came down from 80.2 per thousand in 1970-75 to 53.5 per thousand in 1976-80, which is much lower than Egypt's 85 per thousand in 1978. [13, p. 28; Egypt's and Jordan's data are from 26, 1984 and 1981.]

Similar conclusions follow from noting the calorie supply per capita in various periods. The West Bank increased its calorie supply from 2,344 calories per capita in 1969-71 to 2,786 in 1975-7. Gaza increased it from 2,091 to 2,386 calories in the same period. Israel had a small rise from 3,074 to 3,144, while Jordan suffered a decline from 2,278 to 2,067 calories in that period. Egypt had a supply of 2,760 calories per capita in 1977. [13, p. 22; Egypt's data are from 26, 1981.]

Finally, the West Bank and Gaza residents have experienced a large increase in the ownership of TVs, radios, telephones, private cars, and electric utilities in their homes. The most dramatic change has been in the construction of private homes. The figures on all these amenities compare favorably with both former and present occupiers, in relative terms with Israel and in both absolute and relative terms compared with Egypt and Jordan. The same may be concluded with regard to education, at least in quantitative terms. [For details see: 13, p. 24; 19, chapters 4 and 9.] If so, the occupation cannot be held responsible for not achieving more in the economic and social sectors of the occupied territories.

■ **Costs of Lost Opportunities**

So far we have dealt with the impact of economic policy of occupation, including the policy of do nothing. A different impact may be attributed to lost opportunities or the failure to take advantage of the occupation to improve the chances of peace and prosperity among the warring parties. In 1940 J. E. Meade outlined what has come to be the post WWII international economic order as a basis for peace. [12] Meade's idea was that most wars have an economic origin and therefore peace must be based on economic principles which promote coexistence and advancement of different economic systems. Though the resulting economic order of the IMF and the World Bank have failed to promote economic development of the Third World or guarantee peace, the main idea still holds that peace can be promoted by planning for it before the given war comes to an end.

A similar though broader concept surfaced again when Fred Ikle' urged that plans should be made for the kind of relationship desired after the war, long before the end of the war. [9] Ikle' urged also that the goals for which the war is fought should be kept in view, rather than concentrate on the means and on winning battles, because when the war ends, which it must, we have to live with the consequences. Now we have another theory of how to prevent war or sustain peaceful relations, namely by promoting a "Balance of Prosperity," on the assumption that if mutual prosperity could be made dependent on peaceful relations between any two parties, war between them may be avoided in order to protect their mutual prosperity. [1]

These approaches have at least three points in common: 1) Economic conditions are strategic in war-peace relations; and 2) consideration of the economic welfare of the other party is as important for peaceful coexistence as one's own welfare; and 3) the economic bases of peace can and must be established before a war ends or even before it starts if that is not too late. Failing to do so would entail what may be called the Costs of Lost Opportunities. It should be instructive in this context to recall the U.S. economic policies toward Japan, Germany, and Italy, and its Marshall Plan as means of promoting harmony, or alliance, and preventing renewed conflict. Israel, no doubt, is aware of the significance of these policies, as indicated by the so-called "Marshall Plan for the Arabs" idea recently proposed by Prime Minister Perez. [*See* contribution of Joyce R. Starr in this volume.]

Having reviewed the economic effects of occupation in Palestine, it appears that the occupiers have failed on all three counts, although this argument may be difficult to apply to Jordan and Egypt because they were not at war with the occupied territories but were their protectors. In contrast, it is possible to argue that Israel has paid little attention to the economic relations with the occupied territories as strategic factors in ending the conflict. Israel seems to have paid little attention to the economic welfare of the territories as means to promote future harmony. On the contrary, it seems that the economic welfare of the territories has been depressed by Israel's usurpation of the resources of the territories and by making them progressively more dependent on the economy of Israel. Finally, Israel does not seem to have any economic plans for future healthy economic relations with the occupied territories. Israel's plans, if they do exist, including the so-called Marshall Plan for the Arabs, tend to be aimed at relations with the neighboring Arab countries, rather than with the Palestinians, the closest neighbor and main party to the conflict. For example, there are "open bridges" with Jordan and attempts have been made to "normalize" relations with Egypt, but no known attempts have been made to build economic bridges with the Palestinians.

Several questions may be raised at this point. Could Israel have applied different economic policies to promote peace, and would it have been in Israel's interest to concentrate on relations with the occupied territories? Would it have been feasible to raise the economic level of the territories as a way of reducing conflict? There is little doubt that Israel could have cooperated more closely with the occupied territories to elevate their economic level. First, Israel has the know-how and the capacity to influence the territories, which are much less developed than and therefore susceptible to influence by Israel. Second, Israel has been the occupier and the military power and therefore has the means to enforce policy. Finally, the people of the occupied territories may be presumed to have enough economic rationality not to reject policies that would help the development of their economies, had such policies been proposed and implemented. It is possible that Israel has deliberately ignored the Palestinian inhabitants and concentrated on dealing with the Arab countries for political reasons. If so, no doubt Israel has lost opportunities to utilize economic relations with the Palestinians as a bridge of harmony and peace.

Let us assume, however, that Israel did not deliberately ignore the occupied economies. Would it have been feasible to achieve higher levels of economic performance and well-being in the territories? Such hypothetical questions can be answered only on the basis of certain assumptions. First, let us establish a reasonable scenario for the future of the occupied territories. The occupied territories may become an independent Palestinian state; they may be restored to and unified with Jordan; they may become an autonomous unit under the sovereignty of Jordan, Israel, or both; or they may be integrated into Israel (annexed) to form a unified state. I propose that whichever of these scenarios dominates, Israel could use economic policy during occupation as a bridge to peace and to better future relations. This would be true even of the 2nd scenario which would create a larger and stronger Jordan. On the other hand, an economically developed West Bank and Gaza, helped into development by Israel as the present occupier, would mean an enlargement of the market for inputs and outputs of Israel. Economic development of the territories during occupation would also help to eliminate and prevent the recurrence of duality, discrimination, and conflict on account of economic inequality. The emerging society would be free of the two or three class system that prevails at present in the labor market, which is a cause of grievance and potential conflict.

Second, having assumed an end to the conflict, regardless of the scenario, and that Israel has an excellent opportunity to use economic policy as a bridge toward peace and harmony, how much can Israel do to realize that objective? As a minimum, Israel could develop a plan for the economic transformation of the territories in cooperation with the inhabitants. As a maximum, it could remove the technological and productivity gaps between the economies of the territories and that of Israel. Some experts might argue that removal of the gap is not feasible, at least not within the present framework or the foreseeable time horizon. It is still possible to estimate the cost of lost opportunities accruing from the failure to pursue feasible targets.

In a study of potential development in the occupied territories, Ben Shahar, et al., suggested that "the whole philosophy of development should be to put the territories on a path that will allow sustained growth with all the implications with respect to modernization of their structure." [3, p. 9.] To do so it seemed necessary to promote industrialization which, given existing limitations of entrepreneurial capacity, would have to depend on "exogenous development supported by outside supply not only of capital but also of entrepreneurship and markets for the developing industry." [3, p. 9.] In estimating potential development, the authors projected that agriculture could grow within a range of between 6.7 and 9.9 percent annually between 1968 and 1978, on the assumption that water supply would increase from a little over 200 mm^3 a year to over 600 mm^3 by 1978. Manufacturing would increase at an average annual rate of between 5.8 and 11.4 percent, or between 5-13.4 for the West Bank alone. [3, p. 7.] Labor productivity could increase at rates ranging from 2.4 to 6.0 annually, with the major increase coming between 1973 and 1978. Manufacturing would constitute 9.5 percent of GDP in 1978 and would employ 12.9 percent of the labor force in the occupied territories, while agriculture would produce 38.8 percent of the total output and employ 23.4 percent of the labor force in that year. [3, p. 6.]

These projections were based on assumptions that certain policies would be implemented to realize the potential, such as the relaxation of trade restrictions with the Arab countries, and integration of the occupied economy with that of Israel. In other words, the potential seemed realizable. The results, however, have been far less favorable than predicted. On one hand, most of the growth of income in the territories has come from the sale of services or factor employment outside the territories, and from unilateral transfer payments from the outside. Structural change or development in agriculture and industry has been much less than projected. Industrial growth rates have been declining in the West Bank since 1971, and they have fluctuated more radically in the Gaza Strip, at lower levels than projected. [6, pp. 24-25.] Productivity increase has also been far below the projections, and in the case of industry there has been a decline. The exact deviations from the projections are unimportant and unverifiable because of the incomparability of the data, but the deviations are real and represent a strategic economic loss due to faulty Israeli policies or to the absence of economic policies toward the occupied territories.

The results of Israel's economic policies regarding the occupied territory and population may be summarized as follows. Little investment or facilitation of investment in industry and manufacturing in the territories is evident. On the contrary, obstacles in the way of investment are created by the authorities in the form of red tape or in the name of security, and by rules and regulations which project Israeli industry. The government of Israel has usurped the water resources and the projected increase in water supply has been utilized mostly by Jewish settlements and Jewish consumers. At the same time, the West Bank farmers have lost control over more than a third of the agricultural land. [16, p. 64-66; 4, pp. 30-35.] If we were to make a general assessment of the cost of these policies, we may conclude that the lost output, even relative to the feasible level predicted by Israeli economists, would amount to a growth rate of the GNP of about 3 percent annually. That, however, is the quantitative loss. The structural qualitative loss is certainly

more serious and strategic because it means that the economy of the territories has continued to be underdeveloped when it could have been
developed enough to serve as a basis for more harmonious relations with Israel, before and after the war comes to an end.

■ Implications

Observers from the occupied territories and from the occupying countries
have concentrated their attention on what they considered to be detrimental economic effects of occupation. The complaints have ranged widely,
covering issues such as exploitation of the occupied territories in the form
of cheaper raw material, a guaranteed market for manufactured goods of
higher prices than might be prevailing on the international market, and
cheap labor. Complaints have also been made that the territories do not
receive enough economic support from the central government to permit
development of the economy or advancement of society. Observers from Israel have argued that their economy has suffered because of the occupation
through inflated expenditures, misuse of foreign exchange and increased dependence on cheap, technically backward labor, and retardation in productivity, technical advance, and competitiveness.

Though the measurement of these possible effects may be difficult because of their relative nature, it would be equally difficult to deny their existence, as it would be to deny the existence of benefits for both the occupying
country and the occupied territories. As we have seen, both parties have
benefited from trade, labor exchange, and technical transfer. The conditions of life in the occupied territories tend to document the reality of improved conditions, at least as much as has been the improvement in
comparable neighboring countries. In fact it would be almost impossible to
make a case that the occupation has been such an economic burden as to
necessitate its termination. This of course does not mean that the occupation can be justified on economic terms either. On the contrary, there is
reason to believe that the same mutual benefits (or burdens) would result
from mere interaction between these economies because of the inequality in
their levels of development and technological achievements. If there should
be peace and an end to occupation, and if there should be free trade between
Israel and the West Bank and Gaza, the same effects would be expected.
Free trade and an open market would dictate that the more advanced or
stronger economy would dominate the less advanced or weaker economy.
Therefore, the only way to avoid the exploitive effects blamed on occupation
is to either close the technological and development gaps between the two
economies or resort to protectionism and restriction of free trade. [*For*

details see: 18, Chapter 8.] A hidden cost of the occupation policy has been the cost of lost opportunities. The occupation forces, by failing to implement feasible rational economic policies, have forfeited the potential output that could have been realized; they have failed to build an economic bridge to peace and reduce expenditure on defense; and they have failed to remove economic duality and dependency which are features of the imperialist economy. In other words, the costs of occupation have been embodied in the policies which were implemented and in the failure to implement other policies which might have helped to end the war even before it had started.

Finally, while the economic arguments against occupation may not be strong, there are serious and valid arguments against it which arise from other sources. The complaints against occupation are genuine expressions of the love of freedom and independence by the residents of the occupied territories, and the love of peace, stability, or humanism by Israeli opponents of the occupation. Both groups, however, are in essence arguing for peace and an end to the war and that is where the answer to the grievance of both groups lies: in a peaceful settlement of the conflict, far more than in an end to the occupation.

■ References

1. Arad, Ruth, Seev Hirsch and Alfred Tovias. *Economics of Peacemaking*, MacMillan, 1983.

2. Bahiri, Simcha. *Peaceful Separation or Enforced Unity*, Tel Aviv: International Center for Peace in the Middle East, 1984.

3. Ben Shahar, Haim, Eitan Berglas, Yair Mundlak, and Ezra Sadan. *Economic Structure and Prospects of the West Bank and the Gaza Strip*, Santa Monica, Rand, 1971.

4. Benvenisti, Meron. *The West Bank Data Project*, Washington and London: American Enterprise Institute, 1984.

5. Bregman, Arie. *The Economy of the Administered Areas*, 1974-75, Jerusalem: Bank of Israel, 1976.

6. Gharaibeh, Fawzi A. *The Economies of the West Bank and Gaza Strip*, Boulder and London: Westview Press, 1985.

7. Government of Jordan, National Planning Council. *Five Year Plan for Economic and Social Development*, 1981-85, Amman: 1981.

8. *IBRD. The Economic Development of Jordan*, Baltimore: Johns Hopkins Press, 1957.

9. Ikle', Fred. *Every War Must End*, New York and London: Columbia University Press, 1971.

10. Lustick, Ian. *Arabs in the Jewish State*, Austin and London: University of Texas Press, 1980.

11. Mazur, Michael P. *Economic Growth and Development in Jordan*, Boulder: Westview Press, 1979.

12. Meade, J. E., *The Economic Basis of a Durable Peace*, London: Basis Books, 1940.

13. Meron, Raphael. *Economic Development in Judea-Samaria and the Gaza Strip*, 1970-80, Jerusalem: Bank of Israel, 1983.

14. Milward, Alan S., *War, Economy and Society*, 1939-45, University of California Press, 1979.

15. Rozenkier, Avraham. "The Price of Occupation," *MAPAM*, April 1985.

16. Salhiya, Emile. "Problems of West Bank Development," *J. Palestine Studies*, Volume XI, #2, (1982).

17. *Statistical Abstract of Israel*, various years.

18. Tuma, Elias H. and H. Darin-Drabkin. *The Economic Case for Palestine*, London and New York: Croom Helm and Free Press, 1978.

19. Tuma, Elias H. *Economic and Political Change in the Middle East*, Palo Alto: Pacific Books, 1986.

20. _____. "Economics of War and Peace," Working Paper, presented at Kuwait University, April 12, 1986.

21. United Nations, *Compendium of Social Statistics*, New York, 1980.

22. *UNESCO, Statistical Digest*, 1981, 1983, 1986.

23. U.S. Arms Control and Disarmament Agency, *World Military Expenditures and Arms Trade*, 1963-1973, and 1972-82; Washington, D.C., 1975 and 1984.

24. U.S. Department of Commerce, Bureau of the Census, *International Population Dynamics*, 1950-79, Washington, D.C., 1980.

25. Van Arkadie, Brian. *Benefits and Burdens*: A Report on the West Bank and Gaza Strip Economies Since 1967, New York: Carnegie Endowment for International Peace, 1977.

26. World Bank. *World Development Report*, 1981, 1984.

27. Zakai, Dan. *Economic Development in Judea-Samaria and the Gaza Strip, Jerusalem: Bank of Israel, 1985.*

28. Zarhi, Saha'ul. "The Occupied Territories – Economic Liability," *New Outlook*, Part I, January – February, and Part II, March, 1977.

29. Zureik, Elia T. *The Palestinians in Israel*, London: Routledge and Kegan Paul, 1979.

Section II

Solutions to Conflicts and the Risks of Cooperation

This section contains three studies. These studies are one step further along the road to peaceful cooperation than those in the previous section in that they look at ways to solve conflicts. One looks even further, contemplating the risks that come with the benefits of economic cooperation.

Intriligator and Brito discuss the arms race in the Middle East. They find evidence of both an arms race and arms control efforts in the region, identifying superpower involvement in both. They recommend an arms control scenario that would include a specific Israeli plan for the West Bank and Gaza Strip and a U.S. economic assistance plan for economic regional cooperation.

Schott identifies the circumstances in which economic sanctions might be used to achieve foreign policy objectives in the Middle East. The practice of economic sanctions is not unique to the Middle East, and Schott et al. (1985) documents 103 instances of the use of sanctions since the beginning of WWI. Of these, they define 36 as having been successful. The probability of success increases when the target country experiences economic distress and political instability and/or the target is a close trading partner. Economic sanctions can be used by any country but experience shows that they have been used mainly by the major powers. Thus the risk of the use of intra-regional sanctions in the Middle East is small, especially if the foundations for peace are jointly agreed upon and are based upon common interest.

McGuire looks beyond the first stages of economic cooperation to the interdependence that comes with economic cooperation. It is traditional to assume that cooperation and thus increased welfare serve as incentives for the establishment of peace. However, there are risks that cooperative efforts will fall apart, so participants are exposed to costs that otherwise would not have existed. The magnitude of the costs is proportional to the degree of integration, the highest level of which is the exchange of factors of production. McGuire compares the costs of the possibility of disruption of factor migration with the costs of a break in commodity trade. His study is purely analytical, and thus is applicable to any regional integration framework.

5

Arms Races and Arms Control in the Middle East

Michael D. Intriligator and Dagobert L. Brito

■ **Abstract**

In this paper we identify relevant questions and issues concerning arms races and arms control in the Middle East. We identify for the relevant parties their defense and arms control objectives, their interactions in terms of conflict and cooperation, other factors affecting arms races and arms control in the region, the prospects for arms control, and future scenarios for the region. Our major conclusions are that: (1) There is evidence for both an arms race and arms control in the region. (2) The application of superpower arms race and arms control concepts pertaining to the United States and the Soviet Union is inappropriate or even dangerous in this particular regional context. (3) A more appropriate way of analyzing arms races and arms control in the region is with a multilateral and multidimensional approach which, in fact, may be in the future more and more relevant to the superpower context as well. (4) There are possibilities for further arms control initiatives of various types – unilateral, bilateral, and multilateral – in the region that could be useful steps toward an overall arms equilibrium, but, for the foreseeable future, such an equilibrium will continue to be at relatively high levels of armaments. (5) Probably the most reasonable and desirable future arms control scenario would include Israeli determination of a specific plan for the future of the West Bank and Gaza Strip and U.S. economic cooperation and political dynamism in the region.

■ Major and Minor Actors in the Middle East Region

By the "Middle East" we shall mean the interactions of 14 actors in the region, which we divide into seven major actors and seven minor actors.

The seven major actors are the major confrontation states of Israel, Egypt, Syria, and Jordan; the Palestinians which, while not having their own state, play a major role in the region; and the superpowers of the United States and the Soviet Union, which, while not in the region, have significant influences in the Middle East.

The seven minor actors, being relatively less important, are excluded from considerations for now, recognizing that they may have played major roles in the past and/or that they could play major roles in the future. These include other states in the region, namely Lebanon, Saudi Arabia, and Iraq; states in the broader region, namely Iran and Libya; and major power states of the United Kingdom and France. We exclude Lebanon in view of its virtual collapse as a meaningful state. We exclude Saudi Arabia although we recognize that it plays a major role in terms of providing financing for arms acquisitions by Arab countries in the region and that, while it has no significant land forces, it too may have to be treated in the future as another major actor in the region in terms of its developing air capabilities. We exclude Iraq for the time being largely because it is preoccupied with its war with Iran, recognizing that this is a temporary exclusion and that once that war is over it may be necessary to treat it as a major actor in the region. We also exclude Iran and Libya because of their distance from the region and their preoccupation with other matters, although we recognize that Libya, like Saudi Arabia, plays a major role in terms of providing financing for arms acquisitions by Arab states in the region. Finally we exclude the United Kingdom and France due to their relatively less significant role in the region than that of the superpowers, recognizing that both have played major roles in the region in the past. Thus, while at times past or in the future another definition of the region might be required, for the present and near future the Middle East will be treated as the region defined by the interaction of the seven major actors.

■ Arms Races in the Middle East

An arms race consists of the interactive and dynamic process of weapons acquisition among two or more states. Such arms acquisitions are typically based on perceived security interests, in terms of retaining a balance or equilibrium with rival powers. As each state seeks such a balance the result is an interactive and dynamic arms race. There are, however, other reasons for arms acquisitions, including the role of the army, prestige, the desire for regional hegemony.

In the Middle East region there are, in fact, multiple and many-sided arms races. There is an arms race between Israel and the confrontation states, stemming, in part, from underlying enmity, but further stimulated by each side seeing its security interest threatened by arms acquisitions on the other side, resulting in attempts to correct the perceived imbalance by acquiring additional weapons.[2] This arms race is further intensified and complicated by the arms acquisitions of the Palestinians, which stimulate responses on the part of both Israel and the confrontation states. The several wars that have been fought in the region and the long state of war have aggravated this arms race. In fact there are recurring cycles of military buildup, followed by the outbreak of war, particularly in the case of Syria and Israel. It should, however, not be concluded that arms races inevitably lead to the outbreak of war in the region.[3] Of the major Arab-Israeli wars that have been fought since 1948 perhaps only the 1956 war was related directly to arms acquisitions, in particular, to Israeli concern that the growing supply of Soviet weapons to Egypt would disturb the status quo and lead to an eventual Egyptian strike against Israel.[4]

Another arms race in the Middle East is the arms race among the Arab states. The states are concerned about their own security vis-a-vis one another, but they are also competing for power and influence in the region. The desire of both Egypt and Syria to be the dominant military power in the region further aggravates the Middle East arms race.

A major influence on both arms races is the role of the army in the Arab states of Egypt, Syria, and Jordan, which are, in effect, praetorian guard states with large standing armies. The role of the army in these states is decisive, and they form the backbone of the regime. The army plays a significant political, social, and economic as well as military role in these states. While Israel relies on reserves, its army also plays a significant role going well beyond military considerations. All of these armies will continue to demand major resources, both human and financial, in their procurement policies, virtually regardless of any conceivable circumstance. These resources must be specifically taken into account in considering any future scenario for the region. Ironically, any arms control measures must allow explicitly for resources to be channelled to the armies of each of the confrontation states.

Another major influence on both types of arms races in the Middle East is the presence of significant arms supplies from outside the region, particularly the arms transfers from the United States and the Soviet Union. To some extent, the superpowers use their arms transfers to compete for influence in the region, and these arms transfers, in part, drive the arms race in the region as the transfers by one superpower stimulate both additional transfers by the other superpower and responses from the competing nations in the region. In recent years the United States has played a major role in the supply of arms to Israel, while the Soviet Union has played such a role in supplying arms to Syria. The superpowers have been willing to provide vast quantities of weapons to the region, including certain modern weapons systems, such as high performance aircraft and missiles.

Yet another major influence on arms races in the Middle East is the presence of government assistance programs and private remittances to the states in the region. The superpowers, in addition to providing arms to the region, also provide economic assistance to states in the region, including budgetary and foreign exchange support. Such economic assistance programs give states in the region resources not only for consumption, investment, etc., but also, directly or indirectly, for arms acquisition and maintenance, given the underlying fungibility of economic resources. As to the United States, Israel and Egypt are, in fact, the two largest recipients of U.S. foreign assistance programs: In fiscal year 1985 the United States provided Israel $3.35 billion in economic and military aid and provided Egypt $2.5 billion, the two largest aid levels from a total aid figure for all countries of $13.7 billion. (In 1984 the United States provided Israel $2.61 billion and Egypt $2.5 billion out of a total of $12 billion.) The Soviet Union provides substantial economic support to Syria. Other states and private groups also provide economic assistance to the region, some of which is translated, directly or indirectly, into arms acquisitions. In particular, the oil-producing Arab states provide economic assistance to the confrontation states. Private groups also provide economic assistance, such as the contributions of Jews worldwide to Israel and the remittances of Egyptians and Palestinians working abroad, especially in the oil-producing Arab states.

■ Arms Control in the Middle East

Arms control consists of initiatives undertaken to achieve or to increase strategic stability among the states involved in a potential conflict. With this broad definition, arms control includes any measures that decrease the danger of war.[5] Secondary goals, as in the discussion of arms control in the super power context, would include the limitation of damage in case of war and the reduction in the cost of armaments.[6] While arms control can include limitations or reductions in number of weapons it is not restricted to this approach alone.[7]

Arms control can involve unilateral, bilateral, or multilateral initiatives. In fact all three types of initiatives can be illustrated in the Middle East region, and these illustrations serve to emphasize an important point, namely that arms control, broadly construed as initiatives that reduce the chances of war, *does* apply to this region. In fact, it has played an important role in reducing, but not eliminating, instabilities in the region.[8]

Unilateral arms control measures have included initiatives undertaken by parties both within and outside the region. Israel has exercised restraint in terms of not overtly introducing nuclear weapons to the region. In fact its policy of nuclear ambiguity not only shows self-restraint but it has the effect of limiting nuclear weapons developments by other Middle East states or nuclear transfers from the superpowers through the threat of their overt introduction by Israel. This policy of nuclear ambiguity has, in fact, been a model which has been used in other regional conflict situations, e.g., India-Pakistan, where, as in the Middle East, it induces caution and restraint by both the confrontation states and the superpowers. The possibility of Israeli nuclear weapons would entail destabilizing repercussions and superpower reactions.

Another unilateral action is the refusal of the superpowers to supply certain types of weapons systems to states in the region. While the United States and the Soviet Union are major arms suppliers to the region, both have established certain limitations in terms of which weapons they supply, the numbers of such weapons, and how these weapons could be used. In particular, they have refused to supply nuclear weapons to the region. They have also established quantitative limitations on numbers of high-performance aircraft and missiles supplied to the region. This unilateral arms control action is reinforced by the potential threat of a disruption of weapons supply or an embargo on weapons shipments, which induces caution on the part of Middle East parties in their use of not only the specific weapons supplied by the superpowers but other weapons as well. Such caution adds to stability against war outbreak and thus represents a type of arms control initiative exercised unilaterally by each of the superpowers for the region.

Bilateral arms control also exists in the region, specifically in the Egyptian-Israeli peace treaty. This treaty ended a state of war, which had significantly added to the arms race and instability in the region. Ending the state of war had the effect of significantly reducing regional political tensions and potential instabilities and thus can be considered an important arms control measure.

Even before the Egyptian-Israeli peace treaty there were elements of bilateral arms control in the region, however, in the form of demilitarized zones, buffer zones, limitations on deployments or weapons systems in certain areas, implicit agreements to avoid certain targets, and implicit agreements otherwise limiting the nature of war.

Multilateral arms control also exists in the region in the form of the Camp David agreement, involving Israel, Egypt, and the United States. A specific example of a multilateral arms control initiative is the presence of U.S. observers in the Sinai, agreed to by both Egypt and Israel, to provide early warning and protection for both sides.

Another aspect of multilateral arms control is the cooperation of the superpowers and other nuclear and nonnuclear powers in establishing a nonproliferation regime. In particular, the United States and the Soviet Union have taken an active interest in ensuring that constraints and incentives exist for states in the region not to develop nuclear weapons. These nonproliferation measures, which can be interpreted as a type of arms control initiative, have, to some extent, been offset by nuclear developments in the region and by nuclear exports to the region but, they, together with the unilateral restraint exercised by Israel, have been largely successful in preventing the overt introduction of nuclear weapons in the Middle East. The Middle East could have been significantly more dangerous and unstable in the presence of overt nuclear weapons.

■ Interactions Among the Major Players

Having treated some of the major aspects of both arms races and arms control in the Middle East, we now consider the seven major actors of the region, as discussed earlier, namely Israel, Egypt, Syria, Jordan, the Palestinians, the United States, and the Soviet Union, and, in particular, consider the bilateral interactions between each pair of these seven major actors. Altogether there are 21 such bilateral interactions, and fourteen are ranked in terms of their relative importance, from the standpoint of arms races and arms control, in Figure 5.1. These rankings are subjectively rather than objectively determined, on the basis of judgments.

The most important arms race/arms control bilateral relationship is that of Israel and Egypt, shown as the "1" in Figure 5.1. This relationship is considered the most important in terms of the Middle East arms race, with Israeli weapons acquisition based, in part, on Egyptian capabilities and vice-versa, and in terms of Middle East arms control, of which the Egyptian-Israeli peace treaty is one of the most important examples.

The second most important bilateral relationship is the Israel-Syria relationship, particularly in view of the substantial Soviet arms transfers to Syria, the high proportion of Syrian GNP devoted to arms acquisitions (which even exceeds that of Israel), past wars, and the current perception of Syria as Israel's principal potential enemy in view of the peace treaty with Egypt. Third and fourth ranked of the 21 bilateral relationships are the

MAJOR ACTORS:	E	S	J	P	U	R
Israel (I)	1	2	3	4	5	
Egypt (E)		10	13	14	7	
Syria (S)			9	12		6
Jordan (J)				11		
Palestinians (P)						
United States (U)						8
Soviet Union (R)						

Israeli interactions	1, 2, 3, 4
Superpower interactions	5, 6, 7, 8
Arab interactions	9, 10, 11, 12, 13, 14

Figure 5.1: Rankings of importance of bilateral interactions relevant to arms races and arms control in the Middle East

Israel-Jordan and Israel-Palestinian relationships, based on past wars, terrorism, the continuing Palestinian problem, and the question of the future of the West Bank and Gaza Strip. These four most important bilateral relationships are treated, as a group, as *Israeli interactions* in view of the role of Israel in each. All four of these bilateral relationships derive, in part, from the defense and arms control objectives of Israel, involving a perceived need for military superiority in the region in order to provide some degree of security against a surprise attack. Such superiority would deny any opponent or coalition of opponents the option of resort to force. In addition, Israel is concerned with self-sufficiency in arms, given the fear of a possible arms embargo; acquisition of high technology weapons systems both for security and for certain economic and political goals; a settlement of the Palestinian issue; a reduced burden of military expenditure, given an extremely high ratio of military expenditure to GNP; and certain political objectives.

The next set of four bilateral relationships each involve the United States, the Soviet Union, or both, and are therefore treated, as a group, as *superpower interactions*. These include the United States-Israel interaction, ranked 5, involving U.S. arms transfers and economic assistance, and the Camp David process; the Soviet-Syrian interaction, ranked 6, involving arms transfers and economic assistance; and the U.S.-Egypt interaction, ranked 7, involves economic assistance and the Camp David process. The U.S.-

Soviet relationship is ranked 8, involving both superpower competition in the Middle East and the application of the superpower-supported non-proliferation regime in the region. As in the case of Israeli interactions, the superpower interactions derive in part, from the objectives of each of the superpowers. For the United States its principal concerns are maintaining stability in the region; ensuring the survival of Israel; keeping good relations with Egypt, Jordan, and other Arab countries; maintaining Western access to oil; retaining general influence in the region; and minimizing the influence of the Soviet Union in the region. The region is, in fact, vital to U.S. interests. The Soviet Union is concerned with protecting its client state, Syria, and retaining and expanding its influence, both political and military, in the region. It also appears to have a broader objective of encircling the oil fields of the Gulf region, given its involvement in Syria, Afghanistan, the Indian Ocean, and South Yemen. Such a campaign of encircling the oil fields puts the Soviets in a position both to threaten the economies dependent on this oil, particularly those of Western Europe and Japan, and possibly to obtain oil from this region in the future on concessionairy terms.

The third and final set of bilateral relationships are the *Arab interactions*, involving Syria-Jordan, Egypt-Syria, Jordan-Palestinians, Syria-Palestinians, and Egypt-Palestinians, ranked 9, 10, 11, 12, 13, and 14, respectively, and involving changing patterns over time of conflict and cooperation, with implications for arms races and arms control in the Middle East. As in the case of the two previous sets of bilateral interactions, the Arab interactions derive, in part, from the objectives of the Arab actors. For Egypt the goal is security, particularly against a surprise attack, but in addition, Egypt is concerned with maintaining a military option; preserving its traditional dominant political and military role in the region; settling its economic problems; and resolving the Palestinian issue. Jordan is concerned with security, both in terms of an external attack and in terms of internal revolution. It must also be concerned with the Palestinian issue, particularly the future of the West Bank, but its principal concern is the preservation of its independence and territorial integrity. Syria is concerned with its own defense, with ensuring that it plays a major or even dominant role in the region, and with regaining the Golan Heights. It also has the broader and more ambitious goals of creating "Greater Syria," assuming control over traditional Palestine, including Jordan, Lebanon, and most of Israel. The Palestinians are concerned with their survival and security, establishing a state of Palestine, resolving their factional differences, and ensuring their economic well-being.

The remaining rankings, each involving one of the superpowers, are of lesser importance, and they are not shown explicitly in Figure 5.1, although, over time, they could become more important. Also, over time, other actors might be added, particularly Saudi Arabia and Iraq.

■ The Inappropriateness of Applying Superpower Arms Race and Arms Control Concepts to the Middle East

In analyzing arms races and arms control in the Middle East it is important to take into account the specifics of the region, including the seven major actors and their various interactions, the important role of the superpowers, the lack of (overt) nuclear weapons, the role of the army, and related political and economic considerations. It is inappropriate to consider arms races and arms control in the Middle East region as playing roles similar to those they play in the superpower competition, given these special considerations. The application of U.S.-Soviet concepts relating to defense or arms control can be misleading or even dangerous. In particular, defense and arms control concepts that have been applied to the superpowers, such as mutual assured destruction, counterforce targeting, strategic defense, detente, and strategic arms reductions are probably not applicable to the region.

Given the nature of the region it is necessary to study it in multilateral, rather than in bilateral terms and to treat explicitly the military, political, and economic interests of all parties, rather than focusing on purely bilateral military issues. In fact, if one were to treat the Middle East situation in strictly bilateral military terms, specifically in terms of Arab and Israeli military balances, one might, as a result, overlook the fact that two of the most important potential arms control initiatives for the region are political/economic, not military and unilateral/multilateral, not bilateral, as discussed below.

We also would note that, interestingly enough, U.S.-Soviet strategic interactions in the future may very well also be more appropriately analyzed in such multilateral and multidimensional terms rather than in bilateral military terms, given the planned or expected future deployments of British, French, and Chinese capabilities, and given the important interactions among military, political, and economic variables. Thus, rather than U.S.-USSR strategic relations being a model for studying arms races and arms control in the Middle East, it may be that precisely the opposite is true, with Middle East military, political, and economic interactions being a prototype of eventual global strategic interactions. A major difference between global and Middle East strategic interactions, however, is precisely the role of the superpowers in the region.

■ Future Scenarios: Baseline, Pessimistic and Optimistic

Alternative future scenarios can be envisaged for the Middle East in terms of the possibilities for arms races and arms control. As in quantitative forecasting, it is instructive to bracket a particular forecast with a "low" and a "high" estimate. Here a "baseline" scenario, representing the most likely future, is bracketed by "pessimistic" and "optimistic" scenarios, in terms of potential arms race/arms control possibilities for the region.

The *baseline scenario* is a continuation of the status quo, but coupled with anticipated political, economic, and military developments. In this scenario, as to Israeli interactions the likelihood is that of a continued "cold peace" with Egypt and "cold war" with Syria and Jordan, coupled with political activity and low-intensity conflict of skirmishes and terrorist acts by the Palestinians. In terms of superpower interactions this scenario will likely involve reduced economic assistance to the region. In terms of Arab interactions this scenario will likely involve continued shifting alliances and low intensity conflict. The result would be continued arms acquisitions in the region with no significant arms control initiatives.

Rising and high oil prices in the past led, directly or indirectly to increased arms acquisitions in the region by the Arab parties, through both governmental support of the oil-producing states and remittances from guest workers, especially Egyptians and Palestinians. The recent drastic reductions of oil prices and expectations of continued relatively depressed oil prices over the short to medium term do *not* lead, however, to the reverse anticipations of major reductions in arms acquisitions. Because of the influential role of the army in the Arab states these states would be unwilling to make significant cuts in arms acquisitions, particularly given the high levels and major acquisitions of arms by Israel and the other Arab states.

Thus the result of reduced oil revenues will probably lead not to a significant reduction in arms purchases but rather to a reduction in investment, imports, and living standards.[10] Budgetary restrictions or limitations in the United States may require limiting its economic support for Israel and Egypt in the future. Similarly, the Soviet Union may be required to reduce its support for Syria due to its own economic difficulties, particularly when coupled with falling domestic oil production and international oil prices, given that the bulk of export earnings of the Soviet Union stem from oil sales. Such reduced superpower support could have some effect in terms of reduced arms purchases, but, as in the case of falling oil prices, the more significant effects would probably be reduced investment, imports, and living standards.

The *pessimistic scenario* involves, in terms of Israeli interactions, some or all of: a further deterioration of political relations with Egypt as Egypt seeks to improve its position vis-a-vis other Arab states; skirmishes or even open conflict with the Syrians; the escalation of low-intensity conflict with the Palestinians; and further disaffection, revolt, or uprisings in the occupied territories. Another aspect of the pessimistic scenario could be the overt introduction of nuclear weapons by Israel.[11] Such a step would have significant destabilizing repercussions, including a nuclear arms race in the region and adverse superpower reactions.

In terms of superpower interactions, in this pessimistic scenario there could be added transfers of arms to offset reduced economic assistance and fewer restrictions on numbers or use of weapons supplied to the region as a result of competition from other suppliers.

As to Arab interactions, in this pessimistic scenario there could be greater tensions and conflicts due to reduced external support and the repatriation of Egyptian and Palestinian guest workers. A particularly pessimistic scenario would be severe economic pressures in the Arab states leading to significant reductions in living standards. The result could be economic disaster leading to possible social and political upheaval, conceivably to the advent of revolutionary fundamentalist and apparently irrational regimes in the region. These developments would make the prospects for peace in the region even more remote as, for example, a revolutionary fundamentalist Egypt renounces the peace treaty with Israel and once again, seeks the elimination of Israel.

The *optimistic scenario* involves, in terms of Israeli interactions, a significant improvement in its relationships with Jordan and the Palestinians through a decision on its future role in the West Bank and Gaza Strip. A national debate on future options in these occupied zones could lead to a national commitment to a particular plan and a timetable of actions with regard to its implementation. Such a plan should include specific steps with regard to the future political, security, economic, and legal status of these regions that have been occupied since 1967 and could become more and more areas of unrest and potential flash points for major conflict. Such a plan could play the major role in settling the issue of the future of the Palestinians if it recognizes the interests of the Palestinians and also of all the states in the region in this key issue. Some sort of resolution of this issue which is accepted by all parties would probably represent the most significant arms control initiative for the region, in terms of reducing the chance of war.

In this optimistic scenario Egypt would take significant steps to foster peace in the region by promoting closer ties to Israel, including greater trade, tourism, cultural and scientific exchange, etc. It would also take a greater role in expanding the Camp David peace process, particularly by encouraging the involvement of Jordan.

As to superpower interactions, in the optimistic scenario the superpowers would take some important steps unilaterally or jointly to reduce the chance of war. Most important would be restraints on certain weapons systems, particularly systems that could undermine any arms equilibrium in the region.[12] At the same time the superpowers would ensure continuation of supply of defensive systems. Furthermore, the United States would, in this optimistic scenario, play an active political and economic role to promote arms control. It would promote improved Egyptian-Israeli and Jordanian-Israeli relations via political dynamism in the region, leading, for example, to Jordan joining the Camp David process. The result could be an Israel-Jordan peace treaty, perhaps based on the same "peace for land" formula as in the Egypt-Israel peace treaty. Meanwhile, continuing this optimistic scenario, the Soviet Union could play a similar role in fostering a Syrian or Israeli peace treaty as the United States played in fostering an Egyptian-Israeli peace treaty, including restrictions on deployments and jointly manned, Syrian-Israeli-Soviet observation stations in the Golan Heights to provide early warning and protection of both sides in this sensitive area.

As to Arab interactions, in this optimistic scenario there would emerge greater economic and political cooperation due, in part, to the positive steps of Israel and the superpowers.

■ Prospects for Arms Control

The discussion of future scenarios, baseline, pessimistic, and optimistic, suggests that there are some significant possibilities for arms control in the region that would build on past efforts and help stabilize the region by reducing the chance of war. Nevertheless, for the foreseeable future the region will probably continue to have a relatively high level of armaments.

Certain arms control initiatives could play a significant role in promoting stability in the region. For Israel the most important arms control initiative would be that of determining a reasonable future for the West Bank and Gaza Strip, in recognition of the potential problems of continued occupation of these territories, the attitudes of the people of these territories, the interest and involvement of the other states and Palestinians, and the security concerns of all interested parties. This initiative would be an important and perhaps essential step toward other arms control initiatives, such as an expanded Camp David agreement to include Jordan.

For the United States the most important arms control initiative would be economic and political activities to foster economic cooperation and political dynamism in the Middle East. Only the United States can provide the financing, administrative expertise, and the capability of working as a friendly third party with both Israel and the Arab states of Egypt and Jordan that are all needed to promote economic cooperation in the region. Economic cooperation in the form of expanded trade and investment, joint major capital projects, and labor and capital mobility throughout the region could play a significant role in terms of arms control. Unilateral U.S. initiatives, building upon its interactions with several states in the region, could foster regional economic cooperation which, in turn, could promote political as well as economic cooperation, providing both bilateral arms control results in terms of Israeli interactions and multilateral arms control results in terms of Arab interactions. The region, particularly the Arab states, suffer from chronic economic problems, including lack of skilled manpower, an obsolete and aging capital stock, poor economic planning, overpopulation in Egypt, and a limited national market in Jordan. These traditional economic problems are being compounded by newer problems stemming, as noted, from reduced oil prices, including reduced governmental funding from oil-producing states, reduced remittances from Egyptian and Palestinian workers in such states, and repatriation of these workers. The resulting economic pressures, when combined with demands of the military for continued support, could lead to severe reductions in living standards with possibly disastrous political consequences, particularly in Egypt, which already faces severe economic pressures. Economic cooperation in the region, fostered by the United States as part of its economic support and political involvement in the region, could avoid this disastrous future and thus play a significant role in terms of arms control.

Reference has been made recently to a possible U.S. Marshall Plan for the Middle East. While this is primarily a slogan, and there are dramatic differences between postwar Europe and the Middle East today, it would, in fact, be extremely useful to have an integrated plan and overall concept for economic assistance and cooperation in the region. Other nations, particularly those of Western Europe, and international organizations, particularly the IMF and the World Bank, could also play an important role in fostering economic cooperation in the region. Economic cooperation resulting in economic growth could prevent the advent of revolutionary fundamentalist regimes, could provide the resources needed to keep the armies intact, and could improve the political climate. Such economic cooperation could be an important step in a process of political, military, and social change in the region which would result in greater stability. Economic cooperation, particularly when combined with political dynamism, could, in fact, be one of the most important instruments of arms control in the region.

Both forms of arms control, the political determination by Israel of a future for the West Bank and Gaza Strip and U.S. activities to promote economic cooperation and political dynamism in the region, involve political and economic rather than military initiatives. Each would be initiated by the unilateral actions of one of the major actors in the region, and each could lead to positive bilateral and multilateral arms control responses. Furthermore, they are mutually reinforcing, with a resolution of the status of the West Bank and Gaza Strip helping promote economic cooperation and political dynamism in the region and vice-versa. These two initiatives, particularly when taken together, represent the most reasonable and desirable prospects for arms control in the region. Even with either or both of these initiatives, however, the likelihood is that there will continue to be a relatively high level of armaments in the region for the foreseeable future, given present levels, planned production and transfers, the lack of an overall political solution, and given the significant role of the armies in all states in the region. Nevertheless, arms control, particularly multilateral approaches, involving several parties, and multidimensional approaches, involving political and economic as well as military initiatives, could play an important role in stabilizing the region and avoiding some extremely undesirable alternatives for the Middle East.

	MILITARY	*POLITICAL*	*ECONOMIC*
UNILATERAL	No introduction of overt nuclear weapons by Israel; Refusal by superpowers to supply certain types or numbers of weapons.	*Israel determination of a future for the West Bank and Gaza Strip.*	*United States actions to promote economic cooperation.*
BILATERAL	Egyptian-Israeli peace treaty; Israeli-Jordanian peace treaty.	*Egyptian-Israeli and Israeli-Jordanian improved political relations.*	*Bilateral economic cooperation.*
MULTILATERAL	Superpower cooperation to prevent nuclear proliferation in the region; *Egyptian-Israeli Jordanian peace treaty.*	Camp David agreement of Egypt, Israel, United States; *Expanded Camp David agreement to include Jordan.*	*Multilateral economic cooperation.*

Figure 5.2: Past and possible *future* arms controls initiatives in the Middle East

Note: Future initiatives are in *italics*.

A summary of past and possible future arms control initiatives for the region appears in Figure 5.2. This table highlights some important past steps and possible future ones, particularly the unilateral/political initiatives of Israel vis-a-vis the West Bank and Gaza Strip and the unilateral/economic initiatives of the United States in fostering economic cooperation in the region. Both of these unilateral steps, particularly when taken together, have important potential bilateral and multilateral consequences with military, political, and economic dimensions, including improved political relations between Egypt and Israel and Israel and Jordan, bilateral economic cooperation, an expanded Camp David agreement to include Jordan, and Israeli-Jordanian (or multilateral Egyptian-Israeli-Jordanian) peace treaty, and further bilateral and multilateral economic cooperation in the region.

▪ Notes

*We would like to acknowledge the extremely perceptive observations and useful suggestions of Shlomo Aronson, who is currently visiting UCLA from the Hebrew University, and the research assistance of Daniel Lefler, an intern at the UCLA Center for International and Strategic Affairs. We also received helpful suggestions from W. Seth Carns, Steven Rosen, and Etel Goldman.

1. Our previous work on arms races appear in Brito (1972), Intriligator (1975), Intriligator and Brito (1976, 1984), and Brito and Intriligator (1985). For a review of the literature on conflict theory, including arms races, see Intriligator (1982).

2. For a formal model of this interactive process see Intriligator and Brito (1985a).

3. For a theoretical analysis of the relationship of an arms race to the outbreak of war see Intriligator and Brito (1984). *See also* Mayer (1986) and Intriligator and Brito (1986).

4. *See* Evron (1977).

5. Our previous work on arms control appears in Brito and Intriligator (1977) and Intriligator and Brito (1985b, 1986).

6. For a discussion of the so-called "canonical" goals of arms control, as applied to the superpower arms conflict, see Schelling and Halperin (1961) and Schelling (1963).

7. As has been noted in the general arms control literature, in certain contexts arms *increases* can stabilize an otherwise unstable situation and thus can be considered as arms control initiatives. *See* Schelling and Halperin (1962) and Schelling (1963). For a formal model implying that in certain situations arms *increases* can reduce the chance of war see Intriligator and

Brito (1984). *See also* Mayer (1986) and Intriligator and Brito (1986) for further discussions of the relationships between arms acquisitions and war initiation. Some specific examples in the Middle East were the U.S. transfers of Phantom jets to Israel in 1970 and the Soviet transfer of Scud surface-to-surface missiles to Egypt in 1973. The former strengthened Israel and thus deterred Arab attacks, while the latter forced Israel to restrict attacks to military objectives, avoiding countervalue air strikes against Egyptian population and economic infrastructure in order to avoid Egyptian countervalue retaliation against Israel. For a discussion of these cases of arms transfers as arms control measures in the region see Evron (1977). Evron notes that while the transfer of Phantom jets secured some stability, war was not ultimately prevented. He also notes that while the Scud missiles limited the destructiveness of war by restricting targets to military objectives they did strengthen Egypt's intention to start the 1973 war in the first place.

8. For previous analyses of arms control in the Middle East see Evron (1973, 1975, 1977). *See also* Gray (1975), Mihalka (1973), and Milstein (1972), Rattinger (1976), and Rosen (1978).

9. An exception may be in time of war. During the 1973 war there were reports of possible Soviet nuclear weapons on ships approaching the region.

10. In economic terms, the marginal prosperity to buy arms is high when income is rising, but low when income is falling, a type of ratchet effect.

11. *See* Feldman (1982) and the critiques of his position in Beres, Ed. (1986). *See also* Jabber (1971) and Rosen (1977).

12. An important precedent for supplier cooperation in limiting arms transfers to the Middle East is the Tripartite Declaration of 1950, under which the arms suppliers to the region at that time, the United States, Britain, and France, regulated arms transfers. It was a major arms control agreement which was effective until the emergence of the Soviet Union as a major arms supplier to the region in the Soviet-Egyptian arms deal of 1955.

▪ Bibliography

Beres, Louis Rene, Ed. (1986), *Security or Armageddon; Israel's Nuclear Strategy*, Lexington: Lexington Books.
Brito, D.L. (1972), "A Dynamic Model of an Armaments Race," *International Economic Review*, 13:359-375.
Brito, Dagobert L. and Michael D. Intriligator (1977), "Strategy, Arms Races, and Arms Control," in J.V. Gillespie and D.A. Zinnes, Eds., *Mathematical Systems in International Relations Research*, New York: Praeger.
—(1985), "Conflict, War, and Redistribution," *American Political Science Review*, 79:943-957.

Evron, Yair (1973), *The Middle East: Nations, Superpowers, and Wars*, New York: Praeger.

___(1975), "Arms Races in the Middle East and Some Arms Control Measures Related to Them," in G. Sheffer, Ed., *Dynamics of a Conflict; A Reinterpretation of the Arab-Israeli Conflict*, Atlantic Highlands, N.J.: Humanities Press.

___(1977), *The Role of Arms Control in the Middle East*, London: The International Institute for Strategic Studies, Adelphi Paper No. 138.

Feldman, Shai (1982), *Israeli Nuclear Deterrence: A Strategy for the 1980s*, New York: Columbia University Press.

Gray, Colin S. (1975), "Arms Races and Their Influence upon International Stability, with Special Reference to the Middle East," in G. Sheffer, Ed., *op. cit.* London: Chatto and Windus.

___(1981), *Not by War Alone: The Politics of Arms Control in the Middle East*, Berkeley: University of California Press.

Intriligator, Michael D. (1975), "Strategic Considerations in the Richardson Model of Arms Races," *Journal of Political Economy*, 83:339-353.

___(1982), "Research on Conflict Theory: Analytic Approaches and Areas of Application," *Journal of Conflict Resolution*, 26:307-327.

Intriligator, Michael D. and Dagobert L. Brito (1976), "Formal Models of Arms Races," *Journal of Peace Science*, 2:77-88.

___(1984), "Can Arms Races Lead to the Outbreak of War?" *Journal of Conflict Resolution*, 28:63-84.

___(1985a), "Heuristic Decision Rules, The Dynamics of the Arms Race, and War Initiation," in Urs Luterbacher and Michael D. Ward, *Dynamic Models of International Conflict*, Boulder: Lynne Rienner.

___(1985b), "Non-Armageddon Solutions to the Arms Race," *Arms Control*, 6:41-57.

___(1986), "Mayer's Alternative to the I-B Model," *Journal of Conflict Resolution*, 30:29-31.

Mayer, Thomas F. (1986), "Arms Races and War Initiation: Some Alternatives to the Intriligator-Brito Model," *Journal of Conflict Resolution*, 30:3-28.

Mihalka, Michael (1973), "Understanding Arms Accumulation: The Middle East as an Example," in J. Benkak, Ed., *International Conflicts: The Methodology of Their Assessment*, New York:

Milstein, Jeffrey (1972), "American and Soviet Influence, Balance of Power, and Arab-Israeli Violence" in B.M. Russett, Ed., *Peace, War, and Numbers*, Beverly Hills: Sage Publications.

Rattinger, H. (1976), "From War to War: Arms Races in the Middle East," *International Studies Quarterly*, 20:59-

Rosen, Steven J. (1977), "A Stable System of Mutual Nuclear Deterrence in the Arab-Israeli Conflict," *American Political Science Review*, 71:1367-1383.

___(1978), "What the Next Arab-Israeli War Might Look Like," *International Security*, 2:

Schelling, Thomas C. (1963), *The Strategy of Conflict*, Cambridge: Harvard University Press.

Schelling, Thomas C. and Morton H. Halperin (1961), *Strategy and Arms Control*, New York: Twentieth Century Fund.

6

Economic Sanctions and the Middle East

Jeffrey J. Schott

■ Introduction

It may seem anomalous to discuss economic sanctions in the context of economic cooperation in the Middle East. But as a practical matter, countries resort to both economic assistance and sanctions in pursuit of foreign policy objectives. One must look at both poles of economic statecraft — carrot and stick — to understand international economic relations. The United States has been the most stalwart supporter of Israel, but that has not dissuaded it from imposing limited economic sanctions against Israel on frequent occasions.

This paper will attempt to analyze in which circumstances and in what manner economic sanctions might be deployed in pursuit of foreign policy objectives in the Middle East. As such, the scope of analysis extends beyond the countries of the region to the major powers with substantial political, economic, and security interests in the region.

The paper first reviews the historical experience since World War I with sanctions deployed in pursuit of foreign policy goals. Distinctions are made between types of policy goals and the situations in which sanctions are imposed. Sanctions episodes involving Mideast countries are surveyed, and preliminary conclusions are drawn regarding the efficacy of sanctions in advancing political objectives in the Middle East. The analysis then turns to the question of which countries wield economic influence in the region and how such influence could be applied in the future in pursuit of foreign policy goals.

▪ Economic Sanctions in Pursuit of Foreign Policy Goals

This section will address the question of whether sanctions are effective and, if so, under what circumstances? The analysis draws heavily on the comprehensive study of economic sanctions published by the Institute for International Economics in 1985.[1]

Conventional wisdom asserts that sanctions "never work," that they mask a lack of resolve to deal with problems, and that they inevitably result in the practitioner "shooting himself in the foot." The conspicuous failures of recent episodes involving the U.S. grain embargo against the Soviet Union and sanctions against the construction of the Soviet-European gas pipeline have reinforced this view. Nonetheless, governments repeatedly defy conventional wisdom in resorting to sanctions in pursuit of goals as diverse as the dismantling of apartheid in South Africa to the overthrow of Qaddafi in Libya to the adoption of political reforms in Poland.

To analyze why countries resort to economic sanctions, Gary Hufbauer, Kim Elliott and I documented 103 cases since the beginning of World War I where sanctions were deployed by a number of countries in pursuit of foreign policy goals. We organized the cases by broad policy objective: "modest" or relatively limited, specific goals (i.e., antiterrorism; nuclear nonproliferation; support for human rights); the overthrow of a foreign government (e.g., U.S. sanctions against Trujillo in the Dominican Republic); the termination of limited military conflicts (e.g., the Turkish invasion of Cyprus in 1974); the weakening of the economic/military potential of a major adversary (e.g., the Arab boycott of Israel); and "major" or fundamental changes in the political regime of a target country (e.g., sanctions against apartheid in South Africa).

Why do countries resort to economic sanctions? The answer turns on the alternatives a country has in pursuing a foreign policy objective and the tools it has at its disposal. Basically, a country can address foreign policy disputes in five different ways: diplomacy, political coercion, economic coercion, covert action, and military intervention. Policy responses usually involve a combination of these ingredients. Economic sanctions often emerge as the centerpiece when a balance is needed between actions that seem too soft or those that seem too strident. In such situations, sanctions are seldom regarded as the "ideal" weapon; rather they are seen as the "least bad" alternative.

What about the other weapons in the foreign policy armory? Diplomacy in the classic sense has acquired a bad name. The telecommunications revolution and transoceanic jet travel have undermined the influence of overseas emissaries. Today, diplomats are often used as message carriers (the story of U.S.-USSR diplomacy) or hostages (in Iran and Libya), rather than mediators or negotiators.

Political coercion — marked by breaking diplomatic relations and isolating the target country internationally — has its own drawbacks. A complete break in diplomatic relations establishes a hostile atmosphere and undermines the political leverage available to influence the policies of the target country. Relations between Iran and the United States illustrate this outcome. A campaign to turn the country into an international pariah takes time to implement, time that is often well-spent by the target to achieve a political rescue. This story is illustrated by erstwhile U.S. efforts to isolate Syria.

Covert and quasi-military measures are distasteful to democracies and often yield a domestic backlash which can undercut support for the policy. To avoid this pitfall, governments resort to charades such as covert U.S. aid to the Contras in Nicaragua under the guise of humanitarian assistance. Israel is unique in its bold, nonhypocritical approach to quasi-military and covert actions.

Military intervention may work against certain small and even medium-sized countries (Grenada and Argentina), but it often seems too dangerous in instances where the threat of big-power confrontation lurks (Poland and Afghanistan); moreover, military intervention often proves ineffective in the context of national civil wars (the United States in Vietnam; Israel in Lebanon).

By comparison with other policy alternatives, economic sanctions may not seem so bad. Trade and financial controls are a way to demonstrate resolve, to express outrage, and to seek to deter further abuses without risking dangerous confrontation or embarrassing humiliation.

Are sanctions effective in achieving foreign policy goals? Success is in the eyes of the beholder. Much depends on the type of goal sought, the particular historical context, and the method in which sanctions are deployed. A whole host of factors, both political and economic, may bear importantly on the outcome of a sanctions episode.

The political variables we examined included the health and stability of the target country, the warmth of prior relations between sender and target, international assistance to the target country or cooperation with the sender, the duration of sanctions, and the use of companion policies such as covert and quasi-military measures. The economic variables included the cost of sanctions to both target and sender countries, their trade linkage, the ratio of GNP values, and the type of sanction deployed (trade or financial).

In our analysis, we judged an episode successful if sanctions made a modest contribution to a goal that was at least partially realized. By that definition, sanctions were successful in 36 percent of the cases we analyzed. Episodes involving destabilization and modest policy goals were the most successful; attempts to disrupt military adventures, to impair a foreign adversary's military potential, or otherwise to change its policies in a major way generally failed.

It is important to note, however, that success has proven more elusive in recent years than in earlier decades. Prior to 1973, almost half of all the sanctions cases studied were successful; since 1973 the success rate has dropped to just over a quarter. The growth in global economic interdependence and East-West confrontation have made it easier for target countries to find alternate suppliers, markets, and financial backers to replace goods embargoed or funds withheld by the sender country.

Under what circumstances are sanctions most likely to contribute to the successful achievement of foreign policy goals?

First of all, economic sanctions are a big-power game. In only a handful of the 103 cases were sanctions deployed by countries other than the United States, United Kingdom, USSR, and the Arab League. Indeed, the GNP of sender countries was on average more than 150 times greater than that of the target countries.

That said, sanctions are most likely to succeed if they have a clearly defined and limited objective, if they are imposed decisively rather than incrementally so as to inflict the maximum pain on the target country, and if they do not impose insupportable costs on domestic industries and foreign allies. Furthermore, the probability of success increases if the target country is experiencing economic distress and political instability, and/or if the target is an erstwhile friend or close trading partner. On the other hand, international cooperation with the sanctions is *not* a prerequisite for success, but the converse — international assistance to the target country — often leads to the failure of a sanctions episode.

With these brief rules of thumb in mind, I now examine how sanctions have been deployed in the Middle East.

■ Economic Sanctions: The Mideast Experience

The experience with economic sanctions in the Middle East context follows closely the pattern in the total pool of cases. Sanctions episodes involving Mideast countries accounted for almost 10 percent of all the cases documented. Five of the ten episodes involved modest political objectives such as antiterrorism and embassy relocation; the other five sought more fundamental political changes such as the surrender of territory and the abrogation of treaties and alliances. A summary of the cases appears in Table 6.1.[2]

Consistent with the general findings, sanctions contributed to the successful achievement of foreign policy objectives in 60 percent of the modest policy cases; likewise, there was only one (marginal) instance of success in the five major policy cases. The Middle East is no exception to the rule that sanctions work best when targeted at narrowly-defined and limited policy objectives.

■ Modest Policy Cases

Economic sanctions contributed modestly or importantly to the resolution of foreign policy disputes in three instances: allied concern over the nationalization of the Suez Canal; U.S. concern about anti-American rhetoric by Egypt; and Arab League concern about the prospective move of the Canadian embassy from Tel Aviv to Jerusalem. On the other hand, U.S. attempts to stem support for terrorism by Iraq and Libya were less successful.

U.S., UK, and France v. Egypt (1956). The nationalization of the Suez Canal by Egyptian President Nasser in July 1956 prompted quick retaliatory moves by the United States, United Kingdom, and France to ensure free passage through the canal and to secure compensation for the nationalization. Egyptian assets in the three countries were frozen and the British banned the export of war materiel to Egypt. Canal dues were diverted to a special account outside of Egypt. In October 1956, Nasser sought a compromise solution in the UN Security Council, but talks were mooted by the Israeli attack in the Sinai.

The sanctions created financial constraints which severely cut back Egyptian trade for several months in 1956. Nasser's willingness to compromise reflected in part these economic pressures. Sanctions, however, were only part of the story. More importantly, the British and French wanted to undermine Nasser's domestic political support; sanctions were just a steppingstone to their planned military intervention (which was curtailed by U.S. sanctions against them in November 1956).

U.S. v. Egypt (1963-65). Egyptian intervention in Yemen in 1963 and bouts of anti-American rhetoric (which incited the burning of the JFK Library in Cairo in 1964) led to the suspension of U.S. development assistance in 1964 and subsequent cutbacks in PL-480 food aid in 1965. These sanctions contributed substantially to Egyptian troop withdrawals from Yemen and to the amelioration of relations in 1965 (including the appointment of a moderate

Table 6.1 Economic Sanctions: The Mideast Experience

Cases	Success Score Index[1]	Cost/GNP (%)	Trade Linkage (%)	Int'l Coop Index[2]
Modest Political Objectives				
UK/France/US v. Egypt (1956)	9	3.4	22	2
US v. UAR (1963-65)	16	1.4	14	1
US v. Libya (1978-80; 81-86)	4	0.8	20	1
Arab League v. Canada (1979)	12	negl.	2	3
US v. Iraq (1980-82)	4	0.1	5	1
Major Political Objectives				
Arab League v. Israel (1946-)	4	4.1	2	3
US v. Israel (1956-83)	2	0.1	22	1
US v. Arab League (1965-)	6	negl.	9	3
Arab League v. US/Netherlands (1973-74)	9	0.4	2	3
Arab League v. Egypt (1978-83)	1	(0.4)	4	3

[1]Index scaled from 1 to 16, indicating extent sanctions contributed to a policy outcome: 1 represents no contribution to a failed outcome; 16 represents a significant contribution to a successful outcome.
[2]Index scaled from 1 to 4, indicating the degree of assistance received by the sender country in applying sanctions. Key: none (1); minor (2); modest (3); significant (4).

Source: Hufbauer, Gary Clyde and Jeffrey J. Schott, *Economic Sanctions Reconsidered: History and Current Policy*, (Washington: Institute for International Economics), 1985.

prime minister). The "honeymoon" was short-lived, however; the U.S. rejection of Nasser's call for a substantial *increase* in aid led to renewed attacks on the U.S. role in Vietnam in mid-1966.

U.S. v. Libya (1978-80; 1981-86). The United States has imposed sanctions against Libya on frequent occasions since 1978 in an attempt to quell Libyan support for international terrorism, to counter Libyan military adventures in Chad, and to undermine the Qaddafi regime. U.S. exports to Libya of military equipment were barred in 1978 in retaliation for Libyan support of terrorist groups; export controls on small aircraft, helicopters, aircraft parts, and avionics were added in October 1981. In March 1982, the United States embargoed crude oil imports from Libya and restricted U.S. exports of sophisticated oil and gas field equipment and technology. Virtually all of the above measures were imposed unilaterally and without the support of the Western Allies.

In January 1986, the United States banned all economic transactions between Libya and the United States. Libyan government assets were frozen. All trade was cut off and foreign exchange transactions forbidden. As a result, most U.S. citizens remaining in Libya were forced to leave and U.S. companies were ordered to cease operations (with some oil and oil-service companies given a reprieve until the end of June 1986). These measures have not restricted Libyan oil production nor have they precluded the sale of Libyan oil on world markets. However, Libya has been under severe financial pressure as a result of the sharp drop in oil prices. U.S. sanctions have made it marginally more difficult for Libya to market its oil under current world market conditions.

Arab League v. Canada (1979). Canadian plans in June 1979 to move their Israeli embassy from Tel Aviv to Jerusalem led immediately to threats by the Arab League of a total trade boycott. New Arab League projects in Canada were cancelled or deferred, and Iraq embargoed oil shipments to Canada. By late October, Canada capitulated and canceled plans to move their embassy.

U.S. v. Iraq (1980-82). After citing Iraq along with Syria, Libya, and South Yemen as countries supporting international terrorism, the United States blocked in 1980 the export of $11.4 million worth of engine cores for Iraqi frigates being built in Italy and a $208 million sale of commercial jets to Iraq. In March 1982, Iraq was removed from the list of terrorist nations because of a purported reduction in its support of terrorism, despite conflicting evidence supplied by Israeli intelligence. State Department officials admitted in 1983 that the reason for the lenient treatment was because "the U.S. wants to foster Iraq's independence, keep it from the Soviet orbit and maintain lucrative trade links."[3]

- ## Major Policy Cases

In a region that has seen three major wars in the past thirty years, it is clear that countries will go to war over major policy goals before they would succumb to economic coercion. It thus is not surprising that the track record of such economic influence attempts is poor.

Nonetheless, economic sanctions have been part of the Mideast scene throughout the postwar period. The Arab League boycott of Israel since 1946 and U.S. antiboycott penalties against the Arab League since 1965 still involve important political goals, but their economic impact has dissipated over time. Neither has contributed even modestly to the achievement of their publicly-avowed policy goals. Similarly, U.S. attempts to influence Israeli policy on frequent occasions since 1956 by withholding economic and military aid, and Arab League pressure to get Egypt to abrogate the Camp David accords, also have failed. Only the Arab League oil embargo in 1973-74 was marginally successful (see below).

Arab League v. Israel (1946-). In 1946, the Arab League set up a central boycott office (CBO) and endorsed laws prohibiting the sale of Arab lands to, and the import of products made by, Palestinian Jews in order to block "the realization of Zionist political aims."[4] After the creation of the state of Israel, Egypt closed the Suez Canal to Israeli shipping and all Arab trade with Israel was banned. In the following years, the CBO extended the boycott to firms and individuals that did business or sympathized with Israel, prompting antiboycott measures by Israel and the United States. The boycott has had a negative impact on Israeli economic development, restricting trade opportunities and increasing the cost of imported oil. But the Egyptian experience since Camp David indicates that the boycott resulted in a substantial loss to most Arab nations as well and did so without the achievement of its political and foreign policy objectives.

U.S. v. Israel (1956-1983). The United States has withheld economic and military aid to Israel on frequent occasions since 1956 in short-lived attempts to promote Israeli territorial concessions or to encourage greater flexibility in peace talks on the Palestinian issue. Eisenhower's threats to suspend economic aid led to the withdrawal of Israeli troops from the Sinai in early 1957; Nixon's attempts to influence Israeli policy on border issues after the 1967 war by delaying shipments of military equipment proved less successful. In March 1975, Kissinger blamed Israeli intransigence for the breakdown of talks with Egypt over the Sinai and slowed arms deliveries to try to extract Israeli concessions for disengagement from the Sinai and the Golan Heights; the Sinai II accord concluded in September 1975 required, however, a massive U.S. payment to Israel for its territorial concession. More recently, Reagan delayed approval of the sale of 75 F-16 fighters in April 1983 following the Israeli invasion of Lebanon. Six weeks later the sale was approved following an Israeli-Lebanese agreement on troop withdrawals.

Except for the 1956-57 sanctions episode, U.S. attempts to coerce Israel through aid denial have been short-lived and relatively ineffective. Sanctions against Israel have not had strong U.S. public support; in most instances, Israel has been able to "wait out" the anger of the current administration until Congress pressured for the resumption of aid flows (sometimes with compensation – i.e., converting loans to grants). The United States has tried to exert its influence only in big-stakes cases involving territorial concessions in the Sinai, Golan Heights, and Lebanon. Because of the degree of Congressional support for Israel, efforts were not made to influence Israel on more "modest" issues such as West Bank settlements.

U.S. v. Arab League (1965-). To counter the Arab boycott of U.S. firms doing business with Israel, Congress passed in 1965 an amendment to the Export Control Law of 1949 which, as amplified in 1977, prohibited compliance with the boycott. Penalties for violations were implemented through the denial of DISC tax benefits. Dual jurisdiction by the Treasury and Commerce departments and incomplete reporting has made enforcement problematic, however. The sanctions have proven to be more a symbolic than an effective measure against the Arab boycott.

Arab League v. U.S./Netherlands (1973-74). Following the outbreak of the Yom Kippur war in October 1973, Arab League members cut oil production by 5 percent per month to force Israeli withdrawal from occupied territories and embargoed oil shipments to the United States and the Netherlands for their support of Israel. The production cuts were moderated and then cancelled in December 1973 as tensions eased following the negotiated ceasefire. The embargo was lifted against the United States in March 1974 and against the Netherlands in July 1974 by all countries except Libya and Iraq; ironically, oil from those two countries continued to flow to the United States through the Caribbean throughout this period.

The oil embargo was widely evaded through transhipments, internal reallocation of supplies by the major oil companies, and by several producers themselves that failed to abide by the production cuts. However, the oil embargo did reinforce the oil price increase to $5.12 per barrel announced earlier in October. Several analysts ascribed the impact of the sanctions on oil prices as an underlying goals of the OPEC countries.

The oil embargo did not force Israel to abandon the occupied territories or to persuade the United States to moderate its support for Israel. It did, however, contribute to a pro-Arab shift in Japanese and West European policies as well as bolstering world oil prices. From an Arab perspective, sanctions made a modest contribution to an outcome that, on balance, was positive.

Arab League b. Egypt (1978-83). In the aftermath of the Camp David accord between Egypt and Israel, Arab League members (except Morocco, Sudan, Oman) pledged an economic boycott of Egypt and moved Arab League headquarters out of Cairo in retaliation for the agreement with Israel. In March 1979, the League agreed to a trade boycott of Egypt but decided against financial controls. The impact of these measures was more than compensated by increased U.S. economic/military aid and new trade ties with Israel. In 1983, efforts were begun to restore normal economic ties between Egypt and the Arab League which culminated in a vote by the Islamic Conference in January 1984 to readmit Egypt and in the resumption of diplomatic ties with Jordan in September 1984.

*   *   *

Three observations can be drawn from the preceding consideration of sanctions deployed in the Middle East, which may prove instructive for any prospective use of sanctions in the region. All three mirror conclusions reached in the broader study of 103 sanctions cases.

Sanctions are most effective when applied in pursuit of narrowly-defined and limited policy objectives. The correlation between economic deprivation and political willingness to change is weak, and is most likely to occur in low-stakes confrontations over "modest" policy goals. Nasser was willing to muffle his anti-U.S. rhetoric to avoid U.S. retaliation; similarly, Canada backed down over the relocation of its embassy. Neither case proved more than an embarrassment to the regime of the target country, making their concessions less wrenching in political terms. Obviously, one could not expect such a united domestic reaction if the United States or Israel submitted to the "high-stakes" territorial demands of the Arab League – consequently, the Arab boycott has been much less effective.

Sanctions should be applied decisively and with resolution. A strategy of "turning the screws" invites evasion: it affords the target country time to find alternative suppliers, to build new alliances, and to mobilize domestic opinion in support of its policies. Furthermore, sanctions generally are regarded as a short-term policy, with the anticipation that normal commercial relations will be reestablished after the resolution of the crisis. Public opinion in the sender country may initially welcome sanctions, but support often dissipates over time. In the successful cases in the region, sanctions were imposed immediately at the onset of the crisis. None of these cases lasted much more than one year.

International cooperation is not a guarantee of success because it is generally sought in high stakes cases that are less likely to succeed under any circumstances. Table 6.1 shows that the international cooperation index was much higher in "major" cases than in cases with "modest" policy objectives — but that factor did not correlate closely with success. In cases involving specific and modest goals, international cooperation is not needed to achieve success. One thus could conclude that sanctions should be either deployed unilaterally — because the impact on one's allies is slight — or they should be designed in cooperation with one's allies in order to reduce backlash and evasion.

▪ Prospective Use of Sanctions

Drawing on the lessons of historical experience, what role can sanctions play in pursuit of foreign policy objectives in the Middle East? To answer this, I first look at which countries wield economic influence in the region and then explore which types of objectives may be attainable *inter alia* through the use of economic coercion.

No country in the Middle East has the wherewithal to exploit its economic leverage over other countries in the region with the exception of Saudi Arabia, the dominant economic force in the Arab League. As shown in Table 6.2, all of the countries in the region run substantial current account deficits of between 4.2 percent to 7.7 percent of GNP (except for Saudi Arabia whose current deficit is a staggering 24 percent). However, foreign reserves are adequate in all the countries except Syria.

If economic pressures build for changes in policies of Mideast governments, the impetus probably will come from the intervention of the United States, the USSR, Saudi Arabia and, to a lesser extent, the European Community. Tables 6.3 and 6.4 give a thumbnail sketch of the economic linkages between the major powers and key countries in the Middle East.

The United States has strong ties to Israel and Egypt, and has more modest economic relations with Jordan. The United States accounts for 24 percent and 14 percent of the total trade of Israel and Egypt respectively. More important, U.S. economic aid has represented on average 6.0 percent and 4.4 percent of Israeli and Egyptian GNP respectively over the period 1983-84. When military assistance is included, these ratios climb to 13.5 percent and 9.3 percent respectively. It is unlikely that other powers could replace such large sums in the event of a cutback in U.S. aid; Israel and Egypt essentially are hooked on the U.S. economy. While more modest in comparison, U.S. trade and aid with Jordan is still significant. The U.S. share in total Jordanian trade is 9 percent; the U.S. supplied Jordan with an annual

Table 6.2 Mideast Economic Profile: 1984 ($US million)

	GNP	Exports	Imports	C/A Bal.	Total Reserves (incl. gold)	Exports/GNP (%)	C/A Bal. GNP (%)
Egypt	27,140	3,140	10,766	(2,081)	819	12	(7.7)
Iraq	27,350*	9,050	9,780	n.a.	n.a.	n.a.	n.a.
Israel	23,450	5,808	9,886	(1,411)	3,095	25	(6.0)
Jordan	4,160	695	2,785	(265)	551	17	(6.4)
Lebanon	n.a.	629	2,940	n.a.	988	n.a.	n.a.
Libya	29,360	10,574	6,854	(1,803)	3,759	36	(6.1)
Saudi Arabia	100,820	42,386	33,695	(24,036)	24,906	42	(23.8)
Syria	20,070	1,767	3,470	(852)	83**	9	(4.2)

*Data for 1981
**Data for 1983
n.a. not available

Source:
IMF, International Financial Statistics (October 1986).
IMF, Director of Trade Statistics Yearbook: 1979-85.
OECD, Geographical Distribution of Financial Flows to Developing Countries: 1981-84.

Table 6.3 Trade Linkage: 1985 (in percent)

Country Share of Total Trade of/	Egypt	Iraq	Israel	Jordan	Lebanon	Libya	Syria
United States	14	5	24	9	6	2	2
Saudi Arabia	1	negl.	-	12	8	negl.	negl.
USSR	2	1	-	negl.	n.a.	negl.	6
EC	46	42	36	24	41	70	39

Source: IMF, *Direction of Trade Statistics Yearbook: 1979-85.*

Table 6.4 Economic Aid*: Annual Average 1983-84 ($US million and percent of GNP)

Donor/Recipient**	Egypt	Iraq	Israel	Jordan	Lebanon	Syria
United States	1,221	17	1,338	31	29	15
	(4.4)	(n.a.)	(6.0)	(0.8)	(n.a.)	(0.1)
EC + members	335	4	125	50	32	30
	(1.2)	(n.a.)	(0.6)	(1.2)	(n.a.)	(0.2)
OPEC	5	2	-	664	7	880
	(negl.)	(n.a.)	(16.2)	(n.a.)	(4.8)	
Multilateral	427	51	8	132	42	96
	(1.5)	(n.a.)	(negl.)	(3.2)	(n.a.)	(0.5)
Total	1,988	74	1,471	877	110	1,021
	(7.2)	(n.a.)	(6.5)	(21.4)	(n.a.)	(5.5)

*Total gross disbursements of official development assistance, other official flows (grant element below 25 percent) including official export credits, and funds provided by the official sector to support export credits or direct investment of the private sector.

**Libya received only negligible amounts of economic aid and therefore was not included in the table.

Source: OECD, *Geographical Distribution of Financial Flows to Developing Countries: 1981-1984.*

economic aid package of $31 million in 1983-84; when $85 million in military aid is included, the total aid package is equivalent to 2.8 percent of Jordan's GNP.[5]

Despite its checkered track record, the United States is likely to continue to be the leading practitioner of economic sanctions in the Middle East as in other areas of the world. It has strong economic links to several countries and has major foreign policy interests with both Israel and the Arab states.

By contrast, the USSR has a much more limited role in the economies of Mideast countries, the only significant Soviet trade is with Syria. The USSR accounts for 6 percent of total Syrian trade and for 12 percent of Syrian exports. In addition, Soviet economic aid to Syria in 1983 totalled $326 million, equivalent to 1.7 percent of Syrian GDP.[6] Soviet military assistance to Syria, as well as to Libya and Iraq, is undoubtedly quite substantial, but data is not publicly available. Press reports in April 1984 indicated, however, that the USSR had agreed to provide a $2 billion long-term credit to Iraq for arms purchases.[7]

Given its limited economic leverage, the Soviet Union is not likely to actively exert economic pressure in the region except on Syria. Its military aid, however, could be destabilizing and used to undercut efforts by other countries to deploy sanctions to pursue foreign policy objectives contrary to Soviet interests.

Saudi Arabia has and continues to exercise its economic leverage among its friends in the region (e.g., Iraq, Jordan, Lebanon) as well as its foes (e.g., Israel). Trade ties are strongest with Jordan and Lebanon, accounting for 12 percent and 8 percent of the total trade of each respectively (though the Saudis took 23 percent of Lebanese exports in 1984). Indeed, the Saudis used their leverage in early 1983 to bar all Lebanese imports until Lebanon cracked down on the influx of Israeli-made goods through so-called illegal ports.[8] Saudi trade with other countries in the region is negligible.

Substantial Saudi influence is conveyed via economic assistance. The Saudis contribute a major share of OPEC's economic aid, which averaged $880 million to Syria and $664 million to Jordan in 1983-84 (equivalent to 4.8 percent and 16.2 percent of GNP respectively). In addition, Saudi Arabia has supported Iraq in recent years with substantial bilateral economic aid (including future oil sales).

Saudi Arabia probably will play a less active role in the future in imposing sanctions because of its declining oil revenues and international reserves and because of its sensitivity to a backlash from radical Arab groups. As the keeper of many of the Islamic holy places, the Saudis have to walk a tightrope between religious and political interests. As such, they are more likely to use carrots than sticks, and then only in support of its Gulf Cooperation Council (GCC) partners, Syria (in hopes that economic development will blunt the desire for military adventures) and Iraq (for defensive purposes against Iran).

The European Community (EC), by contrast, has major trade ties with all the countries in the region, ranging from 24 percent of the total trade of Jordan to 70 percent of Libya's trade. The EC has been reticent to exploit this leverage, however, for three key reasons:

—most importantly given their dependence on Mideast oil suppliers, Europeans are sensitive to Arab counter-measures. In addition, they fear the spillover effects of sanctions on overall peace prospects in the Middle East;

—the difficulty in achieving a foreign policy consensus in the EC-10, and even more so now in the EC-12; and

—the opposition in principle of several member countries to the use of sanctions, which are regarded as ineffective.

As such, EC foreign policy is likely to be influenced mainly by commercial considerations when the subject of Mideast sanctions arises. It will take a grave provocation, such as the bombing of the Berlin disco, the U.S. military attack against Libya in April 1986, and the Syrian-inspired attempt to sabotage an El Al jet in April 1986, to jolt the Europeans into even limited action.[9]

For the reasons cited above, the EC will be extremely cautious in its resort to economic coercion. While the Community has followed the UK in banning arms sales to Syria as a result of the El Al incident, the sanctions were limited and half-hearted. The EC probably will impose more stringent sanctions only when it is pressured to join in U.S. actions. Such pressure will be taken more seriously in the future since the United States demonstrated that it would pursue military actions once it had expended its options in the economic and diplomatic fields. As such, EC participation in sanctions episodes could become increasingly frequent to avoid further military confrontations.

Under what circumstances might we see future attempts at economic coercion? And against what countries? Gazing at a crystal ball is not a scientific method, but let me present an educated guess.

Given the political currents in the region, sanctions will most likely be imposed to combat state-supported terrorism and to improve prospects for peace negotiations. The former is a limited, relatively modest objective where sanctions could contribute if they are applied forcefully. To exert sufficient leverage, this will require joint action by the United States and the European Community. The latter objective is a "high-stakes" venture where success is less likely unless more limited goals are targeted. Sanctions will not force territorial concessions, but they could induce minor policy concessions which improve the negotiating climate for peace talks.

Which countries might be the main targets of future sanctions? The above considerations suggest that the main targets, in descending order of probability, could very well be Libya, Israel, and Egypt. Jordan, Iraq and Lebanon are more likely to be influenced by carrots than sticks. While limited sanctions have been implemented recently to punish Syria for its support for terrorism, such measures are likely to be short-lived because of overriding concerns about Syria's military role in Lebanon and because of Soviet offsets and limited trade linkages.

With Libya, I am on pretty safe ground. As this article is being prepared, new diplomatic and economic sanctions are being imposed or planned to undermine Qaddafi and his support for terrorist adventures. These measures would supplement the extensive economic sanctions imposed by the United States and later reinforced by military action. Indeed, the fact that the United States demonstrated that it would pursue a military option in the absence of viable economic alternatives makes it all the more likely that additional joint sanctions will be applied in the future.

The effectiveness of the new sanctions depends on the willingness of other countries to coordinate with the United States. Unilateral actions by the United States do not significantly tax Libyan resources or close the financial spigot which flows to Libyan-backed terrorists. U.S. leverage over the Libyan economy has been sharply reduced since the imposition of sanctions in 1982. The total trade embargo announced in January 1986 affected only a small volume of trade. The United States accounted for only 2 percent of total Libyan trade in 1985 compared to more than 25 percent in 1980. U.S. imports from Libya feel from a peak of almost $9 billion in 1980 to an average of $30 million in 1984-85; U.S. exports also declined, though less dramatically, from $813 million in 1981 to $311 million in 1985.

By contrast, Europeans take the bulk of Libyan oil exports and account for over half of total Libyan imports. Joint sanctions by the United States and Europe could cut sharply into Libyan trade and reduce its oil revenues. First, the Europeans could join the U.S. oil boycott and replace their Libyan oil imports with comparable shipments from countries such as hard-pressed Nigeria. At the very least, Europe should begin to diversify away from Libyan supplies. France already has taken steps in this direction by asking their oil companies to refrain from bringing Libyan oil and refined products into the country.[10]

Second, Europe could complement U.S. financial sanctions (i.e., asset freeze) by barring new official export credits. Fiscal constraints may not change Qaddafi's ways, but they could affect his means to support terrorism.

Coincidentally or not, Qaddafi's adventurism did lessen temporarily in early 1982 after Libya suffered revenue shortfalls due to the glut in world oil markets.

Israel also could come under increasing economic pressure from the United States for two reasons. First, U.S. budgetary constraints will force greater scrutiny of economic and military grants. At the very least, this will result in increased conditionality on aid flows. Second, the increased trade ties that will result from the U.S.-Israel Free Trade Agreement will increase U.S. leverage over the Israeli economy. In addition, it will expose Israeli exports to new or expanded demands by U.S. industries for protection, and in so doing influence Congress in its deliberations on Israeli aid.

Some may argue that the strategic importance of Israel and its close and enduring friendship with the United States would preclude the effective use of economic leverage—it has not happened in the past and the clout of the Israeli lobby on Capitol Hill seems to guarantee that the United States will continue to extend carrots rather than apply the stick to Israel. But in the past the United States has sought only vague redirections of Israeli policy towards negotiations with Egypt and on border questions. With more modest objectives, the threat of reduced economic aid could be an effective lever against a country so dependent on U.S. resources. If the United States sought a limited, specific objective—say, a moratorium on new West Bank settlements—to grease the skids of new peace talks with Jordan, it would be much harder for Israel and its supporters in Washington to oppose the sanctions on national security grounds. Israel should be less confident in the future that a revenue-hungry Congress will restore cuts in nonmilitary assistance.

Egypt could face similar pressures, although U.S. coercion can only go so far before the Egyptians risk a strong backlash from other Arab countries. While such a reaction could be muted by discreet U.S. representatives in Riyadh, if pushed to the wall Egypt could raise the banner of pan-Arabism to enlist support to offset the impact of U.S. sanctions. Obviously, this is not an option available to Israel and one which could have serious implications for the Israel-Egypt peace treaty.

■ Conclusion

One cannot dismiss the prospect that economic sanctions will continue to be a factor complicating the calculus of political relations in the Middle East. Recognition of this factor should not dissuade countries from seeking ways to promote economic cooperation among the countries in the region in order to lay a stronger foundation for peaceful political relations. Carrots and sticks are part and parcel of economic statecraft. When used judiciously, they both can serve constructive foreign policy objectives.

■ Notes

1. Hufbauer, Gary Clyde and Jeffrey J. Schott, *Economic Sanctions Reconsidered: History and Current Policy*, (Washington: Institute for International Economics), 1985.

2. As this chapter was being prepared for publication, limited sanctions were being imposed against Syria for its complicity in the attempt to bomb an El Al airliner in London in April 1986. Data on these measures are not yet available, but the case will be referenced in the text as appropriate.

3. *Washington Post*, 8 October 1983, p. A25.

4. Resolution 16 of the Permanent Boycott Committee.

5. IMF, *Direction of Trade Statistics Yearbook: 1979-85* and AID, *Overseas Loans and Grants*.

6. Cited in CIA, *Handbook of Economic Statistics*.

7. *Keesing's Contemporary Archives*, Volume XXXI, p. 33497.

8. *Wall Street Journal*, 25 February 1983, p. 31.

9. In the latter case, *The Economist* chastised the EC for its "dithering over Syria," noting that "the only common policy which could be agreed upon was a compromise so pale as to make the Community look ridiculous." (*The Economist*, 1 November 1986, p. 14).

10. *Wall Street Journal*, 6 August 1986, p. 20.

7

Factor Migration, Trade, and Welfare Under Threat of Commercial Disruption

Martin C. McGuire[*]

I

One of the motives behind this volume is the hope that economic cooperation among the states of the Middle East might lead to decreasing hostility
and conflict. Economic cooperation may take a variety of forms with diverse
benefits and different distributions among participants. But realistically,
any agreement to cooperate whether explicit or implicit may break down ex-
posing participants to risks and costs they otherwise would not have borne.
These costs will also vary with the form of economic cooperation between
nations and prudence will require that any state contemplating a step toward
closer economic relations carefully weigh these costs as well as the benefits.
The implications of economic cooperation between Israel and the other
countries of the Mid-East would be better understood, therefore, if we examined the implications of the fact that there are risks that cooperation will
fail over the entire spectrum of possible economic relations among nations
in the region. At one end of the range lies complete isolation and autarky;
at the other, complete economic-political unification. Between these ex-
tremes, cooperation begins with limited trade in commodities, shades into
restricted then free commodity trade, followed by preferential trading

[*]Department of Economics, University of Maryland. Research leading to
this paper was sponsored by the Japanese Fulbright Commission and the
Faculty of Economics, Osaka University. The paper is derivative from and
uses constructs contained in the work of H. Shibata (1985) and H. Shibata
and M. McGuire (1986).

agreements, then free trade areas and customs unions, and finally exchange of factors of production including direct foreign investment and labor migration.

Some may disagree as to the ordering of each of these steps from isolation to complete integration – e.g. whether exchange of factors of production should be considered the last step before complete integration or not. However, most would agree that as one proceeds along such a spectrum both the net economic benefits to a cooperating region increase, as well as that the exposure to risk of breakdown in cooperation and the costly consequences of such a breakdown also increase. The purpose of this paper is to lay out certain initial considerations relevant to comparison of the benefits from two general types of cooperation between states versus the costs of a breakdown in such cooperation. The two classes of economic interaction to be compared are trade in commodities on the one hand, and exchange in migration of factors of production on the other.

One of the consequences of international conflict is frequently the disruption of trade among trading partners or between such partners and the rest of the world. Such losses need not be altogether regrettable if they deter or reduce the frequency of conflict (as there is some evidence [Polachek, 1985] to suggest they do). Conflict can cut off or truncate trade between adversaries or among innocent bystanders. It has been recognized at least since the time of Adam Smith that protective measures of trade control taken before trade disruption can limit a country's losses from an autarky imposed by war. Such protectionism may constitute justifiable restriction on free trade.

Smith labored without the benefit of the factor price equalization (FPE) theorem, however, without knowledge of the one-one correspondence between goods price equalization (GPE) and FPE, and therefore without awareness of the perfect equivalence between factor movements and goods movements across national boundaries in a Heckscher-Ohlin (H-O) world. This equivalence, first spelled out by Mundell (1957), has played an important role in modern analyses of the effects of protectionism, of discrimination, and of imperfect competition on the movement of capital, labor or other factors of production across boundaries. This paper begins to merge these two lines of thought to compare the effects of factor migration and commodity trade in an *uncertain* world subject to trade disruption.

II

The classical argument for protection is readily incorporated into a Heckscher-Ohlin trade context with the assumption that factors of production are completely immobile in the short run, both between industries and between countries.[1] Figure 7.1 shows a country's long run production possibilities with a fixed factor endowment as TT. With world prices p and no risk of trade

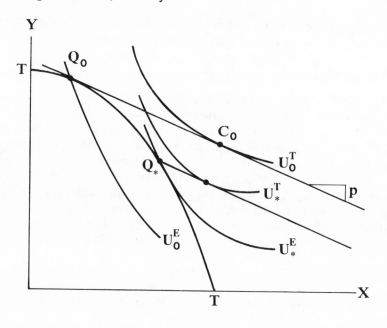

Figure 7.1

disruption, this country should produce at Q_0 and consume at C_0, concentrating in production of Y which it then exports. Now assume trade is disrupted; for simplicity, assume it is totally curtailed. Having locked its productive factors in at Q_0 in the short run, the country must also consume at Q_0. Thus, if the likelihood of trade disruption is, say, $(1 - \pi)$, then *ex ante* the subject country will enjoy utility level U_0^T during peace or free trade with probability π and U_0^E during emergency with probability $(1 - \pi)$. Its *ex ante* expected utility becomes

$$E(U) = \pi U_0^T + (1 - \pi)U_0^E \tag{1}$$

Now through trade restriction of one sort or another such a country might control the pre-emergency allocation of resources so as to discourage the degree of specialization beneficial under certain free trade. Such control might proceed all the way to maximization of utility under pure autarky by restricting production to point Q_*. Then utility if trade is disrupted becomes U_*^E and if trade is allowed U_*^T with expected utility

$$E(U) = \pi\, U_*^T \quad + \quad (1 - \pi)U_*^E \tag{2}$$

It is notable that U_*^T cannot be achieved in the pre-emergency trading situation unless domestic production is subsidized. A tariff or quota alone will choke peace-time consumption down to U_*^E — an outcome approximately observed in autarkic socialist economies. The two pairs of outcomes just identified as U_k^j (j = T, E; k = 0,*) are merely two points on a continuum. For a fixed probability some intermediate restrictions on free trade specialization may be optimal. In the two good small country cases, suppose the world terms of trade between X and Y were given by p, and the small country, transformation function by Y = F(X). Then assuming Y is exported and X imported, maximization of expected utility is derived from

$$E(U) = \pi U[\{X + M\}, \{E(X) - pM\}] + (1 - \pi)U[X, F(X)] \tag{3}$$

where M represents imports of X and pM represents exports of Y. The results are

$$\frac{U_x^T}{U_y^T} = p \qquad ; \text{i.e., MRS = world price in a trading world} \tag{4}$$

$$\frac{dF}{dx} = \frac{\pi\, U_x^T + (1 - \pi)U_x^E}{\pi\, U_y^T + (1 - \pi)U_y^T} \; ; \text{i.e., MRT = probability weighted average} \tag{5}$$

Producer/Consumer Surplus Outcomes

Policy Chosen	State of the World	
	Emergency Autarky	Peace and Free Trade
No Restrictions on Trade	1,2	1,2,3,4,5,6,7
Welfare Maximizing Trade Restriction	1,2,3,4	1,2,3,4, ,6,7
Gain/Loss from Optimum Policy	$(3 + 4)x (1 - \pi)$	$-5x\,\pi$

This result can be visualized easily with supply-demand curves as in Figure 7.2, showing the situation for import-good X. In the absence of trade restriction with no disruption to trade, X_0^P is produced, X_0^C consumed, and the difference imported, while X_0^P is both produced and consumed if trade is discontinued. As a result of trade stoppage consumer surplus in the amount of areas 3 through 7 is lost. Now suppose government interference takes the form of a subsidy, s, to producers of X; production increases to X_*^P; peace time consumption remains at X_0^C; area 5 is lost from producer surplus in peace but areas 3 + 4 are gained when an emergency comes up. Since the marginal subjective valuation MRS^T arises with likelihood π and MRS^E with likelihood $(1 - \pi)$ the optimum value of s and therefore supply price $F_X = dF/dX$, occurs where F_X equals the probability weighted average $\pi MRS^T + (1 - \pi)MRS^E$.

One advantageous feature of this supply/demand presentation is to clarify how gains and losses from trade impairment can actually be measured as areas under supply/demand curves. Estimates of supply and demand schedules for exports and imports are all that is needed to determine how gains and losses depend on the probability of disruption. For each of various guesses as to the likelihood of trade disruption, an optimal trade restriction can then be identified.

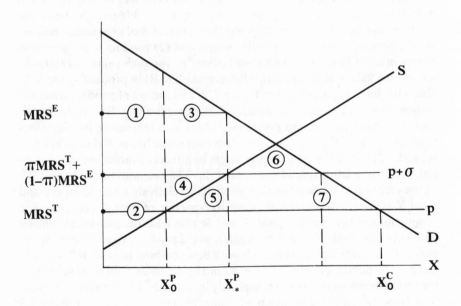

Figure 7.2

III

Every country espouses an objective of national self-sufficiency at least to a degree adequate to national survival. Accordingly, all countries take some measures to limit their vulnerability to trade disruption. Among the alternatives to tariffs or subsidies, etc., for controlling the degree of specialization must be counted preferential trading agreements and customs unions on the international front, and stockpiling, emergency planning or stand-by production base capacities on the domestic front. An important extension of the national defense argument for protection must include these alternatives to protection. Another instrument for influencing a country's vulnerability to trade disruption would seem to be capital/labor migration or movements of other factors into and out of the home country. Although analyses of factor movements have appeared with increasing popularity of late, these all have been with reference to free trade or second best restricted trade conditions – and not the war-peace dichotomy which forms the texture of this paper.

For purposes of the analysis of factor migration as it relates to national self-sufficiency and defense, one theorem of importance is that in a world governed by Heckscher-Ohlin assumptions a country can protect itself completely from the costs of trade disruption by infinitely many alternative changes in its stock of factors of production. Such changes in labor or capital will come about by in-migration or out-migration. Figure 7.3 shows the relationships between (1) the Edgeworth box of factor of production endowments, contract curves, and relative wages and (2) product transformation curves in an H-O world. With world price "p" for each value of capital K_i alternative values of L generate a Rybczinski-line R_i^L in product space X-Y. One such line, R_i^L is labeled in Figure 7.3b and the set of product transformation curves it identifies is included. Movement along R_i^L to the southeast designates production points consistent with increasing immigrations of labor given p. Figure 7.3c shows two entire families of Rybczinski lines, R_i^L and R_j^K, where the latter group refers to effects of variations in the capital stock when labor is held constant at L_j. The orientation of R_i^L and R_j^K derives from the assumption that good X is relatively labor intensive and good Y is relatively capital intensive irrespective of overall economywide proportions of labor and capital. Panel 3c also adds the income expansion path between goods X and Y for a given world price p. This income expansion path will intersect successively with new combinations of R_i^L and R_j^L. Each corresponding combination of K_i and L_j indicates a different set of factor endowments which would completely insulate the small country in question from potential disruption of trade embargoes. Thus, Figure 7.3 demonstrates that through factor migration (immigration *or* emigration) a

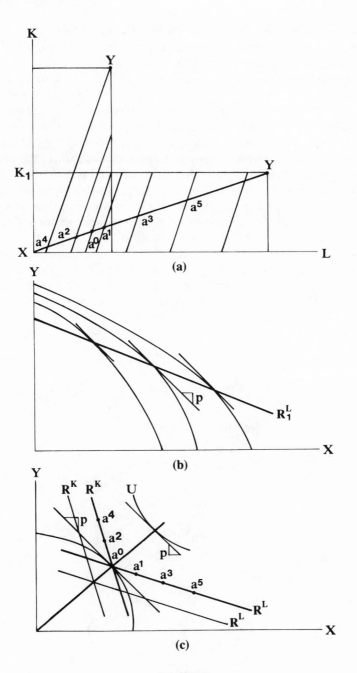

Figure 7.3

country can completely protect itself from trade disruption. (This proposition is valid only under the stringent assumptions of the Hecksher-Ohlin model.) Figure 7.4 continues the argument with an example of a small country with indigenous factor endowment (L_1, K_1), and a set of demands such that it would produce at Q_0 but consume at C_0 importing X and exporting Y. This country can achieve complete autarky and therefore insulate itself totally from trade disruption *either* by importing labor or by exporting capital. Labor imports move it along R_1^L until, at point Q_A, demands for all products can be produced at home. Capital export shrinks the economy along R_1^K until, at Q_B again, all "domestic" demand is met from domestic production. These alternatives are perfect substitutes due to the equivalence between imports of L or exports of K and exports of X or imports of Y; or similarly due to the equivalence between imports of K or exports of L and exports of Y or imports of X.

Thus, we have the rather peculiar conclusion that factor migration can protect a country completely from the losses which would arise when its trade is disrupted without causing any offsetting loss under peace time free trade. If this is true, why do we see so little migration of labor and exchange

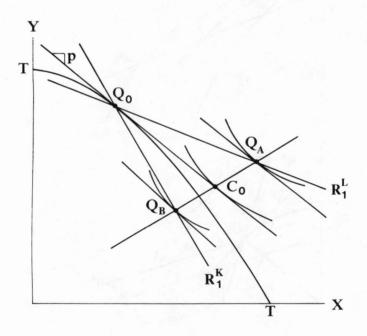

Figure 7.4

of capital relative to huge trade volumes—trade which is subject to disruption with familiar consequences of economic upheaval? Part of the answer to this question is that the conclusion (viz. that factor migration can insulate a country from losses due to trade disruption) is valid only under the assumption that factor migration is *welfare-neutral* for the migrating factor and for the society of origin or destination as well. But this may be a fallacious assumption. Thus, in Figure 7.4 the conclusion that in-migration of L insulates the country from disruption just as would out-migration of K only follows if the home country "natives" are indifferent as to where their capital produces *and* consumes and are indifferent whether they live-work-consume at home or with foreigners abroad. However, a country may not be indifferent about where "its" citizens work, live, consume, and locate capital. Similarly, a country and its government may not be indifferent when foreign capital or foreign nationals enter its borders even if such entry reduced vulnerability to trade stoppage. In this case, factor migration and goods trade may be equivalent only if taxed or subsidized, or not at all. In more technical terms, there may be *public good* considerations effecting the utility of migrant labor in both the country of origin and of destination; or there may be *externalities* transmitted or received by visiting labor. Along another dimension, when factors migrate across countries *irreversibilities* may be anticipated; that is, extracting capital or workforce from a foreign location, whether under peace time normal conditions or more especially under emergency or war conditions may be difficult to impossible. In the latter case, capital may be expropriated, workers and their assets seized, and in the extreme, held hostage. Still another explanation for limits on capital/labor migration short of the prediction of an H-O model may be that the model itself is inaccurate in its assumptions. Thus, decreasing returns to scale may limit factor migration or diverse, specific, immobile factors may contribute to production in different countries causing an ultimate decline in marginal returns to mobile factors. Furthermore, the Hecksher-Ohlin model may be inaccurate in its assumptions of competitive organization, of full information, of free mobility of factors of production, or of exhaustively and appropriately defined property rights.

As a beginning to deal with these possibilities, we can now extend our model of the expected utility maximizing national security argument for protection, to analyze the case for autarky inducing factor movements. Again, we make the initial assumption that good X is imported and Y exported by a small country facing a world price of p, in a Hecksher-Ohlin framework. With indigenous endowments of labor $\bar{L}$ and capital $\bar{K}$, the country will allocate these factors among industries so that the wage rate w and rental rate r of capital are equalized across countries at levels which depend on world factor prices. Now suppose we introduce the possibility that capital may enter or exit from this country in an amount $\hat{K}$. $\hat{K}$ is measured positively for foreign capital inflows and negatively for capital outflows so that the entire capital stock of the country becomes $K_T = \overline{K} + \hat{K}$. If capital flows in, output of the capital intensive industry (assume to be X) will increase, and of the labor intensive industry will decrease. Here one might assume that this capital inflow, $\hat{K}$, if positive, all becomes located in industry X. Our assumption, however, will be that any inflow of capital is uniformly mixed with the preexisting capital and is divided among industries in the same proportions as domestic capital. Evidently, how the in-migrating capital is intermingled with existing domestic capital (which is native to the recipient country) may influence whether foreign capital can be identified and its return taxed adversely or in the extreme confiscated altogether. Here, we are choosing an assumption that domestic and foreign capital are as thoroughly mixed—and therefore probably as indistinguishable—as possible.

If capital is allowed to immigrate, the receiving country's total product increases in value from $w\overline{L} + r\overline{K}$ to $w\overline{L} + r\overline{K} + r\hat{K}$. The amount of that product available for home consumption becomes $w\overline{L} + r\overline{L} - t\hat{K}$ allowing for the possibility that entry of foreign capital imposes an extra cost of t per unit, a cost which we assume is diffused throughout the domestic society. (If capital immigration generated an extra external benefit, then "t" would be negative.) The domestic share, s, of total product then becomes

$$s = \frac{w\overline{L} + r\overline{K} - t\hat{K}}{w\overline{L} + r\overline{K} + r\hat{K}} \tag{6}$$

The amount of goods X and Y *produced* depend simply on factor allocations

$$X = f(L_x, K_y) \; ; \; Y = (L_y, K_y) \tag{7}$$

subject to factor limits

$$L_x + L_y = \overline{L} \tag{8}$$

$$K_x + K_y = \overline{K} + \hat{K} \tag{9}$$

But these amounts are not all available to the native citizenry to consume or trade. Instead, we assume sX and sY are available. These amounts can be traded in world markets at terms of trade, given by p.

With the model now set up, we can explore the interaction between factor movement and trade in commodities under several scenarios.

■ *Optimum Immigration: No Risk of Trade Disruption*

In a world of complete certainty, the policy problem of choosing a level of factor migration which maximizes domestic national welfare then becomes

$$\text{Maximize} \quad U[(sX + M), (sY - pM)] \tag{10}$$

$$\{M, s(\hat{K}), X(\hat{K}), Y(\hat{K})\}$$

The generic solution requires

$$p = \frac{U_x}{U_y} = \frac{\phi_L}{f_L} = \frac{\phi_K}{f_K} \tag{11}$$

and

$$(pX + Y)\frac{ds}{d\hat{K}} = -rs \tag{12}$$

as first order conditions. Interpretation of the first is one of straightforward efficiency in production and exchange. The second condition requires that capital be imported or exported until marginal diversion of total product to foreign immigrant capital equal the average domestic capture of capital product. In the case of no uncertainty and no risk of trade disruption, the optimal capital import or export, $\hat{K}^{opt}$, depends crucially on the value of t, the externality parameter in equation (6). For t = 0, equation (12) solves identically, *indicating that, provided the chance of trade disruption is zero, any value of $\hat{K}$ is as good as any other* since commodity trade can substitute perfectly for goods trade. For t > 0, $\hat{K}^{opt} = -\infty$ for t < 0, $\hat{K}^{opt} = +\infty$. A determinate, interior solution — indicating that some definite amount of capital is most preferred (i.e., national welfare maximizing) — requires a nonlinear externality term in the sharing function of equation (7). Thus, if t instead of a parameter were itself related to $\hat{K}$ — say t = a$\hat{K}$ to signify an increasing quadratic external cost imposed by the immigrating factor in the recipient society — an interior, determinant amount of capital in-migration could be shown to be optimal.

■ *Capital Migration Under Risk of Autarky*

The maximand in the above problem assumes a riskless outcome. We can incorporate risk in the model as in the analysis of free trade restrictions by assuming a known chance $(1' - \pi)$ of trade disruption. Then, expected utility becomes

$$E(U) = \pi U[sX + M), (sY - pM)] + (1 - \pi)U[sX, sY] \tag{13}$$

with the constraints the same as in the riskless case. This maximand represents a hazard that trade will be disrupted and the country forced into autarky.

A crucial feature of these trade disruption scenarios, which might be modelled in diverse ways, concerns the status of the foreign, imported factors of production once trade stops. This status is reflected in the form of $(1 - \pi)U[C_x, C_y]$ where C_x and C_y denote domestic *native* consumption opportunities once trade is curtailed. Various alternative dispositions which might arise include

$$C_x = sX ; C_y = sY \tag{14}$$

which would indicate that foreign factor owners maintain all their claims on production during war or emergency just the same as in peace. As an alternative we might write

$$C_x = X ; C_y = Y \tag{15}$$

to indicate that all foreign assets (including workers) are seized (workers drafted) along with their production. Still another alternative is

$$C_x = f[L_x, (\frac{\overline{K}}{\overline{K}+\hat{K}} K_x)]; C_y = \phi [L_y, (\frac{\overline{K}}{\overline{K}+\hat{K}} K_y)] \tag{16}$$

Foreign capital (or workers as the case might be) is repatriated and factor inputs in domestic production are proportionately reduced. These possible production outcomes are illustrated as points a, b and c in Figure 7.5.

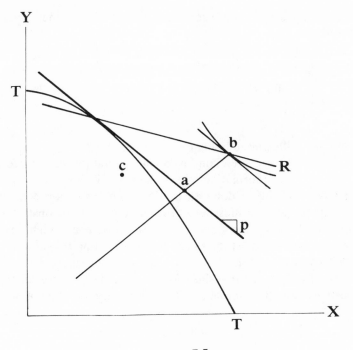

Figure 7.5

As a case in point, assume that foreign factor owners are not discriminated against in the event of trade disruption (i.e., equation (14) above); the relevant objective function becomes

$$E(U) = \pi U[(sX + M), (sY - pM)] + (1 - \pi)U[sX, sY] \quad (17)$$

with the same set of constraints as in the risk free scenario. First order conditions for a welfare maximum are

$$\frac{U_x^T}{U_y^T} = p; \quad \frac{U_x^T + \frac{1-\pi}{\pi}U_x^E}{U_y^T + \frac{1-\pi}{\pi}U_y^E} = \frac{\phi_L}{f_L} = \frac{\phi_K}{f_K} \quad (18)$$

These first order conditions imply that when entry of foreign capital generates no externally (positive or negative) migration should proceed until it just substitutes for trade such that all loss from trade disruption is eliminated and

$$\frac{U_x^T}{U_y^T} = \frac{U_x^E}{U_y^E} = p. \qquad (19)$$

This outcome is illustrated in Figure 7.5 (point a).

If society must pay a premium for foreign capital (by way of internal adjustment costs of one form or another), the effect is the same as a tariff on the importable subsidy on domestic production of the import competing industry. Figure 7.6 both illustrates this optimum and demonstrates that a tariff or subsidy *lowers* the gains from factor movement which was undertaken as protection against the risk of trade disruption (as shown by Bhagwati, 1979). With imported capital generating an external diseconomy, "domestic native" production shifts from Q_0^N to Q_*^N, where relative marginal costs include the external effect. Capital migration then is allowed to

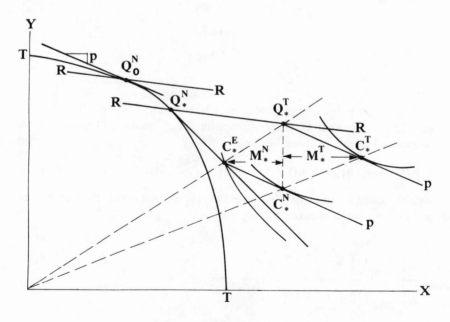

Figure 7.6

proceed to Q_*^T which generates a total of C_*^T of "domestic" (native plus immigrant) consumption in peace time with imports M_*^T. In contrast to M_*^T the amount M_*^N is imported for native consumption. Domestic native consumption during peace is shown at point C_*^N with immigrant's consumption the difference between C_*^T and C_*^N. And C_*^E represents domestic-native consumption in an emergency when trade is disrupted. The optimum mix between factor imports and commodity imports is also readily illustrated in a supply-demand curve diagram as in Figure 7.7. The demand curve D_N refers to demands by domestic natives, while D_T includes all demands, native and immigrant. The optimal amount of capital import under conditions of no external cost is assumed to be $\hat{K}_0$ with marginal product curve as shown. Now assume that external cost "t" raises the relative price of good X by τ. The optimal capital import then yields supply curve $\hat{K}_*$. Consumption during peace time is X_*^T including imports M_*; consumption during trade stoppage when imports are blocked is X_*^E. $\hat{K}_*$ is the optimal supply of capital; for this amount of capital inflow, probability weighted marginal benefits ($\pi MRS^E + (1 - \pi)MRS^T$) just equal externality inclusive marginal cost of production (i.e. p $+\tau$).

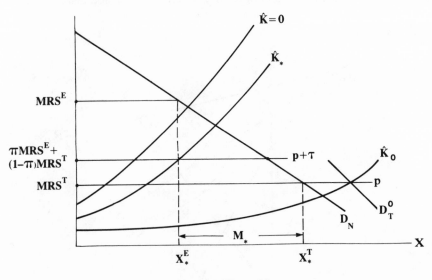

Figure 7.7

IV

In essence, the preceding model of factor migration as a substitute for trade in goods identifies protection from effects of trade disruption as a primary benefit from factor movement within a Hecksher-Ohlin world. Another significant possible benefit is that factor growth through migration will *increase* free trade welfare. This could occur if the home country is specialized completely in the production of its export good. Then in-migration of the factor which is used intensively in the import industry will increase the free trade welfare of the native population. Alternatively, out-migration of the factor used intensively in the export sector will increase the free trade welfare of those left behind. In Figure 7.8, under free trade, production is specialized at Q_O, which is beneath R_O due to a labor shortage; consumption is shown at C_O. If labor is accepted into this economy *native* production under free trade can move to Q_1, and native consumption to C_1.

More than protection from trade disruption, factor immigration may actually make autarky following on disruption preferable for the domestic-native population. Factor immigration beyond that needed to insulate from disruption may reverse trade patterns with the result that *domestic-native utility is greater* at U^E than U^T. Here is a conclusion to suggest a positive benefit from factor movement beyond protection from trade disruption.

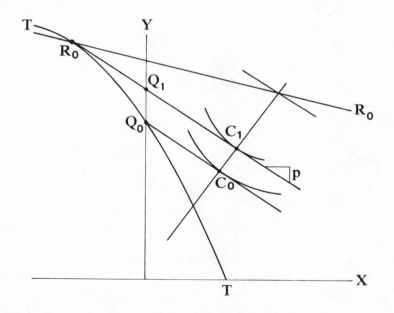

Figure 7.8

If factor movement can substitute for trade, and if costly vulnerability to trade disruption is thereby averted, factor movement may save a country the costs of forestalling (or reducing the probability of) emergency embargo through defense or security efforts, or through other measures such as stockpiling and standby production. And if the amount of trade vulnerability a country allows actually invites embargoes (as Bhagwati and Srinivasan (1976) have argued) — such that more trade makes disruption more likely — then factor movements to diminish commodity trade would actually reduce the likelihood of the embargoes or similar emergencies.

All of these arguments in favor of free factor migration to reduce a country's vulnerability to disruption seem to raise the question whether any discernible *disbenefits* of factor migration can be identified within the Hecksher-Ohlin framework, or must recourse be made to other effects to explain limitations on factor movements in the real world. The answer to this question might depend in part on distinguishing between migration of people and migration of other factors, e.g., capital.

Exchange of factors of production both depend on the risks of emergency (up to and including war) and also will influence the magnitude of such risks. On the one hand, a high risk of trade disruption will reduce factor movement. On the other hand, exchange of factors between states or regions will provide each with incentives to limit conflict. The exchange of factors of production could extend to potentially adversarial states. In this case, such exchanges would probably limit the chances of hostilities breaking out, since once a state of hostility exists previous factor exchanges become similar to an exchange of hostages. For example, as between Israel and its mid-Eastern neighbors, exchange of factors (because of the potential loss if war breaks out) might limit risks of war. On the other hand, such trades might appear so dangerous as to be rejected. The difference between capital and labor as objects of inter-country migration may be crucial at this point. Labor migration seems more risky than capital movement. Human hostages will command more powerful allegiance from governments and therefore expose the immigrant's homeland to stronger pressures to escalate or settle if conflict among neighboring states arises. On the other hand, capital, if exchanged, may be less vulnerable to expropriation because identity of ownership may be more easily concealed and capital may be stored and replaced.

Once we step outside the H-O world of identical technologies and homogenous production functions across all countries, numerous other reasons to explain limits on factor migration are accessible. These alternative explanations include decreasing returns to scale in production, existence of specific immobile factors in different counties, noncompetitive elements in market structure, diverse technologies across countries and so on. Although all these alternatives can change the optimal quantity of factor migration, and may be indeed necessary to invoke an interior limited solution for welfare maximizing factor exchange, none would appear to undermine the usefulness of the idea of factor exchange as protection against costly consequences of trade stoppage, nor to soften the risks of loss which such exchange may induce.

V

The connections between a country's economic position in the world economic system and its strategic position in the world geo-political system must become a topic of growing interest and importance as political and economic dependencies among states continues to increase. This paper addresses a particular rather narrowly defined question from the larger context of how economic relationships may reduce conflict or generate it. In the larger context, the question may be asked whether commercial intercourse among countries reduces or exacerbates their conflicts. Voluntary commercial exchange will always entail mutual accrual of benefits, but the redistribution of power brought on by trade or economic integration within the world political system need not be reciprocal let alone symmetric. Just as economic strength must form the basis for a country's winning its conflicts, political conflict if it induces military competition is a form of economic warfare among adversaries (Wolfson, 1985). Moreover, where countries compete outside their own borders for third markets, their economic rivalry may easily spill over into the political sphere. And every exchange of goods between trading partners insofar as it is a dynamic process can cause dislocation, pain, and resentment in both countries. Adding to these relationships the fact that some trade in goods or factors of production may have special importance to the distribution of military strength, the situation becomes still more complex. Thus, the idea that some countries might wish to insulate themselves partially from their growing dependence on trade with particular rivals and each other is not unintelligible. By allowing factors of production to migrate away countries and to consume their wages/rents/etc., in the country of destination, nations reduce their vulnerability to trade disruption. However, the cost of such insulation must be reckoned if accomplished by factor in-migration as a dilution of national unity, possibly as a necessary compromise in the character of national public goods, possibly as less secure central command over the economy in time of emergency. On the other hand, if insulation from trade disruption were accomplished by means of factor out-migration, then not only is the domestic economy smaller and therefore expectedly less robust in time of war, but domestic interests have become hostage to foreign power, creating a situation which might increase the demands on security from the state.

In the light of the rather general considerations raised in this paper, and our models of trade, protection, and migration, it is clear that policy makers in countries of the Mid-East have no easy task in selecting the best instruments for advancing economic cooperation and possibly some degree of political conciliation. The structure of this paper, however, does suggest that any exchange of capital, workers, technical knowledge, or personnel should be coordinated with commodity trade policy among countries of the region. The costs and benefits of varying degrees of economic cooperation could depend decisively on the risks of trade disruption, the risks of more serious hostilities, the reversibility of commodity-factor exchange agreements, and the potential for loss when cooperation is tested.

▪ Notes

1. This analysis draws heavily on the work of Mayer (1977), Bhagwati and Srinivasan (1976), Shibata (1985), and Shibata and McGuire (1985).

▪ References

Arad, Ruth W. and Arye L. Hillman, 1979, "Embargo Threat, Learning and Departure from Comparative Advantage," *Journal of International Economics* 9, 265-275.

Bergstrom, Clas, Glenn C. Loury and Mats Persson, 1985, "Embargo Threats and the Management of Emergency Reserves," *Journal of Political Economy* 93:1, 26-42.

Bhagwati, Jagdish, 1979, "International Factor Movements and National Advantage," *Indian Economic Review* 14(2) (N.S.), 73-100.

_____, and Ernesto Tironi, 1980, "Tariff Change, Foreign Capital and Immiserization," *Journal of Development Economics* 7, 71-83.

_____, and Richard A. Brecher, 1980, "National Welfare in an Open Economy in the Presence of Foreign-Owned Factors of Production," *Journal of International Economics* 10, 103-115.

_____, and Richard A. Brecher, 1981, "Foreign Ownership and the Theory of Trade and Welfare," *Journal of Political Economy* 89(3), 497-511.

_____, and T.N. Srinivasan, 1976, "Optimal Trade Policy and Compensation under Endogenous Uncertainty: The Phenomenon of Market Disruption," *Journal of International Economics* 6, 317-336.

_____, Richard A. Brecher and T.N. Srinivasan, 1983, "On the Choice Between Capital and Labour Mobility," *Journal of International Economics* 14, 209-221.

Cheng, Leonard, 1985, "Intermittent Trade Disruptions and Optimal Production," unpublished paper, Department of Economics, University of Florida, Gainesville, FL 32611.

Grossman, Gene M. and Assaf Razin, 1984, "International Capital Movements Under Uncertainty," *Journal of Political Economy* 92:2, 286-306.

Helpman, Elhanan, and Razin, Assaf, 1978, *A Theory of International Trade under Uncertainty*, New York: Academic Press.

Hillman, Arye L. and Ngo Van Long, 1983, "Pricing and Depletion of an Exhaustible Resource when there is Anticipation of Trade Disruption," *Quarterly Journal of Economics* 98, 215-233.

Kemp, Murray C., and Liviatan, Nissan, 1973, "Production and Trade Patterns under Uncertainty," *Econ. Record* 49, 215-27.

Loury, Glenn C., 1983, "The Welfare Effects of Intermittent Interruptions of Trade," *American Economic Review* 73 (Papers and Proceedings), 272-277.

MacDougall, G.D.A., 1960, "The Benefits and Costs of Private Investment from Abroad: A Theoretical Approach," *Econ. Record* 36, 13-35.

Markusen, J.R., 1983, "International Factor Movements and Commodity Trade as Complements," *Journal of International Economics*.

Mayer, Wolfgang, 1977, "The National Defense Tariff Argument Reconsidered," *Journal of International Economics* 7, 363-377.

McGuire, Martin, and Hirofumi Shibata, "National Self-Sufficiency Protection and Defense," unpublished paper, Osaka University, Faculty of Economics, Osaka, Japan.

Mundell, Robert A., 1957, "International Trade and Factor Mobility," *American Economic Review*, 47, 321-35.

Polachek, Soloman W., 1980, "Conflict and Trade," *Journal of Conflict Resolution* 24:1, 55-78.

Shibata, Hirofumi, 1985, "A Note on Trade and Security Expenditure and Defense Cost-share Arrangements," unpublished paper, Osaka University, Faculty of Economics, June.

Svensson, Lars E. O., 1984, "Factor Trade and Goods Trade," *Journal of International Economics*, May.

Tolley, George S., and John D. Wilman, 1977, "The Foreign Dependence Question," *Journal of Political Economy* 85:2, 323-347.

Section III

Regional Cooperation: International Experiences and Options and Their Implications for the Middle East

This section contains eight studies. They cover the broad scope of international cooperation, including the role of economic development, a plan for a Middle East "Marshall Plan" and cooperation in scientific technological transfer. The last topics covered suggest that the service sector could be an appropriate starting point for economic cooperation.

Starr concentrates upon the need for and feasibility of a Middle East Marshall plan. Her main idea is that the Middle East needs a something like a Marshall Plan to spur investment and economic recovery. Starr stresses the importance of such an undertaking, due to the severe economic effects of long-lasting military tensions and wars, as well as the belief that a Marshall Plan (with certain modifications) would do for the Middle East what it did for Western Europe forty years ago.

Gafny advocates the Middle East Marshall Plan as an "Economic Strategy of Peace." He suggests learning from the 1947 European Marshall Plan and applying substantial foreign aid to the main problem of the countries in the Middle East – their huge foreign debt. He believes that the debt burden is a major socio-economic constraint upon the area's development. A healthy rate of economic growth is essential for stability and political moderation in the Middle East, and Gafny believes that foreign aid on a substantial scale is necessary to facilitate that growth.

Blejer uses the extent to which regional economic integration has occurred in Latin America as an example of possibilities for formal and informal agreements regarding regional economic cooperation. The main form of cooperation found there is preferential trade agreements. The Middle East countries, like those in Latin America, are developing countries. Thus, implications regarding economic integration in Latin America may also hold true in this region. Blejer emphasized that modifications in traditional approaches to economic integration are needed when dealing with developing countries since certain basic economic characteristics about these economies differ from those in developed countries. Further adaptations may be necessary in applying them to the Middle East.

Concheiro emphasizes the role of technology in economic development and international trade among LDCs. The data he presents show the increasing share of LDCs in world exports, and he predicts that this share will more than double in the next 25 years (by 2010). He also predicts that in the next generation there will be major structural changes in production and in the composition of trade among the LDCs leading to a decline in the share of food, textiles and apparel and to an increase in the share of chemicals, metal products, and machinery in these economies. He analyzes changes in the industrial structure of Israel, Syria, Egypt and Jordan since 1965. Similarities in growth patterns suggest options for intra-industry trade as well as joint ventures.

Nilsson discusses the role of Science and Technology (S&T) in economic development, in general, and in the process of industrialization, in particular. He sees a special role for S&T in the Middle East which is vital to the success of the "Marshall Plan." This possibility arises from the uneven distribution in the quality and quantity of scientific activities among Israel and the Arab countries. Therefore, he suggests that the first cooperative endeavors between Israel and the Arab countries should be in science and technology with emphasis on food and water technologies, plant genetics, and energy.

Hindly views the service sector as the logical place for economic cooperation between Israel and its neighbors to begin. Transport and communications would be a good starting point because of geographic factors. Linked transportation and communication networks will lead to the supply of other services, insurance, repairs, and storage. In order to illustrate the importance of services, Hindly analyzes the role of services in the international economic framework. He uses the results to build the economic case for unilateral liberalization of restrictions on international transactions in services.

8

A Marshall Plan for the Middle East: The U.S. Response

Joyce R. Starr

It was in 1979 that I began a dialogue with Arnon Gafny, former governor of the Bank of Israel, and Dr. David Abshire, former chairman of the Center for Strategic and International Studies (CSIS), on the creation of a Middle East Development Fund—envisioned to serve a role similar to the post-World War II Marshall Plan for the reconstruction of Europe. Through the efforts and resources of CSIS, spurred forward by Mr. Gafny's personal dedication to this concept, two major international conferences were held, involving delegations from numerous countries, and negotiations were begun at an unofficial level with Western leaders and governments.[1] The idea has since won the attention and commitment of former Israeli Prime Minister Shimon Peres.

When we first launched this effort, the Middle East was on the "brink" of peace. The historic treaty between Israel and Egypt had been signed only a few months earlier, in March 1979, and the energy of hope was in abundant supply. Indeed, the U.S. Embassy in Damascus had even drafted a series of optimistic cables in 1978–79 describing how Syria could benefit from the peace process!

As we move into 1987, the Middle East is on the brink of chaos—economies are crumbling, the cancer of impoverishment is overtaking the region, political and religious extremism has become the norm, terrorism is the call to arms for the common man, and hope has all but vanished from the lexicon of the leadership. Forty years earlier, Winston Churchill described Europe as "a rubble heap, a charnel house, a breeding ground of pestilence and hate." Under Secretary of State Clayton reported that every European with whom he talked warned that further deterioration would lead to revolution. Their words ring prophetic in capturing the stark reality of the Middle East today.

Europe was saved through the inspiration, generosity, and hard-headed economic sense of the Marshall Plan. Thus we ask ourselves, cannot the western nations call forth the power, the resources, the sheer will and vision to reverse the awesome desolation overtaking the Middle East?

In raising this question, we must first understand the origins of the Marshall Plan, the form it took, and the challenge it offered. A senior State Department official in 1948 compared the Plan to a *flying saucer*: "Nobody knows what it looks like, how big it is, what its direction might be, where it is moving, or if it really exists." Half of the Americans living today were not yet born when the Marshall Plan was established, and few of those who were have any memory of what it actually entailed.

General George Marshall was Army Chief of Staff during the war. His reputation for exceptional character, leadership and organizational skills was already legend when President Truman appointed Marshall Secretary of State in 1947. Two previous post-war Secretaries had failed in their attempts to raise the Department of State from a malaise that prevented innovative thinking and the development of far-sighted policy responses to Europe's worsening conditions. Marshall succeeded in only a few months to rekindle morale and to provide an environment that encouraged the generation of bold ideas. He also appointed a Policy Planning Staff, which he tasked with preparing the *long view* of foreign policy issues.

The Marshall Plan for the reconstruction of Europe was in fact the creation of George Kennen, the State Department professional Marshall had named as director of the new Policy Planning Staff. Kennen held this position for only ten days when he received the directive to devise an economic plan that would save war-torn Europe. The concepts conceived by Kennen and his team were outlined by Marshall in a commencement speech, delivered at Harvard University in June, 1947.

In this speech Marshall stated, "It would be neither fitting, nor efficacious for this government to undertake to draw up unilaterally a program designed to place Europe on its feet economically. This is the business of the Europeans. The role of this country should consist of friendly aid in the drafting of a European program and of later support of such a program so far as it might be practical for us to do so. The program should be a joint one agreed to by a number if not all Europeans."

It is noteworthy that Secretary Marshall refused to allow the Department of State to transmit his speech to foreign embassies. The great military strategist had made a historic decision to leave the consequences of his remarks to fate. A British diplomat heard about the speech, mentioned it to a colleague from the BBC, who was able to obtain a rare copy from a member of his car pool—an economist working at the Department of State. The BBC reporter carried the substance of Marshall's remarks during his 10:30 p.m. commentary. By chance, British Foreign Minister Bevan was listening that evening to the broadcast. Bevan conveyed the news with great excitement to his European counterparts. But had he retired early that evening, the Marshall Plan might well have been relegated to the State Department file drawers to collect dust.

Instead, the United States would soon undertake a $13 billion initiative (equivalent to approximately $90 billion in 1987 terms) that would change the course of history. It was Senator Charles Vandenberg, arguing before the U.S. Senate on behalf of the plan with compelling intellect and emotion, who galvanized public and congressional support. In eloquent oratory, he urged:

"Mr. President, the decision here which concerns the Senate is the kind that tries mens' souls—I understand and share the anxieties involved. It would be a far happier circumstance if we could close our eyes to reality, comfortably retire within our bastions, and dream about isolated and prosperous peace. There are no blueprints to guarantee results: We are entirely surrounded by calculated risks. I profoundly believe that the pending program is the best of these risks. This legislation, Mr. President, seeks peace and stability for free men in a free world. It seeks them by economic rather than by military means. It proposes to help our friends help themselves in the pursuit of sound and successful liberty in the democratic patter."

Vandenberg went on to stress, "There is only one voice left in the world, Mr. President, which is competent to hearten the determination of the other nations and other people in western Europe to survive in their own choice, or their own way of life. It is our voice. It is in part the Senate's voice. Surely, we can all agree—whatever our shades of opinion—that the hour has struck for this voice to speak as soon as possible."

The Marshall Plan conceived by the Department of State and approved by Congress was first and foremost a self-help program, that necessitated a COLLECTIVE and COOPERATIVE response from the European community. Indeed, the sine qua non of the plan was that the European nations would prioritize amongst themselves the allocations for each country. Moreover, the monies given were primarily in the form of credits for goods and services, two-thirds of which were purchased in the United States.

Can we now imagine the Syrians and Israelis or Iranians and Iraqis readily agreeing to economic assistance for the other—instead of committing their diminishing resources to the other party's destruction? Can we project a new U.S. foreign aid program for the Middle East constructed on a regional, rather than bilateral basis? Certainly the nations presently receiving our aid would welcome additional funds, but doubtfully at the cost of benefits already won. Can we identify leaders of equivalent stature and motivation as Secretary George Marshall to issue the challenge and Senator Vandenberg to enlist public support? Most important, can the United States yet again be a lone actor on the world stage?

The answer, of course, is that we cannot. The tragic drama of the Middle East necessitates an international response, a united and vital western leadership. The United States is no longer in a financial position to undertake even an additional $10 or $20 billion foreign aid program without strong allied participation. Present economic assistance levels to Egypt and Israel, (60 percent of our total foreign aid package), are likely to be reduced in the coming years, not augmented. In 1986, for the first time in our history, the United States became a debtor nation. The ranks of destitute and struggling Americans are growing by the day. The anguish and poverty of our poor is enough to try men's souls, but increasingly middle class America faces a future of economic uncertainty and fear.

A Marshall Plan for the Middle East must therefore contain elements that go beyond all previous thinking on the issue. For example, perhaps we should consider the merits of an Eastern Mediterranean grouping of nations. After all, a clear distinction can be made between the economic position of gulf states like Saudi Arabia or Kuwait, and the bleak situation facing the Mediterranean countries of Egypt, Israel, Jordan, Lebanon, Syria, and Turkey.

Given an Eastern Mediterranean focus, it might also be more in the direct interest of a European country, for instance Italy or Germany, to "father" the plan. (Current European and Japanese enthusiasm for a regional economic initiative — as conveyed in discussions with U.S. officials at the June, 1986 Tokyo Summit — can best be described as lukewarm.) An imaginative scheme of credits, investment, and even debt forgiveness would be required and would eventually mean a reduction or phasing out of bilateral aid.

Whatever the formula, the creation of a regional Marshall Plan would absolutely necessitate cooperation among recipient states and a readiness to join forces against the one enemy they share in common: hopelessness.

■ Notes

1. These efforts were elaborated on in *A Shared Destiny: Near East Regional Development and Cooperation*, ed. by Dr. Joyce R. Starr, Praeger, 1983.

9

The Middle East Development Fund

Arnon Gafny

■ The Economic Consequences of Peace 1919

In the year 1919, a British economist, who later turned out to be one of the greatest and most innovative of them, returned from the Paris Peace Conference deeply enraged and frustrated. He was John Maynard Keynes, who had served during the war years of 1914-1918 in the U.K. Treasury and was also Britain's official representative to the Peace Conference early in 1919. He immediately wrote and published his brilliant dissertation "The Economic Consequences of the Peace," in which he waged a critical attack on the fragile economic foundations laid at the Peace Conference for the postwar era in Europe.[1]

Keynes had developed a novel approach to the economic strategy of peace: "It was the task of the Peace Conference to honor engagements and to satisfy justice; but not less, to reestablish life and to heal wounds."

In order to open the road to world prosperity, the great economist suggested an approach well-accepted today but entirely contrary to the current of opinion at that period and the nature of the treaty of Versailles. First, the entire war debt of the debtor allies should be forgiven by the creditor countries, mainly the United States. "The prospect of being relieved of oppressive interest payments to England and America over the whole life of the next two generations would free the future from excessive anxiety." In addition, an international loan should be arranged, in order to "...meet the ills of the immediate present – the excess of Europe's imports over her exports, the adverse exchange, and the disorder of the currency. It will be very difficult for European production to get started again without a temporary measure of external assistance."

Although it is dangerous to speculate on possible alternative courses that could have substituted for actual history, it may be argued that had Keynes' advice been adopted, the most serious crisis of inflation and depression might have been avoided and world peace might have been more stable.

■ The "Marshall Plan" — 1947

The lesson, however, was learned — at a high price — and Keynes' ideas were embodied in U.S. policy in the aftermath of the second world war. Two years after the war, Europe still suffered from the destruction of its economy and from lack of capital to stimulate industrial productivity. Frustration started to spread all over Europe due to the fact that the high expectations from peace were not fulfilled. It was against this background that the United States devised the European Recovery Program, later known as the Marshall Plan, which was named after George C. Marshall, then American Secretary of State. Marshall understood the gravity of the situation and devised a bold policy to remedy it. During the five years from 1947-1952, the United States provided 12.4 billion dollars in economic aid, as well as plans for the economic reconstruction of Europe. This historic act set into motion the rapid economic growth of Europe and laid the foundation for decades of growth and prosperity.

■ A "Marshall Plan" for the Middle East?

Of late, the need for a "Marshall Plan" for the Middle East has been recognized in various countries.

As thirty years of war in the Middle East have not resulted in physical devastation, our immediate economic problem is not rebuilding ruined economies. The economic loss suffered by the countries of the Middle East due to the state of war is reflected mainly in the constraints placed on the economic and social development of the region. For many years, national security has tied down a large portion of the manpower, and much of the initiative and productive capacity have been diverted to defense purposes. Enormous sums have gone to purchase military equipment and maintain military strength.

The war and defense burden are mainly reflected in the huge foreign debt accumulated in the region. The situation in 1984 of Egypt and Israel indicate the magnitude of the problem. Egypt, with a population of 46 million people, and GNP of $32 billion, had accumulated $23 billion external debt and $3.6 billion annual debt service (30 percent of current account receipts).

Israel, with a population of 4.2 million and a GNP of $21 billion had accumulated $23 billion external debt, which is as high as Egypt's external debt and higher than its own GNP. The annual debt service reached $2.9 billion (also 30 percent of current account receipts).

The external indebtedness of Egypt and Israel has arisen mainly from the defense burden they have had to shoulder for a whole generation. Most of the borrowing was used to acquire arms and maintain defense capacity, rather than to create a productive capacity from whose fruits the people could benefit and the loans be repaid.

A disproportionately large external debt is, undoubtedly, one of the principal constraints on the socioeconomic development capacity of both countries as well as others in the region and may prolong into peacetime the economic loss normally associated with war periods. Therefore, a "Marshall Plan" for the Middle East and Israel must create conditions whereby financial and physical resources may be rapidly allocated for economic development at the same time that the political and social foundations of peace are being laid. Such a plan would enable the large-scale development necessary to ensure significant reduction of the economic and social differentials that marked the years of hostilities in the area. It will also serve the interests of the industrialized countries since, above all, a healthy process of growth at the fastest possible rate is essential for the stability and political moderation of the area, so as to enable promotion of production, international trade, and debt repayment.

Evolution of the Plan

In the years 1979 and 1980, a group of international experts of various nationalities, experts in the field of multinational financing of development, informally exchanged opinions concerning "Marshallian" ideas relevant to the transition from war to peace in the Middle East.

The concept of a multinational development fund evolved as the major practical proposal for a mechanism that will ignite the process of economic growth despite the enormous war debts that serve as the major constraint for the area.

In 1981 the Edmond de Rothschild Foundation in New York commissioned me to perform a study on international promotion of economic development in the context of the peace process in the Middle East. The study was defined as follows:

A) The foundation of a multinational fund for economic development in the cause of peace; membership open to all countries in the region, as well as nonregional countries who support the peace process in the Middle East.

The fund will mobilize the financial resources needed for development; the study shall determine their size, methods of mobilization, the relationship between public and private sources, the need for grants and loans as well as the period of loans.

B) Alternative structures of the fund: membership, board of directors, management, location, methods of disbursements of funds.

C) The role of commercial bank cofinancing.

D) The formation of an international business sector investment corporation whose major task would be to bring together, in the form of joint ventures in the Middle East, finance, enterprise, management, technical skill and know-how, in order to cause efficient economic development within the peace process. The relation between the fund and the corporation would also be studied, the need for two separate entities, the provision of a subsidized multinational political risk insurance for business sector activities.

E) Identification of areas for mutual economic cooperation between countries in the area, projects which would be effectively implemented jointly with international entrepreneurs.

In May and December 1981, the Center for Strategic and International Studies (CSIS), under the leadership of Dr. David Abshire, its chairman and Dr. Joyce Starr, its representative in the Middle East, hosted two international conferences that considered the feasibility of the concept. The participants in these conferences were bankers, businessmen, and officials from the U.S., Europe, Egypt, and Israel. There was a strong and unanimous conviction that greater attention should be focused on steps to reduce conditions of hostility through the alleviation of poverty and the improvement of living conditions as a result of achieving peace. A development approach was seen as a necessary measure to accompany the peace process – the two are inextricably associated.

The proposal for a Middle East development fund emerged in the last conference as a plan likely to provide the institutionalization and tools to implement a "Marshall Plan" adapted to the needs of the area in the 1980s.

Dr. Abshire closed the conference with the following comment: "I believe that we have participated here in a very significant discussion and we must now turn it into action."

In 1982 a detailed proposal was elaborated within the study sponsored by the Edmond de Rothschild Foundation and discussed with experts and leaders from the industrial countries as well as Middle Eastern countries.

The following is the description of the scheme as crystallized in 1982.

The Scheme

The following scheme is intended to join private and public funds and entrepreneurship with governmental support in order to create economic growth that will remunerate both investors and the peoples of the Middle East. Productive investment of this nature and scale is imperative to the improvement of the economic welfare of the peoples.

The scheme consists of three elements:

First, the constitution of a joint Middle East peace commission, whose members would be the respective ministers or top officials of the various countries;

Second, the formation of a multilateral Middle East peace development fund (MEPDF) for the purposes of (A) contributing to the financing of projects significant to the economic well-being of the peoples of the region and thus, to the strengthening of the peace process and (B) providing insurance against political risk to private investors involved in approved priority projects and;

Third, the formation of an international investment corporation owned by private and public financial institutions from various countries. This corporation would identify, develop and mobilize the financing for projects which contribute to the economic progress of the countries of the region participating in the scheme.

■ The Joint Economic Middle East Peace Commission

The purpose of the commission would be: (1) to coordinate the activities within this scheme with the national economic plans of the respective countries; (2) to solve problems encountered by the participants in the scheme; (3) to review periodically at the ministerial level the economic developments; (4) to determine the priority areas in which the investment effort can yield maximum benefit in the terms of reference of this scheme; (5) to mobilize the efforts of their respective governments in support of approved projects; (6) to negotiate the economic incentives to be granted by the member countries.

The representatives of member countries on the commission would be ministers or top officials designated by their respective governments. Once the Middle East peace development fund and the private investment corporation were organized, their chief executive officers would report to the commission and attend all meetings.

The Proposal

For the first two years, the joint commission should meet biannually. The meetings could take place on a rotating basis in each of the participating countries, with the minister of the host country acting as chairman. A permanent secretariat consisting of a nominee from each country would assure effective follow-through in each participating country. The secretariat would prepare the agenda for each meeting and report results of actions agreed upon at the previous meeting. The joint commission should recommend to the MEPDF areas of the highest economic priority in which feasibility studies should be performed. The joint commission would engage in policy-making and reviewing functions rather than operational tasks.

What makes this scheme potentially unique is that it combines (A) a high level joint commission, (B) a public financing and risk insurance entity (MEPDF), and (C) a business investment vehicle (the corporation), all linked to the common objective of advancing peace and development through the financing and implementation of projects which are economically viable.

The Operating Entities

It is proposed that separate entities be formed to channel flows of private and public capital. Within the context of separate entities, the flexibility and initiative of the private investors would be guaranteed. Indeed, the operating styles of private investment entities and publicly funded institutions are sufficiently different for them to be separated. However, through the joint commission, both entities would be assured of a strong backing at the ministerial level and coordination of their objectives, policies and operations. Thus the overall scheme seeks to maximize the advantage of each form of operation, while providing effective operational coordination and governmental support.

The Middle East Peace Development Fund

The question will be raised whether a new regional fund should be established when the world is awash with development institutions that have difficulty in obtaining domestic political backing in most of the industrialized countries. Therefore, it must be clearly understood that this is not just another economic development initiative. This is a unique scheme which is directly and specifically tied to a clearly identifiable objective; consolidating peace through specific economic linkages, while encouraging other countries to join in the peace effort. Thus, the objectives are more clearly defined and less open-ended than those of the more conventional multilateral development institutions. It is for this reason that the existing institutions cannot achieve the objectives which are the basis for the creation of the MEPDF. The World Bank, for example, is universal in scope; hence, operations financed by it must meet overall World Bank policy and operational standards, and cannot be tailored to the particular circumstances created by peace efforts. Similarly, the aid bilateral program is, by definition, a program between a given country and the United States. It does not build cross linkages between countries in the region, which is one of the important objectives sought through the proposed scheme.

The MEPDF would be staffed in part by nationals of countries in the region and would be engaged in a continuing process of project identification, preparing and financing. As the projects were implemented with mutual benefits to the peoples of those countries, there would be created over a period of the next ten years an experience of joint economic activities. Although less ambitious than the European Economic Community, the effect could be much the same: the creation of institutions which provide the means for continuous involvement in the resolution of common economic problems.

Functions

The MEPDF would use its resources within the above-mentioned framework:

(A) To finance economically feasible projects and programs in countries of the area. Due attention should be given to projects beneficial to more than one country;

(B) To undertake or participate in the study and preparation of public and private projects;

(C) To promote investment in development projects in the countries of the area;

(D) To mobilize public and private capital resources for the financing of development projects and programs;

(E) To provide or help mobilize technical assistance necessary in the implementation of projects or programs;

(F) To provide insurance to private foreign investors engaged in such projects against risks such as expropriation, inconvertibility of currencies, war and civil insurrection.

Organization

(A) MEPDF would be created through an agreement between the governments of the initiating countries and open to all countries that wish to join it. The charter of the MEPDF should be negotiated and agreed upon by all the member countries.

(B) A Board of Directors would be created. The government of each of the regional members would nominate a director and an alternate. The nonregional members could also nominate a director and an alternate but should they outnumber the regional countries they would elect among them an equal number of directors to the regional countries. Should the commission decide to allow issue of shares to private and institutional shareholders, it would agree on the number of directors to be elected by them.

(C) The fund should have a minimal competent professional and administrative staff. But in order to limit administrative expenditure, it should use as much as possible the manpower of existing international and national organizations which provide similar services on a contractual basis.

Needs and Resources

The needs of MEPDF would depend on the extent of its regional membership, as well as their national development needs. It should be determined according to the amounts necessary to create long-term sustained high rate of growth in each of the regional members, taking into consideration their economic and social absorptive capacity.

But in order to establish its credibility and enable it to function immediately, the nonregional members should make a binding commitment of U.S. $30 billion over the first ten years, of which U.S. $3 billion (10 percent) should be paid in at once (U.S. $300 million per annum cash) to provide immediate liquidity.

Another trench of U.S. $3 billion (10 percent) would be contributed by the nonregional countries into a special fund according to a timetable based on the need to meet financial obligations; this contribution would not carry any voting rights.

The "special fund" would be used for:

A) Creation of reserves needed by the risk insurance facility;

B) Participation grants in feasibility studies and other research and development;

C) Subsidizing interest rates to priority infra-structure projects and in periods of high market rates.

The remaining commitment of U.S. $24 billion (80 percent) would serve to back guarantees for borrowed capital and would be called upon only if and when needed to meet obligations on the Fund's borrowing. The sum of U.S. $24 billion would thus be mobilized over 10 years through:

A) Bond issues to be sold on the money markets;

B) Syndicated loans from commercial banks in the form of cofinancing projects;

C) Cofinancing with other international or regional organizations.

The callable capital would serve as a guarantee fund—a contingent liability on the subscribers.

The amounts borrowed of the MEPDF would not exceed, at the first stage, the sum of the callable capital. Later, after establishment of credibility in the markets, it may be extended through establishment of a gearing ratio. In this way, the capital subscription can be leveraged to broaden the financial base of the institution's operations.

It is suggested that part of the repayments of the regional countries defense loans, in the coming decade, to the U.S. and other member countries who own such assets, would be made to the MEPDF. These payments may be made to the fund in the local currency (Egyptian pounds, Israeli shekels, etc.) and would be used for financing projects chosen by the corresponding country. Such an arrangement is of course dependent on bilateral agreements between the relevant countries.

Operations

The fund will implement its purpose and functions by providing loans, equity financing and technical assistance to the countries of the area. It will also be authorized to guarantee loans to the same countries.

The limits to the amount to be lent or guaranteed would be at the beginning the capital prescriptions, surpluses and reserves of the Fund. But, in order to eliminate unnecessary restrictions, a study should be made of how to broaden the scope of operations (by establishing a gearing ratio) without requiring additional governmental subscriptions.

Contrary to the practice of the World Bank, it is proposed that the MEPDF will finance both the local and foreign currency components of the projects. This element is vital in order to encourage local participation in the development process itself and thus build up local production.

It is proposed that loans would be granted for periods up to 25 years for infra-structure and 15 years to industrial, agricultural and similar projects. Also facilities for medium-term financing (up to 5 years) would be established for small projects with rapid returns.

It is proposed that in order to maintain stable expectations which are necessary in the economies emerging from war to peace, a ceiling for the long-term interest rate would be fixed by the board of directors. In periods of higher market rates the difference would be paid out of the special fund. For some priority areas, mainly infrastructure with significant social benefits, a special lower rate should be approved, say 4-5 percent. Again, the difference would be paid out of the special fund.

An essential ingredient to economic development is the ability to prepare projects and programs. The fund shall have the authority to provide technical assistance for this purpose and at least partially finance it by grants and loans. In this context the fund shall also be involved in training of professional personnel to plan, manage and operate projects. This will be done directly as well as in cooperation with other organizations.

In contrast to conventional multilateral development institutions, the fund would not be expected to attempt to influence development policies, macro or sectorial, of the member countries in which projects are being financed, except where such policies have a direct impact on the financial or economic feasibility of the project being financed or insured. While the fund would be governed by economic feasibility in determining projects to be financed or investments to be insured, due consideration should also be given to the degree and the manner in which they advance the peace process.

Insurance Operations

With respect to risk insurance, it is considered necessary to attract significant foreign investors, given the history of the area. The proposal may be based on a pooled insurance concept encompassing all member countries.

The investment must consist of new capital, or technical skills that qualify as foreign investment under the laws of the host country, being contributed to the project.

Insurance would cover losses due to expropriation, inconvertibility, war, revolution, or insurrection. As a general rule, coverage will extend for a period between seven and fifteen years. Expropriation will be defined to include "creeping" appropriation.

A minimum reserve of an amount to be decided would be established at the outset, and the administrator will manage the fund's operations with a view toward increasing that reserve.

The fund would develop a premium structure which will permit the recognition of changing conditions and make possible premium and coverage adjustment during the policy term.

The investors would be required to bear a portion of the insured risk themselves so as to have a meaningful amount of their own resources at stake in the projects.

The Investment Vehicle (The Corporation)

A private investment entity would have to have the following characteristics:

1) A special-purpose investment corporation would be established to concentrate on project and project-related financing.

2) The entity could commit its own resources for investment purposes but would also seek maximum participation by other investors in projects in which it is prepared to invest or lend;

3) The new entity would be responsible to its shareholders; it would operate under the laws and regulations of countries in which it is headquartered and conducts business;

4) A firm decision on the size and nature of capital of the private investment entity would be made after potential investors have been canvassed. The need to call up capital, increase shares, etc. would be determined by the board of directors according to needs and circumstances;

5) The entity would aim to earn an adequate return on capital and avoid losses which impair earnings or capital;

6) The new entity's investment and lending criteria would be guided by the need to achieve and maintain its own credit-worthiness and to ensure the confidence of its shareholders. The aim would also be to have an asset portfolio which gives the new entity a very high credit standing for itself.

7) The new entity would fund itself from world financial markets. It could make loans or investments in any currency. Matters like country risk, hedging against foreign currency exchange risk, liquidity and capital adequacy would be decided by the management, including the board of directors, on private investment principles within the framework of promoting sound development within the host countries.

8) The capital of the new investment corporation should be sufficient to provide the base for its operations; the aim would be to build capital from profitable activities over the years ahead. Declaration, magnitude and timing of dividends would be decided by the board of directors upon the recommendation of management. Investors could not expect dividends until profits were earned.

9) The new entity could have its headquarters in Europe in a financial center suited to its purposes. The venue of the corporation would be decided by the shareholders.

10) The new entity would aim to have a minimum staff of the highest professional quality and reputation, able to evaluate project proposals from the viewpoint of economic viability. Full use would be made of existing private and public institutions in host and creditor countries.

11) The new entity would aim to achieve international standing needed to make possible substantial leveraging of its capital. It would aim for a leveraging capacity equal to that of top experienced lenders. In its earlier years, it would not be expected to achieve the maximum levels of leveraging because prime importance would be attached to careful asset acquisition and avoidance of loan losses.

12) The investments and loans made by the new entity would probably average longer than the maturities of ordinary commercial banks; shorter maturities would also be available for project and trade-related purposes; general purpose loans would be avoided. Portfolio diversification would be a guiding principle of lending and investing.

▪ Recent Developments

The war in Lebanon and its following complications, the "cold peace" relations between Israel and Egypt since then, forced the slowdown of the efforts to actively promote the scheme during 1983 and 1984.

In 1985, however, the Middle East confronted a new situation: a steep decrease of oil revenues and its effect on employment and economic conditions in the region. The deterioration of the economy endangered the stability of moderate regimes. The prime minister of Israel, Mr. Shimon Peres, was the first head of state to point out publicly the immediate need for an arrangement that would ignite economic development and growth in order to restabilize the region and continue the peace process. Being familiar with the concept of a Middle East development fund, Mr. Peres decided to promote it among the leadership of the industrial countries as a realistic mechanism, through which the urgent needs of the region should be provided.

The concept attracted the attention and interest of most heads of state of the industrial countries and is now placed on their agenda.

The reduction of oil prices has hurt even non-oil producing countries in the Middle East by reducing their employment and industrial and agricultural export opportunities. On the other hand, the industrial countries have gained substantially and their capital and money markets are booming.

Thus, at present, urgent economic and political needs exist in the Middle East and new international resources are available to the industrial countries. The time may be just ripe to turn the ideas into action.

■ **Notes**

1. Keynes, John Maynard, *The Economic Consequences of the Peace*, Macmillan & Co., Ltd. (London, 1920), p. 23.

10

Regional Integration in Latin America: The Experience and the Outlook for Further Cooperation

*Mario I. Blejer**

The attempt to reach formal and informal agreements among groups of countries encouraging economic cooperation and establishing tariff and other trade-related preferences for the members of the group is not a new phenomenon. The most notorious historical example of a customs union is the *Zollverein*, formed in 1834, which led to the eventual political unification of Germany. In our days, particularly in the postwar period, many attempts at economic integration have taken place in different areas of the world and, among them, the best known and probably the most successful case is that of the European Economic Community.

Since many of the earlier and better-known cases of integration took place between countries that had reached a relatively high level of economic development, most of the attention of policy-makers and theoreticians was primarily directed to the analysis of these cases without considering the particular circumstances and interests of less developed economies. The advocacy of economic integration between developing countries became a very topical issue in the 1960s, particularly after the establishment of the Latin American Free Trade Area (LAFTA), and, motivated by the growing number

---

*The views expressed are strictly those of the author. This paper is a summary of "Economic Integration: An Overview" prepared by the author at the invitation of the Inter-American Development Bank and published as the Introduction to the 1984 Annual Report of that organization. A shortened version of that paper was published in 1985 by the *IMF Survey*.

of integration attempts in different areas of the world, the interest of the economic profession started to shift toward the specific aspects present in developing countries.

In this light, the first section of the paper very briefly surveys the main elements of the traditional approach to economic integration with its standard extensions and then turns to the modifications introduced to deal with developing economies. The second section is the core of the paper and focuses on the Latin American experience. The last section reviews the implications of recent developments regarding the prospects for regional cooperation.[1]

▪ The Theoretical Framework

The Traditional Approach

The traditional approach to economic integration is based on the pure theory of customs unions. It is a "trade" approach in the sense of dealing with the liberalization of the current account and neglects other aspects of international economic relationships such as tax agreements, the harmonization of fiscal and monetary policies, liberalization of capital flows, the free movement of labor, and many other forms of international cooperation. The traditional approach is largely based on the evaluation of the static welfare implications of altering the existing patterns of production and trade following the formation of a customs union. Jacob Viner (1950) showed that the welfare effects of a customs union are ambiguous, since its establishment gives rise to two opposite effects: trade creation and trade diversion. Clearly, welfare increases if trade creation effects dominate trade diversion.

This traditional view of the welfare effects of customs unions is based on a large number of stylized assumptions that raise questions about the appropriateness of this model for the case of developing countries. The central assumptions include perfect competition in factor and goods markets, fixed terms of trade, full employment, constant returns to scale, no externalities, no transport costs, identical production functions, constant technology, constant tastes, and constant quality and quantity of factors of production. Despite the restrictive nature of these assumptions, they helped to establish a taxonomical approach for the characterization of those potential partners which are more likely to benefit and those which are more likely to reduce their welfare as the consequence of a customs union. In addition, a rationale for the theory of the "second best" was presented, a theory later elaborated by Meade (1955) and Lipsey and Lancaster (1956), and which expanded to many other fields of economic theory. The central tenet of this theory is that, in the presence of many distortions, the addition of others or the elimination of some do not affect welfare in an a priori known direction. The message within the context of economic integration was that, although the establishment of a customs union is a step in the direction of free trade, a first-best in this neoclassical paradigm, its ultimate effect on the economic welfare of the participants could not be evaluated ex ante.

The theoretical conception regarding economic integration was therefore set on the premise of the superiority of free trade and the negation of protectionism as a channel eventually conducive to first-best solutions. In the best of cases, integration could improve welfare above autarky levels but, generally, the gains were lower than those attainable through nonpreferential commercial liberalization.

This type of argumentation, however, was not well received in political and economic circles of many developing countries where integration was seen as a step to counterbalance the economic weight of the industrial world and as a way to solve some of the structural problems affecting the developing countries, such as a very narrow market size and the secular deterioration of the terms of trade. The desirability of the idea, however, had to be sustained by a set of economic arguments in order to provide a rationale for the implementation of integration policies.

The Development Approach

The analytical framework supporting economic integration among developing countries is based on various departures from the original theoretical framework. Those departures are of three main types: (a) extensions to the basic model, especially changing the assumptions but without altering the general analytical structure; (b) the elaboration of arguments rationalizing economic integration in terms of alternative objectives and social welfare functions; and (c) the consideration of the effects of distortions and the introduction of dynamic elements to the cost-benefit evaluation.

(a) Two sets of departures from the assumptions of the basic model provide some theoretical arguments relevant for supporting economic integration in developing countries. The first relates to changes in the terms of trade, and the second to the presence of economies of scale.

The consequences of allowing for terms-of-trade effects are related to the proposition that a country with monopsonistic power in world markets improves its terms of trade by imposing tariffs. But it is only when each individual member is small but the combined union has market power that a terms-of-trade argument for small countries may be made. However, the attainment of terms-of-trade improvements may require a very high common external tariff with the consequent high probability that negative welfare effects will arise from trade diversion. Moreover, the argument seems to apply more to the formation of consumer cartels than to favoring economic integration.

A second set of modifications refers to the achievement of economies of scale following the formation of a union. The central idea is that, following the enlargement of the market for some commodities being produced at high costs by members of the union before its formation, what, on the surface, appears to be trade diversion will ultimately be beneficial to all the members since the average cost of production will fall as production expands. However, in order to raise welfare, the economies-of-scale effect should lead to a final price lower than the world price, which implies that the country could, in principle, have become an exporter to world markets even without the union. The point in question is then one of achieving market access and not of granting discriminatory protection. In addition, the argument about economies of scale applies only at the level of the production unit and is not relevant for the combination of total production of multiple individual units. This carries the implication that, in order to attain economies of scale, single members of the union may have to capture the entire market of specific products with others totally abandoning its production. This, of course, raised the critical issue of the distribution of gains and location of industries within the union.

(b) In the attempt to support the push for economic integration among developing countries, a new approach emerged. This new approach accepts protection and trade restrictions as tools of economic policy which is not necessarily inferior to the free-trade system. Such advocacy of tariff protection is viewed as justified when the social welfare function is redefined to include future as well as current consumption and other noneconomic objectives, and when there are imperfections, externalities, and distortions in commodity and factor markets. In all those cases, an optimal trade policy seeks the attainment of dynamic transformations in the economic structure, which would lead to a different pattern of specialization reflecting the concept of dynamic comparative advantage.

The "development approach" to economic integration is, therefore, theoretically grounded on the nonsuperiority of free trade over protection when nonstandard economic objectives are considered or when commodity, factor, and foreign-exchange markets are distorted. Accepting this idea, the "development approach" does not view customs union formations as a second-best policy.

When considering nonstandard welfare functions, the attainment of industrialization plays a central role in the design of the alternative social objectives. The structuralist approach to development has been based on this type of reasoning. Because of specific rigidities, lags in technological transfers, and the pricing mechanism predominant in the world economic system, structuralists view industrialization as the core of economic development. Given the perceived superiority of the industrial strategy, the conservation of the domestic market together with the enlargement of other marketing horizons becomes the centerpiece of this development approach. But why is economic integration the most appropriate trade policy to reach this objective? The answer appears to rely on the belief that some members of a customs union have an advantage within the union but suffer a definitive comparative disadvantage with respect to the rest of the world. In addition, the potential optimality of integration policies to attain industrialization is supported by the view that customs unions tend to enhance the bargaining power of the participants. In this context, some authors (e.g., Meade, 1955) have stressed the increased bargaining power of the union as a whole when negotiating with third parties. The threat of the union to increase the common external tariff, unless some advantages in third markets are granted, may be more credible and effective than the possibility of individual retaliatory actions. Although it may indeed be factual that unions carry more weight than individual participants, it is not obvious that setting up common barriers is a precondition for expanding the bargaining power of the countries of a region. It is certainly conceivable to work out ad hoc regional arrangements with the specific purpose of improving the negotiating stance of the group which do not necessarily require trade integration.

(c) The advocacy of economic integration in developing countries, however, rests mainly on arguments based on the achievement of dynamic effects in the presence of distortions and market imperfections. The introduction of nonstatic cost-benefit analysis into the context of economic integration is an extension of the concepts of the infant industry and of a dynamic comparative advantage. However, when these notions have been elaborated in connection with economic integration, they have been largely linked to the issues of market constraints and to an extended variant of the economies-of-scale argument.

A common version of the traditional infant-industry claim asserts that the observed patterns of international trade only reflect the structure of comparative advantage at a given point in time. However, this structure is not static and developing countries may emerge, after a learning process, with a comparative advantage in many industrial sectors which, at present, show a negative relative cost ratio. The unfolding of such a comparative advantage requires the preservation of the domestic market for those industries identified as likely to benefit from increases in the volume of production. This is therefore an argument for temporary protection, leading first to import substitution and, potentially, to exports and competitiveness in world markets.

The economic rationale of the infant-industry argument is based on a dynamic variant of the economies-of-scale notion. It claims that the complete structure of average and marginal costs, even if increasing in a static sense, falls as production proceeds. The downward displacement of the cost structure is caused by technological gains, productivity rises, and human capital improvements, which can be achieved only through learning by doing and cannot be disembodied from the production process itself.

When utilizing the infant-industry argument in the context of economic integration, an additional element plays an important role: the indivisibility of plant size. Individual country markets may be large enough to suffice for efficient primary import substitution, but further import substitution involving intermediate imports, consumer durables, and capital goods requires an even larger market size to attain a dynamic comparative advantage. This is so because in many of those sectors there are minimum plant sizes which are a prerequisite to even start the process of production at reasonable costs, and production at those levels of plant sizes requires more than individual national markets. Therefore, in their quest for enlarging the scale of import substitution, developing countries are constrained by limited national markets which do not allow the establishment of efficient size plants that will be conducive to subsequent improvements in productivity and competitive production costs.[2] In this light, economic integration is viewed as a way to overcome the limitations of the national market by allowing the establishment of economically efficient plants designed to produce for larger union markets.

The standard criticism to the infant industry argument can, however, be applied to its extension to the customs union context. In the first place, we confront the empirical issue about eventual cost reductions following increases in the levels of production. But even if initial costs decrease as the volume produced rises, the case for protection can be made only if the total discounted welfare costs arising from protection are lower than the present value of the social benefits which will accrue to the country as the industry becomes efficient and competitive in world markets. But even granting that the dynamic cost-benefit ratio clearly shows a positive balance, the question is why private initiative, without protection, would not exploit a profit opportunity expected to yield net benefits over time.

There are a number of answers to this type of criticism. In the first place social and private costs and benefits probably differ due to externalities and to the inability of private firms to fully capture the returns from accumulation of human capital, which tends to be nonfirm and even nonindustry-specific. In addition, the horizon over which benefits are discounted as well as the rate of discount may differ when social, rather than private, considerations are taken into account. Moreover, distortions and imperfections in financial markets may limit the access of private enterprises to the capital resources needed to finance projects even if they are indeed profitable in the long run.

However, as most of these factors arise from market-specific distortions and imperfections, direct intervention in those markets may have a lower social cost than the roundabout method of protecting the product markets.

Apart from the analytical issues mentioned there may be some practical considerations related to the infant industry argument which are of special relevance in the context of customs unions. Since the degree of protection needed to attain dynamic benefits may differ widely across members, depending on their level of technological development and industrialization, this would give rise to a conflict about both the level and the time profile of reductions in the common external tariff. Furthermore, since the argument is based on the need to expand the market due to the indivisibility of plant size, it has implications for the issue of the location of new industry together with the dismantling of some already existing industry in other members. This is a central matter regarding the distribution of gains from a union and may become a stumbling block in many integration schemes.

▪ The Patterns of Economic Integration in Latin America

The first steps toward Latin American integration were taken in the decade of the 1950s but no concrete framework emerged until 1960. Since then, three different models of integration have been implemented with different degrees of success. The first model is represented by the Latin American free trade area (LAFTA), which was an attempt to gradually eliminate barriers to intra-regional trade without establishing a common external tariff or designing any other substantial measure of domestic or external policy coordination. The second type is the creation of subregional common markets, like the Andean Group, the Caribbean Community (CARICOM) and the Central American Common Market (CACM). These are devised as true customs unions that have also attempted to implement a larger degree of homogeneity in internal policies. The third model is that embodied in the more recently established Latin American Integration Association (LAIA),[3] which sets up a framework for negotiations with the objective of achieving multilateral trade agreements based on initial bilateral negotiations. The operational structure of this framework could, therefore, be characterized as a regional GATT.

Some of the attributes of these three models of integration, as well as the problems that they encountered, are analyzed in this section.

The Free Trade Area Model (LAFTA)

In the late 1950s, many of the leading economic and political forces in Latin America arrived at the conclusion that the deterioration in their terms of trade, which was a central problem during the decade, was a very short-run phenomenon of the world economy. At the same time, the larger countries in the area started to realize that the strategy followed in the postwar period, basing economic development on import-substitution industrialization, was facing some constraints due, among other factors, to severe domestic-market limitations and to the significant magnitude of the investments needed to deepen the process of import substitution beyond the stage of consumer goods into the intermediate and capital goods levels. At the same time, the degree of competitiveness in foreign markets of most of the Latin American countries remained low, making more difficult the transition from an inward-looking to an export-led development strategy.

In these circumstances, regional economic integration appeared to be the most promising alternative which would, at the same time, break the domestic market limitations and avoid the need to penetrate the industrialized countries' markets. Therefore, economic integration was basically regarded as a channel for the continuation of the process of import substitution. The opening of a larger market, which would remain highly protected from the rest of the world, would enable the deepening of the import-substitution process, now at the regional rather than at the national level. In this conception it is already possible to discern, to some extent, the seeds of the problems which later plagued the first formal attempt of integration, since a scheme based on these grounds was bound to result in a very unequal distribution of benefits, following the different levels of progress of the various members in the process of import substitution.

The widespread acceptance of economic integration as the proper channel to continue the process of economic development led to the signature, in 1960, of the Montevideo Treaty which established LAFTA.[4] Operationally, the agreement envisaged only the multilateral negotiation of regional tariff reductions and the elimination of other barriers limiting the volume of intra-trade. There were no provisions for the coordination of external commercial policy, and no rules were set up for the harmonization of internal policies.

LAFTA established a transition period of 12 years during which the member countries would gradually eliminate most of their mutual trade barriers following product-by-product negotiations. Two principles were supposed to serve as guidelines for the implementation of the agreement: the principle of reciprocity and the "most favored nation" clause. The reciprocity principle was a procedure designed to allow those members for which trade flows with the rest of the area did not increase or become largely unbalanced, to request compensation. The "most favored nation" clause is similar to the GATT principle, by which each member country should generalize to all the other members any tariff advantage granted to third countries (whether the third country is or is not a party to the agreement). However, in order to be consistent with the principle of reciprocity, member countries could grant to some other members tariff reductions not extended to the rest, provided that the beneficiary was a country of a relatively lower level of economic development. This discriminatory rule could have avoided extensive trade diversion, but it was never clearly established which ones were the relatively less developed countries.[5]

The instrumentation of the agreement was based on three mechanisms of negotiation: the national lists, the common lists, and the agreements for industrial cooperation. The national lists contained those products for which an individual member country agreed to reduce its tariff level by at least 8 percent after each round of negotiations. The common lists were to be negotiated every three years in a multilateral forum and would include those commodities for which all the members collectively agree to fully eliminate all internal trade restrictions over the formative period of 12 years. The agreements for industrial cooperation were conceived as bilateral understandings between members of the region, leading to the coordination of their industrial policies with the objective, to incentivate, in an ordered fashion, the production of commodities not yet subject to intra-regional trade. These agreements would be mainly bilateral but any member could join through negotiations.

The expectation that LAFTA would lead toward the elimination of trade barriers in the region never actually materialized. It did not achieve even the short-term goal of establishing a free trade area by fully eliminating the tariffs on the common lists. The national lists were of little practical importance and their enactment all but stopped with the creation of the Andean Group in 1969. Only one single common list was approved in 1964 and it never became effective. After 1969, the focus of negotiations in LAFTA shifted from trade issues to the agreements for industrial cooperation. However, these agreements included very few sectors, generally dominated by multinational corporations and mostly located in the three larger countries – Argentina, Brazil, and Mexico.

The standstill reached by LAFTA in 1969 and its decline thereafter are reflected in the percentage of negotiated commodity trade from total intraregional trade. This percentage reached a peak of 88.7 percent in 1964–66 and fell to 40 percent by the end of the 1970s.[6] This means that intra-regional imports not subject to LAFTA agreements grew faster than, and currently exceed, those which were negotiated, and on which some type of tariff reduction was reached. In addition, an even more striking fact is that imports subject to LAFTA agreement were no more than 6 percent of the total imports of the region from the rest of the world in 1979.

What are the main underlying reasons for the weaknesses of LAFTA? The vulnerability of LAFTA could be traced to the very nature of the agreement which took a pure trade approach to integration. It did not include any concrete mechanism to guarantee the even distribution of the costs and benefits from the potential increase in trade flows, and there were no instruments for the planning of multilateral industrial investments adopting a regional rather than national scope. In addition, there were no provisions for the harmonization of domestic monetary, fiscal, and exchange rate policies. Confronted with this situation, the smaller countries in LAFTA, which were interested in advancing beyond the pure trade approach, sponsored the creation of instruments which would use the integration process as a framework for the implementation of collective development initiatives. Thus, in 1964 a resolution was approved establishing formal mechanisms for the programming of regional investments. This decision was, however, never implemented.

This very partial approach to integration, an approach based on the expansion of the national markets in order to increase the flows of trade, directly reflects the predominant conception that regarded the process of integration simply as the continuation of the process of import substitution and not as a tool to further collective regional growth. But even within this narrow scope, LAFTA had quite a short and limited success. Tariff reductions applied mainly to commodities which were already subject to regional trade and, consequently, LAFTA only helped to consolidate traditional trade.

In practice, particularly after 1964, most of the attempts to further reduce or eliminate tariffs were frustrated by sectorial opposition. Progress took place only when the interests of one member country to capture the market of another did not affect any particular sector in that country. Although it is reasonable to anticipate that those industries which are losing protection would react negatively to any sort of trade liberalization, the nature of the integration process as envisaged in LAFTA did not necessarily have to lead to this type of confrontations. A negotiated mutual liberalization of trade could avoid the total elimination of the industries with higher costs if some sort of intra-industry specialization could be assured. This requires that each country should specialize, within each industry, in those varieties and qualities in which it has, or is likely to attain, a comparative advantage. Although a strong case for such specialization could be made, it is not simple to determine in isolation in which products each industry would have a comparative advantage in a regional context. In those circumstances, some degree of centralization in the establishment of the patterns of industrial specialization may be more conducive to the attainment of an efficient structure. As mentioned above, no mechanism for such centralization was created within the LAFTA framework.

Moreover, the agreement did not provide for mechanisms designed specifically to deal with the issues arising from the creation of new industries as a response to the enlargement of the market. The geographical placement of new industries is a crucial factor for the determination of the trade effects of a union. To the extent that new regional industries produce commodities previously originating outside the union, there will be export gains for the new producers but a trade-diversion effect for the rest of the members, giving rise to opposite welfare costs. In those cases where LAFTA provided incentives to the creation of new industries, the location and structure of those industries were left to be determined by market forces, without any concrete attempt to overview the process. Since Argentina, Brazil, and Mexico were at a significantly higher degree of industrial development, free market forces would have led to a concentration of new industries in those countries. The deepening of the integration process within a scheme like LAFTA would have resulted in the reproduction, at the Latin American level, of the world pattern of trade, with the more advanced countries reaping most of the benefits of industrial development, and the rest of the members concentrating in the production and export of primary commodities. Such a model of integration was rejected by the smaller countries and was a central reason for the stalling of the process.

An additional major limitation of LAFTA was the total lack of harmonization of the members' domestic economic policies. Thus, exchange rate, fiscal, and monetary policies continued to be designed in each country without any coordination with the other members and without regard for the stated objective of increasing cooperation within the region. In addition, there were no attempts to collectively exploit possible externalities in the process of export promotion (like developing common marketing strategies, or exploiting common lines of credit). Moreover, since there was no agreement about a common policy regarding the treatment of foreign investment, LAFTA offered, in a number of areas, large profit opportunities for some foreign-owned firms which could take advantage of the larger market size by locating their operations in the countries with a more favorable treatment. This type of situation may result in distortions and trade diversion due to the relocation of industries from one country member to another for reasons which have little to do with underlying comparative advantages but, rather, with the different financial treatment of foreign investment.

The Common Market Model (The Andean Group)

The limitations and contradictions of interests within LAFTA paralyzed the process and convinced many members that a different type of integration model was required if, indeed, integration was going to play a pivotal role in achieving sustained development through trade. For that reason, the countries in the Andean region which felt a stronger need to expand their markets than the larger countries in the region, decided to follow a different, much more ambitious pattern of integration. This led to the signature in 1969 of the Cartagena Accord which formally created the Andean Group.[7] With the intention of correcting the shortcomings of LAFTA, the Andean Group established the following mechanisms of operation:

mutual trade liberalization within the subregion would be carefully planned at a global level;
a common external tariff would be gradually established;
the problem of distribution of costs and benefits would be attended to mainly by the implementation of regional investment programs;
there would be concrete attempts to harmonize domestic economic policies, starting with the treatment of foreign investment; and
special treatment would be given to the two relatively less developed countries in the area, Bolivia and Ecuador, which would be allowed to implement the agreements at a slower pace.

In principle, the Andean Group looked much more promising than LAFTA since it was apparent that the members had less structural dissimilarities and less conflicts of interest. Moreover, in order to minimize frictions, the process of negotiation would be more global and automatic instead of item by item as in LAFTA. The project envisaged a specific horizon for the adoption of a common external tariff and faced immediately the task of planning the pattern of subregional industrial development. These two instruments proved, however, to be much more difficult to implement than originally thought, and soon became important stumbling blocks in the advancement of the Andean Group. In addition, other factors precluding sustained progress included the lack of compatibility of exchange rate policies of individual countries with the subregional liberalization policies and the absence of coordination of their export promotion strategies. Also, the issue of intra-region factor mobility was almost totally disregarded in the Cartagena Agreement.

Since the establishment of a common external tariff and the adoption of a subregional program of industrial planning were recognized as two of the basic innovative tools of the Andean Group, some detailed analysis of the problems involved in their implementation is in order. A central conclusion which can be reached is that, although both instruments are indeed appropriate means to deal with the issues of policy harmonization and distribution of costs and benefits, their actual implementation is a strenuous endeavor inasmuch as significant conflicts of interests remain between the accepted common objectives of the group and the basic development strategies of the individual countries. A corollary of the above is that a successful integration process requires not just an understanding regarding the harmonization of policies but also the elimination of major discrepancies among the members about their long-term development strategies. A compromise about this last issue seems to be a more important ingredient in the process than the actual implementation of specific policies.

As a case in point, the complications arising from the process of designing the common external tariff could be mentioned. The countries of the Andean Group agreed to establish a common external tariff by 1980 and, by the same time, the level of intra-regional tariffs should have been reduced to zero for a large number of commodities. This was not fully implemented, reflecting the basic conflicts of interest between members. A genuine adoption of the type of commercial policy envisaged by the Accord requires that countries surrender their autonomy regarding a number of policies, since the objective of increasing intra-regional trade would not be reached if exchange rate policies, indirect taxation, and nontariff barriers are not subject to coordination. This type of coordination is not easy to achieve.

The acceptance of a common trade policy carries, therefore, political and economic costs. The economic cost may be substantial if the volume of intraregional trade was very low prior to establishing the tariff, since the common external tariff would certainly lead to significant trade diversion.[8] To be acceptable, this cost should be compensated for by the gaining of access to an enlarged export market. Since, within the Andean Group, the potential for expanding industrial exports was extremely different across countries, a serious distributive problem was bound to arise. Thus, the adoption of a common external tariff, together with the elimination of the internal barriers, may result in an intraregional transfer of income of a magnitude which would depend on the level and the dispersion of the common tariff. The higher the common tariff, the higher the potential internal redistribution if the assumption is that the level of the tariff reflects the cost differential between the world price and the most efficient regional producer. Therefore, in the absence of a comprehensive compensation policy, the level and coverage of the common tariff would become a matter of serious contention. But the evaluation of the compensation size and the mechanism for its implementation are indeed a very difficult issue.

An additional source of difficulty regarding the common external tariff is the lack of consideration given within the Andean Group to the interrelationship between commercial and exchange rate policies. Clearly, the degrees of intra- and extra-regional competitiveness are jointly determined by the tariff and the exchange rate levels. When a country devalues its currency, it increases the level of protection granted by a given common tariff and the magnitude of its incentives for intraregional exports. On the other hand, countries with an overvalued currency will need a higher common external tariff in order to preserve its internal market and to restrict external competition for its exports to other countries of the region. This source of conflict is exacerbated when countries in the region do not share the same outlook about the role of the external sector in the development process. Thus, in the discussions within the Andean Group there were two opposite positions: Colombia (joined later by Bolivia and Peru) favored a lower external tariff, mainly for efficiency reasons and following its more export-oriented strategy and its policy of maintaining a realistic exchange rate for its manufacturing sector. Chile actually broke from the Group over its insistence, basically guided by free-trade ideology, that external barriers should be uniform and minimal. On the other hand, Venezuela insisted on a high common tariff in order to compensate for the large productivity gap between its petroleum sector, which determines its exchange rate, and the other sectors of the economy.

The second innovative element incorporated within the Andean Group is the important role given to industrial planning. The priority given to this element arises from the need to solve the location problem, one of the sources of inequity in the distribution of costs and benefits, and from the emphasis given within the Andean Group to the protectionist approach geared to the continuation of the import substitution process at a regional level. The purpose of industrial planning is to obviate the market process and directly determine the location of new industries. The objective is to maximize the benefits, for the Group as a whole, of the establishment of new industries aiming, at the same time, to achieve an equitable distribution of these benefits. It is clear that the two objectives may not be consistent since maximization of benefits should follow the pattern of intraregional comparative advantage which may not satisfy regional equity considerations. In addition, the implementation of industrial planning is largely biased in favor of the producers and disregards the implied costs for the consumers and the distribution of these costs. If these costs are unevenly distributed, pressures to stall the plans are certain to mount.

The potential conflict between efficiency and distributive equity may certainly threaten the viability of industrial planning. A popular proposal to solve this problem has been the separation of location from ownership. New industries could be owned by multinational corporations formed by all the member countries, with the distribution of dividends linked to the level of benefits and to some agreed criteria for distributional equity.[9]

Two additional difficulties related to regional industrial planning are the delegation of authority to a multinational entity and the issue of labor mobility. Regarding the first problem, the conflict is similar to the one arising in relation to the common external tariff. If the long-term development approaches of the member countries do not coincide, the sectoral priorities arising from the national development strategy may clash with those established by regional industrial planning. With respect to factor mobility, the issues of labor migrations and capital flows were never settled within the Andean Group. The presence of different levels of labor utilization and wages have some implications for the integration process. One practical consequence is the fact that, without labor mobility, the divergence between the social and the private costs of labor tends to be different in each member country if employment levels are different and, as a consequence, the social costs of producing the same commodity differ, even if the private costs are equalized across countries. This creates additional tensions in the design of common policies since, for example, the equalization of social costs would require different external tariffs,[10] which is incompatible with the principles of a common market.

A Loose Arrangement Model (LAIA)

With the stagnation of LAFTA and with the complications faced by the more comprehensive arrangements established within the Andean Group, there was a feeling in Latin America that the formal framework of integration should be reshaped. Against this background, a new organizational structure, the Latin American Integration Association (LAIA), was created in 1980 to replace LAFTA. The new organization is a much looser framework, with a smaller scope than LAFTA. The two basic instruments of LAIA are negotiated partial agreements and regional tariff preferences. The partial agreements are bilateral tariff reductions containing a "convergency" clause which allows other members to negotiate their inclusion. The regional tariff preferences are limited reductions in the external tariff of each member, which apply to all the members of the Association. This is not a common lower tariff among all the member countries since each country maintains the level of its tariff with third countries but grants a specific preference to the other countries of the region. Therefore, members have preferential access, relative to the rest of the world, to other member markets, but intraregional tariffs continue to differ for the same commodities.

Thus, with the establishment of LAIA, the global program of regional liberalization which characterized LAFTA is replaced by a formal framework aimed at setting up an area of mostly *partial* economic preferences. Although it is apparent that this shift indicates a weaker commitment, especially of the non-Andean countries, to the idea of economic integration, in fact, it is a reflection of a more realistic and pragmatic attitude. The trade negotiation process in LAIA takes a distinctive bilateral nature, particularly since the abandonment of the most-favored-nation clause, which was a centerpiece in LAFTA, makes the issue of generalizing preferences a nonbinding but a negotiated process. This facilitates the reaching of agreements between countries with some commonality of interests, which may not be shared by the rest of the countries of the area. This approach may have a higher potential for increasing intraregional trade flows, resulting in an environment more conducive to regional cooperation in other areas. Also, it is more likely that bilateral agreements will be reached by countries which already have trade relationships, increasing the potential for trade creation and reducing the risk of trade diversion.

Regarding the regional tariff preferences, they may be a source of contention. The reason is that by not adopting a unified tariff for intra-trade, the degree of access that each country is granting to the other members may vary dramatically. If, for example, there is water in the tariff of country A while the tariff of country B is very low, the same margin of preference may still deny regional access to the market of A, while entry into B may be free for member countries. This is bound to create friction, which will limit the number of agreed tariff preferences.[11]

So far the actual performance of LAIA has not been better than that of its predecessors. In general terms, LAIA currently sells to countries within the region no more than 20 percent of its total exports, buying within the region a similar percentage of its total imports. Individual countries show quite a different picture as can be seen from Table 10.1. The table also shows that, following a substantial increase in the volume of intratrade until the mid-1970s, there has been a reversal, with a particular downturn in the early 1980s. To stop this trend, the 1985 Annual Meeting of LAIA decided to adopt some new measures intended to increase the volume of trade within the region. The new measures are based on multilateral mechanisms for the reduction of nontariff barriers and a request to the public sector of each country to channel its own foreign trade toward the Latin American region. There is also an intention to intensify counter-trade and barter mechanisms which would reduce the need for the use of foreign exchange. The perspectives for success are, however, not better with the adoption of those mechanisms because the basic barriers to the integration effort have not been removed.

Table 10.1 Intra-Regional Exports as a Percentage of Total Exports, Latin America, 1962-1979/82

	1962	1965	1970	1975	1979	Most Recent Year
LAIA						
Argentina	13.0	16.8	21.0	25.9	26.3	20.3 1/
Brazil	6.4	12.8	11.6	15.6	17.1	15.0 1/
Chile	8.5	8.3	11.2	23.8	...	24.7 2/
Mexico	5.0	8.2	10.4	12.6	6.7	...
Paraguay	32.6	30.7	38.5	36.0	34.4	...
Uruguay	...	...	12.6	28.8	40.2	28.7 3/
Andean Group						
Bolivia	4.1	2.7	8.5	35.0	31.5	...
Colombia	5.5	11.1	13.5	20.8	17.9	20.7 1/
Ecuador	6.0	10.6	11.1	37.8	24.1	...
Peru	9.6	9.4	6.4	16.9	21.3	15.6 1/
Venezuela	10.1	12.6	12.5	12.3	11.7	16.9 3/

Source: United Nations international trade tapes.

1/ 1982
2/ 1980
3/ 1981

▪ Recent Developments and the Outlook for Further Regional Cooperation

This section discusses the impact that recent global and regional developments may have on the process of integration, and considers a number of options for intensifying other forms of regional cooperation.

A number of significant developments have taken place over the past decade and have affected the conditions, as well as the sociopolitical milieu, within which the process of integration evolved in Latin America. Among the most consequential are: (a) the differential impact on the region of the oil shocks and countershocks; (b) the adoption, in some of the countries of the region, of comprehensive trade liberalization programs; and (c) the eruption of the world financial crisis, centered on the very high volume of the Latin American foreign debt.

The Oil Shocks and Countershocks

The oil shocks of the 1970s as well as the sharp fall in oil prices after 1985 had a global effect on the Latin American economies, but it also had a marked differential impact in the various countries of the region. It is quite evident that the major global effects arise from the consequences on the industrial countries of the violent changes in the relative price of oil and the nature of the links that those countries maintain with the developing world. Following the oil shocks, many industrial countries experienced serious economic recessions which were propagated to the periphery, among other channels, through the downturn in the growth of international trade, with the consequent shrinkage in the export markets for LDCs, and the deterioration in the price of primary commodities. It is apparent that, in those circumstances, a deepening of the integration process could have served as a palliative and the process could have been strengthened from this development. On the other hand, the current renewal of the growth of industrial countries and the reduction in the oil-induced balance of payments burden of these countries could be seen as leading toward the weakening of the integration efforts, given the higher potential for extra-regional exports.

That these worldwide fluctuations in economic conditions have not had a clear impact on the integration efforts in Latin America could be, at least partially, explained by the differential incidence that the oil price changes had on the various countries of the area, depending on their relative position in the world oil market. Clearly, in the 1970s, oil exporters, particularly Venezuela and later Ecuador and Mexico, largely strengthened their external payment position while oil importers, like Brazil and most of the Central American countries, suffered a dramatic deterioration of their external balance. This change in internal distribution and in the value of the countries' endowments was instrumental in making less operative the set of common goals established by the standing integration frameworks. A clear expression of this new reality was the changing priorities of the members, evidenced by development strategies which became increasingly more divergent. A practical consequence of this situation was the adoption of domestic incentives and of exchange rate and fiscal policies geared toward the achievement of a new set of priorities, even if the characteristics of these policies were detrimental and inconsistent with the attainment of regional objectives and with the aims of the integration process.[12]

The substantial change in the relative price of energy had very serious consequences for the viability of some operational aspects of the integration agreements already established. The energy shock changed the pattern of internal comparative advantage, altering the considerations, particularly within the Andean Group, which were guiding the establishment of new industries. Furthermore, the changes in regional income distribution was bound to affect the distribution of gains and losses from the process, in general, and from industrial planning, in particular. Therefore, the need to reassess the criteria for reallocation of resources and for subregional specialization slowed down the process of integration in the late 1970s.

An additional negative impact on interregional trade relationships has arisen from the oil countershocks, that is, the sharp reductions in the nominal and relative prices of oil. The reason for this development is that some of the countries in the region, mainly Mexico and Venezuela, which largely expanded their trade following their terms of trade gains, are faced with strict external limitations which caused them to drastically reduce their imports, including those from the other countries of the region. From the ideological point of view, however, the oil countershocks may be seen as providing further support to the industrialization-cum-protection approach, since they prove that even countries with large supplies of what is considered a valuable natural resource are not immune to world fluctuations, which could be extremely damaging for their stability if they relay heavily on primary commodity exports.

Liberalization Policies

A second salient event taking place during the past decade was the adoption of comprehensive trade-liberalization programs in Latin America, particularly in the Southern Cone countries of the region (Argentina, Chile, and Uruguay). In general, the late 1970s witnessed a growing disposition in the region to turn away from protectionism and to allow free-trade mechanisms to play a more prevailing role. The stated purpose of the new trade policy was to open the economy to foreign competition by reducing and standardizing tariffs and other foreign-trade restrictions, and by relaxing the limitations on foreign investments and foreign credit. This policy marked the abandonment of import substitution, at least at the ideological level, and the adoption of a development strategy based on the gains from free trade.

The implementation of these policies had a number of consequences for the integration process. At the operational level, contradictions arose between the liberalization policies and the contractual obligations undertaken by some of the countries in the framework of the existing integration schemes. The most dramatic event in this context was the conflict between Chile and the Andean Group. In October 1976, tariff reforms, as well as a new liberal treatment of direct foreign investment, led Chile to abandon the Andean Group and to pursue independent trade and investment policies.[13]

In addition, the liberalization attempts coincided with a period of innovation, on the one hand, and of turbulence, on the other, in the foreign exchange market of many countries. Some of the adopted policies, like using the exchange rate as a counter-inflationary mechanism and preannouncing and lagging the rate of nominal devaluations, resulted in broad fluctuations in the value of the real exchange rate and in dramatic swings in the direction of intraregional trade. This was motivated by profit opportunities constantly shifting across the borders. In addition to payment imbalances, such a situation created confusion and turmoil in the trade relations of the countries involved, disrupting regular commercial ties, and disturbing the conventional mechanisms which affect the nature of trade flows. This turn of events certainly had upsetting effects on the evolution of the integration process by weakening the concept of unified regional markets and by lowering the likelihood of attaining any sort of exchange rate policy coordination.

The most important manner by which the advent of liberalism to the region hindered the process of integration was at the doctrinal level, since it gave renewed impetus to the debate about the adequacy of the development model upon which integration was founded. The process of integration in Latin America was conceived as an essentially inward-looking process, an extension, within an enlarged setting, of the postwar pattern of development based on import substitution intended to preserve the domestic market for local producers.[14] The liberal approach was directed against the continuation of import substitution which was regarded as a source of distortions, inefficiencies, and misallocations. Liberalization, on the other hand, was promoted as an outward-looking approach designed to incentivate competition, efficiency, and modernization. As such, it was, in some sense, the antithesis of the view upon which integration was established since it advocates low and nondiscriminatory tariffs and more reliance on the free market mechanism for the allocation of resources.

The conflicting ideologies had a detrimental effect on the integration process by promoting, even in those quarters rejecting liberalization, a reassessment of the integration policies. Here, once again, we can point to the same source of tension that was mentioned before: the main stumbling blocks to the process of integration are not the result of antagonistic interests about rather limited specific issues, but reflect fundamental divergencies of views regarding long-term development strategies.

Despite these divisive events, the process itself did not suffer a fatal blow, largely due to the apparent failure of the liberalization attempt. For a diversity of largely country-specific reasons, most of the countries were forced to abandon the reform packages which included commercial opening up as a centerpiece. Although it can be argued that the type of free trade policies adopted were not reason for the collapse of the programs (Blejer, 1983), it is evident that the demise of liberalization in the early 1980s reversed the trend against economic integration which was growing in the previous decade. The emerging negative attitude regarding liberalization was strengthened by the bad timing of the Southern Cone experience, which coincided with the intensification of protectionist tendencies in industrial countries. These tendencies reinforced parallel trends in the developing world and restored respectability to protectionist policies as a desirable option, thus reestablishing the ideological basis upon which the Latin American integration movement was established.

▪ The Financial Crisis

The third global development which is affecting the integration process is the four-year old financial crisis arising from the large foreign debt of the Latin American nations. The common denominator across the region in the 1980s is the unprecedented stocks of foreign liabilities which have caused a drastic reduction in available foreign financing, and the need to curtail domestic expenditures in order to generate the trade surpluses which would allow servicing of the foreign debt. Although very impressive balance-of-trade surpluses have been registered since 1981 (*see* Table 10.2), a large portion of the surpluses are generated by import cuts and there are only few signs that nontraditional exports are expanding enough to play a significant role (Table 10.3). It is quite clear, therefore, that the adjustments have been trade-depressing, which can have a number of repercussions for intraregional commercial relations.

In the first place, there is evidence that the contraction of intraregional trade has been proportionally larger than the overall trade reductions. If this only represents reciprocal cuts on imports, it will certainly not result in foreign exchange savings for the region as a whole. On the other hand, the simple promotion of growth of intraregional exports will also not, per se, generate additional hard currency to service the foreign debt. The claim that economic integration should be intensified as a response and as a solution to the foreign debt problem may be justified only if intraregional exports substitute imports from outside the region. In such a case, foreign exchange is regionally saved, but this, by definition, implies trade diversion. Moreover, it is important to establish the source of those additional intraregional exports. If there is a simple redirection of exports away from extraregional destinations, no additional foreign exchange is gained. If, on the other hand, exports are produced drawing resources from the nontraded sector or, more important, if idle resources are utilized, there is a net gain of foreign exchange for the region as a whole. In the case of intersectoral factor mobility, the welfare cost of trade diversion still persists, but if

Table 10.2 Trade Balances, Selected Latin American Countries, 1980-85
(*Cumulative, in billions of dollars*)

	1980-82	1983-85
Argentina	2.1	12.5
Bolivia	0.9	0.6
Brazil	-0.8	32.0
Chile	-3.4	2.0
Colombia	-4.1	-2.3
Ecuador	0.6	3.0
Mexico	-1.4	34.3
Peru	-0.1	2.3
Uruguay	-1.0	0.6
Venezuela	18.8	24.4
10 major Latin American countries	11.5	109.3

Source: Morgan Guaranty Trust Company of New York, *World Financial Markets*, February 1986.

Table 10.3 Imports and Nontraditional Exports, Selected Latin American Countries, 1981-85

	Nontraditional Exports (As a percent of total exports)		Imports in 1985 (Percent change from 1981-82 average)	
	1981-82	1985	Value	Volume
Argentina	30.0	37.0	-45.4	-43.4
Bolivia	5.0	--	-11.7	-8.5
Brazil	51.0	54.0	-36.4	-26.4
Chile	55.0	55.0	-42.1	-34.8
Colombia	52.0	53.0	-20.7	-22.6
Ecuador	6.0	5.0	-26.9	-26.1
Mexico	27.0	31.0	-29.1	-28.9
Peru	22.0	27.0	-46.8	-45.5
Uruguay	55.0	65.0	-41.1	-46.1
Venezuela	4.0	10.0	-48.7	-28.1
10 major Latin American countries	30.0	35.0	-36.9	-29.8

Source: See Table 2.

intraregional export growth generates employment, trade diversion has a very low social cost and there is a genuine gain for the region as a whole. In sum, the intensification of integration may play a role in the overall solution of the debt quagmire and help to activate the economy, only if it is export-oriented and if it can mobilize unemployed capacity and resources without diverting those already engaged in extra-regional exports.

Options and the Outlook for Further Cooperation

It is possible to think about additional mechanisms which could promote regional cooperation in areas beyond the already established formal frameworks.

An area which deserves attention is intraregional capital flows and the integration of financial markets. Intraregional capital flows have been, in general, very unstable, reflecting the lack of well-organized capital markets.[15] Capital movements often represent trade credit or the financing of specific projects rather than the free flow of financial capital. The obstacles to the growth of regional capital flows have been of a different nature. In the first place, in Latin American countries as a whole, capital is a scarce resource and, therefore, the financial systems in these countries are designed to attract funding from outside the region rather than to facilitate the flow of capital within it. The widespread use of an exchange control system designed to alleviate balance of payments difficulties has been more important. This type of currency controls has tended to impede the internal flow of capital.

The actual volume of capital flows have been, however, influenced by the development of intraregional trade, given that it requires suppliers' credit and the strengthening of ties between the banking and the financial systems. Also, some of the formal integration frameworks, which result in the organization of subregional financial institutions functioning as clearing houses or as financial corporations, had some influence in increasing intraregional capital flows.

Table 10.4 shows the total of intraregional loans included in the external public debt of Latin American countries for the period 1970-82. The table shows an increase in the loans approved during the period, but the fluctuations are erratic and there is no clear trend. Clearly, the most important type of loans are official bilateral loans, followed by loans from financial institutions, and then by suppliers' credits. The official bilateral loans have been used merely to finance the export of basic commodities from some countries of the region, largely oil from Venezuela and Mexico.

Table 10.4 Intra-regional Loans Included in the External Public Debt, Latin America, 1970-82 1/ (*In millions of 1980 dollars*) 2/

	Intra-regional Total	Supplier Credit	Loans by Financial Institutions 3/	Official Bilateral Loans
1970	104.3	44.1	--	60.2
	(1.7)	(2.3)	(--)	(4.6)
1971	127.0	64.1	12.5	50.4
	(1.8)	(4.0)	(0.3)	(3.2)
1972	290.9	77.3	56.2	157.4
	(3.0)	(4.5)	(1.0)	(6.4)
1973	397.8	45.2	58.3	294.3
	(2.9)	(2.8)	(0.6)	(9.5)
1974	816.7	283.5	37.9	495.3
	(4.5)	(11.8)	(0.3)	(12.3)
1975	575.1	24.5	98.2	452.4
	(3.4)	(1.0)	(0.8)	(18.7)
1976	1,153.2	141.3	398.3	613.6
	(4.8)	(6.8)	(2.3)	(13.5)
1977	464.2	65.1	22.7	376.4
	(1.9)	(3.6)	(0.1)	(17.3)
1978	672.7	108.4	185.1	379.2
	(1.9)	(5.5)	(0.7)	(6.6)
1979	823.9	68.5	401.5	353.9
	(2.1)	(1.9)	(1.2)	(14.7)
1980	1,443.1	42.5	699.8	700.8
	(5.7)	(3.3)	(3.5)	(18.0)
1981	791.7	31.8	256.8	503.1
	(2.5)	(1.4)	(1.0)	(14.3)
1982	557.2	51.2	75.1	430.9
	(2.2)	(4.1)	(0.4)	(10.7)

(In parentheses: ratio of intra-regional loans to total external public debt.)

Source: IDB (1984).

1/ External debt includes all debts guaranteed by the government of debtor countries with maturities of more than one year.

2/ The U.S. GDP deflator was used to convert original data into 1980 dollars.

3/ Except those financial institutions located in the Bahamas and in Panama.

It is important to stress, however, that the ratio of intraregional debt to total external public debt is extremely low (never exceeding 6 percent), as can be seen from the figures in parentheses in Table 10.4. It is clear therefore that there is ample room for developing mechanisms to incentivate the intraregional mobility of capital and, in the light of the current financial crisis, this could contribute to greater and more effective regional cooperation. To attain this objective, it will be necessary to reach some degree of financial market integration. This is, however, one of the most advanced stages of cooperation, which usually takes the form of a monetary union involving the establishment of fixed exchange rates along with the harmonization of monetary and fiscal policies. This requires a high degree of policy synchronization and, in general, requires that a customs union be in place before a monetary union could be established. Moreover, it can be argued that the free movement of goods, services, and factors of production is a necessary prerequisite for a successful monetary union. Under these circumstances, it would be hard to foresee any type of monetary integration in the Latin American context, given the slow progress of the integration movement. This, however, should not preclude the pursuit of some type of coordination in the management of exchange rates and the promotion of cooperation agreements in the financial area.

It is perhaps interesting to mention in this context that, unlike in the commercial area, not too much effort has been devoted to the promotion of mutual understandings in the area of invisibles trade, in general, and of financial services, in particular. To some extent, goods entering world trade could be regarded as composite commodities, comprising the good itself and the variety of financial, informational, communications, and other types of services which took part in the process of transferring them from the producers to the foreign consumer. Many of these services, particularly in the financial area (such as insurance, banking, credit information, etc.), are increasingly becoming subject to international trade. For this reason, the determination of the pattern of comparative advantage may not be solely dependent on the relative costs of producing the commodities themselves but on the composite cost of bringing them to the world market.

Although it would be difficult to argue that developing countries have any type of obvious competitive edge in the provision of financial and other trade-related services, it is likely that there are economies of scale in providing these services and, therefore, regional sharing and other cooperative agreements on this field may result in lower financial and other service costs throughout the region. This could lead to both an intensification of existing trade flows and a redirection of trade from outside the region, arising from a more competitive position of member countries when a whole-inclusive measure of the cost of trading is considered. In other words, imports from inside the region may be cheaper than those from outside when financial and other service costs are included, if agreements reducing those costs for intraregional trade are reached. Specific mechanisms of cooperation, which could lead to such a reduction in trade-related service costs, include the collective provision of insurance services, nondiscriminatory practices regarding commercial banks of other countries in the region, incentives for the operation of regional banks geared to the provision of trade services, the promotion of specialized credit lines, the pooling of marketing and advertising information, etc. Another potential area for increased cooperation in this context relates to financial market taxation. Differential taxation gives rise to abnormal patterns of capital flows which may distort trade patterns, particularly if they generate under- and over-invoice practices to avoid exchange controls.

Some Concluding Remarks

The process of economic integration in Latin America was largely based on the "development approach" which relies on protection in order to enlarge the size of the market to attain economies of scale and gain dynamic benefits arising from increased productivity. In fact, most countries viewed the integration schemes merely as a channel for the continuation of the import-substitution process. They looked at the potential larger market as the way to overcome the limitations imposed by technology and by indivisibilities in plant size when import substitution is deepened beyond the final and the intermediate goods level.

It would be quite accurate to state that the main objectives of economic integration in Latin America have not been achieved. Although it is possible to point out a number of sources of the complications, it is the lack of convergency of the conceptions of the various countries regarding their long-term development strategies which have been indeed the most important stumbling block for the process. Countries find it difficult to relinquish, even partially, their national autonomy in favor of global considerations when there are very large discrepancies regarding the desired long-run path for the economy. It is, therefore, difficult to envisage a very successful integration process between countries with conflicting views about the social, political, and economic characteristics of economic growth. Moreover, even if the importance of policy harmonization within any integration framework cannot be overemphasized, from past experience it is possible to claim that the harmonization of policies is in fact a precondition for success and not an additional stage in the process. A feasible course of action is the encouragement of cooperation in many areas outside the formal frameworks of integration. Regional trade would tend to prosper if countries could provide a stable environment conducive to an intensification of mutual relations. The search for stability includes the affirmation and clarification of the rules to be observed in policies governing all types or regional relations. This is necessary if there is to be a reduction in the degree of uncertainty inhibiting those transactions and preventing related cross-country investments. A clarification of the rules that apply and a realistic appraisal of the costs and benefits are crucial elements to assure the progress in the process of regional cooperation.

▪ Notes

1. For a more extensive discussion of these topics, see Blejer (1984). The *1984 Annual Report of the Inter-American Bank* was devoted to the issue of economic integration in Latin America and is an extensive source of historical, statistical, and analytical information on the subject.

2. On the issue of plant size and its impact on developing countries, see Teitel (1975).

3. Asociación Latinoamericana de Integración (ALADI).

4. The Montevideo Treaty was signed by Argentina, Brazil, Chile, Mexico, Paraguay, Peru, and Uruguay. In 1961, Brazil and Colombia added their signature. Venezuela joined LAFTA in 1966 and Bolovia in 1967.

5. In practice, however, Bolivia, Ecuador, Paraguay, and Uruguay were considered to belong to that group.

6. Trade is measured by imports.

7. The original signatories of the Accord were Bolivia, Chile, Columbia, Ecuador, and Peru. In 1973, Venezuela joined the agreement while in 1976 Chile decided to separate from the Group.

8. Assuming that there was some trade with the rest of the world in the commodities in question before the formation of the union.

9. See Schydlowsky (1978).

10. Because the equalization of social costs requires a differential between the private costs (and prices) of the various countries.

11. In addition, LAIA requests that all members eliminate nontariff restrictions on -intra-regional trade. This has been implemented to a very limited extent.

12. It should be remembered that the first oil shock coincided with a commodity boom which improved the terms of trade of some other countries of the region, reducing their perceived need for integration as a central piece of their devlopment strategy.

13. The source of the conflicts was the opposition of Chile to both the common external tariff and the Andean Code regulating foreign investments.

14. It could be mentioned in this context that this approach is not very different from the view taken by the European Common Market with respect to the agricultural sector. In fact, it could be argued that there is more merit to protecting industry in developing countries than to protecting agriculture in Europe, which could only look to a declining future. There is, therefore, no normative implication in the assertion here about the protectionist characteristics of the integration process in Latin America.

15. See IDB, 1984, Chapter III.

■ References

Blejer, Mario I., "Liberation and Stabilization Policies in the Southern Cone Countries: An Introduction," *Journal of Interamerican Studies and World Affairs*, 25, November 1983.

___, "Economic Integration: An Overview," in Inter-American Development Bank, *Economic and Social Progress in Latin America*, Washington, D.C., 1984.

Inter-American Development Bank, *Economic and Social Progress in Latin America*, Washington, D.C., 1984.

Lipsey, Robert G. and K. J. Lancaster, "The General Theory of Second Best," *Review of Economic Studies*, 24 (1), 1956–57.

Meade, John E., *The Theory of Customs Unions*, Amsterdam, North Holland Publishing Company, 1955.

Schydlowsky, Daniel M., "Criterios Amaliticos para la Formulación de una Political Economica Subregional Andina," in E. Tironi (ed.) *Pacto Andino, Caracter y Perpectivos*, IEP, Lima, 1978.

Teitel, Simon, "Economies of Scale and Size of Plant: The Evidence and the Implications for Developing Countries," *Journal of Common Market Studies*, 13, 1975.

Viner, Jacob, *The Customs Union Issue*, New York, Carnegie Endowment for International Peace, 1950.

11

Technology: Development, International Trade and Cooperation*

Antonio Alonso-Concheiro

■ Introduction

Technology has been made both goddess and scapegoat of a thousand things. No one can deny technology is certainly a very important factor in economic development, international trade or military strength. But technology has also been mystified to a great extent, for it does not and cannot account for everything, or even most things. Understanding technology as "applied knowledge with a productive purpose," one may be tempted to consider almost everything to be technology (from devices to politics, from machines to social ways of organization). Yet, even in such an ample definition there is scope for other factors. Esthetical and/or ethical values, which are used by societies as rules of preference, as part of the cultural fabric, also play their part.

There certainly is a high correlation between economic development and investment in scientific and technological research and development (R&D) activities. Still, it seems valid to ask whether the relation between the two is causal and, if so, the direction of causality. Of course many indicators point to a more complex relationship between the two than simple causality, regardless of its direction. Technology certainly contributes to a betterment of economic conditions and this in turn provides the necessary funds for research and development activities. However, the highest rate

---

(*)Part of this work was funded by the National Council of Science and Technology of the Mexican Government.

209

of economic growth, measured by Gross Domestic Product (GDP) has been achieved in the last decades by the developing countries, who in general expend a smaller percentage of their GDP in scientific and technological development. Thus a word of caution seems appropriate before equating economic or social development with technology. Particularly if technology is interpreted as "advanced technology," or as new and modern gadgets, as it is frequently done (sometimes even unconsciously) by many of us. Yet, having said this, the links between technology and everything else are sufficiently strong to benefit from a closer retrospective and prospective look at them.

Any attempt to look at the future is a risky business (risky in the sense of reaching images that never come true or that we deeply dislike). As Niels Bohr pointed out, "it is very difficult to make accurate predictions ... particularly about the future." In a recent paper, R. Ackhoff states as a paradox that "the more accurately we can predict, the less effectively we can prepare; and the more effectively we can prepare, the less we need to predict." Thus I will not try to make predictions, but rather to imagine some possible futures. It is obvious that the future can only be imagined and thus no value of truth can be assigned to the scenarios. No matter how convinced I may be personally about the validity of the images of the future that I will discuss, I recommend to the reader to maintain an alert and critical attitude towards the contents of the paper, and to feel free to disagree with parts or all of it. On the other hand, no matter how risky it may be to search into the future, it is also absolutely necessary if we want to improve our capacity to explore future alternatives and to examine possible menaces and opportunities lying ahead; not only because this is part of actually building the future, but because looking at the past *and* the future will allow us to better understand the present and thus to improve our decision-making process. As Albert Camus wrote: "Each generation believes it is destined, without doubt, to rebuild the world. My generation knows, however, that it will not do it. But its task is perhaps more important: To stop the world from its own destruction."

■ Structural Changes in World Industry and Manufactures Trade

The growth of world industry has been accompanied since the 1940s by a steady and important structural change, both in the kind of products manufactured and in the countries manufacturing them. In other words, industrial growth has not been evenly spread between industries or between countries. Perhaps the perceived structural change is not unique to this period of time, but rather a permanent feature of world evolution. Relative or comparative advantages in labor and capital, the mastering of technology, and a myriad of other factors, bring about changes in the rates of growth of different industries and countries. Technology brings about changes in the products and the ways of manufacturing them. The relative importance of the manufacturing branches changes as new products and production processes come into being and new needs are perceived by society.

Although starting from a small industrial base, the developing countries were able in the last decades to increase their share of the world manufacturing value added. However their advances were not as rapid as the group of countries with centrally-planned economies, who devoted the largest proportion of their national resources to industrialization. On the other hand, the group of developed countries steadily reduced its share of world manufacturing value added; perhaps this is only a further sign of their moving towards a post-industrialized era, with economies dominated by the services sectors. If this trend would continue in the future, by the year 2000 the developing countries would account for around 13 percent of the world manufacturing value added, with 45 percent going to the group of countries with centrally planned economies and nearly 41 percent to the developed countries with market economies. According to this scenario, somewhere between 1995 and the year 2000 the centrally planned economies could have overtaken the developed market economies in their share of world manufacturing output (Table 11.1).

Table 11.1
Share of world manufacturing value added by regions (percentages)

Year	Developing countries		Centrally planned economies		Developed market economies		World
1966*	7.19		19.33		73.48		100.0
1973*	7.95		23.15		68.95		100.0
1980*	8.75		29.37		61.88		100.0
1985	9.9	± 0.3	31.8	± 1.0	58.3	± 1.5	100.0
1990	11.1	± 0.5	26.0	± 1.5	52.9	± 2.0	100.0
1995	11.8	± 0.5	40.3	± 2.0	47.9	± 2.5	100.0
2000	13.0	± 0.7	44.8	± 2.5	42.2	± 3.5	100.0
2005	14.1	± 1.0	49.0	± 3.0	36.9	± 4.0	100.0
2010	15.3	± 1.5	53.3	± 4.0	31.4	± 4.5	100.0

*Data taken from Leechor *et al* (1983)

This could probably bring a very unstable and tense world situation around the years 2000 to 2010, for it would modify the relative strength of the two main competing systems of today.

In spite of the evident gains in world manufacturing value added obtained by the group of countries with centrally planned economies, their share of the world manufacturing exports has been declining; meanwhile, that of the developed market economies has remained almost constant, with perhaps a slight decline in recent years, in spite of the ground lost by them in the world manufacturing value added. If the trends of the last 20 years were to continue, the scenario of Table 11.2 is considered to be highly likely. Many explanations of how and why such a scenario could happen are possible. One of them would suggest that the scenario is the result of the so called

Table 11.2

Share of world manufacturing exports by group of countries (percentages)

Year	Developing countries			Centrally planned economies			Developed market economies			World
1966*	4.52			8.55			86.93			100.0
1967*	5.49			10.27			84.24			100.0
1968*	5.63			10.04			84.34			100.0
1969*	5.97			9.48			84.55			100.0
1970*	6.10			9.30			84.60			100.0
1971*	5.84			9.16			85.00			100.0
1972*	6.09			9.36			84.55			100.0
1973*	6.98			8.03			84.19			100.0
1974*	7.32			7.83			84.86			100.0
1975*	6.52			8.74			84.74			100.0
1976*	7.54			8.21			84.26			100.0
1977*	7.72			8.19			84.08			100.0
1978*	7.90			8.01			84.09			100.0
1979*	8.50			7.63			83.86			100.0
1980*	8.81			7.32			83.86			100.0
1985	11.4	±	0.5	7.3	±	0.48	1.3	±	2.5	100.0
1990	13.6	±	0.8	6.5	±	0.67	9.9	±	3.0	100.0
1995	16.3	±	1.0	5.9	±	0.87	7.8	±	4.0	100.0
2000	19.3	±	1.5	5.3	±	1.07	5.4	±	5.0	100.0
2005	22.7	±	2.0	4.8	±	1.37	2.5	±	6.0	100.0
2010	26.7	±	2.7	4.3	±	1.56	8.9	±	7.0	100.0

*Based on data from Leechor et al (1983)

"industrial reallocation process" and the relative specialization of the developed market economies in the trade of services.

Within this framework, the industrialized countries could be in the process of abandoning certain industrial sectors which could be taken by the developing countries. In general these would be energy, labor, or raw material intensive industries. The industrialized countries would then specialize in the "knowledge industries." The insistence of the United States and other industrialized countries to bring the services sector under the General Agreement on Tariffs and Trade (GATT) seems to render further support to this kind of argument. However this cannot explain the whole picture and it seems too simplified a scheme. Some traditional sectors, such as footwear and leather or textiles, which in the last decades were located in developing countries, with relative comparative advantages of low wages and availability of resources could, in the process of redeployment, be transferred to the industrialized countries. These sectors have not had major technological changes for a long time. With technology already available today (particularly electronics and materials), they may be changed to favor the advantages of the developed countries. This could represent a countertrend to that shown in the scenario described above. In any case, it seems logical that with a high rate of population growth, urbanization and industrialization, the manufacturing infrastructure of the developing countries will have to grow if any degree of social stability in them is to be expected — and likely at a higher rate than that of the developed countries, who have a relatively stable population and have practically ended their urbanization and industrialization process.[1] Linked with all this, and possibly pushed by protectionist measures taken by the industrialized countries, there has been, since at least 1965, a clear trend to an increased south-south trade. In 1970 intradeveloping countries trade accounted for 26.4 percent of the total exports of manufactures from the developing countries. In 1975 the share increased to 34.4 percent and in 1980 to 36.5 percent. If this trend would continue, the scenario of Table 11.3 is likely. My impression is that although south-south trade will continue to increase its share, the gains will be less than those shown in Table 11.3. I believe that the need for a real transfer of resources from North to South will be required to maintain some degree of stability in the world economy and this will mean an increase in trade from south to north. Thus, perhaps intra-developing countries trade of manufactures could approach with higher probability, say 41 percent by 1990, 45 percent by the year 2000, and 47 percent by 2010.

Within the developed countries with market economies there have also been changes in the importance of specific countries. Germany and Japan have increased their share in both total production and trade, in particular of manufactures, while the United States, and above all, certain European countries, such as Great Britain, have decreased it. In parallel there has

Table 11.3
Share of intra-developing countries trade in manufactures

Year	Intra-DC manufacturing exports as a % of total manufacturing exports of developing countries		Intra-DC manufacturing exports as a % of world manufacturing trade	
1970*	27.1		1.65	
1975*	34.4		2.13	
1980*	36.5		3.21	
1985	39.1	± 0.5	4.5	± 0.4
1990	43.1	± 0.7	5.9	± 0.7
1995	45.3	± 0.8	7.4	± 0.9
2000	50.4	± 1.0	9.7	± 1.3
2005	53.9	± 1.3	12.2	± 1.5
2010	56.9	± 1.5	15.2	± 2.0

*Data taken from Leechor et al (1983)

been a shift in the center of trade from the Atlantic to the Pacific. A combination of Japan, China, and the newly industrialized countries of Southeast Asia (Singapore, South Korea, Taiwan, etc.), with a huge internal market (headed by China), capital technology and material resources, could prove to be a formidable focal point that may shape the world's economic and trade patterns of the future.

The shifts mentioned above for manufactures as a whole are only a part of the changes occurring. Not all the manufacturing branches have behaved in the same manner, and countries have shown different patterns of specialization.

For example, the share of the developing countries in the value added of capital goods changed from 3.74 percent of the world total in 1963 to 4.32 percent in 1970 and 5.77 percent in 1979. This can be unfavorably compared with their share of the world total manufacturing value added of 6.63 percent in 1963, 7.58 percent in 1970 and 8.93 percent in 1979; i.e., the developing countries have even less relative importance in capital goods than in total manufactures. Further, within the capital goods, they only account for 1.3 to 1.5 of the world value added in professional and scientific equipment (ISIC 385), where one can assume that the technology factor is more important than in other groups of products. Just as an example, within the value added of capital goods generated by the developing countries, the share of different groups of products has been shifting towards electrical and non-electrical machinery, with transport equipment and other capital goods losing ground. If the observed trends were to continue in the future, the scenarios of Tables 11.4 and 11.5 seem possible. In one it is assumed that electrical machinery would have reached a maximum percentage share sometime near 1985, with nonelectrical machinery growing steadily. In the second scenario the share of electrical machinery is assumed to grow in the future following a logistic curve, while nonelectrical machinery shows signs of moderating its growth. In my opinion, this second scenario seems more likely.

It should also be noted that the relative weight of the manufacturing sector in the total exports is much greater for the developed market economies (around 75 percent) than for the centrally planned economies (between 50 and 55 percent) and the developing countries (20-25 percent). These values remained relatively constant from 1969 to 1980, but with higher variations in the group of developing countries. It is also interesting to note that about two-thirds of the manufacturing of the developing countries go to developed market economies, and that the developing countries buy about one-quarter of the total manufacturing exports of the developed market economies. If recent trends continue, by the year 2000 probably between 46 and 50 percent of the manufacturing exports of the developing countries could go to developed countries, and between 32 and 36 percent of the total manufacturing exports of the developed countries could be destined to developing countries (Table 11.6).

It is also important to notice that the exports of labor-intensive manufactures have greatly reduced their share on the total manufacturing exports of the developing countries. It should be pointed out that, understandably, they have always had a lower share in the intra-developing countries trade as compared with exports destined to developed countries or centrally planned economies. With high probability this trend will continue in the future and, if it does, a likely scenario would be that of Table 11.7 (and Figure 11.7).

▪ Structural Changes in the Composition of Manufacturing Product and Trade

During the last 20 years the two manufacturing groups which have shown a more dynamic growth of value added are chemicals and metal products and machinery, both characterized by a relatively high technology in the production processes and a high proportion of skilled labor force. The

Table 11.4
Value added of capital goods in the developing countries. Share of groups of products as a percentage of total value added.
Scenario A.

Year	Non-electrical machinery (ISIC 382)	Electrical machinery (ISIC 383)	Transport equipment (ISIC 384)	Professional and scientific equipment (ISIC 385)	Other capital goods (ISIC 390)	Total capital goods
1963*	20.44	22.67	40.45	2.60	13.83	100.00
1967*	22.66	25.11	36.86	2.40	12.98	100.00
1970*	22.12	28.06	38.54	2.45	8.83	100.00
1975*	26.78	25.71	37.91	2.39	7.20	100.00
1977*	28.14	27.35	34.55	2.53	7.44	100.00
1979*	26.71	28.63	34.45	2.58	7.62	100.00
1985	31.5 ± 1.5	27.6 ± 1.0	32.4 ± 0.4	2.5 ± 0.2	6.0 ± 0.4	100.0
1990	34.4 ± 1.8	27.4 ± 1.5	30.7 ± 0.5	2.5 ± 0.2	5.0 ± 0.5	100.0
1995	37.9 ± 2.5	26.5 ± 2.0	29.1 ± 0.6	2.5 ± 0.3	4.2 ± 0.5	100.0
2000	41.2 ± 3.0	25.3 ± 2.5	27.5 ± 0.7	2.5 ± 0.4	3.4 ± 0.5	100.0
2005	44.4 ± 3.5	24.0 ± 3.0	26.0 ± 0.8	2.5 ± 0.5	2.9 ± 0.6	100.0
2010	47.9 ± 4.5	22.7 ± 3.5	24.5 ± 0.9	2.5 ± 0.7	2.4 ± 0.8	100.0

*Calculated from data given in UNIDO, *Industrial Development: Global Report 1985*, United Nations, New York, 1985

Table 11.5
Value added of capital goods in the developing countries. Share of groups of products as a percentage of total value added. Scenario B.

Year	Non-electrical machinery (ISIC 382)	Electrical machinery (ISIC 383)	Transport equipment (ISIC 384)	Professional and scientific equipment (ISIC 385)	Other capital goods (ISIC 390)	Total capital goods
1963*	20.44	22.67	40.45	2.60	13.83	100.00
1967*	22.66	25.11	36.86	2.40	12.98	100.00
1970*	22.12	28.06	38.54	2.45	8.83	100.00
1975*	26.78	25.71	37.91	2.39	7.20	100.00
1977*	28.14	27.35	34.55	2.53	7.44	100.00
1979*	26.71	28.63	34.45	2.58	7.62	100.00
1985	28.8 ± 1.2	30.3 ± 1.5	32.4 ± 0.4	2.5 ± 0.2	6.0 ± 0.4	100.0
1990	30.1 ± 1.7	31.7 ± 1.8	30.7 ± 0.5	2.5 ± 0.2	5.0 ± 0.5	100.0
1995	30.9 ± 2.3	33.3 ± 2.2	29.1 ± 0.6	2.5 ± 0.3	4.2 ± 0.5	100.0
2000	31.6 ± 2.8	34.9 ± 2.8	27.5 ± 0.7	2.5 ± 0.4	3.4 ± 0.5	100.0
2005	32.3 ± 3.2	36.3 ± 3.5	26.0 ± 0.8	2.5 ± 0.5	2.9 ± 0.6	100.0
2010	32.7 ± 3.5	37.9 ± 4.0	24.5 ± 0.9	2.5 ± 0.7	2.4 ± 0.8	100.0

*Calculated from data given in UNIDO, *Industrial Development: Global Report 1985*, United Nations, New York, 1985

Table 11.6
Manufacturing trade links between developing countries and
developed market economies.

Year	% of manufacture exports from developing countries to developed market economies	% of manufacture exports from developed market economies to developing countries
1966*	69.8	19.4
1967*	70.9	21.8
1968*	71.3	21.4
1969*	70.8	20.5
1970*	68.4	19.6
1971*	67.6	19.7
1972	66.1	19.1
1973*	68.2	19.3
1974*	65.5	22.3
1975*	61.4	26.0
1976*	65.7	25.4
1977*	63.3	25.8
1978*	64.9	25.4
1979*	63.8	23.8
1980*	59.7	25.3
1985	58.0 ± 2.0	27.0 ± 1.5
1990	54.6 ± 2.5	29.2 ± 1.8
1995	51.2 ± 3.0	31.5 ± 2.2
2000	47.9 ± 3.5	33.8 ± 2.8
2005	44.1 ± 4.0	36.5 ± 3.3
2010	40.5 ± 5.0	39.0 ± 4.0

*Historical data taken from Leechor C, *et al* (1983)

chemical industries were the most dynamic in the developed countries.
Machinery had a higher growth in both developing countries and centrally-
planned economies. It should be noted that, in general, the chemical
industries are more capital intensive as compared with machinery branches,
so that the specialization pattern should not be surprising. As can be seen
in Tables 11.8 to 11.10, the structural change taking place in manufacturing output is similar in form for all three groups of countries (except in food
and beverages, which has remained practically constant and it is estimated
will continue to do so in the developed market economies, while it has lost

Table 11.7
Exports of labor intensive manufactures as a percentage of total manufacturing
exports from the developing countries, according to countries of destination.

Year	To developed market economies (%)	To centrally planned economies (%)	To developing countries (%)
1966*	91.2	92.3	71.4
1968*	90.5	88.4	70.9
1970*	85.8	85.1	69.8
1972*	80.7	86.4	63.5
1974*	76.7	84.0	60.4
1976*	77.5	81.3	59.1
1978*	74.4	81.2	65.6
1980*	72.4	74.0	56.7
1985*	60.6 ± 3.5	69.7 ± 3.5	50.3 ± 2.8
1990*	50.0 ± 3.8	61.6 ± 3.8	44.4 ± 3.2
1995*	37.3 ± 4.0	53.0 ± 4.0	38.7 ± 3.7
2000*	27.0 ± 4.3	44.1 ± 4.5	33.0 ± 4.2
2005*	19.0 ± 4.8	32.7 ± 5.0	28.0 ± 4.6
2010*	12.9 ± 5.2	28.0 ± 5.5	23.5 ± 5.0

*Historical data taken from Leechor C, *et al* (1983)

ground to the other two groups of countries). What is different is the relative strength of each branch of products and the speed with which branch substitution is taking place. This substitution process seems to be in a more advanced state in the developed market economies, where it could be expected that the metal products and machinery will reach their maximum share of the manufacturing output between 1990 and 1995, beginning to decline thereafter.

A similar situation will probably not be reached by the other two groups of countries before the year 2010. It is also interesting to notice that, not surprisingly, the pattern of change in trade follows closely that of the manufacturing output. In general it can be said that all three groups of countries are gradually shifting their manufacturing output towards heavy manufactures.

The degree of specialization can be better perceived comparing the growth of the manufacturing branches by countries or groups of countries. Taking 1965 as the base year and setting the value added of each manufac-

Table 11.8
Structure of manufacturing product in developing countries (in percent)

Year	Food beverages and tobacco	Textiles	Apparel leather footware	Chemicals coal and rubber products	Metal products and machinery	Other manufactures	Total manufactures
1966	23.0	13.0	5.7	16.8	16.7	24.8	100.0
1968	22.4	12.9	5.5	17.7	17.3	24.2	100.0
1970	22.3	12.3	4.9	18.7	18.5	23.3	100.0
1972	20.7	11.6	4.6	19.8	19.9	23.4	100.0
1974	19.6	10.8	4.7	19.7	23.0	22.2	100.0
1976	20.0	10.6	4.7	19.1	23.9	21.7	100.0
1978	19.6	9.6	4.3	19.9	23.7	22.9	100.0
1980	19.6	9.3	4.2	19.1	25.0	22.8	100.0
1985	18.0 ± 0.8	8.2 ± 0.4	3.8 ± 0.2	21.3 ± 1.0	27.1 ± 1.0	21.6 ± 0.8	100.0
1990	16.8 ± 1.0	7.2 ± 0.4	3.4 ± 0.2	22.4 ± 1.3	29.2 ± 1.3	21.0 ± 1.2	100.0
1995	16.0 ± 1.3	6.3 ± 0.5	3.1 ± 0.3	23.3 ± 1.6	30.9 ± 1.8	20.4 ± 1.5	100.0
2000	15.0 ± 1.5	5.5 ± 0.5	2.7 ± 0.4	24.2 ± 2.0	32.6 ± 2.5	19.9 ± 1.8	100.0
2005	14.2 ± 1.8	4.8 ± 0.6	2.5 ± 0.5	25.4 ± 2.5	33.9 ± 3.0	19.2 ± 2.0	100.0
2010	13.2 ± 2.0	4.3 ± 0.6	2.3 ± 0.6	26.5 ± 2.8	35.1 ± 3.5	18.7 ± 2.2	100.0

*Data from 1966 to 1980 taken from Leechor C, et al (1983)

Table 11.9
Structure of manufacturing product in developed market economies (in percent)

Year	Food beverages and tobacco	Textiles	Apparel leather footware	Chemicals coal and rubber products	Metal products and machinery	Other manufactures	Total manufactures
1966	12.4	4.7	4.8	12.0	37.5	28.6	100.0
1968	12.2	4.6	4.3	13.1	38.1	27.7	100.0
1970	12.1	4.6	4.0	14.1	38.1	27.1	100.0
1972	11.9	4.6	3.9	14.8	37.8	27.0	100.0
1974	11.7	4.2	3.6	15.0	39.4	26.1	100.0
1976	12.2	4.3	3.7	15.4	39.0	25.4	100.0
1978	12.0	3.9	3.4	16.0	40.0	24.7	100.0
1980	12.1	3.8	3.2	15.9	40.6	24.4	100.0
1985	12.1 ± 0.6	3.5 ± 0.2	2.8 ± 0.2	18.3 ± 0.8	40.4 ± 2.0	23.1 ± 1.0	100.0
1990	12.1 ± 0.8	3.2 ± 0.2	2.5 ± 0.2	20.0 ± 1.0	40.4 ± 2.3	21.8 ± 1.2	100.0
1995	12.1 ± 1.0	2.9 ± 0.3	2.2 ± 0.3	22.1 ± 1.3	40.2 ± 2.8	20.5 ± 1.5	100.0
2000	12.1 ± 1.2	2.6 ± 0.4	1.9 ± 0.3	24.2 ± 1.8	39.6 ± 3.3	19.2 ± 1.8	100.0
2005	12.1 ± 1.5	2.3 ± 0.5	1.7 ± 0.4	26.5 ± 2.3	39.4 ± 3.8	18.0 ± 2.0	100.0
2010	12.1 ± 1.8	2.2 ± 0.6	1.5 ± 0.5	29.3 ± 3.0	38.0 ± 4.0	16.9 ± 2.0	100.0

*Data from 1966 to 1980 taken from Leechor C, *et al* (1983)

Table 11.10
Structure of manufacturing product in centrally planned economies (in percent)

Year	Food beverages and tobacco	Textiles	Apparel leather footware	Chemicals coal and rubber products	Metal products and machinery	Other manufactures	Total manufactures
1966	17.9	8.5	7.3	9.7	31.8	24.8	100.0
1968	16.9	8.0	7.6	10.3	33.8	23.4	100.0
1970	16.0	7.6	7.6	10.6	35.2	23.0	100.0
1972	14.9	7.2	7.1	10.6	36.9	23.3	100.0
1974	14.1	6.7	6.6	10.7	38.6	23.3	100.0
1976	12.9	6.5	6.4	11.0	40.6	22.6	100.0
1978	12.3	6.2	6.1	11.0	42.4	22.0	100.0
1980	11.8	5.9	6.1	10.7	44.0	21.5	100.0
1985	10.0 ± 0.5	5.2 ± 0.2	5.3 ± 0.2	11.5 ± 0.5	47.4 ± 2.5	20.6 ± 1.0	100.0
1990	8.5 ± 0.7	4.5 ± 0.3	4.9 ± 0.3	11.9 ± 0.7	50.5 ± 3.0	19.7 ± 1.3	100.0
1995	7.2 ± 0.8	4.0 ± 0.4	4.4 ± 0.4	12.3 ± 0.9	53.3 ± 3.8	18.8 ± 1.5	100.0
2000	6.1 ± 0.9	3.5 ± 0.5	3.9 ± 0.5	12.9 ± 1.2	55.6 ± 4.5	18.0 ± 1.8	100.0
2005	5.2 ± 1.0	3.1 ± 0.6	3.5 ± 0.6	13.2 ± 1.5	57.7 ± 5.0	17.3 ± 2.0	100.0
2010	4.4 ± 1.2	2.7 ± 0.7	3.2 ± 0.7	13.8 ± 1.8	59.4 ± 6.0	16.5 ± 2.5	100.0

*Data from 1966 to 1980 taken from Leechor C, et al (1983)

turing branch in that year as 100, Figures 11.1 and 11.2 plot the growth of each of sixteen branches for the years 1970 and 1980[2], both for developed and developing countries. As can be seen in this more detailed picture, the developed countries show a high degree of specialization above all in plastic products (ISIC 356) and to a lesser degree in chemicals (ISIC 351, 352), with electrical and nonelectrical machinery following close. On the other hand, the developing countries show, first, a less clear pattern of specialization, and second, preference for electrical and nonelectrical machinery and chemicals (although the latter only after 1970). Within this global framework it is interesting to review the evolution of certain countries. The graphs corresponding to Japan and France are shown in Figures 11.3a and 11.3b and those of the Federal Republic of Germany and the United States in Figures 11.4a and 11.4b. Two different and distinguishable patterns of change emerge, with Japan and the United States showing a more pronounced process of specialization. The pattern of Germany and the United States is very similar to that of the developed countries; this is only natural because of their big share of the manufacturing value added of the group. But Japan and France have had a structural change more like that of the developing countries, apparently specializing above all in electrical machinery. One may suspect that, at least in the case of Japan, this has to do with the emergence of the electronics industry. In any case, the branches of specialization of the developed countries apparently correspond closely with those which "export" more innovations to other branches (i.e., chemicals, mechanical engineering, instruments and electrical and electronic products).[3] Among the developing countries, in particular the newly industrialized countries, those which show clear specialization patterns – e.g., South Korea (Figure 11.5b), Singapore, Hong Kong and even Brazil (Figure 5a) seem to have done better in the past than those who present a more uniform development – e.g., Mexico and Argentina (Figure 11.6b). It is also interesting to note that the Soviet Union has had a structural change of its manufacturing sector which very much looks like the union set, in the set theory sense, of those of the United States and Japan plus an important growth in metal products and transport equipment (see Figure 11.7).

Figures 11.8 to 11.10 show the structural change of the manufacturing sector of some countries of the Middle East. The specialization pattern of Israel is less marked than those of the other countries included, and it is similar to that of the Soviet Union (except for a greater importance in petroleum and coal and a lesser importance of metal products and nonelectrical machinery). One may note that, with the exception of chemicals, in each of the specializing branches chosen by Israel there is at least another Middle East country which is also specializing in it. From the point of view of trade this could mean, in general terms, either more competition, if one thinks of interindustries trade, or more possibilities for an increase in commerce, if

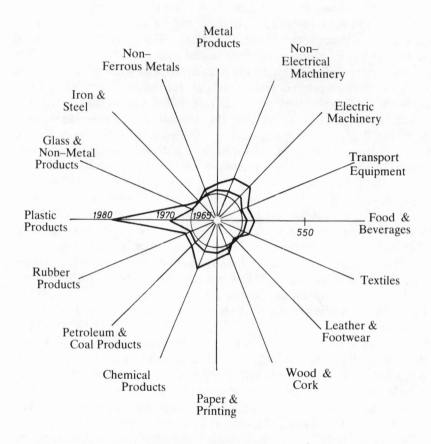

Metal
Products

Non–
Ferrous Metals

Non–
Electrical
Machinery

Iron &
Steel

Electric
Machinery

Glass &
Non–Metal
Products

Transport
Equipment

Plastic
Products

1980   1970   1965

550

Food &
Beverages

Rubber
Products

Textiles

Petroleum &
Coal Products

Leather &
Footwear

Chemical
Products

Wood &
Cork

Paper &
Printing

Figure 11.1 : **Developed Countries: Industrial Structural Change**
(Index Value Added 1965 = 100)

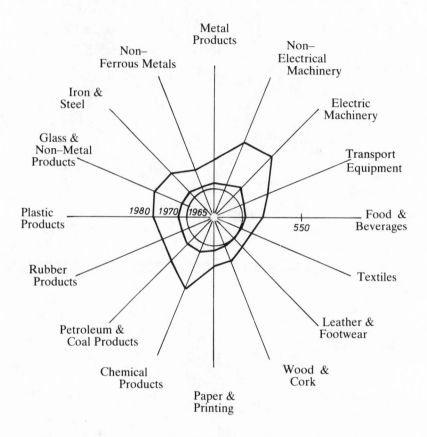

Figure 11.2: Developing Countries: Industrial Structural Change
(Index Value Added 1965 = 100)

226

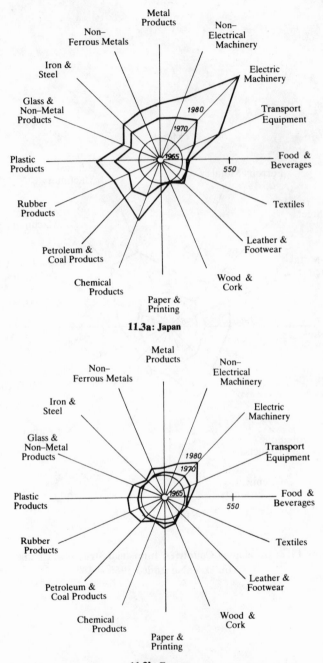

11.3a: Japan

11.3b: France

**Figure 11.3: France and Japan: Industrial Structural Change
(Index Value Added 1965 = 100)**

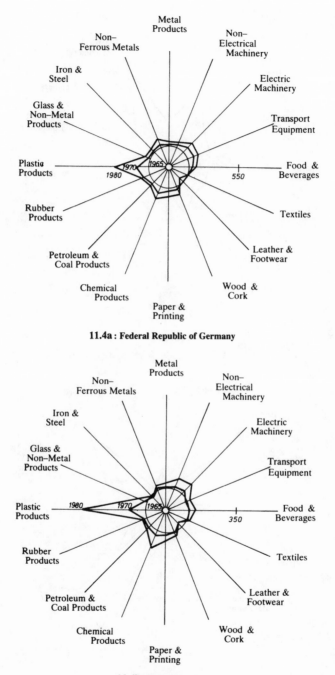

11.4a : Federal Republic of Germany

11.4b : United States

**Figure 11.4 : Germany and the United States: Industrial Structural Change
(Index Value Added 1965 = 100)**

228

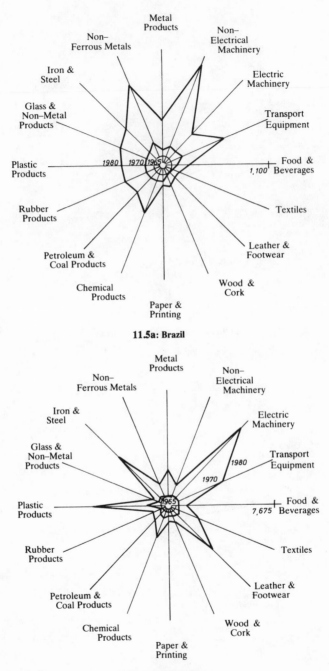

11.5a: Brazil

11.5b: Republic of Korea

Figure 11.5: Brazil and Korea: Industrial Structural Change
(Index Value Added 1965 = 100)

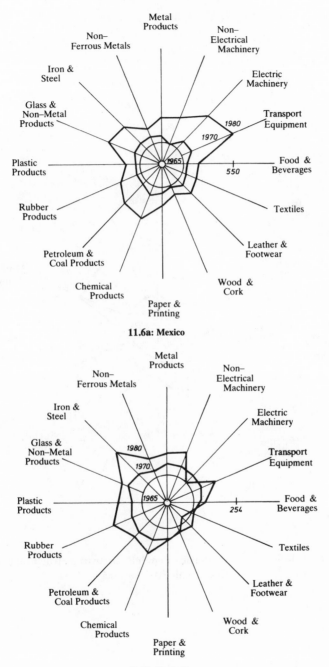

11.6a: Mexico

11.6b: Argentina

Figure 11.6: Mexico and Argentina: Industrial Structural Change
(Index Value Added 1965 = 100)

230

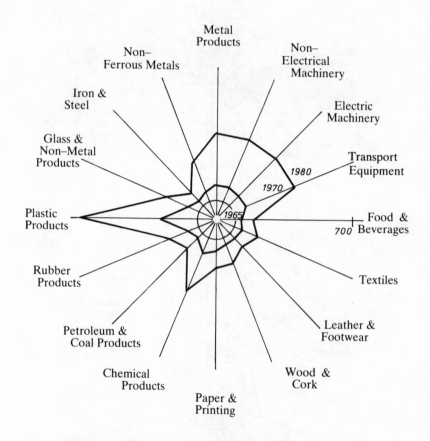

Metal
Products

Non–
Ferrous Metals

Non–
Electrical
Machinery

Iron &
Steel

Electric
Machinery

Glass &
Non–Metal
Products

Transport
Equipment

1980

1970

Plastic
Products

1965

Food &
Beverages

700

Rubber
Products

Textiles

Petroleum &
Coal Products

Leather &
Footwear

Chemical
Products

Wood &
Cork

Paper &
Printing

Figure 11.7: Union of Soviet Socialist Republic: Industrial Structural Change
(Index Value Added 1965 = 100)

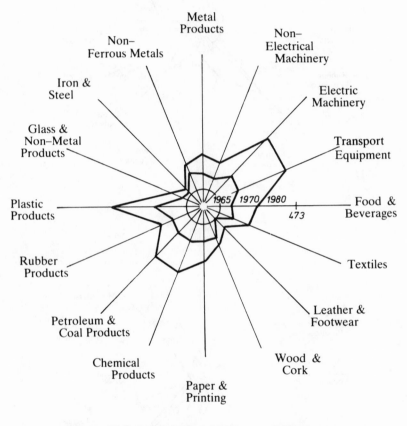
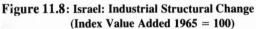

Figure 11.8: Israel: Industrial Structural Change
(Index Value Added 1965 = 100)

232

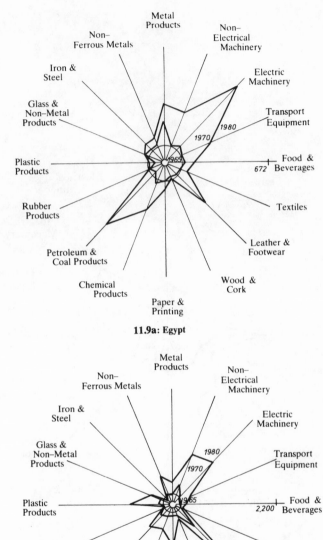

11.9a: Egypt

11.9b: Syria

Figure 11.9: Egypt and Syria: Industrial Structural Change
(Index Value Added 1965 = 100)

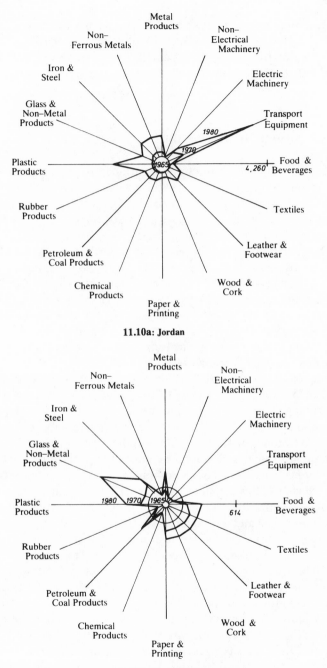

11.10a: Jordan

11.10b: Saudi Arabia

Figure 11.10: Jordan and Saudi Arabia: Industrial Structural Change
(Index Value Added 1965 = 100)

one thinks about intraindustries trade. Perhaps a more detailed analysis of the kind suggested here could reveal where the most promising cooperative efforts are within the region in manufactures. It may also be useful to extend this kind of analysis if joint ventures were thought to be a suitable means of cooperation between countries of the region.

■ A Technological Dimension

The changes in products and trade mentioned in previous sections have been occurring in parallel with a multidimensional substitution process of the means used to satisfy the world needs and of technology. Several of the individual substitution processes have been documented (for example, see Marchetti, 1984, for the case of energy).

It has been advanced (e.g., Mensch, 1979) that technological inventions and innovations occur in waves and closely linked to long economic cycles. Such a statement should not be taken, in my opinion, to mean that the evolution of the economy or technology can be described in a mechanistic manner, but rather as an indication that under present production relations they follow certain rules. Given that, the present and next innovation waves are likely to be centered around technical advances in electronics, new materials and bioprocesses (e.g., Raz B and Eres B, 1985).

The technology factor in both trade and development has been widely studied (see for example Vernon R, 1970), but still much remains to be said. However, recognizing my own limitations on the topic, I will not attempt to elaborate on it. Instead, I will just sketch a couple of points I consider of interest for developing countries and the Middle East region.

It is frequently said that developing countries copy the industrial patterns of the developed world. Although this may be true, in the case of trade in a sense it reflects itself as a counter-pattern. The most advanced developed countries have more dynamic innovation processes, partly due to heavier spending in research and development, partly due to a bigger participation of the private sector in it and to stronger links between productive activities and research and development activities. It is generally in the developed countries where new products originate. Due to multiple reasons, external markets for these products are soon sought and found. Thus, trade shows no imports and growing exports. But soon after, other countries who technologically follow closely, start producing the same product, innovate the production process, and capture part of the international market. Thus, the country where the product originated is likely to gradually reduce its exports (due to competition) and even to begin importing. The developing countries, on the other hand, at first only have imports. It is only some time later, when they adopt the technology, that they start their own production. And only then, by making use of comparative advantages, they may capture a part of the international market. Therefore they begin with a high imports coefficient (imports to consumption) and a low (or null) exports coefficient (exports to production) and only gradually they move to a more equitable position. Thus, trade possibilities should be treated differently if they refer to new or to established and mature products. The point at hand can be illustrated with the case of Mexico.

One last thought. If imports and/or exports of manufactured products are ordered using their price per unit weight, the list obtained is very similar to that resulting from an ordering based on research and development spending as a percentage of total sales. This is so even without normalizing for the differences in price of raw materials used in each product. Thus, value added is in a sense technology incorporated in a product. And it is interesting to note that in developing countries, when there are exports and imports in the same category of products, in general the price per unit weight of exports is smaller than that of the imports; i.e., imports have more incorporated technology than exports. Thus, even in the manufacturing sector it seems to be true that the developing countries export mainly their materials (or at least more so than developed countries). If economic cooperation in the Middle East (or any other region) is to be based on a more equitable basis, it is my opinion that trade arrangements should take into account possible unbalances in value added per unit weight and not be based merely on total value. This would increase the hope of building a sustainable cooperation effort and not only an increased economic exchange of goods, materials or services.

■ **Notes**

1. Understood as a transformation process of the productive activities from the primary sector to the secondary sector.
2. The data and graphs were taken from UNIDO (1985).
3. See Pavitt K (1984).

■ **References**

Ackhoff, R. L., "Beyond Prediction and Preparation," S[3] papers, No. 82-6, Social Systems Sciences Department, The Wharton School, University of Pennsylvania, Philadelphia, PA, 1986.

Alonso A. and Rivas, S., *Tecnología y Comercio Exterior de México: Primer Informe Parcial,* Report of Fundación Javier Barros Sierra AC of restricted circulation, México, DF, November 1984.

Leechor, C., et al, *Structural Changes in World Industry,* A World Bank Technical Paper, Industry and Finance Series, ISSN 0253-7494, v. 1, November 1983.

Marchetti, C., "Innovation, Industry and Economy; A top-down analysis," Professional Paper, International Institute for Applied Systems Analysis, Laxenburg, Austria, December 1983 (25p).

Mensch, G., *Stalemate in Technology,* Ballinger Publishing Co., Cambridge, Massachusetts, 1979.

Pavitt, K., "Sectoral patterns of technical changes towards taxonomy and a theory," *Research Policy,* North Holland, 13, 1984, pp. 343-373.

Raz, B., Eres, B., "2010: Technological Options and Uncertainties," Proceedings of the Workshop "Mexico 2010: Views from Abroad," Fundación Javier Barros Sierra AC, México DF, August 26-29, 1985.

UNIDO, *Industrial Development: Global Report 1985,* United Nations, New York, 1985.

Vernon, R., (ea). *The Technology Factor in International Trade,* National Bureau of Economic Research, distributed by Columbia University Press, New York, 1970.

12

The Effect of Science and Technology in Regional and Global Development

Sam Nilsson

■ SCIENCE AND TECHNOLOGY AFTER WORLD WAR II

World War II marked a "scientification" of technology not only for war purposes but also for the civilian market which was emerging after the war. Let us only mention such results as DDT (Muller Nobel Prize), nerve gases (the understanding of the neurophysiological reactions to organic phosphorous compounds), the radar (microwave propagation), the jet engine, and, of course, the atom bomb (the result of the largest research and development effort ever undertaken).

The extraordinary results of organized R&D led to the *institutionalization of science and technology*. Governments, especially in the West, created national research councils, national research labs, and some governments even created special ministries for science. The Organization for Economic Cooperation and Development, OECD, which emerged from the European Steel Union, installed a special directorate for Science, Technology and Education whose first director general was the British chemist Dr. Alexander King. He had been one of the leading science advisors in the UK during WWII and was behind the large-scale production of DDT to be used in the later phases of the war. When Alexander King retired from OECD in 1974 he became the chairman of IFIAS and stayed in that position until 1984. Under the leadership of OECD's Secretary General Thorkil Kristensen and Alexander King, a special Science Policy Office within OECD was created which organized independent evaluation teams of high-level scientists who visited the OECD members for assessment and critique of the Policy and Organization of Science and Technology and Higher Education in the member countries.

I believe this is one of the best examples of "regional" (OECD now also includes the U.S., Japan, Canada, and Australia) cooperation of Science and Technology for economic development. To the best of my knowledge, this has not been tried in an organized manner in any other region of the world. The only other example I know is perhaps the late attempts by the six ASEAN countries in Southeast Asia to coordinate and cooperate in Science and Technology for development.

The UN organization and some of its agencies, notably UNESCO, have organized Science and Technology programmes for developing countries. Two large UN conferences on science and technology for development were organized in 1963 in Geneva and 1979 in Vienna. None of these have had any significant impact on the regional cooperation among developing countries.

Organized and institutionalized science and technology took a firm hold only in the industrialized countries where it became more and more integrated into the economic development process. Let us only think of the powerful role of MITI in Japan. Nothing like this exists in developing countries.

■ Industrialization of Science and Technology

With the increasing "scientification" of technology and innovations, the industry in advanced societies has moved closer to university research. In the U.S., there has always been a close relationship between university research and commercial applications. It started with the so called Route 128 phenomenon when enterprises grew up along Route 128 around Boston and Cambridge in New England.

It must be recalled, however, that many of the new "high-tech" companies in this case originated from contracts to MIT, Harvard, and Yale from the Department of Defense in the U.S. This tradition is very strong in the U.S. and the most recent example is the Strategic Defense Initiative (SDI). However, today there is a growing direct commercial interest in university research by the U.S. industry. A few examples suffice to show this.

Using a $10 million donation from 16 companies, Stanford University has created a Center for Integrated Systems. The chemical giant DuPont is investing $6 million in Harvard University's new genetics department, while three large companies – Union Carbide, Eastman Kodak, and Corning Glass – have pledged contributions of up to $2.5 million annually over the next six years to set up a biotechnology institute at Cornell University.

In Houston, Texas, they hope to create the biggest medical applications center in the country and perhaps in the world.

We now see similar patterns emerge in Europe. Increased international competition and declining productivity have given corporations an incentive to find new ways to keep up with the quickened pace of change.

In Sweden, there is a science and technology park or innovation center at every major university.

The university-industry interaction is becoming well-organized and part of the national S&T policy in most industrialized countries. In Japan, where the traditions of university-industry cooperation are not so well developed, one is talking about "directed" basic research which is largely determined by the powerful MITI (Ministry of Trade and Industry).

With the increasingly intimate relationship between research and commercial applications, the situation for the universities and other teaching institutions has changed dramatically. Many think that the present university system is out of tune with the development in society in general. This may also be one of the reasons why separate institutes must be created for the innovations and practical applications based on research. In most developing countries, including countries in this part of the world, one can see clearly how the burdens of the past — colonial or noncolonial — make the universities even more unadaptable to the needs of society. Many think that the closer relations between commercial interests and research at the universities constitute a threat to basic research and I believe that the worries are justified to some extent.

The same worries have arisen at many U.S. universities in connection with the Strategic Defense Initiative (SDI). I believe, however, that we are at a transition point in organized research which opens up great opportunities for harmonization of directed basic research with the industrial applications and innovations for societal purposes. Universities, like industry, are confronted with major structural changes which need not be only bad for research.

■ Role of Industry

In free-market as well as centralized planned economies, industry is seen to be the most effective means of producing and marketing the products.

A special position is taken by the Transnational Corporations (TNCs). Their role has long been a subject of great controversy, especially in relation to developing countries. I believe that the criticism and skepticism of the TNCs (especially the American) has been considerable among the Arab countries in North Africa and the Middle East.

For the UN conference on Science and Technology for Development, UNCSTD, in Vienna in 1979, IFIAS carried out a study called "Science and

Technology for Development – Role of TNCs." It was done with a team of two developing country researchers (from Mexico and India) and two persons from two of IFIAS' corporate affiliates, i.e., Unilever in the Netherlands and Atlas Copco in Sweden. The team was coordinated by the well-known Dutch physicist Professor H. B. G. Casimir who for several years was the research director of Philips in the Netherlands. This study disclosed a number of considerable misunderstandings on both sides, but especially concerning the structure and "life" of TNCs. In particular it was pointed out that TNCs prefer not to set up R&D units in developing countries, mainly for two reasons. It is too expensive and there is a lack of qualified experts in many developing countries. The TNCs are not altruistic institutions and the host countries must learn the painful lesson of building up their own self-reliant capacity in science and technology. This takes a long time. There are no shortcuts to technology transfer. In my view, technology cannot be transferred – it can only be developed. Where there is a scientific and technological capability, there is a greater chance for investments by foreign companies. I mention this here because I believe the difference in the level of S&T capability between the countries, especially between Israel and the neighboring countries, is such that it would make a harmonious cooperation in S&T rather difficult.

■ A CHANGING WORLD

In 1974, the UN held a special session of its General Assembly on "a new economic world order" – an initiative originally promoted by the late president of Algeria, Mr. Boumidienne.

As usual, not many tangible results came from the rhetoric of this session, but it did bring out in the open several of the questions on the minds of Third World countries such as pricing of raw materials and other commodities, protectionism, technology transfer, and foreign investments.

The so called North-South dialogue was started and at this time (1974-1980) the "South" was negotiating from a morally strong position in view of the oil price escalations at three different occasions during this period. Now, about ten years later, the situation is significantly different for several reasons:

(1) The role of OPEC is dramatically weakened for a couple of reasons which will not be discussed here;

(2) The North-South dialogue is practically dead;

(3) The UN system and its credibility is weakened considerably and many think that the UN will be weakened very much before it can be strong again.

I met recently people in the U.S. who think that the UN will collapse entirely. The crisis is particularly bad with UNESCO, one of those UN agencies which has been helpful in regional development involving science and technology.

(4) The present development of science and technology is almost entirely dominated by the race between the U.S., Japan and Western Europe. The USSR and Eastern Europe are still many years behind in high-tech areas and I would even pretend that such countries as India, Taiwan, South Korea and Brazil are more advanced in many areas than the Soviet Union and Eastern Europe.

Another clear tendency in the "changing world" is the *increasing role of the private sector*. Both at the national level — especially in the welfare states such as Sweden — and at the governmental level, notably the UN but also regional organizations such as EEC, OAS (Latin America), OAU (Africa) and ASEAN (Asia), there are great disenchantments with the effectiveness and capacity of the governmental sectors of society.

I believe that in sector after sector we will see private and other non-governmental initiatives supplement state activities.

In the U.S. this is a well established tradition and the increasing privatization of research is one example which we discussed earlier.

However, the U.S. is now looking at the research capabilities also in other countries for the realization of some key high-tech areas. The *Strategic Defense Initiative* (SDI) is a case in point and it has stirred a lot of emotions not only at American universities but also in the allied countries with whose researchers and industry the U.S. wants to have formal agreements of cooperation.

Its objective is not research for a product or a class of products as were the large research projects of the past — Manhattan and even Apollo — but the building of a complex and interconnected system, open in terms of technologies and products to be adopted for its implementation. The SDI is a systems programme with a precise objective which accepts technologies and products only if they are completely in line with the required performance and characteristics.

The European response, EUREKA, is not a systems programme but rather an assembly of assorted and substantially independent products and technologies. Although the EUREKA proposal may give a large degree of freedom in choices of technologies on the one hand, it neglects one of the most obvious and striking aspects of the newest stages of technological development, namely integrated systems management of technologies, which is both a generator of results and itself a source of overall flexibility and reliability.

Even if there is an effort to define technological and industrial objectives precisely within EUREKA, such specifics do not currently reflect any well identified demand from a market. This problem has permanently plagued

European technology policy. The French call EUREKA "technology à la carte" which means that any company from any country in Western Europe is welcome to cooperate with other European companies. Much skepticism has been expressed among government officials in European countries about the real value for science and technology and ultimately for the competitiveness of Europe. The industrialists seem to be more enthusiastic but it is justified to ask whether the projects approved at the ministerial meeting in Hannover in January 1986 would not come about anyhow by the normal processes of the market. The first EUREKA projects are listed below:

(1) European standard for microcomputers for business and home uses; Partners: France, UK, Italy

(2) A Compact Vectorcalculator; Partners: France, Norway, (Italy)

(3) Production of amorphous silicon; Partners: FRG, France

(4) Robots for textile industry; Partners: France, Portugal, (Spain), (Turkey)

(5) Development and production of filter membranes; Partners: Denmark, France, (Netherlands)

(6) Euro-laser (CO2), mainly for materials cutting and production; Partners: FRG, France, UK, Italy

(7) Eurotrac; Experiments on transport and transformation of environmental trace elements in the troposphere of Europe; Partners: FRG, Finland, Netherlands, Norway, Austria, EEC, (Denmark), (Italy), (Sweden), (Switzerland), (Turkey)

(8) European research network; Partners: FRG, France, Finland, Netherlands, Austria, Sweden, Switzerland, EEC, (Belgium), (Greece), (UK), (Italy), (Luxembourg), (Ireland), (Norway), (Portugal), (Spain), (Turkey)

(9) Development of diagnostic methods based on mono-clonal antibody technique for diseases; Partners: UK, Spain

(10) Flexible production systems based on opto-electronics; Partners: France, Italy, (Switzerland)

It is becoming evident from what has happened in Japan since the end of WWII that military objectives are not essential for the large-scale applications of science and technology.

Japan, too, is worried about the consequences of SDI for the competitive strength of the U.S. in a number of high-tech areas. At the recent summit meeting in Tokyo, the Japanese hosts proposed a worldwide cooperative R&D programme in biotechnology for civilian purposes, such as health and medicine, agriculture, energy, industrial production, and environmental problems. This proposal is called the "Human Frontier" programme and would require about $5 billion. What was decided in Tokyo on this proposal I don't know, but IFIAS has become intimately involved with a related Japanese proposal which was first made around 1976. Mr. Nakajima, a previous President of Mitsubishi Research Institute in Tokyo, proposed as a "global" programme that a Global Infrastructure Fund, GIF, of $500 billion should be built up gradually between 1980 and the year 2000. The fund should be an independent, nongovernmental institution for the promotion and initial funding of large-scale infrastructure projects for civilian peaceful purposes. Such projects as "Greening of the Deserts," a "new" Panama Canal, a global railway, a global highway, a tunnel at Gibraltar to Africa, a tunnel between Japan and the Republic of Korea, are in the list first presented by Mr. Nakajima. All projects should stimulate technical development, employment, economic progress, and peaceful cooperation. It should be recalled that the GIF proposal was first presented when the world was in the middle of the oil crisis and Mr. Nakajima saw it as a sort of planet-scale application of Keynesian theory – a global Marshall Plan.

IFIAS will organize a workshop in Anchorage, Alaska, the first week of July, 1986 at which criteria, methods for analysis, and consequences of large-scale projects will be discussed. A number of specific project proposals will also be presented and hopefully the Anchorage workshop will be followed by multidisciplinary feasibility studies of a few selected projects. It may interest you to know that one of the projects presented is by Professor Amos Richmond from the Jacob Blaustein Institute for Desert Research at Sede Boqer in the Negev. His paper is called "Greening of the Deserts – a Case for the Development of Arid Lands."

Let me finally mention another proposed global cooperative programme which, however, is entirely in the area of Science which is presently under consideration by ICSU, the International Council of Scientific Unions. The proposed programme is called the *Global Change Programme*. It was first suggested by NASA and a few U.S. scientists in 1982–83 under the name "Global Habitability." It was later changed to IGBP = International Geosphere and Biosphere Programme. The purpose is to try to launch a ten-year research programme that would use the latest means of analysis and observation (balloons, satellites, computers, etc.) for a complete survey of the state of the global geosphere, lithosphere, and biosphere in order to see if major global changes can be detected and how they interact. The "Global Change Programme" will be carried out between 1990 and 2000. Great interest has been expressed for cooperation from a number of countries, including the USSR. ICSU will present its final proposal in September 1986. IFIAS has been contacted by NASA concerning the possibility of becoming the implementation agent for the Global Change Programme.

From the few examples given above, there is no question in my mind that the very global nature of science and technology will generate more and more of regional and global cooperative programmes. I think we should welcome this both for the sake of science and technology itself and for the long-term stability of the world. But we should also be aware of the fact that any regional or global cooperation in science and technology will be successful only if it supports the policy of the partners (nations) involved. It has to be a positive-sum-game with long-term gains for everyone involved.

■ THE SPECIAL CASE OF THE MIDDLE EAST

Prime Minister Shimon Peres has proposed a "Marshall Plan" for the Middle East. When the political peace process for the region is making only modest or no progress, the economic cooperation is seen as a more practical option, according to what I have read in the newspapers. The plan would involve the U.S., West Germany and Japan and comprise some 20-30 billion dollars. It would be the reverse of recycling of petro-dollars which was on everybody's mind some ten years ago. From what I have heard, these plans were not discussed at the latest summit in Tokyo. As much as I have great sympathy with the idea I can see great difficulties in realizing such a plan.

■ Role and Potential of Science and Technology in the Region

One of the difficulties has to do with the uneven quality and quantity of scientific activities between Israel and the Arab countries in the region.

Prof. Antoine B. Zahlan, a Palestinian Christian, originally from the American University in Beirut published in 1980 a book called *Science and Science Policy in the Arab World*. From his thorough and objective analysis it is clear that most of the scientific research in the Arab countries are at a very low level. He states that the number of universities is growing steadily and around 1980 there were about fifty, and all together they enroll almost one million students. However, the research activity in most Arab universities is very limited, states Professor Zahlan. For instance, the level of support received for scholarly and scientific research at the *University of Khartoum in the Sudan* may be taken as a typical average. In 1974 the budget for research was £S20,000 out of a £S 9 million budget for the entire university. During the past ten years, however, a certain improvement can be seen in a few isolated places. The *Kuwait Institute of Scientific Research* (KISR) increased its research budget from KD 1.33 million in 1975–76 to KD 4 million in 1976–77, and in 1977–78 it was KD 6 million. Most of the research is of applied nature and related to the practical problems of development of Kuwait.

The University of Petroleum and Minerals (UPM) in Dhahran on the Gulf in Saudi Arabia has expanded into a full-fledged and extremely well-equipped university. A special Research Institute at UPM carries out advanced research in areas of direct interest to Saudi Arabia. The Institute has six technical divisions, i.e., Petroleum and Gas Technology; Energy Resource; Geology and Minerals; Water Resources and Environment; Metrology, Standards and Materials; Economic and Industrial Research. The Research Institute at UPM is very well equipped with satellite image interpretation and is the center in Saudi Arabia for space technology and remote sensing. It is a member of IFIAS and I was much impressed by the quality and programmes when I visited it in September 1985. In 1978, the Saudi Arabian *National Centre for Science and Technology* (SANCST) was established by virtue of a joint U.S.-Saudi Arabian agreement.

Space research and remote sensing seem to become prominent areas for the scientific institutions in Saudi Arabia, which was much boosted by the participation of one of the Saudi princes in the space shuttle crew in September 1985.

Probably the most impressive progress in scientific activities is that of *Jordan*. The enrollment of students (men and women) at the four universities is around 30,000 which is much for a population of 3.5 million.

Several other scientific institutions have been created recently both for basic research and for research on problems related to the development of Jordan. One of these is the *Royal Scientific Society* (RSS) which was founded in 1970 on initiative by its Chairman Crown Prince Hassan. RSS is a member of IFIAS and Prince Hassan is one of IFIAS' special advisors. His role in the development of science and technology in Jordan seems to be of very great importance. The budget of RSS is around $12 million. Like most other research institutions in the Arab countries its activities are directly related to the development needs of the country which is reflected in the departments of RSS; Mechanical Engineering; Solar Energy Research; Industrial Chemistry; Building Research; Electronic Services; Computer Services; Economics. A fully equipped electronics laboratory was a gift by Japan ($5 million) a few years ago.

On Prince Hassan's initiative has recently been established the *Jordan National Geographic Centre* in Amman which will be responsible for a modern land map system using the latest of remote sensing techniques. Not surprisingly this Centre has a high degree of military involvement in its activities. Judging from the visits in several Arab countries I have the impression that the interest in science and technology is much deeper and more widespread among the students in Jordan than in most other Arab countries.

In *Egypt* there are well established traditions in research and in the linking with Western industrialized countries, notably the U.S. and England. The educational standards are probably the highest among the Arab countries and the research is generally at a high level, for instance in medicine. However, when it comes to utilizing science and technology for industrial and other development purposes Egypt seems to have a long way to go. One reason is the lack of a widespread infrastructure (everything is concentrated to Cairo and Alexandria); another reason is the chaotic economic and social situation. *The National Research Centre* (NRC) is the largest science and technology center in the Arab world. It has more than 2000 employees and is strongly oriented towards the development problems of Egypt, i.e., agriculture, water resources, energy, building technology, metallurgy, etc. NRC is a member of IFIAS and I have visited it several times. I am much impressed with the level and commitment of the research staff at NRC but less so with the equipment and organization. I believe that the bureaucracy in general in Egypt is a great handicap for the effective development of the country.

I have had firsthand impressions of the science and technology institutions in the Arab countries mentioned above by personal visits just as I have firsthand information by many visits to the Weizmann Institute and the Jacob Blaustein Desert Research Institute in the Negev which are both members of IFIAS.

I know less about the science and technology institutions in such countries as Syria, Iraq and Lebanon. In the latter there was once a very active scientific community, also in basic research, at the American University in Beirut.

If we look at the *scientific manpower* in the Arab countries we find a constant expansion of educational facilities and popularization of education.

The Arab population of university graduates has been growing at a steady exponential rate, doubling every 5.3 years since the early 1950s. By 1980 there were about 1.5 million graduates in the Arab countries. At the present rate of growth we can expect about 12 million Arab university graduates by the year 2000.

However, we know that far from all of those who earn higher academic degrees are engaged in scientific research and not all who perform research actually make any significant or useful contributions. Accurate and regular surveys of the scientific manpower in the Arab countries do not seem to exist. If one uses the figure of 3000 for the number of full-time researchers in Egypt (a UNESCO study from 1976) and adds up the figures given for other Arab nations, one finds a total of some 7000 full-time researchers in the Arab world, an average of five (5) research workers per 100,000 of the population. The number of R&D workers in the "advanced" R&D countries (Egypt, Lebanon, Iraq) is about 10 per 100,000 of the population. In the rest of the Arab countries investigated in the UNESCO study, six countries had about one (1) per 100,000, and the remaining twelve are close to zero per 100,000.

The production of scientific publications shows a very low output for the Arab countries: around 930 papers in 1973 – instead of some 14,000 based on the normal average of two papers per full-time researchers.

I have gone into some detail of the infrastructure of science and technology in the Arab countries only to show that one can expect great difficulties in any major collaborative effort involving both Israel and the neighboring Arab countries, perhaps with one exception and that is Jordan.

Even if the funding and infrastructure situation in the Arab countries has improved somewhat since Zahlan published his report in 1980, the present sense of frustration is adequately expressed in a report from 1978 which tried to come to terms with one of the most difficult problems, that of integrating scientific research, economic development and the transactions with technology under way in the Arab world.

This report was a proposal for establishing an Arab Fund for Scientific and Technological Development with specific reference to the Arab world. The report concluded that:

"Scientific and technological impotency is only a natural concomitant of a society which is still characterized by widespread poverty, high levels of illiteracy, sometimes obsolete social attitudes, a work force still maintaining its present orientation, a class of cadres often demoralized and frustrated by their environment and the attraction of emigration and, last but not least, an elite that has amply proved in various circumstances the limits of its capacity to launch the economy towards 'take-off' into the industrial age."

I believe that the reasons for the relative backwardness of science and technology in the Arab countries are to be found not only at the infrastructural and organizational level but at a deeper level of values and attitudes vis à vis the role of science and technology in society and its practical utilization.

The well known Pakistan Nobel Laureate in physics Abdus Salam has presented a very outspoken statement on the failings of Arab science in the *Middle East Magazine* (June 1986). Salam concludes:

"Of all the civilizations on earth it is the Islamic one — both Arab and non-Arab — which is weakest in science. No other civilization talks of science in this way. It seems that those who do not want to do real science talk of Islamic science."

▪ The Challenges

In June 1981 IFIAS organized in Stockholm the first seminar in a series on "Science and Technology in Islam and the West." It was an attempt to begin to look carefully at the role of culture and values in the pursuit of science and technology. The Stockholm seminar was on "knowledge and values" while the other seminars in the series dealt with more specific subjects such as architecture, environment, and agriculture.

The seminar series resulted in a book called *The Touch of Midas: Science, Values and Environment in Islam and the West* (Ed. Ziauddin Sardar).[1] The present (value) crisis in science both in the West and Islam was at the center of discussion during this seminar series. It was stated that "Science is an activity of human beings acting and interacting, thus a social activity. Its knowledge, its statements, its techniques have been created by human beings. Scientific knowledge is therefore fundamentally social knowledge. As a social activity, science is clearly a product of history and of processes which occurred in time and place and involved human actors. These actors had lives not only in science, but in the wider societies of which they were a part." Dr. Helga Nowotny, Austria, who was one of the participants in the seminar series stated that "science has completed its programme of 'inner colonialization' and is now ready to drop its protective shield of providing well-being for all, as 80 percent of its research and development budget is directed towards military objectives." We are now forced to realize, continues Nowotny, that science and technology cannot be separated from their applications, use and abuse; neither can they be divorced from the social forces that are inherent in them. The challenge that the epistemology of science now faces is how to build new institutions of science which are at the same time concordant with its traditional concept of knowledge and can face the challenge coming from the outside.

■ Food Security in the Middle Eastern Region

February 8-10, 1986 the Arab Thought Forum arranged a symposium in Amman called "Food Security in the Arab and Third World." IFIAS Executive Committee was invited by Crown Prince Hassan to participate in the symposium. He is the founding chairman of the Arab Thought Forum. It was abundantly clear from the symposium that the Arab countries are moving fast away from a situation of self-sufficiency in food. Today the Arab countries import food worth $18 billion (Saudi Arabia's share is $5 billion). It is expected that the imports will increase to $27 billion in 1990 and $60 billion in the year 2000. The rapid population increase is one of the reasons. In 1986 there were 200 million inhabitants in the Arab countries which are expected to grow to about 300 million in the year 2000. Of these 70-80 percent are in African Arab countries which does not make the situation better. The Arab symposium participants were very open and frank in their criticism of the food situation in the Arab world. It was pointed out that India with only 30 percent more fertile land than Sudan but with a population of 740 million against Sudan's 22 million is able to feed itself while millions in the Sudan live at constant catastrophe. It was also mentioned that Pakistan is able to export food worth about $1 billion.

Reference was made several times to the need for a functioning Arab common market but it was also pointed out that only 10 percent of the food export from Arab countries goes to other Arab countries.

Crown Prince Hassan mentioned that he had given up hope to achieve food self-sufficiency through the political channels in the Arab countries and that he was now discussing with private investors and companies in London and on Wall Street investment possibilities in major food and agriculture programmes. According to him, there is a need for a new opening for European-Arab country cooperation in this area.

At the Arab summit in Amman in 1981 it had been agreed that $5 billion should be invested in food production in the Arab world during a development decade. Still today nothing has happened, which is not due to lack of a framework or lack of money. It was generally agreed at the Amman symposium in February that the inaction is because the political management of the Arab economic system is defective. Even if Saudi Arabia alone could afford the entire investment in the Sudan to make its enormous agricultural potential effective it will not be done because of political uncertainty and mismanagement. The Sudanese potential is about 40 million hectares but only 8 million are now being cultivated.

The Arab world should — it was agreed — concentrate on *one* major common issue, that of food security.

Food vulnerability leads to cultural vulnerability, technical vulnerability, political vulnerability and military vulnerability. This can only be overcome by a joint Arab action which would also involve a great portion of science and technology programmes. There was, however, not much hope that an Arab common market would function soon and it was concluded that each individual country should improve its own food security as much as possible before relying on food trade with other Arab countries.

One of the key problems for improved food production is the *access to water*, either in rivers, aquifers or from rain. Israel is said to use five times as much water per head as its less industrialized and intensively-farmed neighbors. It is essential that new sources of water are exploited and better use of existing sources is implemented in the region. It was pointed out that no study of the Jordan valley water situation had been done since the Arab water summit in 1964. Reference was made to the fact that the Nubian sandstone aquifer under the Sinai and the Negev holds 200 billion cubic meters of water, 70 billion cubic meters of which are under the Negev. Agricultural settlements in the Negev suggest that the water is low enough in salt content to be suitable for irrigation. Since the water, like that found under the Sahara and Arabia, cannot be replenished, its extraction is analogous to the extraction of oil. *A long-range plan must be devised for managing these resources*, which should be a challenging goal for any regional cooperation. The financial, legal, social, environmental and technological aspects of regional utilization of aquifer water should constitute a sufficiently challenging task for scientists and engineers in the region. It is a true large-scale infrastructure project.

In parallel with the enhancement of the water utilization in arid zones should be launched a *research programme in plant genetics and biotechnology* for improvements and adaptation of plants to the special prevailing ecological conditions in arid zones. This and *Controlled Environmental Agriculture* (CEA) have been discussed in the paper by Amos Richmond "Greening of the Desert," mentioned earlier.

Another area of modern technology related to large-scale resource utilization is that of *Remote Sensing* which should also be very suitable for regional cooperation. Space photographs allow us to map unknown regions, to locate fertile soils (reflectively of Kaolinite), and select areas with potential groundwater resources. In desert regions and arid areas that are prone to droughts these points can make a difference between life and death. The space sciences applications to agricultural development are many and promising.

The well-known former science advisor to the late President Sadat of Egypt, Dr. Farouk El-Baz, has made a proposal for the creation of an *International Centre for Desert Research* (ICDR) somewhere in the Middle East.

It is now generally accepted that a fundamental understanding of deserts and arid regions can only be achieved through a broadly based interdisciplinary approach. In this approach it is essential to consider the desertification mechanisms as complex interactions of both physical and ecological processes. The proposed ICDR will involve a large community of scientists in many disciplines to be involved in planning and execution of projects, seminars, and training programmes.

IFIAS has been approached as a possible partner in the effort to establish ICDR somewhere. Two strong candidates for the location seem to be Jordan and Saudi Arabia.

Still another area in which regional cooperation in science and technology might prove useful is that of *Energy*. Not all countries in the region have access to cheap oil or natural gas and some countries have fuel wood as the dominating source of energy. Solar energy is abundant and Israel has come very far in the technical utilization of solar energy. Even Jordan and Egypt have quite advanced R&D programmes in solar energy.

Several other areas of science and technology could be mentioned which would be good candidates for regional cooperation in the Middle East. The problems to get such cooperation started are, however, not scientific or technological but political and psychological as was pointed out earlier. A few necessary, but not sufficient conditions for regional cooperation in science and technology can be given:

(1) The level of science and technology of the countries involved in a particular field must be reasonably equal so as to provide for a genuine "give and take."

(2) The strategy must be that of a positive-sum-game, i.e., everyone should gain somewhat in the long run.

(3) The participation of at least one outside neutral party from another region (e.g., Europe) or organization (e.g., IFIAS) might facilitate the cooperation in science and technology.

(4) The role of the private sector (industry, banks, nongovernmental research organizations) will probably be of great importance.

(5) Begin with a few concrete projects, for instance, a water plan for arid zone development ("Greening of the Deserts").

■ Notes

1. Manchester University Press, 1984.

....

13

Liberalization of Service Transactions

Brian Hindley

The current state of relations between Israel and her neighbors inevitably means that much discussion of economic cooperation is in fact about how to obtain a position in which economic cooperation becomes feasible. My topic yields little contribution to that debate, although a service – the transfer of know-how – is widely regarded as the largest economic inducement to cooperation that Israel can offer its neighbors.

It is also important, however, to have some idea of what a state of cooperation might entail, both in terms of possible economic configurations and of the legal structures that would underpin them. From this point of view, two factors, both concerned with geography, suggest that in a state of peace, services might be important in trade between Israel and its neighbors.

The first is that the most direct transport links between Israel's neighbors run through Israeli territory. In a state of peace, therefore, a variety of transport and communications links between neighboring states would cross Israel.[1] Transport and communications are themselves services. In addition, however, the supply of these services would necessarily entail the supply of others – insurance, repair, storage and so on.

The second point concerns proximity. Many services probably are more easily supplied at close range than at a distance. The geographical proximity of economies in the Middle East therefore implies the possibility that services might eventually be more important in commerce between Middle-Eastern states than between states in the world at large.

The possibility of realizing this potential obviously depends primarily upon circumstances in the region. However, the probability of realization will also be influenced by events in the world at large.

The attention given to international service sector issues by governments anywhere in the world, for example, will depend upon official perceptions of the significance of those issues – and those perceptions have visibly changed over the past decade. But such attention also will depend on whether fruitful means of negotiating on international service issues emerge from the current diplomatic initiatives. What I propose to do, therefore, is to present some notion of how matters stand in the world at large with respect to these questions.

■ Services in Current International Economic Diplomacy

The fact that international transactions in the service sector are close to the center of current international economic diplomacy is due almost entirely to the efforts of the United States. The U.S. has been pressing hard to place trade in services on the agenda of the forthcoming round of General Agreement on Trade and Tariffs (GATT) trade talks. It also has insisted that the subject should have a high priority in a variety of bilateral contexts, notably including that of the Israel-U.S. free trade area.

International trade in services is a new topic for diplomacy and also for academic research. Current interest in the subject had its origins in neither of these areas. It stems, rather from the business concerns of U.S. service suppliers, who believe that their development of foreign markets is seriously inhibited by restrictions placed upon their activities by governments abroad. Both diplomats and academics concerned with trade policy have (truth to tell) been dragged in the wake of events created by this concern.

These commercial antecedents persuade some that the subject lacks intellectual interest or policy importance. Whatever the impetus for inspection of the service sector and international trade in services, however, examination of the basic facts makes it quite clear that it would be foolish to accept that position. As a recent UNCTAD document[2] puts it, "The importance of the services sector in the world economy is demonstrated by its large share of world GDP (amounting in 1980 to some 65 percent) and by its share (25.4 percent or roughly $610 billion) of current account credits." The exact numbers that are attached to the size of the global services sector obviously depend upon the definition of services employed. The more important point is that services are not on any definition trivial.

It is a fact, moreover, that international trade treaties focus on goods and neglect services. The GATT, for example, makes virtually no mention of services; and where they do appear, it is largely as a complement to trade in goods. As a result, governments are almost entirely unrestrained by legal factors either in the level of protection they may offer to domestic service producers or the means by which they can provide it. In this state of affairs, many governments supply to their domestic service industries a level of protection against foreign competition that appears extraordinary when compared with manufacturing industry.

This fact, together with the point noted above that the effective supply of many services requires geographic proximity of buyer and seller, may go some way to explain the discrepancy between services as a fraction of GDP and of international trade. It may also go some way to explain the hostility aroused by the United States proposals for negotiating rules on services in GATT. Developing countries, especially, have been antagonistic to those proposals.

▪ Defining Services

Despite the fact that services are a focus of international economic diplomacy and despite the attention they recently have received from academic economists, there is no generally accepted definition of the term "services." The literature nevertheless abounds with attributions of characteristics to services.[3]

For example, services are often said to be technically unprogressive.[4] Economic models of international trade which turn upon the presence in the economy of nontraded goods often expressly identify nontradeables with services. And a recent piece asserts that "According to conventional wisdom, services are income-elastic, labor-intensive, and have a high value-added share" but, failing to find empirical conformation for these propositions, seems inclined to conclude that there is no real difference between goods and services.[5]

There are also several substitutes for a definition. One widely-used example of this is the characterization of services as a residual. For calculations of the importance of services in the GNP or in employment, for example, services implicitly are defined as what is left over after agriculture and fishing, extractive industries, and manufacturing have been removed.

A problem with residual definition, however, is that the residual might contain more than one class that it would be useful to separate for some purposes. As the residual not-mining contains agriculture and manufacturing, which for some purposes are usefully distinguished, so the residual that is not-extraction, not-agriculture and not-manufacturing may contain several classes of activity that it would be useful to distinguish. This problem may be particularly acute in the case of services. As noted above, in many economies the residual "services" is larger than what is positively defined.

Another widely-used substitute for a definition is a list. Many discussions of services are prefaced with a list. For example "A typical list of services might include accounting; advertising; banking and financial services;

communications; education; engineering; architecture and construction; franchising; health care; insurance; legal services; recreation and entertainment; transport; and travel and tourism."[6]

For many purposes — including specification of what one wants to negotiate about — a list might be adequate. For purposes of analysis, on the other hand, a firmer base for conceptualization than is implied by resort to a list seems desirable.

Probably the most useful and intellectually stimulating effort to define "services" is that of Professor Hill (1977). Hill's basic definition of a service is:

> . . . a change in the condition of a person, or of a good belonging to some economic unit, which is brought about as a result of the activity of some other economic unit, with the prior agreement of the former person or economic unit.(p. 318)

There are three important elements in this definition (which, of course, Hill elaborates upon in his article).

The first is that service brings about a *change* in condition. This carries the implication that services are not, as sometimes described, like goods that perish especially quickly, but are in a different logical category than goods.

The second is that service occurs *between* economic units. This element gives rise to substantial problems of measurement. The same activity might sometimes be classified as one thing and sometimes as another. If households start washing their own clothes instead of taking them to a commercial laundry, for example, the activity will disappear from the national accounts; and painting a car might sometimes be part of a manufacturing process and sometimes a service.

More generally, the share of "services" in GDP or employment could show very large changes without any change in the activity of the bulk of persons within the economy. If a firm primarily engaged in manufacturing supplies its own advertising or accounting or window-cleaning in-house, the persons engaged in these activities will be classified as employed in manufacturing. The firm might decide to organize these activities in new companies, however, and to purchase the services from them on an out-of-house basis. Then (even though the same persons might provide the service in either case) the activities will be classified as services and the recorded share of services in employment will rise.

The third element in Hill's definition is the condition of prior agreement. Remove that clause from the definition above, and what remains is the definition of an externality.

That these are all essential elements of a satisfactory definition of a service seems beyond doubt. Even Hill's definition, however, does not self-evidently extend to activities such as banking and insurance (nor does the discussion in his article remove that difficulty). These activities conventionally are regarded as services, and surely *are* services on any satisfactory definition of that term.

The problem might be fixed by defining "the condition of a person" in the quotation above to include the property rights owned by that person. Nevertheless, it seems as useful, for present purposes, to return to the notion of services as a residual and the problem of different types of activity that it might be useful to distinguish. Services can be divided into three functional types of activity that exhaust the category that we wish to refer to as services. They are:

(a) *Locational Services* (transport, posts and telecommunications, TV and radio, and perhaps water, gas and electricity . . .) in which the essence of what is done is the conveyance of something from one geographical location to another.

(b) *Services based upon ownership of specialized human or physical capital* (lawyers, doctors, sportsmen and other entertainers, key-cutters, TV repairers . . .). Many of the activities in this category require, or traditionally have required, geographical proximity of the provider of the service and the person or good that is the subject of the activity. The extent to which this is true, however, depends upon the development of locational services. It is possible for a person in San Francisco to use a lawyer based in New York or London. Haircuts and surgery still require physical proximity – but that may not be a permanent state of affairs.

(c) *Intermediary Services* (banking, insurance, wholesale and retail trades, bookmaking, auto rental, libraries, stockbroking, real estate sales . . .). The essence of these activities is that they provide a contact between pairs of persons with offsetting excess demands. In a world of zero search and transaction costs, therefore, these activities would not exist, or would exist in a different form and with different primary functions than they have today – house-sellers and house-buyers would not need to pay an agent to find one another; and groups of persons could club together to place funds in trust for those of their number who suffered specified misfortunes.

It also follows that changes in search costs (as brought about by technical change in locational services) will affect these activities. Though the ultimate nature of this effect is unclear, a current manifestation is the internationalization of many of the activities in this category – they have provided much of the pressure for the introduction of services into the GATT.

There are obvious overlaps and combinations between these types of activities. For example, running an airline calls for the possession of specialized human capital – but the object of the demand of the purchaser of airline tickets is transportation, not, except as a derived demand, the skill of the manager of the airline. On the other hand, that manager might supply his skill directly to another airline as a consultant – he would then be supplying a different category of service.

What is more immediately relevant is that these categories of service have different attributes and raise policy problems. Technical progress, for example, has been, and continues to be, extremely rapid in locational services. A string quartet, it is true, still calls for the same labor input as two centuries ago: the number of ears that a single performance can reach is vastly greater, however.

In terms of policy, locational services traditionally have been subject to problems of natural monopoly. The provision of these services tend to require specialized routes (roads, rails, cables, pipes, satellites . . .) and/or apparatus for transmitting and receiving (telephone exchanges, airports, ports and harbors . . .) which, if privately owned, preclude any approximation of perfect competition.

There is a variety of regulatory responses to this problem. State ownership probably is the most common. The powers of nationalized PTTs now constitute major problems for the international organization of telecommunications and for industries based upon telecommunications.

Natural monopoly is not an issue in either of the other categories, and regulation of them has different forms and rationales. In the case of services based upon the ownership of specialized human capital, regulation typically takes the form of certification of the competence of suppliers by governments or by agencies appointed by governments. Such certification is often a necessary legal condition of practice.

Producers of intermediary services, on the other hand, are usually subject to fiduciary regulation. Insurance companies and banks, for example, are typically required to hold some specified minimum level of reserves against their liabilities.

Although natural monopoly is not an issue in these two categories, they most certainly are not free from problems of imperfect competition. Certificating authorities, for example, have the potential, through their control of entry, of creating monopoly rents for members of the relevant profession or craft. One powerful theory of regulation is that regulatory powers are "captured" by the suppliers putatively subject to them and used by them to suppress competition.[7]

■ Differences Between Goods and Services

Hindley and Smith (1984) argue that the theory of comparative advantage applies to services as well as to goods. That proposition obviously does not imply that goods and services are the same in all respects. Here, I shall focus on some of the differences.

There are at least three differences that are relevant to policy. They are:

(a) the *means* by which domestic service suppliers are protected;

(b) the fact that efficient delivery of many services requires the producer of the service to have a presence in the buyer's market, so that international service transactions often entail some form of international factor movement;[8] and

(c) the frequency and type of regulation of service industries.

I shall discuss each of these in turn.

■ Protection Against Foreign Producers

Because of the "invisible" properties of services, domestic service suppliers cannot usually be protected against foreign competition by means of tariffs. Service industries typically are protected by means which are analogous to "gray area measures" or nontariff barriers (NTBs) to trade in goods.

Thus, protection is provided by methods such as outright prohibitions on foreign suppliers or by laws, regulations, and administrative actions which bear with a particularly heavy weight on foreign suppliers. Protection is also supplied to domestic producers (to jump ahead) by barriers to the establishment of foreign service suppliers.

This characteristic of protection in service industries goes some way to explain both the past neglect of services in the General Agreement on Tariffs and Trade (GATT) and the current interest in them. When the GATT was formed, in the aftermath of World War II, border measures affecting trade in goods—tariffs and quotas for example—were a severe and evident problem whose solution took a natural priority. But since trade in services is not controlled by those means, the focus on border measures had the effect of excluding trade in services from attention.

As border measures affecting trade in goods were reduced through successive GATT negotiations, however, an array of nontariff barriers appeared, some of which held (and hold) the potential to neutralize or reverse the effects of negotiated declines in tariffs. An attempt to come to grips with this problem was a major part of the business of the last round of trade talks (the Tokyo round). But if efforts were to be made in the GATT to deal with this kind of problem for *goods* trade, there seemed no good reason (especially to service suppliers in the United States) to ignore the same kind of problem in *services* trade.

The GATT process, however, so far as been much more successful in reducing tariff rates than it has in controlling nontariff barriers. Moreover, the fact that no such central and transparent means of protection as tariffs exists for the service sector raises a further problem.

The GATT (and virtually every other treaty concerning trade) contains a variety of safeguard clauses, permitting increases in, or restoration of, protection when "vital interests" are threatened by trade. GATT Article XIX, for example, allows GATT members to use tariffs to protect import-competing industries that are threatened by "sudden surges of imports." That an agreement on services should fail to contain some equivalent is inconceivable: many governments have objectives with regard to service industries which they take to be vital.

Since service industries can only be protected by nontariff means, however, this leads to the question of what NTB will be approved, and in what circumstances, for use in safeguard actions. This is not an issue that occurs in goods trade, where tariffs provide a "transparent" means of protection.

▪ International Service Transactions and Factor Movements

As noted above, many of the most effective barriers to international transactions in the service sector take the form of restrictions on establishment. Complete liberalization of services transactions therefore probably would lead to an increase in the international movement of factors for the purpose of supplying services.

In the GATT context, the issue is often raised by developing countries, and therefore appears as a problem of foreign *investment*. That it should appear in this form, however, is a consequence of the way in which services issues have been posed. From an analytical point of view, the need of service industries that are capital or skilled-labor intensive to locate those factors in potential markets in order to sell their products is symmetrical with the need of producers of labor-intensive services to locate that factor in potential markets in order to sell their services.

In an effort to avoid the difficult and contentious issues raised by direct foreign investment and by any claim of a "right of establishment" in a foreign market (and also, perhaps, to avoid the at least equally contentious issues that would be raised by a counter-claim by developing countries for a right of temporary residence abroad of labor for the purpose of selling services), the United States government has suggested that negotiations should be restricted to nonfactor services. Thus, it proposes that the focus should be on services that can be traded in the conventional sense of a person or firm in one country selling something to a person or firm located in another country without relocation of either buyer or seller.

The attempt to avoid one problem, however, creates others. One of these appears in the form of a conflict within the U.S. on its negotiating position. Whatever the tactical advantages of an approach to a GATT negotiation that focuses on traded services, many U.S. service suppliers perceive their major international problem as the lack of a right of establishment in foreign markets. They, therefore, see little point in a negotiation that does not cover rights of establishment, and are pressing for its inclusion in the U.S. negotiating position.

The focus on tradeable services raises a different problem when viewed from the standpoint of developing countries. Although it may be true that service suppliers based in developed countries would find it easier to sell services from local establishments, it is also true that almost all of the services for which trade without establishment is possible are services in which developed countries currently appear to possess a comparative advantage (for example, banking and financial services and insurance). Any successful measure of liberalization in this restricted sense therefore probably would mean that developing countries increased their imports of services from developed countries without any compensating increase in their exports of services.[9]

In GATT terms, this raises a major problem. A GATT negotiation centers upon an exchange of "concessions," where a concession is defined as a reduction in restrictions on imports and where concessions from other countries are won at the "cost" of relaxations in one's own import regime.

Economists are inclined to scoff at the language of GATT negotiations. Ricardo's demonstration of the principle of comparative advantage, they say, destroyed once and for all the possibility of regarding increased openness to imports as a cost. Economic analysis, however, offers no solution to the *political* problem that is addressed by concessions in the GATT process.

The structure of protection in a particular country at a particular time must be taken to represent the outcome of some process of *political* equilibration. To change the protective structure, therefore, it is necessary to change the factors that support the underlying political equilibrium.

A multilateral exchange of concessions offers one means of achieving this. By changing the opportunities available to actors in the domestic political process—by providing exporters, for example, with a direct connection between the barriers they face in foreign markets and their own country's level of protection against imports—the multilateral process alters their economic interests. Hence, the offer of an exchange of "concessions" is likely to help a government that would like to liberalize but faces domestic opposition, and to put pressure on a government that is not persuaded of the case for liberalization.

The United States suggestion that the GATT negotiation be restricted to tradeable nonfactor services, however, defines services in such a way that comparative advantage lies predominantly with developed countries. Hence, the great bulk of potential GATT concessions in services lie in the gift of the developing countries, and this seems to preclude the possibility of an equal *exchange* of concessions between developed and developing countries within the service sector. This may be a cause of the hostility of some developing country governments to the suggestion that services should be discussed in the GATT. It certainly has done nothing to relieve that hostility.

One response to this problem has been to point to the economic gains available to developing countries as a result of liberalization in their service sectors. That such gains exist seems very likely.[10] To point to them in this context, however, misses the point. These gains are available from unilateral action; but the governments of developing countries have not exercised their option to act unilaterally. The offer of gains that they could obtain through unilateral action seems unlikely to persuade them to join a multilateral liberalization. (Though if the tactic *were* successful, it could be applied to many aspects of developed country trade policy — for example, to protection of agriculture by Japan or the EEC or to protection of textiles and clothing by the EEC and the U.S.).

These two problems — the wish of U.S. service suppliers to obtain rights of establishment and the lack of "concessions" for developing countries — have a single potential solution. It is to introduce rights of establishment defined so as to include a right to temporarily locate labor in a country for the purpose of supplying a service.[11]

This course is widely rejected as politically infeasible. The judgment may be correct. Nevertheless, the analytical basis for the suggestion that developing countries will gain from liberalization of heavily-protected service sectors also leads to the suggestion that developed countries will gain from liberalization. A construction company, for example, cannot construct a road or factory at home and ship it abroad. A right to temporarily locate labor in a foreign country for the purpose of construction might well permit developing country "exports" of roads and factories to the mutual benefit of developing and developed countries.

■ Regulation

The third relevant characteristic of services is that the industries producing them are often subject to regulation. It is clear that regulatory powers can be used to create barriers to trade (so that from that point of view they could be treated as a particular form of NTB). Regulation of service industries, however, is widely-regarded as a justified measure of public policy and as essential to the efficient supply of the regulated service. As when health and safety regulations are used to impede trade in goods, therefore, identification of the point at which legitimate action ends and protection against foreign competition begins is not easy.

From the point of view of international transactions, however, the central problem is created by the mere fact of regulation. It is that services are regulated within national jurisdictions but that the form and/or level of regulation differs between jurisdictions.

Regulation, however, is likely to affect the costs of producers of the service. Hence, when producers subject to the regulations of country A are free to sell services in country B without being subject to the B regulatory system, there is not only competition between A and B producers — there is also competition between the national regulatory systems of A and B. Thus, suppliers subject to a system which requires larger reserves, more years of education, or higher minimum prices are likely to claim that they are at a competitive disadvantage against suppliers who are subject to less stringent requirements.

The problem can appear either as an issue of trade or as one of establishment. It is likely to occur as a matter of establishment in services based upon the possession of specialized human-capital, where transactions demand proximity. If standards of certification for medical practice are higher in A than in B, for example, but certification in B implies a right of establishment in A, practitioners in A are likely to protest against the dilution of standards.

The trade aspect of the problem is more interesting in the present context. It occurs when producers established in B are free to sell services in A without being established in A or otherwise subject to the A regulatory system. The efficiency basis for objections to trade in nationally-regulated services is that suppliers subject to the heaviest regulatory requirement will be penalized in competition.

The argument assumes one of two things, however. Either it assumes that the more stringent requirements are not valuable to buyers of the service (or, more precisely, that buyers do not value them at a level commensurate with their cost) or that buyers are ignorant of the advantages that will accrue to them from dealing with suppliers subject to these more stringent requirements.

Buyers may perceive the value to them of the more stringent regulation but not think it worth the extra cost (as they might prefer to buy a VW rather than a Mercedes). In that case, suppliers subject to the more demanding system will lose as a result of trade. However, their losses in this case do not seem to provide a secure basis in the public interest for protecting suppliers subject to the more demanding regulatory system from the effect of competition.

Arguments for preventing competition between regulatory systems, however, are likely to be based on one of the classic rationales for regulation, which is that buyers are not well-informed. Specifically, the argument is likely to be based on the proposition that buyers do not correctly perceive the value to them of the more stringent regulations.

Suppose that country A has a demanding regulatory system, and country B a less demanding one. Producers of services established in B therefore are able to offer a service which, at least on the surface, is more attractive than that offered by producers established in A. The problem is that if suppliers from B can freely sell in A, some buyers in A might buy the B service under the mistaken impression that it also offers the advantages, whatever they may be, of the A regulatory system.

The opening of trade in the service between A and B certainly creates a class of potential gainers (those whose interests dictate the purchase of the foreign service and who are now able to purchase it). However, it also creates a class of potential losers (those who ought to buy the A service but are now free to make the mistake of buying the B service). Moreover, since the argument turns upon misinformation, there is no obvious way of assessing the losses relative the gains.

The problem could be avoided by harmonizing the requirements of the A and B regulatory systems. Yet there is then a question that turns upon the difficult issue of the structure of an optimal regulatory system. Should A accept B's regulations or *vice versa* of what compromise should be struck?

This problem is particularly evident in the EEC. The Treaty of Rome is a much stronger instrument than it would be possible to negotiate in the world at large, and includes an independent Court of Justice to rule on its interpretation. Despite that, progress towards liberalization of trade in services within the EEC has been stalled for some considerable time on exactly the issue of competition between regulatory systems.[12]

An exponent of the public interest theory of regulation might have expected that it would be easier to obtain agreement among the regulatory authorities of the EEC than has in fact proved to be the case. On the other hand, these difficulties will not cause great surprise among adherents of the capture theory of regulation.

■ Concluding Comment

At the start of this paper, I commented that to sustain interest on multilateral arrangements for international trade in services, it would be necessary to develop and demonstrate fruitful modes of negotiating on services. I hope that point of the comment has been made clearer by the intervening pages. The economic case for *unilateral* liberalization of international trans-actions in services is very strong. The technical difficulties in the way of achieving an enforceable *multilateral* agreement are very great (and the difficulty of solving them is, of course, increased by political difficulties).

Negotiators in the 1980s have one major asset. It is that there is now a great deal of *evidently* protectionist action in service sectors. There is therefore a layer of actions that it will be technically easy to strip away (though the politics of the operation is unlikely to reflect that fact).

If such a layer exists for the world at large, however, a much thicker one exists in the case of Israel and its neighbors. If there is *any* movement in this area, therefore, there is a good distance to be travelled before the subtleties discussed in this paper become relevant. It is unusual to wish upon people that they should have to cope with intractable technical problems of law and economics relating to trade. In the case of the countries of the Middle East, however, that wish seems appropriate.

■ Notes

1. I believe that an unactivated clause of the Peace Treaty between Egypt and Israel calls for a road connecting Egypt and Jordan.

2. UNCTAD Secretariat: *Production and trade in services, policies and the underlying factors bearing upon international service transactions* (TD/B/941, March 1, 1983)

3. Riddle (1986) provides a particularly good survey.

4. Bhagwati (1984) provides a stimulating discussion of technical progress in services. Good discussions of the problems of measurement of productivity in services (and of sector economies in general) appear in Inman (1985).

5. The quotation is from Norman and Strandenes (1985).

6. The quotation is from a forthcoming *World Development Report.*

7. The classic sources on the capture theory of regulation are Stigler (1971) and Peltzman (1976). Rottenburg (1980) provides a useful survey of relevant theory and evidence.

8. Samson and Snape (1985) provide a useful review of this aspect of international transactions in services.

9. Problems of the balance of payments and a variety of other developing country concerns regarding the service sector are analyzed in Hindley (1982).

10. Hindley and Smith (1984) consider arguments to the contrary in some detail.

11. Jagdish Bhagwati in the *Financial Times* of November 27, 1985 has urged forcefully that balance in the negotiations requires this extension.

Another possibility, of course, would be to exchange concessions in services for concessions in goods; but what concessions on goods trade the developed countries might be willing to make is entirely unclear — their current posture seems rather to make the withdrawal of such concessions likely.

12. Hindley (1986) gives a detailed discussion of the problems of the service sector in the EEC.

■ References

Bhagwati, Jagdish (1985) "Trade in Services and Developing Countries" Xth Annual Geneva Association Lecture delivered at the London School of Economics, November: forthcoming in *Geneva Papers on Risk and Insurance*.

Bhagwati, Jagdish (1984) "Splintering and Disembodiment of Services and Developing Countries" *The World Economy* (June).

Hill, T. P. (1977) "On Goods and Services" *Review of Income and Wealth* (December).

Hindley, Brian (1982) *Economic Analysis and Insurance Policy in the Third World* (London: Trade Policy Research Centre).

Hindley, Brian and Alasdair Smith (1984) "Comparative Advantage and Trade in Services" *The World Economy* (December) pp. 369-389.

Hindley, Brian (1986) "Trade in Services within the European Community" paper prepared for a conference on *Protection in the World Economy* Weltwirtschaft Institute, Kiel, June.

Inman, Robert P. (Ed) (1985) "Managing the Service Economy" (Cambridge: Cambridge University Press).

Norman, Victor D. and Siri P. Strandenes "Trade-in Services and Developing Countries: Some Comments" Forthcoming with Bhagwati (1985).

Peltzman, Sam (1976) "Towards a More General Theory of Regulation" *Journal of Law and Economics* (August) pp. 211-240.

Riddle, Dorothy L. (1986) *Service-Led Growth* (New York: Praeger).

Rottenburg, Simon (Ed) (1980) *Occupational Licensure and Regulation* (Washington D.C.: American Enterprise Institute for Public Policy Research).

Gary P. Samson and Richard H. Snape "Identifying the Issues in Trade in Services" *The World Economy* (June, 1985).

Stigler, George J. (1971) "The Theory of Economic Regulation" *Bell Journal of Economics*.

UNCTAD Secretariat (1983): *Production and trade in services, policies and the underlying factors bearing upon international service transactions* (TD/B/941, March 1).

Section IV

Suggestions for and Analysis
of Specific Projects
in the Middle East

Each of the six studies in this section analyzes a specific aspect of peace. Topics covered include trade, economic ties, and use of water resources. Fishelson's paper is a summary of potential areas of cooperation on which initial analysis has already been done by the Armand Hammer Fund for Economic Cooperation in the Middle East at the Interdisciplinary Center for Technological Forecasting.

Hirsch describes the trade regime that could be constructed in the region once the political situation makes it feasible. Such a regime would increase the economic welfare of all the countries concerned and create vested interests in peace. The trade involved would be determined by two major factors, proximity and economies of scale. These two factors would lead to export creation and increased output. Hirsch uses the textiles and clothing industries and fertilizers as examples of industries in which industrial cooperation would be likely to be part of the trade regime.

Meital surveys the agreements and arrangements that were included in the framework of normalization of economic relations between Egypt and Israel. He reports and comments on one aspect of peace—the flow of tourists in the 1979-84 period.

The flow of tourists is quite stable. Israeli tourists to Egypt are numerous enough to be important to the Egyptian tourist industry. The flows of Israel-Egypt and Egypt-Israel tourism are about equal. However, while about 17 percent of the flow from Israel to Egypt is Israelis, the share of Egyptians in the Egypt-Israel flow is very small. These results are significant in themselves and have important implications in coming stages of the peace process.

Kally focuses on one aspect of cooperation, that of water resource development. He feels that cooperation in water resource development can make a more significant contribution to the establishment of peace than any other form of cooperation. The importance of water is so great because water played a key role in past regional conflicts, and there is currently a desperate need to solve the regional water crisis. Furthermore, cooperation in water resources development would contribute directly to the welfare of the West Bank and Gaza and thus, help to solve part of the economic issues that are unique to these areas and are likely to undermine peace efforts.

Raz concentrates on a specific project that cannot be undertaken without initial steps towards peace but once completed it would help in the adherence to peace; the Arava port he describes would serve both Israel and Jordan. Raz elaborates upon the technological aspects and potential of this port and its economic significance for the two countries, the entire region, and the world. Once in operation, it would be in the interest of all concerned parties to keep it operational, and with it, peace.

Ajami presents a proposal for economic cooperation between Israel and Southern Lebanon(SL). The main purpose of such cooperation would be to stabilize a region that is currently stricken by political uncertainty, military unrest, and poverty. The success of the project requires economic aid from outside the region. Such a multinational economic aid program would also ensure the active involvement of the countries providing the aid.

The major resource of SL is its labor force. Ajami sees good potential prospects for its gainful employment once Israeli know-how and management are brought in.

Fishelson reports on the projects that have been analyzed by the research team at the Interdisciplinary Center for Technological Analysis and Forecasting (ICTAF) as part of the Armand Hammer Project for Economic Cooperation in the Middle East. The criteria for choosing the projects were:

1) They involve more than one country
2) They yield net benefits to each participating country
3) They further strengthen the vested interests of participant countries in peace

The projects undertaken, which fulfilled these criteria, are distributed over numerous fields ranging from infrastructure (water, transportation, ports) to economic sectors (agriculture, energy, tourism) and to specific industries (fertilizers, cement, textiles and clothing).

Inter-country trade, mainly in the form of trade diversion, received a special treatment at the conference.

From their short description, their analyses project a clear message to "start these projects."

14

Trade Regimes in the Middle East

Seev Hirsch

■ Introduction

Discussion of trade regimes within the context of the Middle East peace process at this time seems utopian indeed. Obviously, a political settlement of the extremely difficult questions facing Israel and its Arab neighbors must precede any discussion of future economic relations. Moreover, it can be rightly argued that it is the nature of the political settlement which will provide the framework for economic relations and not the other way around.

The resolution of the Palestine question, to give but one example, will surely have most profound effects on the kind of economic relations which Israel and its neighbors can expect to develop. The six years that have passed since the conclusion of the Egyptian-Israel peace treaty have clearly shown that at least as far as the Middle East is concerned, political considerations dominate economic ones. Economic constraints may limit the capacity of the parties to wage war against each other; they are unlikely to move them towards peace.

Having acknowledged the primacy of political considerations it still makes sense to engage in speculation about the possible nature of trade regimes in the Middle East. This view can be justified by the history of the Middle East Peace process. To date, the Middle East peace process encompasses only Israel and Egypt, the most populous Arab country, the traditional leader of the Arab world, and leading proponent of the war between Israel and its Arab neighbors, up to and including the Yom-Kippur war of 1973.

Extension of the peace process to other countries and to the Palestinians has thus far proved impossible. This is no accident. It is extremely difficult to devise a viable and mutually acceptable solution which reconciles the national claims, aspirations and security requirements of Israel and its Arab neighbors. Let us recall, however, that some of the specific studies financed by the Hammer Fund for Economic Cooperation in the Middle East – for example, the Nile Water project — were first conceived during the Yom-Kip-pur war of 1973. Four years later the world held its breath as President Sadat stepped out of his plane at Ben-Gurion Airport and declared his country's readiness to engage in the peace process with Israel. The gulf which still separates us is surely less wide than the bridges already built.

Under these circumstances, it makes sense to plan ahead for the day in which the major remaining political obstacles to peace will be removed. Bearing in mind, moreover, that all economic transactions contain elements of conflict and that it takes time and efforts to minimize these elements, it is surely not too early to start thinking about the nature of future Arab-Israeli economic relations under conditions of peace. Economic relations in general and trade regimes in particular have an important role to play in this context.

The remainder of this paper outlines a framework for such a regime. Due to the reasons mentioned above it deals only with those aspects of future trade regimes which are insensitive to the specifics of the political settle-ment. The discussion which follows explicitly recognizes the supremacy of political over economic considerations when considering alternative institu-tional arrangements.

■ Political and Economic Criteria for a Middle East Trade Regime

Any Middle East trade regime (METR) will be based on the participat-ing countries' present economic realities which cannot be expected to change drastically in the short term. It will have to take into account the ex-treme diversity characterizing the region's economies, which vary in size, dis-tribution of resources and of income, level of economic development and industrialization, importance of foreign trade, availability of foreign ex-change, economic organization, degree of government control, as well as size and role of the public sector.

More important perhaps, a METR will have to contend for the foresee-able future with continued opposition to peace. Being motivated by deep-seated religious and political considerations this opposition is likely to be a potent factor which cannot be ignored in the process of designing a METR, which is supposed to enhance the peace process.

Seeking a formula which makes it possible to take into account political as well as economic factors within the peacemaking context, the present author, together with his colleagues, Ruth Arad and Alfred Tovias, developed the concept of vested interest in peace (VIP). An economic transaction is deemed to have a positive effect on VIP if it increases the welfare of those affected parties which have political clout. Transactions which reduce the welfare of such parties are assumed to have a negative impact on VIP. For the purpose of the analysis, distinction was made between two groups of actors: producers and consumers. It was assumed that producers, who can easily identify situations where they gain, and where they lose, and who are, as a rule, well organized, have political clout. Consumers, who are less well organized, are assumed to have no group interest in the peace process.

Bearing the VIP concept and its implications in mind, it is suggested that a viable METR should be constructed so as to ensure that transactions between Israel and her neighbors should satisfy simultaneously two criteria:

They should be economically feasible in the conventional sense, i.e., they should increase economic welfare and they should increase or at least not have a negative effect on VIP. To satisfy the second criterion it is necessary that producer's interests should on no account be adversely affected by intercountry transactions.

Adoption of these criteria implies that integration theory based on concepts developed by Viner, Mead, Lipsey and other international economists, is not expected to provide policy guidelines for interregional arrangements in the Middle East.

The unsuitability of received integration theory for the purpose at hand is due to its neglect of political factors which, for reasons discussed above, are assumed to predominate in the Middle East situation. Adoption of the VIP framework which specifies that producer interests take precedence over consumer interests, imply rejection of those gains from trade which are generated by Viner's "trade creation." The VIP criterion is not satisfied by the theoretical possibility of compensating producers for their losses from the extra resources made available to the economy by international exchange utilizing its comparative advantage. As long as there is no actual mechanism which guarantees compensation, the VIP criterion disallows transactions which hurt the politically-articulate producers.

This outcome could lead to the conclusion that the political constraints, introduced into our framework, preclude altogether the utilization of accepted economic criteria, when specifying the conditions for bilateral relations between the parties involved in the Middle East peace process. This, however, is not necessarily the case; suspension of economic welfare maximizing criteria is suggested here only in respect to transactions which involve redistribution of costs and benefits associated with existing economic activities — existing industries, and existing trade.

In fact the inadequacy of traditional integration theory for the present purpose is partly due to its exclusive concern with existing activities and with questions of redistribution. Peace facilitates a host of transactions which had, in the past, been completely ruled out. Redistribution is unlikely to be the sole or even a major economic issue when peace makes it possible for past belligerents to engage in economic transactions totally forbidden under prepeace conditions.

■ Characteristics of Transactions Between Recent Belligerents

Two factors—proximity and economies of scale—are likely to have a profound influence over the variety and complexity of the transactions facilitated by the peace process.[1]

The term "proximity factor" pertains to the fact that distances between Israel and its Arab neighbors are considerably smaller than distances between these countries and their extra-regional suppliers or markets.

The proximity factor (largely ignored by integration theorists who assume zero transport costs) increases the profitability of trade between neighbors. This factor appears to be responsible for the empirical importance of "border trade" (i.e., trade between adjacent countries which maintain low trade barriers).[2]

In the context of peacemaking, the proximity factor is likely to encounter limitations due to the constraints imposed by the VIP criterion which disallows trade in products and services which compete with existing enterprises. Under such conditions only import substitution may be facilitated by the proximity factor while the more traditional benefits which trade theorists label "trade creation" will be discouraged due to political constraints.

Classes of two transactions "Output Creation" and "Export Creation" which satisfy both economic and the VIP criteria were outlined in *The Economies of Peacemaking*. These transactions are economically viable due to the combined effects of the proximity factor and declining costs facilitated by economies of scale. A brief description of these transactions follows:

Assume a world consisting of three countries, A and B the recent enemies, which have common borders, and R—the rest of the world, which is distant from both. Peace, which enables A's and B's firms to have access to each other's markets, allows these firms to take advantage of the proximity factor and economies of scale.

Thanks to the proximity factor, firms from A and B benefit from low transportation costs in relation to R's firms, in both their home and respective markets. Economies of scale facilitate unit cost reductions when output in A or B is expanded so as to serve the neighboring market.

Note that it is the proximity factor which can give country A firms a competitive edge over country R firms in B's market. Note also that if it were not for economies of scale, which facilitate unit cost reduction accompanying expansion of output, trade between A and B could not increase welfare of consumers and producers in *both* countries relative to pre-peace conditions.

"Export Creation" and "Output Creation" transactions are distinguishable from each other in the following sense: "Export Creation" denotes activities which, before peace, were located in either A or B, and which can, thanks to peace, serve the other country. "Output Creation" refers to activities which, before peace, were invisible in both A and B, because they could not compete with imports from R. Peace makes it possible to establish an operation which can compete with extra-regional imports, as producers with access to both A and B markets are able to benefit from economies of scale. It is possible to conceive of yet another group of transactions which involve lowering of long run costs by combining inputs from both A and B.

By combing inputs, say labor from A and raw materials from B, costs can be lowered below import prices. Cooperation between A and B makes it possible to substitute local production for imports, or even to establish export industries capable of competing in the world market.

Downward sloping cost curves are in fact unnecessary when the establishment of an internationally-competitive industry is facilitated by combining inputs from two or more countries in the region. In this case, which is more general, (since it applies to both upward and downward sloping cost functions) the combination of inputs from A and B facilitates shifting of the cost curve.

If the downward shift of the new cost curve is sufficient, industries able to compete in A and B and even in R become economically viable.

The transaction classes discussed above satisfy the VIP conditions—they have no adverse effects on existing producers. Note, moreover, that they offer additional benefits—they increase (or at least do not reduce) consumer welfare, thus also, satisfying the traditional Viner, Mead criteria.[3]

▪ Policy Implications for Trade Regimes

The policy implications which follow from the analysis in the last section are straightforward: METR should be constructed so as to promote establishment of new production capacity or expansion of existing capacity which will have some or all the following characteristics:

(1) There are economies of scale in production.

(2) It makes economic sense to use raw materials or intermediate inputs sensitive to transportation costs from at least two countries.

(3) A market potential in third countries exists.

Where does all this lead us in terms of trade regimes? Can we think of a set of relatively simple rules which might guide a bilateral or multilateral Arab-Israel commission established to supervise trade and investment flows between the recent belligerents?

There is unfortunately no straightforward answer to the above question. The difficulty involved in providing our hypothetical commission with a set of simple guidelines stems from the nature of the transactions which it is supposed to oversee. As was noted above, few of these transactions involve existing activities – to be realized, new productive capacity must be created and this implies new capital investments, establishment of new firms in some cases, expansion of existing ones in others. In such cases establishment of permanent, or at least long term, links between organizations across the border will be a precondition for the transactions in question.

A trade regime which provides a suitable framework for such transactions implies a fairly high degree of economic integration. This appears to contradict our earlier conclusion, which ruled out even fairly elementary forms of integration such as a free trade area.

(1) The predominance of the VIP criterion thus leads to the rejection of trade regimes based on comprehensive, economy-wide, integration. An institutional arrangement avoiding this type of integration, while allowing comprehensive sectorial cooperation was advocated in *The Economics of Peacemaking* for a specific industry (textiles and clothing). The sectorial integration approach draws its inspirations from the European Iron and Steel community which preceded the establishment of the European Economic Community. It is important in this context to bear in mind both the similarities and the differences in the two cases.

The Coal and Steel community (ECOSOC) was concerned with reconstruction and with rationalization of operations based on the complete elimination of national trade barriers. Such barriers, involving raw materials such as coal and iron ores, had in the past given artificial advantage to the industry of one country over the other. Elimination of barriers to inputs and outputs was in the view of Robert Schuman and his colleagues a necessary step to economic and political arrangements which would make future wars between the West European countries unthinkable.

The ECOSOC was intended, amongst other things, to prevent the reemergence of prewar rivalries. The institutional mechanism chosen to supervise the new arrangements involved the setting up of supra-national agencies which required giving up some degree of national sovereignty.

The Middle East situation is different in several respects. On the one hand institutional arrangements need not be concerned with old economic rivalries. The political conflict between the parties was so all-encompassing as to eliminate all direct economic transaction. Under these conditions there was no economic rivalry of the kind which usually evolves, even between friendly nations. The purpose of any Middle East trade regime must be (as long as the peace process is fragile), to prevent commercial rivalry, which is the logical by-product of any competition between firms, from spilling over into the political arena.

On the other hand it is difficult to expect that the Middle East countries, which differ from each other in so many respects, and which have had little experience of previous economic cooperation of any kind, would be ready to consider surrendering even a minimum degree of national sovereignty to a supra-national authority of whatever kind. Under these circumstances, looser arrangements involving no infringement of sovereignty may make more sense. Free trade zones, possibly of the kind established in recent years by the Republic of China could serve as a model. Free trade zones are established by unilateral decision taken by governments. Their purpose is usually to attract foreign investment and trade. To that end rules and regulations involving, for example, foreign exchange, licensing, and taxes may be amended so as to create a regulatory environment acceptable to foreign investors.

The important point to bear in mind is that free zones are and remain under the national jurisdiction of the country in whose territory it is located regardless of how liberal their trade, foreign exchange, and tax regimes. Free zones involve no loss of sovereignty of any kind, and concessions granted by the governments to local or foreign firms may be withdrawn at any time. These characteristics favor the free zone approach over other alternatives.

The rules and regulations applying to the free zones in different countries may, but need not, be identical or even similar. Their establishment does in fact not depend on bilateral or multilateral agreements. It is, however, possible and even likely, that if the parties to the Middle East peace process decide to use the free zone approach to strengthen their economic ties, they will seek agreements over certain sets of principles which each participating country will undertake to include in its own national free zone legislation.

Harmonization of national regulations might be increased over time and could eventually lead to formal agreements whereby governments grant each other's companies reciprocal rights. Questions of mutual interest in this context are likely to be numerous and quite complex. They can be expected to pertain to issues such as the right of establishment of domestic and foreign firms, right of employing domestic and foreign labor, importing and exporting capital, raw materials, intermediate inputs and outputs, access to national capital markets, exchange controls, taxation, repatriation of profits, etc.

The free zone approach, as its title suggests, can be applied to geographic regions. Free zones in specifically designated areas do in fact exist both in Egypt and in Israel. The approach can also be applied to specific industries or to combinations of industries and regions.

Examples of such an application are discussed in the following section.

■ Examples of Industrial Cooperation Between Egypt and Israel: Textiles and Clothing and Fertilizers

Studies of specific industrial cooperation projects carried out by the Hammer Fund concluded that the textiles and clothing and fertilizers industries of the two countries are characterized by a wide range of complementarities which make them suitable candidates for cooperation of the kind envisaged in section 5.[4] In this concluding section we review these findings and investigate the possibilities of utilizing the free zone approach for the purpose of extracting additional returns from intra-regional cooperation involving these industries.

■ Textiles and Clothing

Egypt's textile and clothing industry has been the country's leading industry employing over 350,000 workers at the beginning of the eighties, who accounted for about one third of industrial employment. Over two-thirds of the output was accounted for by spinning and weaving, mostly (about 80 percent) by state-owned enterprises. Clothing and wearing apparel, representing the balance, have been growing at a more rapid rate. The share of the private sector in this segment of the industry has been far higher, reaching about 60 percent.

The industry's major exports are textile yarn and thread, though cotton cloth and fabric have also been quite important, reaching about 20 percent of total exports of nearly $250 million in 1981. Despite Egypt's comparative advantage in labor-intensive clothing and wearing apparel, it represented only about 10 percent of the industry's exports and about 6 percent of its output. In addition, nearly $500 million of raw cotton, mainly the long staple variety, was exported in 1981.

Israel's textiles and clothing industry (which is mostly in the private sector) accounts for 18 percent of industrial employment and has a gross output of about $1200 million, of which about 37 percent or $450 million was exported, mainly to Western markets, in 1980. Of this, nearly two-thirds was in clothing and ready-made articles.

The share of the industry in value added of the manufacturing sector has been declining, although it has been growing in absolute terms. Among the different sub-sectors, yarn and cloth have been declining, while clothing has been growing as in Egypt. Israel has also been a cotton-growing country (mainly medium staple cotton); its exports in 1980 reached $100 million.

■ Fertilizers

Of the three primary fertilizer ingredients, nitrogen (N), phosphorus (P, P_2O_5, phosphate) and potassium (K, K_2O, potash), Egypt possesses the mineral resources needed to manufacture nitrogen and phosphate fertilizers, and Israel has the mineral resources to manufacture phosphate and potash fertilizers. Jointly, the two countries cover all three ingredients, and this may confer on them a competitive advantage in the international fertilizer markets.

Israel's two million ton net output in 1980, represented nearly 2 percent of the world NPK output and over 4 percent of world NPK trade. The industry is dominated by the state-owned Israel Chemicals Limited (ICL), which controls over 80 percent of output, employment and exports (which accounted for over two-thirds of output).

ICL is further expanding its capacity of downstream products for international marketing. The industry depends, however, on imported ammonia which is based on oil or gas.

Egypt's fertilizer industry has developed more slowly than Israel's. In 1980 it produced about 0.5 percent, and consumed about 0.6 percent of world NPK output. In the present decade, however, Egypt is expected to achieve self-sufficiency at about 750 thousand tons. Nevertheless, due to a shortage of specific items and surpluses in others, imports may still be required, especially to supply the growing need for potash.

Following the loss of the fertilizing effect of the Nile waters, Egypt has been developing an ever-growing need for chemical fertilizers. Availability of a compound NPK fertilizer would simplify the application of all three elements by a farming sector not easily guided by economic incentives.

Though different in many respects the two industries share several characteristics which are particularly pertinent in the questions discussed in this paper in general and to the specific regime advocated in this paper in particular: They exhibit significant complementarities which could be utilized, by means of judicious cooperation between Egyptian and Israel's enterprises, to lower production costs, enlarge the range of products, improve quality and capture important regional as well as extra-regional markets.

In textiles and clothing Egypt could supply Israel with cotton yarn and cloth; Israel could reciprocate with synthetics. Israel might become an importer of Egyptian long staple cotton and Egypt might import the short staple variety grown in Israel.

The most interesting potential for cooperation is to be found, however, in the clothing industry. In this case both countries could learn a great deal from the West European industry, which managed to survive despite fierce competition from both within and outside Europe, by breaking down the production process into several stages, and by performing each stage in locations enjoying competitive advantages vis-a-vis the rest of the world.

The Israeli clothing industry is, as was noted above, characterized by a strong export orientation. Over the years it has established a reasonably strong market position in Western Europe, and to a lesser degree in the United States with which it established a free trade area agreement in 1985. Israel also has a free trade area agreement with the European Economic Community. These agreements guarantee most of its manufacturers access on terms equal to those of domestic manufacturers. Further expansion of exports from Israel appears to be hampered by supply bottlenecks, especially shortage of labor.

Cooperation with Egypt could alleviate some of these shortages. Since Egypt has an obvious advantage in labor-intensive operations such as sewing, Israeli and Egyptian firms could cooperate either by subcontracting or by establishing joint ventures. Egyptian firms, in turn, could take advantage of Israel's capabilities in design, printing, dyeing, and in finishing. Geographic proximity is of great importance in this context since it facilitates communication and physical shipment of goods at short notice and at low cost.

In the longer run the more dominant method of cooperation will probably consist of direct investment which will include establishment of subsidiaries integrated with the present companies. This form of business has advantages over more loose forms of cooperation because it facilitates closer coordination and more efficient utilization of centralized functions such as marketing, design and quality control.

The strategy of establishing manufacturing operations which draw on the competitive advantage of Egypt (cotton, yarn and cloth production, sewing and other labor-intensive processes) and Israel (design, printing and finishing as well as international marketing) may be attractive not only to Egyptian and Israeli firms. Firms from third countries especially those which have preferential trade agreements with either Egypt or Israel or both countries might take advantage of potentially competitive new sources of supply.

In the fertilizer industry, cooperation between Egypt and Israel can, at a minimum, entail bilateral supply arrangements covering missing ingredients: potash from Israel to Egypt and ammonia from Egypt to Israel. More ambitious schemes might consist of long-range supply contracts which may justify expansion of production capacity of ammonia in Egypt and potash in Israel, and of plants using these materials in both countries.

Cooperation may be taken a step further by establishing an integrated complex producing NPK fertilizers, based on an ammonia unit located in Egypt, drawing its potash requirements from Israel and its phosphoric acid from either Israel or Egypt. The complementary requirements for PK or NP combinations could be supplemented from existing facilities in Israel until such time as the volume grew to justify the establishment of Egyptian based production units of PK and NP.

Ultimately cooperation might take the form of a fully-integrated joint venture, pooling resources from both countries for the purpose of jointly servicing third country markets. Bearing in mind that Israel already has an established position in the European and U.S. markets, and that both Europe and Asia are substantial importers of fertilizers, one is led to conclude that the type of cooperation envisaged above could turn the partners, who between them have easy access to the three fertilizer ingredients, into a formidable power in the world fertilizer market.

To conclude, this short review confirms that the textiles and clothing and the fertilizer industries of Egypt and Israel exhibit a wide range of potential complementaries, and that cooperation between them could yield very substantial dividends in the form of new markets and lines of business. Although initially cooperation is likely to consist of specific supply agreements between Israeli and Egyptian companies, this could in time develop into joint projects.

Cooperation could be further enhanced by suitable institutional arrangements intended to facilitate easier movement of goods, processes, capital and know-how between enterprises in the two countries. Such a policy can improve the competitive position and export performance of the industries of both. It is also likely to contribute to an increase in investments from both domestic and foreign enterprises.

To the extent that Egypt and Israel decide to intensify their economic relations by adopting the free zones approach they might consider trying it out first on these two sectors where prospects of success appear to be reasonably good. Their prospects might be further enhanced by third party involvement which might consist of providing capital, managerial, and technical know-how and, most important of all, providing access to markets.

By pooling resources and allowing national firms to cooperate along the lines suggested in this section Egypt and Israel can substantially increase their joint returns from investments in the textile and clothing and the fertilizer industries. To achieve this objective it is not necessary for either side to give up sovereignty. Many of the benefits which economic integration can confer may be gained by steps taken by each of the two countries unilaterally involving the establishment of free zones within their jurisdiction.

Given the advantages inherent in cooperation between firms from the two countries, it can be expected that such cooperation will indeed develop, provided the regimes which govern the operations of the free zones grant foreign firms the right of establishment, the right to tariff-free imports of raw materials and intermediate inputs from third countries, to employ expatriate specialists, to sign long-term supply agreements with domestic companies, and finally to repatriate capital and profits under reasonable conditions. It is desirable, but not absolutely necessary, that foreign firms be allowed to establish joint ventures with domestic firms.

Note that neither reciprocity nor intergovernmental agreements are required in order to initiate inter-firm cooperation. For such cooperation to get underway, it is sufficient for one government, say Egypt's, to decide on the free zone policy, and to invite foreign firms, including firms headquartered in Israel, to operate in Egypt under its provisions. The other country, Israel in our example, can, but need not, reciprocate with a similar policy. Israel-based firms can be expected to take advantage of the opportunities inherent in an Egyptian free zone regime provided they are allowed to do so by their government.

The element whose presence is likely to be most important in enticing firms to cooperate under such circumstances is confidence: confidence that policies proclaimed by the Egyptian and/or Israeli governments will indeed be adhered to, and that contracts entered into with the other side will be honored. Bilateral agreements between the two governments could serve to build such confidence. So could insurance schemes underwritten by either party or better still, by both. Confidence could be further increased if appropriate insurance programs were to be included in bilateral or multilateral agreements involving both governments and international agencies.

This, however, takes us beyond the scope of this paper. It is sufficient to conclude that many of the potential advantages outlined in this section may be realized in a bilateral context if one country decides on a free zone policy, if the other country allows its firms to operate in the first country and if an insurance scheme unilateral, bilateral or multilateral encourages the firms in question to take the political risks inherent in cooperation with firms located in the territory of the former enemy.

▪ Concluding Remarks

The point of departure of this paper is that in the context of Middle East peace process, economics cannot take precedence over politics, even though the conflict itself, surprisingly enough, has few economic causes. If there is a political will for peace, economic considerations are bound to figure prominently in the peace process. It is of vital importance to make sure that the process, which is bound to be slow and arduous in any case, is not encumbered by unnecessary strains, generated by the elements of conflict which inevitably accompany all economic arrangements in general, and trade regimes in particular. Economic Integration conceived by M. Schuman and his colleagues as a mechanism for preventing future wars in

Western Europe, which proved so successful after World War II could, in the very different circumstances of the Middle East, have quite undesirable consequences. This conclusion derives from the high probability that inter-country disparities in endowment, social organization, levels of development and other important economic characteristics, will increase the adjustment costs, which inevitably accompany economic integration, to an intolerable level. Add to these the fragility of the peace process and the deep-seated opposition it encounters in all the countries of the region, and one is driven to the conclusion that even mild forms of integration such as a free trade area cannot be contemplated for the time-being.

Because of these considerations, this paper advocates a trade regime which explicitly recognizes the supremacy of political over economic considerations, and recommends specifically that inter-country trade be limited to transactions which satisfy the vested interest in peace criterion; i.e., they must not adversely affect the welfare of established producers.

It would be idle to deny that adherence to the VIP principle might substantially curtail intraregional trade. This, however, does not imply that economic transactions will necessarily remain at a low level. While conventional trade, if these recommendations are adopted, will be limited to items involving substitution of imports from extra-regional sources, there will be opportunities for new kinds of transaction, not covered by conventional trade and integration theories. Included in this category are goods and services whose competitiveness depends on complementarities between different kinds of natural and man-made resources from the countries of the region. The list of potential candidates for such transactions is considerably expanded when the proximity factor and economies of scale are taken into account. These elements combine to give cooperation between neighbors an economic advantage which can prove to be of significance.

Conventional trade regimes, however liberal, are not in themselves sufficient to encourage transactions of the kind discussed above. Realization of their potential requires institutional arrangements which facilitate long-term inter-firm relations, establishment of joint ventures and inter-country investments.

A modest but vital step in this direction may be taken as individual countries establish free zones covering areas, industries or combinations of both within their jurisdiction.

Adoption of the free zone approach in no way infringes on national sovereignty. It may, but need not, involve reciprocal arrangements between different countries; it could indeed be pursued on a unilateral basis and still make it possible for the countries in question to benefit from many of the advantages which recent enemies may derive from opening their borders to trade and other economic transactions.

A final point: Vergetius, a Roman writer living in the fourth century, offered the following piece of advice to his countrymen:

"He who desires peace should prepare for war." The essential point of this paper might be stated as an appendix to Vergetius' message: He who desires peace should prepare for war. He should, however, also plan for peace. Surely that much can be expected from countries which have each decided to try to overcome the political obstacles which have in the past hampered economic cooperation between them.

■ **Notes**

1. For a more detailed discussion of these factors *see* R. Arad, S. Hirsch and A. Tovias, *The Economics of Peacemaking—Focus on the Egyptian Israeli Situation* (London Macmillan for the Trade Policy Research Centre, 1983) chapter 3.

2. *See ibid* chapter.

3. Note that even the more innocuous Most Favored Nations principle advocated by the GATT may be in conflict with the VIP principle. This could happen when, due to the proximity factor, existing producers in country A who are able to compete effectively with extra-regional suppliers, are underpriced by suppliers from neighboring country B (the ex-enemy).

4. The Armand Hammer Fund for Economic Cooperation in the Middle East Research Project for Economic Cooperation in the Middle East, Tel Aviv University, Tel Aviv, May 1986, p. 1-31 *mimeo*, and individual studies.

15

The Economic Relations Between Israel and Egypt: Tourism, 1979—1984

Yoram Meital

■ INTRODUCTION

The economic relations that have come into being between Egypt and Israel in the years since the signing of the peace agreement in March 1979 are varied. Foremost among them are trade in oil, trade in agricultural products, and cooperation in the sphere of agrotechnology, as well as tourism between the two countries.[1] This paper attempts to survey the development of the tourist traffic in its various aspects in the years 1980–1984. We have chosen to focus on tourism because inaccurate generalizations have taken root regarding this subject.

Arrangements for the passage of travellers between Egypt and Israel are covered in the peace agreement. It states that each party will allow freedom of movement to the nationals and vehicles of the other party into its territory and within its territory, in accordance with regulations applying to nationals and vehicles of other countries. Neither party will impose discriminatory restrictions on the movement of persons and vehicles into the territory of the other party.[2] The first public declaration on the free movement of citizens was made in the presence of President Sadat and U.S. Secretary of State Cyrus Vance at El-Arish (27 May 1979), when the Israeli Prime Minister Begin stated that "The President and I declare from here, El-Arish, that the borders between Egypt and Israel are open. Egyptian citizens may visit Israel and Israeli citizens may visit Egypt."[3] The principle of freedom of movement for citizens of Israel and Egypt is the legal basis for all cooperation within the sphere of tourism between the two countries.

Israel and Egypt are signatories to a number of agreements and memoranda of understanding in the areas of tourism, aviation, and land and sea transport. On 14 February 1980 a memorandum of understanding was signed that sets out procedures for civil aviation between the two countries.[4] Within the framework of the committee for the normalization of relations between Israel and Egypt, a subcommittee was established whose purpose was to prepare a tourism agreement that would cover passenger traffic on land, by sea, and by air between Israel and Egypt. Following the work of this committee a memorandum of understanding was signed on 10 March 1980 between the ministries of tourism of the two countries.[5] The memorandum covers the entire complex of tourism links between Egypt and Israel, which is in fact a standard agreement on cooperation in accordance with the principles of the World Trade Organization.

- ## ENTRY OF VISITORS TO EGYPT FROM ISRAEL

Most of the passenger traffic between Israel and Egypt in both directions is by land. The geographical proximity and the low cost make this route preferable to most visitors. About one-third of the visitors between the two countries travel by air or by sea. Full data exist for visitors by land but passenger lists for the air and sea routes are incomplete. Official sources do not publish details of the composition of groups of passengers to and from Egypt by air and sea.[6]

Table 15.1 shows the distribution of visitors from Israel to Egypt by route taken. The table demonstrates that between 1980 and 1981 the number travelling from Israel to Egypt doubled. Also, 1982 was the peak year and since then the number of visitors from Israel to Egypt has declined. The table does not include visitors travelling by sea owing to the difficulty in obtaining manifests and in classifying the visitors; sea passengers sail on liners calling at a number of ports around the Eastern Mediterranean, and it is difficult to estimate the proportion that land at any given port.

Table 15.1 indicates that during the first five years following the opening of the borders between the two countries, 980,383 visitors crossed from Israel to Egypt. To analyze more exactly the nature of the tourism links between the two countries, it is necessary to look at numbers of travellers according to various groupings: Israeli passport holders, residents of the West Bank and Gaza Strip, visitors holding passports of the Arab countries and other foreign passports. Examination of the composition of each visitor grouping individually may help to clarify the special nature of these tourist links.

Table 15.1
Distribution of Visitors Travelling from Israel to Egypt by Route, 1980-1984*

| | By Land | | By Air | | Total | |
Year	Visitors	%	Visitors	%	Visitors	%
1980	73,048	75.0	24,327	25.0	97,375	100.0
1981	148,210	78.6	39,973	21.2	188,183	100.0
1982	205,600	86.7	31,543	13.3	237,143	100.0
1983	197,913	87.3	28,696	12.7	226,609	100.0
1984	203,408	88.0	27,665	12.0	231,073	100.0

*Excluding visitors arriving by sea.

Sources: Transit data for visitors arriving by land derived from passenger manifests of the Airports Authority - Land Terminal Network; figures for visitors arriving by air derived from data of El-Al Airlines.

■ Entry of Israeli Passport Holders to Egypt

From the time when travel restrictions between Israel and Egypt were lifted until the end of 1984, 161,010 Israelis visited Egypt, amounting to 16.4 percent of the total number of visitors from Israel to Egypt. These numbers indicate that there was a strong desire to get to know Egypt, the former enemy and future partner. The low costs of the journey to Egypt and of accommodations there also encouraged many Israeli citizens to visit.

Table 15.2 shows the number of Israelis entering Egypt by land and by air. The term "Israeli" includes all passengers holding an Israeli passport. Students constituted the largest numerical group among Israeli passport holders entering Egypt. In 1980 they accounted for 46 percent of the total number of Israelis passing through the land crossing into Egypt, while since that year it is estimated that the figure has been constant at about 30 percent.

■ Travel to Egypt of Residents of the West Bank and the Gaza Strip

A considerable part of the overall passenger traffic through the land crossing between Israel and Egypt is made up of residents of the West Bank and the Gaza Strip. For many of them the border constitutes a partition separating families, friends and business associates. In the more than 30 years prior to 1979 the state of war between Israel and Egypt caused this population

Table 15.2
Entry of Israeli Passport Holders into Egypt, 1980-1984

Year	Rafa crossing Visitors	%	Taba crossing Visitors	%	By Air Visitors	%	Total Visitors	%
1980	13,953	76.5	--	--	4,300	23.6	18,249	100.0
1981	29,336	82.6	--	--	6,175	17.4	35,511	100.0
1982	33,516	87.9	1,313	3.4	3,281	8.6	38,110	100.0
1983	24,172	69.9	8,467	24.5	1,950	5.6	34,589	100.0
1984	22,871	66.2	9,680	28.0	2,000	5.8	34,551	100.0

Sources: Derived from data of the Airports Authority - Land Terminal Network, *Annual Report for 1980-1984.* Figures for air passengers derived from data of the Central Bureau of Statistics, *Israel Statistical Monthly*: Central Bureau of Statistics, *Statistical Quarterly for Tourism and Guest Services*, Vol. 13, 1985.

great harm. The signing of the peace agreement and the subsequent removal of travel restrictions between the two countries presented the residents of the West Bank and Gaza Strip with opportunities for reuniting of families, visiting relatives, and establishing business connections.

Table 15.3 indicates the firm socioeconomic ties between residents of the West Bank and Gaza living in areas controlled by Israel and residents of territory under Egyptian rule. The strength of these ties is shown by movement of a large number of visitors and goods each day. Most of the residents of the West Bank and Gaza crossing to the Egyptian side are not tourists in the full sense of the word for in the judgment of border terminal staff and ministry of tourism experts, the overwhelming majority of them travel to Egypt on business or to visit relatives and return within a day or two. From the table it emerges that this average group constitutes 37.6 percent of the total visitors going from Israel to Egypt by land.

Table 15.3 indicates that between 1980 and 1982 the number of West Bank and Gaza residents crossing from Israel to Egypt increased by 241 percent. The peak year for this traffic was 1982. Like with Israelis, the number of such visitors has also steadily declined since that year.

▪ Entry of Visitors Holding Arab Passports to Egypt from Israel

This grouping includes holders of Arab passports other than Egyptians. The lifting of travel restrictions enabled nationals of Arab states who entered Israel-controlled territory via the Jordan bridges to continue their journey

Table 15.3
Entry of Residents of the West Bank and Gaza Strip to Egypt from Israel, 1980-1984

Year	West Bank and Gaza Strip residents		West Bank and Gaza Strip residents
	Visitors	% Growth	as % of total land visitors
1980	22,741		31.1
1981	57,303	152.0	38.7
1982	77,509	35.3	37.7
1983	66,017	-14.8	33.3
1984	61,841	-6.3	30.4

Source: Derived from data of the Airports Authority - Land Terminal Network, *Summary of Passenger and Goods Traffic at the Land Crossings between Israel and Egypt,* reports for 1980-1984.

and visit Egypt. Table 15.4 shows that in the years 1980–1984, a total of 92,528 visitors holding passports of Arab countries crossed from Israel to Egypt by land; 12.8 percent of the total number of visitors arriving by land crossings between Israel and Egypt and 11.1 percent of the total visitors traffic to Egypt. Unlike other groups of visitors, the number of visitors holding Arab passports reached its lowest point in 1982, apparently owing to the outbreak of the Lebanon War.

In 1983 the number of visitors in this category rose sharply by 30.8 percent.

Table 15.4
Entry of non-Egyptian Arab Passport Holders to Egypt from Israel by Land, 1980-1984

Year	Visitors	Change in %	% of total visitors by land
1980	10,442	--	14.3
1981	20,966	100.8	14.1
1982	16,918	19.3	8.2
1983	22,144	30.9	11.2
1984	22,058	-0.4	10.8

Sources: Derived from data of the Land Terminals Network, *Summary of Passenger and Goods Traffic at the Land Crossings between Israel and Egypt,* reports for 1980-1984.

▪ Entry of Holders of Western Passports to Egypt from Israel

Since the opening of the borders between the two states to free movement of travellers, 391,512 visitors holding Western passports travelled from Israel to Egypt. Since 1980 the number of Western visitors arriving in Israel and continuing thence to Egypt has risen steadily, as shown in Table 15.5. Whereas in 1980 this group accounted for 3.6 percent of the total number entering Egypt from Israel, the proportion had reached 11 percent in 1984. It is interesting to note that hostilities and other political events did not exert any appreciable effect on the number of Western visitors entering Egypt from Israel until 1984, and that this group has grown an average of 37.7 percent per year.

In summarizing discussion on the passage of visitors from Israel to Egypt it is worth noting that in the first five years after the lifting of travel restrictions between the two countries, about one million visitors entered Egypt from Israel. Table 15.6 gives the percent of each of the visitor groups entering Egypt via Israel. The table shows that the largest group is that of Western passport holders (39.9 percent), followed by West Bank and Gaza Strip residents (29.1 percent) and Israeli nationals (16.4 percent).

▪ Tourism from Israel as a Percent of Total Tourist Traffic to Egypt

A survey of data on visitor traffic from Israel to Egypt in 1980–1984 shows that in this period 980,383 visitors, constituting 13.7 percent of the total number of visitors arriving in Egypt in this period, entered by land and air routes from Israel. Table 15.7 shows the proportion of visitors arriving from Israel out of the total number of visitors entering Egypt. The table indicates that between 1980 and 1984 the traffic from Israel to Egypt increased by 137.3 percent. The figures show clearly the relatively high proportion of passenger traffic that arrived in Egypt via Israel.

Data of the tourism industry in Egypt indicates that Arab visitors form the majority of tourism to Egypt. The proportion of tourism from Israel may be estimated by calculating the percentage of tourist arrivals from Israel out of the total number of visitors reaching Egypt from Western countries. Because tourist traffic from Israel is composed of several types, arrivals from Israel should be divided and examined in two groupings. First, the proportion relative to total Western tourism to Egypt which come from Israel should be

Table 15.5
Entry of Holders of Western Passport to Egypt from Israel, 1980-1984

Year	By Land	By Air	Total	Change in %	% of total leaving Israel
1980	16,961	18,553	35,514		3.0
1981	33,398	32,051	65,449	84.3	5.8
1982	53,940	26,640	80,580	23.1	8.9
1983	75,047	25,455	100,502	24.7	8.9
1984	85,071	24,396	109,467	8.9	8.8

Sources: Derived from data of the Land Terminal Network and El-Al Airline and from Central Bureau of Statistics, *Statistical Yearbook.*

Table 15.6
Visitors from Israel to Egypt by Origin 1980-1984

	Visitors	%
Western nationals	391,512	39.9
West Bank and Gaza Strip residents	285,411	29.1
Israelis	161,010	16.4
Arab nationals[a]	92,528	9.4
Others[b]	49,922	5.1
Total	980,383	100.0

[a]Excluding Egyptian passport holders and visitors arriving by sea.
[b]Primarily UN personnel and members of the Multi-National Peace-Keeping Force in Sinai.

Sources: Based on data from the Land Terminal Network and El-Al Airlines.

determined; then the proportion of foreign (i.e., non-Israeli) tourists. Table 15.8 shows the proportion of visitors from Israel out of total Western tourism to Egypt. It is seen from this table that visitors from Israel amount to 27.1 percent of the total number of Western visitors to Egypt. It should be emphasized that the figure for visitors from Israel includes all persons who crossed from Israel to Egypt, not only those who are actually tourists.

Table 15.9 indicates the proportion of tourists holding Western passports who visited Egypt via Israel relative to the total number of Western visitors to Egypt. The data show that in the years 1980–1984 an average of 11.0 percent of all Western visitors to Egypt entered from Israel.

▪ Visitors Holding Israeli Passports Among the Total Western Tourism to Egypt

In Egyptian tourism records, Israel is classified with Western countries. It is thus of interest to examine the relative importance of Israeli tourism in overall Western tourism to Egypt. Table 15.10 shows that in 1980–1984 on average Israelis accounted for 4.6 percent of total Western tourism to Egypt.

The central position of Israel as a source of tourism for Egypt is attested to by the fact that from 1981 to 1984 Israel reached sixth place among Western countries in terms of numbers of visitors to Egypt.

▪ ENTRY OF PASSENGERS TO ISRAEL FROM EGYPT

Political considerations aside, Egypt constitutes a significant potential market for tourism to Israel. In recent years it has, however, been claimed in Israel that tourism between the two countries is "one-way," namely that visitor traffic from Israel to Egypt is disproportionately larger than the traffic in the other direction.[7] We asked ourselves whether this claim is numerically correct. Table 15.11 indicates the distribution of entry of visitors to Israel from Egypt by land and by air. The table shows that in 1980–84, 907,992 visitors entered Israel from Egypt. Also, while in 1980 the figure was only 93,308, in 1981 it doubled, and from then until 1984 the numbers steadily increased. On average 18 percent of all visitors to Israel from Egypt arrive by air and 82 percent by land routes.

Table 15.11 shows that at least in terms of the numbers of visitors reaching Israel annually from Egypt, the term "one-way tourism" is not accurate. To estimate in greater detail the nature of the tourist ties between the two

Table 15.7
Visitor Traffic from Israel and Total Visitors to Egypt, 1980-1984

		Visitors from Israel	
Year	Total visitors[a]	number	% of total
1980	1,253,000	97,375	7.8
1981	1,376,000	188,183	13.7
1982	1,423,000	237,143	16.7
1983	1,498,000	226,609	15.1
1984	1,560,000	231,073	14.8

[a]Excluding visitors arriving by sea.

Sources: Egyptian data from publications of EGAPT, *Egypt Tourist Statistics 1980-1984*, p. 18. Figures on visitor traffic from Israel processed from data of the Airports Authority - Land Terminal Network and from El-Al Airlines.

Table 15.8
Visitors Arriving from Israel and Total Western Visitors to Egypt, 1980-1984

		Visitors Arriving From Israel	
Year	Total Western Visitors	number	%
1980	663,816	97,375	14.7
1981	664,749	188,183	28.3
1982	676,663	237,143	35.0
1983	758,572	226,609	29.9
1984	822,804	231,073	28.1

Sources: Figures for total visitors to Egypt are derived from EGAPT, *Egypt Tourist Statistics Information* 1980-1984, p. 25. Figures for passengers from Israel are from Airports Authority - Land Terminal Network and from El-Al Airlines.

Table 15.9
Visitors from Western Countries to Egypt, 1980-1984

Year	Total Western visitors to Egypt	Western visitors to Egypt via Israel Number	%
1980	663,816	37,638	5.7
1981	664,749	67,375	10.1
1982	676,663	80,751	11.9
1983	758,572	99,438	13.1
1984	822,804	108,586	13.2

Sources: Figures for visitors from Western countries processed from EGAPT, *Egypt Tourist Statistics Information*, 1980-1984, p. 18; figures for visitors from Israel processed from data of the Airports Authority - Land Terminal Network and El-Al Airlines.

Table 15.10
Israeli Passport Holders As Percent of Total Western Visitors Travelling to Egypt, 1980-1984

Year	Visitors from Western countries	Israeli passport holders[a] % of total
1980	663,816	2.6
1981	664,749	5.3
1982	676,663	5.8
1983	758,572	4.9
1984	822,804	4.4

[a]Excluding Israeli visitors reaching Egypt by sea or who visited Sinai for a period of less than seven days.

Sources: Figures for visitors to Egypt from Western countries processed from EGAPT. *Egypt Tourist Statistics Information, 1980-1984*, p. 18. Figures for Israeli visitors processed from data of Airport Authority - Land Terminal Network and El-Al Airlines.

Table 15.11
Distribution of Visitors from Egypt to Israel by Route,[a] 1980-1984

Year	By Land Visitors	%	By Air Visitors	%	Total Visitors	%
1980	68,959	73.9	24,349	26.1	93,308	100.0
1981	139,287	76.8	42,121	23.2	181,408	100.0
1982	165,435	82.5	35,122	17.6	200,557	100.0
1983	182,506	85.4	31,206	14.6	213,712	100.0
1984	187,602	85.7	31,405	14.3	219,007	100.0
Total	743,789	81.8	164,203	18.1	907,992	100.0

[a]Excluding visitors arriving by sea.

Sources: Figures for entry of visitors arriving by air processed from Central Bureau of Statistics, *Israel Statistical Yearbook.* Figures for visitors arriving by land processed from Airport Authority - Land Terminal Network, summaries for 1980-1984.

countries, it is useful to examine the entry of visitors from Egypt according to different categories. We distinguish between holders of Egyptian passports, nationals of other Arab countries, and Western tourists.

■ Entry of Egyptian Passport Holders to Israel

On the eve of the tourism agreements and the lifting of travel restrictions between Israel and Egypt, expectations and estimates in Israel on the numbers of Egyptian tourists who would visit Israel each year were high. In 1980 the population of Egypt reached 42 million. However, large sectors of this population live in conditions of poverty and hardship. Yet Egyptian society also includes middle- and high-income groups for whom Israel is a potential tourist attraction. Table 15.12 examines the entry of Egyptian passport holders to Israel by means of arrival. It is seen that the number of Egyptian nationals is low. In the five year period 1980–1984 a total of 17,958 Egyptian nationals visited Israel, amounting to 1.9 percent of the total tourist traffic from Egypt to Israel.

Official and other sources in Israel have stated that the number of Egyptian tourists visiting Israel is hindered by restrictions and statements made by the Egyptian authorities regarding Egyptian citizens interested in visiting Israel. In Israel this attitude was seen as a serious infringement of the agreements which the two states had signed. Official spokesmen in Egypt

Table 15.12
Entry of Egyptian Passport Holders to Israel, 1980-1984

Year	By air	By land	By sea	Total	Change in %
1980	1,474	578	69	2,121	--
1981	1,747	945	23	2,715	28.0
1982	1,622	2,489	48	4,159	53.2
1983	1,291	3,070	39	4,400	5.8
1984	1,269	3,215	79	4,563	2.8
Total	7,403	10,297	258	17,958	--

Sources: Central Bureau of Statistics, *Quarterly Statistics for Transport*, Jerusalem, 1982-1984; CBS, *Tourism to Israel 1984*, Jerusalem, 1985; CBS, *Israel Statistical Yearbook*, Jerusalem, 1981-1985; WTO, *World Travel and Tourism Statistics Yearbook*, various issues.

frequently denied these claims and announced that in Egypt there was no legal or administrative restriction preventing Egyptians from visiting Israel. According to these sources the checks and interrogations applied by the Egyptian Interior Ministry to Egyptian citizens wishing to visit Israel were aimed at preventing the entry of elements hostile to Israel.

Every Egyptian citizen wishing to visit Israel is obliged to obtain a special exit permit, in common with travellers wishing to visit the Communist countries. As described by the director of the Israel Tourism Bureau in Cairo, an Egyptian wishing to visit Israel has to go through a process of several time-consuming stages including questioning, and is even subjected to pressure to cancel his trip. First he must apply to the Interior Ministry and for an exit permit to Israel; in his application he has to note the purpose of his visit (tourism, business, family visit). At the Interior Ministry the applicant undergoes interrogation by Egyptian internal security personnel. He has to undergo another such interrogation as he enters the Israeli embassy in Cairo at the Egyptian security checkpoint located there. If the citizen is determined to visit Israel he will eventually be permitted to enter the offices of the Israel embassy. There he requests an entry visa to Israel. As he leaves the building the citizen will be called on yet a third time to answer a further series of questions put to him by Egyptian security personnel.

When Egyptian officials have been asked to explain why, in their view, the numbers of Egyptian citizens wishing to visit Israel was so low, they mentioned several factors. President Sadat in an interview with Anis Mansour, editor of the weekly *October*, said that "we must distinguish between the Egyptian character and the Israel character, between the pace of life in Israel and the pace of our life here. We are different, and so we shall remain."[10] In an interview by the Egyptian Tourism Minister Gamal al-

Nazir to the Egyptian newspaper *al-Musawwar*, the minister noted additional factors preventing large numbers of Egyptians from visiting Israel. In his
view Israel did not possess tourist attractions for the Egyptian visitor, and
the Egyptian tourist did not have sufficient information about the tourist
locations that do exist.[11] The underlying obstacle was political, the minister
believed. First, the holy sites that the Egyptian citizen would be interested
in visiting were considered Arab possessions under Israeli occupation, and
a visit to these places would be equivalent to recognition of the legitimacy
of the occupation; hence, Egyptians refrain from such trips. Secondly,
"Egypt has made it clear that an increase in the number of Egyptian tourists
to Israel is bound up with withdrawal by Israel from the occupied territories,
and any progress in the political negotiations will bring about an increase in
the number of Egyptian tourists."[12]

A harsher note was introduced into these statements at the time of the
Lebanon War. With the withdrawal of Israel from Lebanon a change also
took place in the tone of statements made by Egyptian officials. In May 1985,
on the eve of the Israeli withdrawal from Lebanon, Dr. Mustafa Halil, personal advisor to President Mubarak, stated: "Egypt has taken a clear-out
decision to improve its relations with Israel. About a year ago, when the Israeli army was still in Lebanon, you would not have heard such a declaration
from us."[13] A similar statement was quoted also from a senior Egyptian official, who informed the director of the Israel Tourism Bureau in Cairo that
"a change has taken place in the policy adopted so far, and the Egyptian
authorities will in the spring permit a number of tourist groups from Egypt
to visit Israel and instructions on this matter have been sent to the Egyptian
interior ministry."[14] These declarations leave no doubt as to the intervention by the Egyptian authorities directly and indirectly in the number of
Egyptian tourists wishing to visit Israel.

Israel possesses a wealth of places holy for Christianity that are revered
by the Coptic community also. There were high hopes in Israel that the
removal of travel restrictions between the two states would bring many Coptic pilgrims to Israel. In the years 1980–1984 only a few dozen members of
the large Coptic minority in Egypt actually came. This fact may be explained
on two levels. The first is primarily legal: the Coptic and the Ethiopian
churches are in conflict over the question of proprietorship of the Dir al-
Sultan monastery situated in the heart of the Holy Sepulchre Church in
Jerusalem. Israel has adopted the traditional policy of nonintervention in
the conflicts between the churches. At the beginning of the 1970s relations
between Israel and Ethiopia improved, and as a gesture of goodwill Israel
transferred control of Dir al-Sultan to the representatives of the Ethiopian
Church. Since then changes have taken place in Ethiopia, in Israel, and in
Egypt. Following the signing of the peace agreement, the Egyptian government, under pressure from the Coptic community, raised the demand that

control of the monastery be restored to Coptic hands. Israel undertook to study the request and placed the matter in the hands of Dr. Yosef Burg, Minister of the Interior. In practice representatives of the Ethiopian Church continue to hold the site, and the issue has not been resolved. On the second level, it should be borne in mind that the Copts are Egyptian citizens and as a minority their position is in any case delicate. In addition, they are subject to the same administrative obstacles and are exposed to the same declarations by officials and in the Egyptian media as other Egyptians. In the words of the Patriarch Shinuda III, the Head of the Coptic community in Egypt, there is additional reason for the dearth of Coptic visitors to Israel. In an interview in the Kuwaiti newspaper *al-Siyasa*, Shinuda declared that personally "he would not go to Jerusalem until the city is liberated from Israeli occupation, even if the problem of Dir al-Sultan is solved."

■ Entry of Citizens of Arab States to Israel from Egypt

One of the interesting effects of tourism cooperation between Israel and Egypt is the entry of passengers holding passports of Arab states (other than Egypt) into Israel from Egypt. For many of them Israel does not represent a vacation resort but a stopover. Some of these travellers cross the land border between Israel and Egypt and continue thence by land to the Jordan bridges; some come to visit relatives living in the territory of Israel.

Table 15.13 shows that between the opening of the land crossings on the Israel-Egypt border and 1984 the number of passport holders of Arab states crossing from Egypt to Israel grew by 84.8 percent. In this period, 94,527 passengers crossed from Egypt to Israel by land, accounting for 13.2 percent of the land passenger traffic from Egypt to Israel. The figures show that in spite of the Lebanon War and accompanying tension the number of Arab visitors arriving from Egypt continued to rise. It is worth noting that throughout the period under discussion the number of visitors from Arab countries was far higher than the number of Egyptian passport holders visiting Israel.

■ Entry of Western Tourists to Israel from Egypt

From 1980 to 1984, the number of Western tourists coming to visit Israel via Egypt grew continually. Two factors contributed to this trend: the signing of the peace treaty between Israel and Egypt, which changed the attitude of the Western tourist regarding the stability of the area,[15] and the lifting of travel restrictions, which for the first time made direct visits between the two countries possible. Table 15.14 shows the marked growth in the numbers of

Table 15.13
Entry of Arab passport holders to Israel from Egypt, 1980-1984

Year	Visitors	Change in %	% of all visitors by lands
1980	11,805		17.1
1981	20,820	76.4	15.0
1982	17,271	-17.0	10.4
1983	22,689	31.4	12.4
1984	21,942	-3.3	11.7

Sources: Based on data from the Land Terminal Network and El-Al Airlines.

Table 15.14
Entry of Western Visitors to Israel from Egypt, 1980-1984

Year	Western visitors	Change in %	% of total traffic[a]
1980	34,233	--	36.7
1981	63,397	85.1	35.0
1982	67,165	5.9	33.4
1983	88,794	32.2	41.5
1984	99,996	12.6	45.7

[a]*Traffic by air and land.*

Sources: Based on data from the Land Terminal Network and El-Al Airlines.

Western tourists entering Israel from Egypt in the years 1980–1984. A total of 353,585 Western visitors arrived, accounting for 38.9 percent of the total passenger traffic from Egypt to Israel. Most of the tourists arrived via land (60.6 percent), the remainder by air (39.4 percent). (The number of visitors arriving by sea is not available, for reasons explained above.)

■ Egyptian Tourism Relative to Overall Tourist Traffic to Israel

The importance of Egypt as a source of tourism for Israel should be examined not only in terms of the numbers of Egyptian passport holders visiting Israel but principally in terms of the total number of visitors reaching Israel from Egypt. Tourism constitutes one of the major sources of foreign currency for Israel and efforts and capital are invested in enlarging the number of visitors reaching the country each year. The place of origin of the visitors is of interest, but in economic terms the industry is measured by the numbers of tourists and how much they spend, and the greater these figures the larger the amounts of foreign currency accruing to the Israeli economy. Examining tourism links between Israel and Egypt from this view, we find that the latter country constitutes the departure point for tens of thousands of visitors entering Israel.

Table 15.15 shows that in the years 1980–1984, 907,992 passengers entered Israel from Egypt, amounting to 15.8 percent of overall tourist traffic entering Israel in this period. It is evident that since the lifting of travel restrictions between the two states the number of visitors entering Israel from Egypt has steadily grown each year. Even in years that were difficult for Israeli tourism (1982) the numbers of travellers entering from Egypt continued to rise.

Table 15.16 shows the proportion of Western passport holders entering Israel via Egypt out of total Western tourism to Israel. The table indicates that Egypt serves as the departure point for tens of thousands of Western tourists who visit Israel after having visited Egypt. In the years 1980–1984, 353,590 Western passport holders entered Israel from Egypt, comprising 6.16 percent of the total tourism volume to Israel. Since 1980 the numbers of such tourists have risen steadily each year.

The proportion of Egyptian nationals in the overall tourism to Israel is extremely small. Table 15.17 shows that in 1980–1984 Egyptian passport holders amounted to no more than one quarter of one percent (0.26 percent) of total tourism to Israel. Since the opening of the borders of the two states to civilian traffic no significant change has taken place in the numbers of Egyptian nationals visiting Israel.

▪ BALANCE OF ISRAEL-EGYPTIAN TOURISM

Study of the balance of tourism between Israel and Egypt shows that since the lifting of travel restrictions there has been a lively movement of travellers between the two states. In the five year period 1980–1984, 1,888,375 travellers crossed between Israel and Egypt, 907,992 of them from Egypt to Israel and 980,383 of them from Israel to Egypt, as shown in Table 15.18. The balance is thus 72,391, in Egypt's favor. These figures argue against the claim of "one-way" tourism, which has become a commonplace in describing the tourism links between the two countries. At the same time, the small number of Egyptian nationals visiting Israel is glaringly evident.

Several important questions still remain open. The most serious of them is in the contribution of the tourist traffic described above to the incomes of each of the two countries in foreign currency. In the absence of data on

Table 15.15
Visitors from Egypt - As percent of total visitors to Israel, 1980-1984

Year	Total visitors	Visitors from Egypt number	%
1980	1,175,000	93,308	7.9
1981	1,137,000	181,408	15.9
1982	997,500	200,557	20.1
1983	1,166,000	213,712	18.3
1984	1,259,000	219,007	17.4

Sources: Central Bureau of Statistics, *Israel Statistical Yearbook*, (1981-1985); Airports Authority - Land Terminal Network, Reports for 1980-1984.

Table 15.16
Western visitors arriving from Egypt as percent of total Western visitors to Israel, 1982-1984

Year	Total Western visitors to Israel	Western visitors arriving from Egypt number	%
1982	915,721	67,165	7.3
1983	1,026,612	88,799	8.6
1984	1,142,189	99,996	8.7

Sources: Central Bureau of Statistics, *Israel Statistical Yearbook*, (1983-1985); Airports Authority -Land Terminal Network, summaries for 1982-1984.

Table 15.17
Egyptian visitors as percent of total visitors to Israel, 1980-1984

Year	Total tourism	Egyptian tourists	% of total
1980	1,175,000	2,121	0.2
1981	1,137,000	2,715	0.2
1982	997,500	4,159	0.4
1983	1,166,000	4,400	0.4
1984	1,259,000	4,563	0.4
Total	5,734,500	17,958	0.3

Sources: Central Bureau of Statistics, Israel Statistical Yearbook (1981-1985);
Airports Authority - Land Terminal Network, Summaries for 1980-1984.

Table 15.18
Balance of Israel-Egyptian travellers, 1980-1984

Year	Total arrivals from Egypt	Total departures from Israel	Difference
1980	93,308	97,375	4,067
1981	181,408	188,183	6,775
1982	200,557	237,143	36,586
1983	213,712	226,609	12,897
1984	219,007	231,073	12,066
Total	907,992	980,383	72,391

Sources: Central Bureau of Statistics, *Israel Statistical Yearbook, 1980-1985*;
Airports Authority - Land Terminal Network, summaries for 1980-1984.

patterns of expenditure of the Israeli tourist in Egypt and of the Egyptian tourist in Israel it is not possible at this stage to answer this question satisfactorily. It is to be hoped that with the continuation of the tourist traffic it will become possible to evaluate its contribution in these terms also.

■ Notes

1. This paper is based on my thesis: "Economic Relations between Egypt and Israel: Agriculture, Tourism and Oil Trade, 1980–1984," University of Haifa, 1986. (Hereafter, Meital, "Economic Relations.") I am grateful to Prof. Gad Gilbar for his generous professional supervision and guidance.

2. See peace treaty between Israel and Egypt in: State of Israel, Ministry for Foreign Affairs. *Israel's Foreign Relations: Selected Documents*, Vol. 5, Jerusalem, 1981, p. 709. (Hereafter, *Israel's Foreign Relations*.)

3. Gammer, M. *The Process of Normalization between Egypt and Israel: Selected Documents*. Tel-Aviv University, 1981, p. 16.

4. *Israel's Foreign Relations*, vol. 6, pp. 392–395.

5. *See*: "Tourism Agreement between Egypt and Israel – 10 March 1980" in: Meital, "Economic Relations," pp. 203–204.

6. In order to prevent double counting, Israelis and Egyptian citizens are counted only on their exit from their borders.

7. *See*: Shipler, David, "Egypt-Israel Tourism: Mostly One-Way." *New York Times*, 15.3.1981. Mcdermott, Anthony. "Egypt and Israel: Empty Relations," Middle East International, No. 187 (12.11.1982). Beinin Joel. "The Cold Peace," *MERIP REPORTS*, (Jan. 1985), pp. 3–9, and Alper, Joseph and Leon Tamman. "Egypt's Frosty Friendship with Israel," *Newsview*, No. 29 (26.7.83), pp. 10–14.

8. *See*: De-Shalit, Meir. "Tourism" in: Hareven, Alouph (ed). *A Chance for Peace: Risks and Hopes*. Jerusalem, Van Leer, 1980, pp. 174–176.

9. *Jerusalem Post*, 29.6.81.

10. *October* 24.2.80.

11. *Al-Musawar*, 13.11.81, pp. 11.

12. Ibid.

13. *Yediot Ahronot*, 17.5.85.

14. *Maariv*, 11.3.84.

15. That concerns only the period 1980–1984, and doesn't include the strong effects of the 1985–1986 terrorists activities, and their harmful influence on tourism to the Middle East.

16

The Potential for Cooperation in Water Projects in the Middle East at Peace

Elisha Kally
Edited by Hilary Wolpert

■ INTRODUCTION

Conflicts over utilization of the region's water resources have appeared repeatedly in various stages of the protracted Arab-Israeli conflict, but were never central to it.

Agreements on the cooperative use of the region's water resources or indeed, of any other resources, would be a major building block in the construction of peace in the area. Binational and multinational projects for the utilization and distribution of shared water resources rank high in the list of instruments that may bolster the peace process. Cooperation in this field should be given high priority; some of these projects are so indispensable for the consolidation of peace in the region that failure to implement them will keep existing tensions unresolved. This may sow the seeds of future conflicts over water or could weaken or jeopardize any peace agreement which is reached. The most important project among the possible cooperative projects described here is the supply of water to the Gaza Strip and the West Bank from external sources. Other projects described here are less essential politically, but would yield immediate, clear welfare benefits to the countries involved.

Among the projects to be outlined below, some are bilateral and others are multilateral.

The first two projects described here, the conveyance of Nile water eastward to the Gaza Strip, and further, and a joint Jordanian-Israeli project for utilizing the Yarmuk River, are conventional joint water projects while the others are complexes of projects whose parts are intertwined. The bilateral Jordanian-Israeli project for the exploitation of the Yarmuk River might supply the water required for the West Bank; the conveyance of Nile water northward might fulfill the same role with respect to the Gaza Strip.

Some of the projects are interchangeable. Nile water might be an alternative to supplies originating in Lebanon. If a given project were not going to be implemented, then its alternative would become more urgent. The description that follows will further elucidate these interdependencies. Each project is independently feasible, but technical, economic and political conditions as well as other projects being done in this framework will determine whether a project is implemented. It is therefore possible to envisage different combinations of various projects, and only the concrete shape of the peace will determine the "basket" of projects that could be undertaken.

■ A PROJECT FOR THE EASTWARD CONVEYANCE OF NILE WATERS

Background and Rationale

The rationale underlying this project comes from the substantial surpluses of Nile water in Egypt. The quantity of water under discussion is tiny by comparison with Egypt's total water resources, about half a per cent of her consumption, but would be sufficient to solve most of the water problems of the other areas. These waters can be conveyed to the north and east to the Gaza Strip, the Israeli Negev and, in certain conditions, also to the West Bank and Jordan, at a reasonable cost.

The political ramifications of such a project are immediately apparent: Egypt and Israel would have to cooperate in any project to convey Nile water through Israeli territory to third parties. Together they hold the key to what might become a major regional peace-promoting undertaking. Israel would be an indispensable partner in any multinational water plan, and particularly so in schemes of water exchanges between the countries and territories of the region.

Egypt can expect to have water surpluses more than sufficient for the transfers discussed here for many years. At present these surpluses result from the capacity of Lake Nasser to supply several billions of cubic meters more water per year than is required in Egypt. Future agricultural, industrial and urban development will not absorb these surpluses before new additional supplies become available to Egypt.

Plans to conserve water through the introduction of more efficient irrigation methods in order to increase agricultural production and preserve soil fertility will be implemented regardless of how the water conserved is to be used. Water conserved through these improved methods are expected to result in savings of some 10 billion cubic meters of water a year. Even a massive extension of Egypt's cultivated area will not exhaust these additional supplies before a new source of water, Egypt's share of the water to be provided by the Jonglei Project in the Sudan, becomes available, and this may amount to some 10 billion cubic meters a year.

Egypt already plans to convey Nile waters to the Sinai Peninsula and to construct irrigation works there. This project, which entails construction of a canal along the Mediterranean shore, might benefit from economies of scale by being expanded to transport Nile water further northward and eastward.

Finally, it would be cheaper to supply Israel's Negev with Nile waters than, as at present, to pump water from the Sea of Galilee at an energy cost of 2–3 kwh. per cubic meter of water. Conveying water from the Nile to the Negev would cost less than one kwh. per cubic meter. This large cost difference suggests the possibility of an exchange of water. If Israel could obtain water from the Nile, the water thus released from their present use in the Negev might be conveyed from the Sea of Galilee to closer destinations on the West Bank and, particularly, to Jordan (to which the cost of conveyance would be even lower). The natural terrain is highly favorable to such a multilateral exchange of water between Israel and her neighbors.

Nevertheless, it should not be overlooked that such a scheme would have to overcome considerable political difficulties. In addition to resistance of an ideological nature, such a project would create an imbalance of benefits and risks between the suppliers of water and its users.

The economic gains to the provider (Egypt) would be small, on the order of some $10 million a year from the export of several hundreds of millions of cubic meters of water at a cost of a few cents per cubic meter. The consumers, in contrast, would become highly dependent upon the system thus created, and for them the economic cost of dissociation would be much higher than for the providers. Therefore, the feasibility of the project would depend on whatever *political* costs and benefits that might be attached to taking part in such an exchange or to dissociation from it by one of the parties involved. The political and economic considerations supporting such a project and those that might inhibit it, from the probable Egyptian viewpoint, are summarized in Table 16.1.

Table 16.1
Supporting and limiting factors in the Nile water exporting project

Considerations Destination	Engineering and Economic Factors and Considerations	Political-Ideological Factors and Considerations
Gaza Strip	This is the destination closest to the projected Egyptian Sinai project; it is at the same elevation--some 50 meters above sea level. It is also relatively simple to implement as an extension of Egypt's Sinai project. The Gaza Strip may also absorb winter surpluses of water to replenish the aquifer.	Egyptian commitment to the Gaza Strip is relatively high, among other reasons because between 1949 and 1967 the territory was under Egyptian administration.
Israeli Negev	Somwhat more distant than the Gaza Strip and also at a higher elevation, of up to 200 meters; the extension of the Sinai project to reach the Negev is therefore more complex. The use of winter water surpluses for storage is more difficult because suitable aquifers are lacking.	Strong Egyptian reluctance to supply Nile waters to Israel is likely to persist; even the authority of Sadat was unable to overcome the opposition. This reluctance may be reduced in the case of a multilateral exchange scheme.
West Bank	Involves an exchange of water with Israel, thus making the project more complex.	Egyptian commitment to the West Bank is less than to the Gaza Strip; an exchange of water with Israel will give the appearance of Nile waters being supplied to Israel and may encounter ideological resistance.
Jordan	As for West Bank, but more econo-mical, because conveying water from the Sea of Galilee to the Ghor Canal is cheaper than pumping it to the West Bank.	As for West Bank.

■ Description of the Project

The project will start with the widening of the El-Salaam Canal which is fed by the Damietta branch of the Nile Delta and its continuation by the Egyptian Sinai canal, so as to attain the necessary carrying capacity (see Map 16.1).

The cost of the water will depend on the carrying capacity of the Egyptian Sinai project and on whether the investment in its extension would be charged to it as a marginal or as a proportional user of the entire project. Assuming that the Sinai project will have a carrying capacity of 1 billion cubic meters a year, and that its extension to the Gaza Strip and the Negev would be charged proportionally, the investment costs would be as shown in Table 16.2. The resulting cost of the water, in U.S. cents per cubic meter, is shown in Table 16.3.

Benefits in terms of cost per cubic meter from a water exchange project in which Israel receives Nile water for the Negev in exchange for water from the Sea of Galilee, which would then be supplied to the West Bank and Jordan, are shown in Table 16.4.

Table 16.4 shows that within the framework of an exchange, the cost of water provision would be some 20 cents per m^3/year for water brought to the West Bank, and only 5 cents per m^3/year for water brought to Jordan, due to favorable topography and use of the existing Ghor Canal. Both of these prices are well within the range of the marginal product value of water, between 10 and 30 cents per cubic meter, in Israel, Jordan, the West Bank and the Gaza Strip. The estimates for the West Bank, however, assume that the water will be pumped only to the lower-lying areas of Samaria, up to an elevation of 200-300 meters above sea level.

■ A JORDANIAN-ISRAELI PROJECT FOR EXPLOITING THE YARMUK RIVER

The Yarmuk River is one of the bigger water resources in the region, with an annual flow of some 500 million cubic meters. By tacit agreement among the riparian countries, Syria, Jordan and Israel, most of the river's water is allocated to Jordan. Jordan exploits primarily the Yarmuk's summer flow, diverting it to the Ghor Canal which irrigates the Ghor Valley east of the Jordan River over its entire length. Although the river runs through a region

MAP 16.1: YARMUK DIVERSION TO THE SEA OF GALILEE

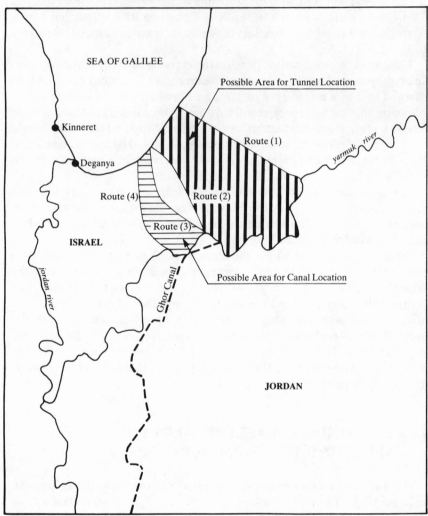

Source: E. Kally, The Armand Hammer Fund for Economic Cooperation in the Middle East, A MIDDLE EAST WATER PLAN UNDER PEACE, Tel–Aviv University, March 1986.

Table 16.2
Investment in the Nile Water Project, 1984 Prices

	Investment, US$ per m^3 per annum		Total Investment, in US$ millions	
	(capacity - 10^6 m^3/year)			
	100	500	100	500
Investment Required				
Widening of Sinai Canal	1.02	0.76	102	380
Extension of Sinai Water Carrier to Gaza Strip and Negev	0.56	0.63	56	315
Total cost of project	1.58	1.39	158	695

Table 16.3
Estimated Cost of Water, in US Cents per M^3 1984 Prices

Capacity	100M.m^3/year	500M.m^3/year
Investment Component		
Capital costs, at 5% per annum	8.7	7.6
Maintenance, operation, treatment	3.5	3.0
Energy costs for pumping, at 7 cents/kwh.	5.2	5.2
Cost of water at source	4.0	4.0
Total cost per cubic meter	21.4	19.8

Table 16.4
Estimated Change in Water Cost from an Exchange Project (US cents per cubic meter)

Destination Cost Component	West Bank (low-lying areas of Samaria)	Jordan (Ghor system)
Energy savings compared with pumping Sea of Galilee water to the Negev	-17	-17
Cost of pumping to destination	14	1
Capital cost of conveyance systems	3	1
Total cost difference per m^3	± 0	-15

short of water, the bulk of its water remains unutilized because most of its flow consists of winter floodwaters. These can be utilized only if some means of off-season storage is available.

The Yarmuk's winter floodwaters might be stored either by constructing upstream dams or by diverting them to their natural reservoir, the Sea of Galilee. Both alternatives are at present beset by political difficulties. The upstream damming of the river is problematic politically because the Yarmuk is an international boundary line along almost its entire length. Its southwestern bank lies in Jordan while its north-western bank is in Syria or in the Golan Heights under Israeli rule.

In addition, the investment in any of the technically feasible upstream dams would raise the cost of water thus obtained above the level justified by its value in agricultural production. The cost of the downstream dam at Nuheiba has been estimated at some $500 million, while that further upstream, at Maqarin, may require an investment of as much as $1 billion. This amounts to an investment cost of $2–3 per cubic meter per year, which is far in excess of the economic value of the water.

The alternative, of diverting the Yarmuk's winter floodwaters to the Sea of Galilee, is precluded by the existing state of war between Jordan and Israel, but it is the technically easiest and most economical solution to Jordan's water problems in the near future. The cost of this project would be only a few percent of what would be needed for the construction of upstream reservoirs.

The storage capacity of the Sea of Galilee, Israel's central water reservoir, is limited, and at present stands at some 500 million cubic meters, although there are plans for increasing it to 750 million cubic meters. Thus nearly half of the waters diverted from the Yarmuk to the Lake of Galilee would run off in winter and remain unutilized.

Nevertheless, the quantity of water that might be made available to Jordan through storage in the Sea of Galilee is quite substantial – an additional 100 million cubic meters a year. This quantity is sufficient for Jordan's short-term requirements, so that this is the most promising supplemental water supply for Jordan in terms of quantity and cost.

This proposal is advantageous to Israel as well: Israel could make use of the Yarmuk's winter floodwaters, which Jordan cannot utilize because of insufficient storage facilities, by pumping them south for subterranean storage in aquifers of Israel's central region. Another benefit to Israel would be the sweetening of the Sea of Galilee water, which today has a high salt content of 800 parts per million. The diversion of the Yarmuk waters into the Lake could reduce this salinity by 20 per cent. Possible sites for the project are shown in Map 16.2.

Pumping the stored water from the Sea of Galilee into the Ghor system will require coordination with pumping into Israel's National Water Carrier.

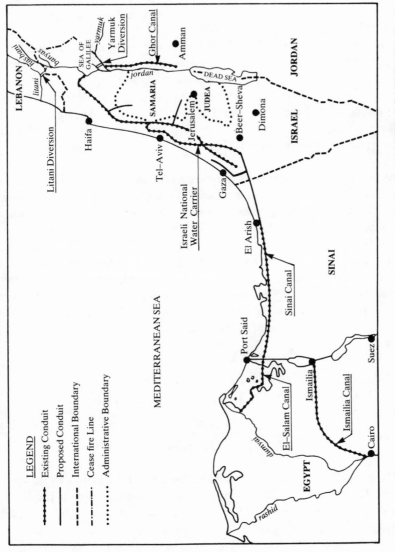

MAP 16.2: SINAI CANAL AND MAIN REGIONAL CONDUITS

LEGEND

Existing Conduit
Proposed Conduit
International Boundary
Cease fire Line
Administrative Boundary

Source: E. Kally, The Armand Hammer Fund for Economic Cooperation in the Middle East, A MIDDLE EAST WATER PLAN UNDER PEACE, Tel-Aviv University, March 1986.

A simulation model of the proposed project has shown that the more intensive pumping into Israel's National Water Carrier will have two contradictory results with regard to the project's objectives. On the one hand, it will reduce the losses of Yarmuk winter surpluses by feeding them into Israel's aquifer in the winter, but on the other hand it will increase the risk of water shortages in Jordan in summers following particularly dry winters.

Therefore, a compromise will have to be found to optimize Israeli and Jordanian consumption in both wet and dry seasons, while allowing for fluctuations in rainfall. Water from the Yarmuk might be supplied to the West Bank via either existing Israeli or Jordanian pumping stations, or through additional pumping stations. This will be described further on. If this were done, the project would have to be operated so as to provide an optimal distribution among the three participating entities, with storage capacity that minimizes runoff of winter water without creating too high a price per m^3 for water.

As previously mentioned, the physical limits and technical constraints on the operation of the proposed scheme do not detract from its economic desirability. The investment in the installations listed above is estimated at $21 million, which would make the cost of the water made available by it (some 180 million cubic meters a year) only 1.5 cents per cubic meter. The cost of pumping the water from the Sea of Galilee to Jordan's Ghor system would cost only about one-tenth of a kwh. per cubic meter (0.7 US cents). The alternative, pumping via Israel's National Water Carrier, would be much more expensive. The investment and the costs of water for Jordan under three different schemes are shown in Table 16.5.

■ COMPREHENSIVE JORDANIAN – ISRAELI COOPERATION IN THE USE OF WATER

General Background

The entire border between Israel and Jordan runs through a hydrological center. Hydrological systems common to both countries include the Jordan and Yarmuk Rivers, the Dead Sea, the Arava Wadi and the Gulf of Aqaba-Eilat Gulf of the Red Sea. In addition, the two countries have common aquifers, mainly in the Yarmuk basin and in the Arava. This shared geography invites cooperation in the development, use and management of shared water resources. The possibility of storing Yarmuk water in the Sea of Galilee was already discussed above.

Table 16.5
Investment and cost to Jordan of storing Yarmuk water for three different alternatives

Cost Component	Storage Project Dam within Jordanian- Israeli territory	Dam within Jordanian- Syrian territory	Diversion to the Sea of Galilee
Investment, US$ millions	500	1,000	21
Capital costs, US cents/m^3, at 10% per annum	14.9	34.6	1.4
Capital costs, US cents/m^3, at 5% per annum	8.4	19.4	0.8
Costs of pumping (+) or power generation (-), in US cents/m^3	-2.0	-3.0	+0.1
Other costs, US cents/m^3	2.0	4.0	0.2
Cost of water, US cents/m^3, with capital costs at 10% p.a.	14.9	35.6	1.7
Cost of water, capital costs at 5% per annum	8.4	20.4	1.1

The areas of potential cooperation extend beyond the possibilities afforded and invited by shared water resources. Jordan, whose water requirements exceed the resources readily available within her territory, has already exhibited her interest in imports of water from other countries in the past, by her participation in the Arab League scheme for diversion of the Jordan River's headwaters into the Yarmuk, and, more recently, through the proposed importation of water by pipeline from Iraq. The two countries that might export water to Jordan at an economic cost are Egypt and Lebanon, and both these sources will be accessible to Jordan only with the consent of Israel, through whose territory such waters would have to be conveyed. Another possible form of cooperation in water resource use between Jordan and Israel would be joint projects for increasing precipitation by cloud-seeding. One project that would involve joint management of the Dead Sea is the joint Two Seas Project. These cooperative projects are described below. The projects' dependence on the level of relations between the two countries is summarized in Table 16.6.

■ Cooperation in the Management of Common Aquifers

Israel and Jordan already cooperate tacitly in the simultaneous exploitation of surface waters. However, they use their common aquifers in the

Table 16.6
Options for cooperation in water use and level of political accord required for each

Subject / Level of Relations	Sharing of Yarmouk water according to existing agreement	Coordination in groundwater exploitation	Active cooperation in ground water use	Artificial rain in Jordan	Storing of Yarmouk Water in Sea of Galilee	Joint Two-Seas Project	Conveyance of water from third country
Coordination in certain subjects	XXXX						
Pre-peace agreement		XXXXXXXX	XXXX	XXXX			
Peace between Israel and Jordan					XXXX	XXXXX	
Regional peace							XXXX

Yarmuk basin and in the Arava with virtually no coordination, to the detriment of both countries. The lack of coordination carries risks for both, such as that of deteriorating quality of water as a result of over-exploitation, or damage to other water sources currently in use. In view of the past experience in tacit cooperation in the use of the water of the Yarmuk River, a greater measure of coordination would appear to be possible even before peace between the two countries is attained.

▪ External Supplies of Water for Jordan

Water from external sources, either from the Nile or from Lebanon, might be conveyed to Jordan (in the case of Egypt, through a water exchange) by transferring the necessary water from the Sea of Galilee to the Ghor Canal. The manner in which the availability of such water supplies in the Sea of Galilee would be assured would depend on the source of the potential imports. If the source were Lebanon, Litani River water would be diverted into the drainage basin of the Jordan River, from where it would reach the Sea of Galilee for transfer to the Ghor Canal. If the source of supply were the Nile, the water supplied to Jordan would be that conserved, by no longer being pumped from the Sea of Galilee for irrigation of the Negev.

Furthermore, transfer of water from the Sea of Galilee would not, at least initially, have to involve any physical conveyance of water from the Sea. Israel could merely waive her right to the Yarmuk waters she is now using. Only water resource use in excess of Israel's present share would require construction of pumping installations.

▪ A Cloud-Seeding Project

Since the Sixties, Israel has carried out experiments to examine whether the quantity of natural precipitation can be augmented by seeding rain clouds with silver iodide. This seeding is carried out by airplanes as well as by ovens stationed on the ground. The experiments have shown with a high degree of certainty that cloud-seeding can increase precipitation in the north of the country by 15–20 per cent. In the South, the results of the experiments have been less favorable, apparently as a consequence of the origin and temperature of the clouds there. In the 70s, a special experiment was carried out on the basis of these results for the drainage basin of the Sea of Galilee, and today Israel carries out routine cloud-seeding in that area.

The findings from these experiments indicate that cloud-seeding might increase precipitation in Jordan as well, but only practical experience could show how much of an increase is possible. The two main regions in which artificial rainmaking might be carried out are the Ghor Valley, Jordan's main agricultural area, and the Yarmuk River basin, which is Jordan's main source of surface water. In addition, the drainage basins of the Jordan River's eastern tributaries might also benefit. Most of the cloud-seeding that might benefit these areas would have to be done over Israeli territory, at a distance of several dozen kilometers to the south-west of the target areas. Based on Israeli experience with regard to the Sea of Galilee basin, cloud-seeding will probably be more successful in the Yarmuk basin than in areas further south.

A project of this kind, which does not involve a high degree of day-to-day cooperation, might well be undertaken even in advance of a peace agreement. The interdependence created by it would be low, as would be the cost of dissociation for either party.

▪ Use of the Ghor Canal

The Ghor Canal was originally built to supply water to the West Bank while that area was under Jordanian rule, as well as to Jordan. As a result, the Canal is under-utilized today. It may therefore be used to supply water to several groups of consumers west of the Jordan River. The settlements in the Israeli part of the Jordan Valley and the Beit She'an Valley presently receive their share of the Yarmuk water all the way from the headwaters of the Yarmuk and the Jordan (via Israel's National Water Carrier). Supply of the same quantities of water from the Ghor Canal, via a pipeline crossing the Jordan's riverbed westward, would save energy *and* supply sweeter water.

Similarly, the eastern part of the West Bank might be supplied with water pumped from the Sea of Galilee into the Ghor Canal and thence, again, via a pipeline crossing the Jordan's riverbed. This would eliminate the cost of building a conveyance system from the Sea of Galilee to the south-west. Finally, the cheapest way to supply the lower western Jordan Valley with water would also be through the Ghor Canal. This would eliminate the need for a parallel conveyance system or, alternatively, of utilizing the saline waters of the lower Jordan.

▪ Cooperation in Exploiting the Lower Jordan River

In addition to the above suggestions, Israel and Jordan might cooperate in the erection on the lower Jordan. At present, such dams are not very attractive economically, due to the salinity of the water involved. They will become even less worthwhile if the Yarmuk River water is stored in the Sea of

Galilee. However, in the more distant future, increased demand for water may make it necessary to consider more expensive water supply projects such as this one.

■ A Joint "Two-Seas" Project

The "Two-Seas" Canal Project offers the potential for joint management of the shared Dead Sea basin. Each country, separately, as if the other did not exist, has drawn up plans for conveying water from the Mediterranean (an Israeli plan) and the Red Sea (both Jordan and Israeli plans) to the Dead Sea, which lies 400 meters below sea level, for the generation of hydroelectricity. Both projects rely upon the evaporation rate of about 1 cubic km^3/year from the Dead Sea, and have been rendered feasible by the roughly equal volume of fresh water that previously flowed into the Dead Sea which Israel and Jordan now draw off annually for irrigation purposes by Israel and Jordan.

This double planning is absurd. The same resource cannot be exploited twice. Also a project of this scope can be carried out economically only if it is financed by a "soft loan," which will probably be forthcoming only for a joint project. A joint project would also constitute a significant additional benefit of constituting another benefit of peacemaking. (See Map 16.3.)

■ COOPERATIVE WATER PROJECTS BETWEEN LEBANON AND ISRAEL

Cooperation between Lebanon and Israel might include electrical power generation from water now flowing into Israel as part of her share in common water resources, and transfer of Lebanese water to Israel for the twin purposes of power generation and supply to additional consumers. These customers, as already described, could be in Israel, Jordan or the West Bank.

The Hasbani River, and to a lesser extent the Ayoun River, could be used for the generation of hydroelectric power. Hydroelectric power generation from the Hasbani would not be very significant quantitatively, only 40 million kwh. a year. A bigger and considerably more significant area of cooperation between Lebanon and Israel would be the conveyance of Lebanese water surpluses through Israel, for sale to Jordan, the West Bank, or to Israel itself.

Such a transfer is feasible through the diversion, by tunnel, of part of the Litani's flow into the Hasbani River (See Map 16.4) or into the Ayoun River. The flows of the upper Litani are already used by the Karoun reservoir which

318

MAP 16.3: THE TWO–SEAS PROJECT
ROUTES OF THE ISRAELI, JORDANIAN AND BI–TERRITORIAL ALTERNATIVES

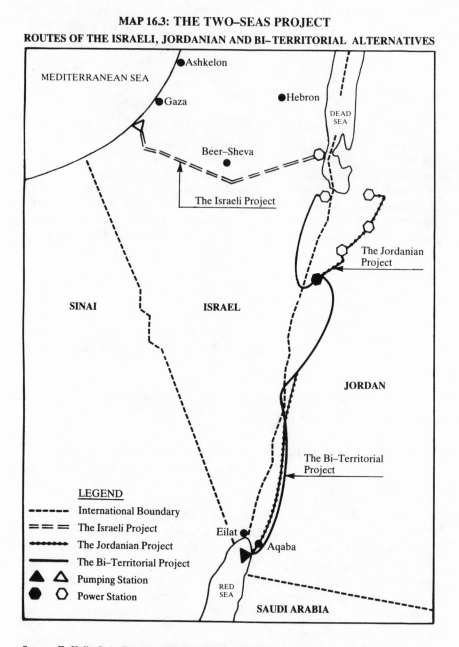

Source: E. Kally & A. Tal, The Armand Hammer Fund for Economic Cooperation in the Middle East, MIDDLE EAST REGIONAL COOPERATION IN THE USE OF ENERGY RESOURCES UNDER PEACE, Tel–Aviv University, November 1986.

MAP 16.4: DIVERSION OF LITANI WATER TO THE JORDAN RIVER BASIN

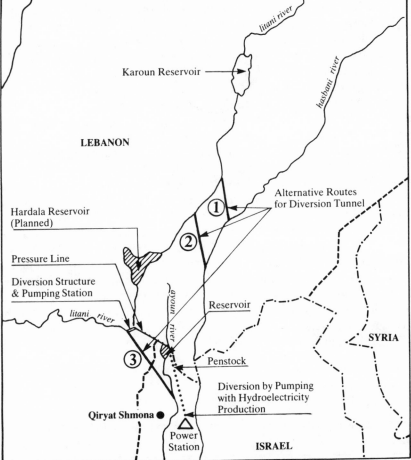

Source: E. Kally, The Armand Hammer Fund for Economic Cooperation in the Middle East, A MIDDLE EAST WATER PLAN UNDER PEACE, Tel–Aviv University, March 1986.

lies 850 meters above sea level. From the Karoun reservoir, the water is fed into a tunnel towards the Mediterranean seashore, generating electric power on its way. This leaves the possibility of generating electricity from the flows of the lower Litani, which may be utilized by the planned Hardala reservoir, at an elevation of 230 meters, upstream from where the Litani changes its course from a southward to a western direction. At this bend the water comes closest to Israeli territory, and could be diverted to Israel.

Most of the hydroelectric power within such a scheme would be generated by the Almagor power station planned to be built above the northern tip of the Sea of Galilee in order to use the Jordan River flow there. The addition of water from the Litani to the presently available flow would make the Almagor project more efficient. It might also reduce existing opposition to the project in Israel because of its environmental impact. As presently conceived, the project would lead to a partial drying out of the Jordan's riverbed in an area that has been declared a nature preserve. Additional water from the Litani could partially overcome this problem.

The diversion of the lower Litani to the Sea of Galilee would produce additional electric power, but would diminish the water resources at the disposal of Lebanon. At present, the lower Litani has surplus water, but this situation may change in the future, as the demand for water in Lebanon grows.

Therefore, the diversion of the Litani waters considered here should be limited to some 100 m³ per annum. Lebanon's limited water surpluses may also require the development of supplementary water resources along the course of the lower Litani to make up for the diverted waters. Such water sources would be more difficult to exploit and they would have to be paid for by the recipients of the water in lieu of or in addition to payment for the diverted Litani waters.

The estimated cost of diverting the Litani to the Sea of Galilee is shown in Table 16.7.

Table 16.7
Costs of diverting Litani waters to the Sea of Galilee basin, in US cents per cubic meter

Cost of water at the source	10
Cost of diversion	4
Value of electric power generated	-6
Total cost per m³	8

■ THE SUPPLY OF WATER TO THE WEST BANK AND THE GAZA STRIP

The West Bank and Gaza Strip have the most limited water resources of any locality in the region. They require external water sources—the West Bank, for its further development, and the Gaza Strip—even for maintaining the level of existing consumption. This places a special political importance on the solution to the water problems of these territories.

Solution to the water shortages of the West Bank and the Gaza Strip, at present, and even more acutely so for the future, is possible only within the framework of a resolution to the regional conflict.

The cultivated areas of the West Bank lie 200 to 700 meters above sea level. Conveying water for irrigation to the upper elevations is questionable on economic grounds, in view of the large differences in elevation between these areas and the potential sources of supply. It will therefore be necessary to consider alternative supply sources, and economic considerations which suggest restricting the supply of irrigation water only to the lower-lying areas, against the political considerations that may favor supplying of irrigation water to higher locations as well.

The Nile is the preferable source of supply of water for the Gaza Strip, for geographic/topographic as well as political reasons. The best source for the West Bank is less self-evident but the Yarmuk and the Litani may be considered as the most obvious choices. Under either of the latter two alternatives, the imported waters would have to be conveyed via the Sea of Galilee.

The demand for irrigation water in the West Bank and the Gaza Strip by the end of the century is forecast at between 290 and 475 million cubic meters a year, depending on whether only the low-lying irrigable areas in the West Bank are to be supplied or the lands at higher elevations as well. In the first alternative the irrigated area would be 48,000 hectares; in the second alternative—74,000 hectares.

Predicted demand for water for nonagricultural purposes is based on Israel's per capita consumption of water when its per capita gross national product was at the level forecast for the inhabitants of these territories by the beginning of the next century, some $1,700 a year. On that basis, total nonagricultural demand for water is expected to reach some 125 million cubic meters.

The local water resources of the West Bank and the Gaza Strip amount to some 143 million cubic meters a year. Table 16.8 summarizes the alternative sources by which the limited local water supplies of the West Bank and the Gaza Strip might be augmented to meet predicted demand.

Table 16.8

Possible additional water supplies for the West Bank and Gaza Strip in millions of m^3 per annum (in brackets - the "Lebanese" solution)

Source	Destination West Bank	Gaza Strip	Total External Supplies
Nile	81	91	172
	(-)	(91)	(91)
Yarmuk	41	-	41
	(35)	(-)	(35)
Litani	-	-	-
	(87)	(-)	(87)
All Sources	122	91	213
	(122)	(91)	(213)

Total external supplies to be brought in are estimated at 213 million cubic meters. This figure would have to rise to 360 million cubic meters in order for irrigation water to be provided for agricultural land in the West Bank which is more than 200 meters above sea level. This alternative, part of the "All Egyptian" solution, is shown in Map 16.5.

The investment required for the various components of this project consists of the capital needed to convey the water from its respective source (Nile, Yarmuk, Litani) and that for the distribution systems. The total required investment varies with the combination of sources chosen. Table 16.9 presents the "Egyptian" alternative, both its limited and expanded versions. The investment necessary for the limited version is considerably smaller. It is assumed that the rate of interest charged to the investment in this project will be five percent a year. At the presently prevailing costs of

Table 16.9

Investment and cost of water in the "Egyptian" alternative of supplying water to the West Bank and Gaza Strip, 1984 prices

Destination	Gaza Strip		West Bank	
Alternative	Investment, US$ millions	Cost of Water US cents/m^3	Investment, US$ millions	Cost of Water US cents/m^3
Limited "Egyptian"	127	21.2	227	20.8
"All Egyptian" Alternative	127	21.2	514	24.7

323

MAP 16.5: POSSIBLE EXTERNAL WATER SUPPLIES FOR THE WEST BANK
AND GAZA STRIP
("ALL EGYPTIAN" ALTERNATIVE)

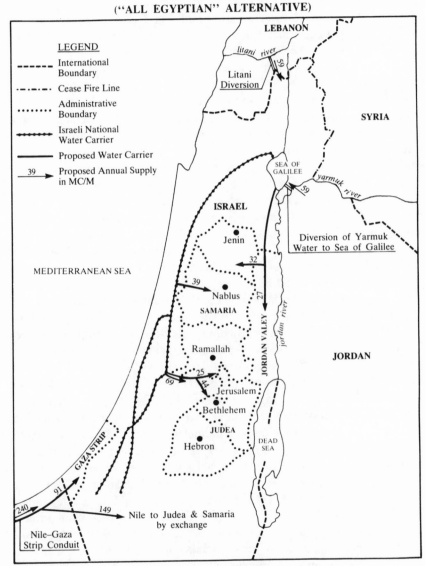

Based on Source: E. Kally, The Armand Hammer Fund for Economic Cooperation in the Middle East,
A MIDDLE EAST WATER PLAN UNDER PEACE, Tel-Aviv University, March 1986.

capital, this represents a subsidization of the project. It is, however, customary to subsidize infrastructure projects of this type through their capital costs. The non-economic benefits of this project, and its dependence on such a subsidy, makes this a reasonable assumption.

The resulting cost of water is rather high in relation to the agricultural product-value per cubic meter, but does not exceed present product values in Israel and Jordan. The relatively low cost estimate obtained for the West Bank is due to the low cost of pumping water from the Sea of Galilee to the Jordan Valley, and the higher cost of the expanded alternative is caused by the high costs of pumping water to the upper elevations in the West Bank.

Resolution of the future of the Palestinians is inextricably tied up with the issue of water supplies for the West Bank and the Gaza Strip. Additional water supplies can be brought from their possible sources only via Israel and with her consent and cooperation. A region-wide agreement on the development and distribution of water resources is therefore indispensable.

As mentioned above, the interdependence that would be created by the projects described in this chapter is not symmetrical between net suppliers and net users of water. While the economic cost of dissociation might be low for Egypt as well as, in some possible alternative scenarios, for Israel and for Lebanon, the cost of dissociation to the recipients – the West Bank and the Gaza Strip – would be very high.

An integrated scheme of supplying the West Bank and the Gaza Strip with water from the Nile and the Litani, involving an exchange of water with Israel, would leave these territories completely dependent on these sources and transfers. Egypt, and to a lesser extent Israel as well, might theoretically be in a position to dissociate themselves without incurring an excessive economic cost. However, Egypt has a commitment to the Palestinian cause, and is unlikely to deprive the inhabitants of the Gaza Strip, as well as those of the West Bank of vital water supplies once they have been made available. Similarly, if Israel were to attempt to dissociate herself from such a scheme, this would be regarded by all the other parties concerned as a hostile act. The political cost of dissociation for Israel would therefore be very high, and this would reduce the risks involved for the West Bank and the Gaza Strip.

Similar considerations apply to Jordan. Jordan would be less dependent than the West Bank upon a joint project with Israel for the exploitation of the Yarmuk River, but an asymmetry vis-a-vis Israel would remain. However, economic costs of dissociation combined with political costs would probably be enough to generate sufficient incentives on all sides for the continuation of the water exchange.

■ SUMMARY

A settlement of the Arab-Israeli conflict and the establishment of peace in the region will require the implementation of binational and multinational water projects. Cooperation in the development and utilization of water resources has a much greater political and economic significance than cooperation in most other infrastructure projects and productive enterprises. Indeed, failure to incorporate such cooperative projects into the peace agreements themselves, and to implement them, may perpetuate a situation of latent conflict over water resources. Such conflict may jeopardize the stability of peace in the region. Conversely, the successful implementation of the cooperative projects described here will strengthen and stabilize the peace.

■ REFERENCES

Elisha Kally and Abraham Tal, "Possible Cooperation between Israel and Jordan in Storing the Yarmuk River Winter Floods in Lake Tiberias" (Hebrew), The Interdisciplinary Center for Technological Analysis and Forecasting, Tel Aviv University, March 1983.

Elisha Kally and Irit Amittay, "Water Supply to the Autonomy Areas from External Sources" (Hebrew), The Interdisciplinary Center for Technological Analysis and Forecasting, Tel Aviv University, February 1984.

17

A Proposal for a Cooperative Water Project: The Aqaba-Eilat Canal/Port

Baruch Raz

Water, a shared natural resource, has caused both conflict and coopera-tion in the Middle East since biblical times. Though water is not usually cited as the primary basis for wars in the region, throughout history it stands out as a source of conflict. Since it is the limiting factor to life and economic growth, consensus in water exploitation has often been hard to reach.

Modern technology offers a multitude of possible projects that could con-tribute to peace through cooperative management of water resources. A variety of water projects are summarized in a table in Appendix II. They can be divided into three basic categories:

1) Projects to maximize water utility, i.e., water transport from areas where it is not used up to areas in dire need of it. This maximizes economic return for water by moving it from areas of low water value to areas of high water value.

2) Projects to better exploit existing water resources in each country. These include projects like modern irrigation, cloud-seeding, and desalina-tion.

3) Engineering projects for extra-agricultural benefit. These include projects like salt water for aquaculture, water cooled power plants, and the Aqaba Eilat canal/port.

The Aqaba Eilat canal/port is particularly suited for implementation be-cause it can be technologically feasible, economically enticing, ecologically sound, providing for intensive use of a salt water resource, and it may be politically possible and stabilizing. For all these reasons, combined with a relatively affordable cost, this project was chosen to represent possible ven-tures for consideration in the framework of the Megaproject Plan.

■ Elaboration of the Aqaba Eilat Canal/Port Project

From the myriad of possible Middle East water-related projects we choose to focus on one example by reviewing its technological, ecological, economic and political ramifications. The Aqaba Eilat projects is relatively manageable from the point of view of size. It brings a variety of immediate benefits to both its users, Jordan and Israel, and to other countries involved. Participation of a third party from outside the Middle East might be a decisive factor in its feasibility. The project can be realized only with tacit consent of both sides. Cooperation between Jordan and Israel is not as elusive as it may seem to an outside observer. Actually, there is a history over the years of informal cooperation. This is true particularly in limited interaction situations in which each side ignores the fact of benefits to the other side. Limited interaction could be achieved under the sponsorship of a neutral party like the U.S., the E.E.C. or Japan in the Aqaba Eilat canal/port project.

Types of previous joint efforts include transfer of technology concerning production of minerals, transfer of techniques of modern irrigation, establishment of a Jordanian bank in the West Bank, and trade across the Jordan River. There is accumulated evidence that these countries do behave cooperatively whenever the price of noncooperation is high enough. Although never formally accepted, the U.S.-initiated Johnston Water Agreement of the 1950s was one such example.

Because of acute water shortages, a variety of economic projects of mutual benefit can be implemented through tacit cooperation of Jordan and Israel. Such projects could contribute to peace when political conditions are ripe.

■ Description of the Present Situation

The Gateway of the Far East and Africa to European markets currently is limited to the Suez Canal. The other arm of the north end of the Red Sea ends in a cul-de-sac, the Gulf of Aqaba. Here Japanese products such as cars and steel enter Israel and Jordan and materials, e.g., phosphates and oil distillates are returned to the Far East. The population of both Aqaba and Eilat is around 22,000 each. Aqaba is the only port of Jordan, while Eilat is the third largest port of Israel, after Haifa and Ashdod. The port cities of Aqaba and Eilat share the Gulf physically, but for political reasons have almost no contact.

The warm sunny coral beaches here 29.5 north of the equator, are a haven for hundreds of thousands of tourists, but are increasingly encroached upon by a bay full of ships. Between them, the two ports service and anchor up to 30 ships a day.

Recently, there has been a proposal to construct a pipeline from Iraqi oil-fields through Jordan ending in the port of Aqaba. This pipeline would enable Iraq to avoid sending oil through the troubled Hormuz Straits and considerably shorten the current shipping route from Iraq to European markets via the Suez Canal.

This increase of oil shipping, loading and unloading at Aqaba would serve to exacerbate pollution of the area and lead to further deterioration of this unique coral reef environment. The other major pollution problem of the area is phosphates which cause increased algal growth and eventually lead to death of the corals. There is a citizen outcry against port expansion based on the fact that more tankers will most probably mean more pollution and less tourism.

One way to separate the two main sources of income, recreation and shipping activities, is a canal extending due north of Eilat and Aqaba approximately 11 km on the Jordan/Israel border. A length of 11 km seems to afford ample length to deal with oil spills, phosphates and other pollutants before they affect touristic areas and coral reefs to the south. Eleven km north of the cities, the broad Arava Valley, with alluvial soil, is only 25 meters above sea level, a fact that would make excavation economical. The canal, approximately 30 m deep and 300 m wide would be large enough to handle all trade arriving into the bay.

The implementation of this plan would solve primarily an oil/phosphate pollution problem that stands to worsen with the possible introduction of the Iraqi pipeline. It could also provide an environment conducive to bilateral economic cooperation which would serve to strengthen a commitment to peaceful coexistence. Foreign investment in such a project not only promises high economic returns but also political perks because the investor would be seen as a contributor to peace and stability in this area.

■ Benefits

An Eilat Aqaba harbor could have far-reaching effects. A port 11 km inland would provide an excellent location for a coal-fueled water-cooled power plant of any economically-determined size. This would be especially important to Jordan, since it has only one marine outlet where water cooled power can be generated. Desalinated water could be a byproduct of the power plant. In this area, heavily dependent on water, prices can go as high as $1/m^3$ for fresh water. Salt water agriculture is an additional source of income that can be adopted in the Arava region. Water drawn from the canal can be used employing state-of-the-art technology to make feasible: fish ponds, shrimp, and algae production.

Moving the ports up the canal frees the natural coasts for recreational activity. Aqaba and Eilat would be opened to their full potential in tourism without concern for future oilspills and degradation of the natural marine environment. As demonstrated recently in the third oil spill on the Delaware River this year, length ensures containment of oil. Further studies in containment and hydrodynamic processes are ongoing in oceanographic research institutes worldwide. These may provide proven techniques for modelling and containment of pollutant dispersal in the Red Sea.

The Aqaba Eilat port would provide the opportunity for development of a land bridge connection from the Far East to Europe as an alternative to the Suez Canal. This land bridge would have the international trade benefit of always maintaining a price ceiling on the use of the Suez Canal. In such a scheme, Japanese goods sent to the area could be stored in a dry, noncorrosive environment in a region of very low cost land in the Arava. These goods would then be repackaged conforming to European distribution channels and destinies, thus lowering storage costs in Europe. This land bridge would be complete with a railroad making the 400 km connection to the Mediterranean. Such a railroad could be built by an international consortium and leased to the countries involved.

Jordan and Israel would benefit from desalinated water to enhance agricultural productivity. They would also benefit from other activities associated with the port project including increased tourism, construction of housing for new residents and jobs from associated industries. The international community would benefit from increased trade and increased stability in an otherwise troubled area.

We would like this rather short document to become a precursor of activity that would lead to a prefeasibility study of one or more of the water projects discussed in this document. The possible advantages of the Aqaba Eilat project are displayed in Table 17.1.

Table 17.1
Summary of Benefits - Aqaba Eilat Canal/Port

Ecological	Economic	Political
1. Containment of oil spills	1. Desalinated water available for use	1. Bilateral economic advantages
2. Control of phosphates	2. Water cooled power plant	2. Stability
	3. Aquaculture	

■ Outline of Next Phase

The following is a list of studies and tests that would need to be conducted for the proposed preparative study of this project.

I. Preparation of a Geological Survey
   A. Collection of existing data.
   B. Specification of testing to be done.
   C. Preliminary assessment of geologic risk.

II. Comprehensive Ecological Impact Statement
   A. Marine life
   B. Water quality
   C. Land and air quality

III. Economic Feasibility Study
   A. Cost of port construction
   B. Cost of land bridge
   C. Land use study
   D. Civil engineering (roads, soil removal, communications, and other infrastructure)
   E. Economic analysis of an aquaculture project
   F. Tourism – potential and required investment

IV. Power Plant
   A. Most economic size
   B. Development of alternative energy sources
   C. Use of desalinated water
   D. Ecological impact

V. Accessory Transportation Requirements
   A. Airport
   B. Railway

VI. Legal Aspects
   A. Compatibility and differences between Jordanian and Israeli relevant legal systems
   B. Investment incentives
   C. Creation of appropriate legal standing for the operating company in each country

The prefeasibility study will consider several options for the realization of the project under prevailing political considerations. It will also explore past and current know-how in similar projects abroad.

Appendix I

Examples of Mideast Water Projects	Description	Economic and Political Considerations
A. Nile Canal	Involves extension and enlargement of already approved Sinai Canal to supply mainly Gaza Strip and Israeli Negev possibly extending to West Bank and Jordan.	Possible because amount to be diverted is less than 1/2% of the current Egyptian consumption which is 50 Km^3/yr. Surplus in Nile water exists and will increase with modern irrigation. Cost is 1/3 price to get water via National Carrier from Galilee, necessitates Egypt-Israel cooperation.
B. Yarmuk Storage	Storage of 1/4 of Jordan's winter flood water in the Lake of Galilee would help solve summer shortage.	Alleviates costly upstream projected damming of the Yarmuk River. Currently, project is precluded by state of war between Jordan and Israel.
C. Ghor Canal to West Bank	Pipelines could be built across Jordan riverbed to supply West Bank with additional, sweeter water.	Most economical way to supply lower western Jordan valley area. Alternative to building parallel canal on Israeli side of Jordan.
D. Iraq to Jordan Pipeline	Projected importation of Water from Euphrates River via a 650 km pipeline to Jordan supplying 120M m^3/yr.	Initial cost of pipeline very high. Militarily quite vulnerable. Continuation contingent on goodwill of Iraq.
E. Litani River to Israel West Bank and Jordan	Diversion of the Litani River via 6-8 km Tunnel to Ayoun or Hasbani River for storage of water in Lake of Galilee.	Project would pay for itself easily by power generated at generated at existing Israeli Almagor station. Relations with Lebanon preclude venture for Israel.
F. Damming of Lower Jordan	Involves cooperation in construction of dams on Jordan for electricity and water shortage.	Currently not economical, especially if Yarmuk water were stored in Lake of Galilee.

Appendix I (continued)

Examples of Mideast Water Projects	Description	Economical and Political Considerations
G. Gaza Strip and West Bank Aquifer Recharge	Water importation from the Yarmuk, Nile or Litani Rivers to overcome present over-draft of up to 90M m^3/yr in the aquifer.	These aquifers are becoming increasingly salty from sea water seepage. Any fresh water sources involve coop-eration with Israel. Could be major step towards peace.
H. Irrigation Techniques	Introduction of modern irrigation techniques, especially applicable in Egypt. Have already been applied extensively in Israel and Jordan to solve water shortages.	Will cost $1000/hectare to introduce in underdeveloped areas.
I. Desalination	Production of fresh from salt water. Energy for the process may be solar or from association with conventional power plant.	Will become more feasible as future demand exceeds supply in areas of the ME. Involves no cooperation between the countries.
J. Rain Intensifi-cation by Cloud Seeding	Silver iodide supplied to clouds by airplane or from stationary ovens on the ground.	Experiments in Israel since 1960s indicate 15-20% in-crease in rainfall in North-ern regions. Seeding done in Israel could benefit the Yarmuk drainage basin in Jordan.
K. Litani Hydro-electric Plant	Storage of water in Lebanon diverted to power plant in Israel via Ayoun River.	Utilizes 200 meter fall to Lake of Galilee rather than to Mediterranean. More efficient power production. Diverted water could also be sold to Israel.
L. Aqaba Eilat Canal/Port	Construction of a Canal from cities of Eilat and Aqaba-11 km northward for use as a bi-national port.	Eliminates pollution problem from tourist area; provides shipping route alternative to Suez Canal.

18

The Multinational Business Development Fund: A Framework for Economic Cooperation and Peace in the Middle East

Riad Ajami

■ Introduction

This proposal presents ideas and suggestions for establishing the Multinational Business Development Fund (MBDF) as a framework for viable economic ventures in Lebanon and along its borders. These ideas and suggestions will be outlined in terms of their long-term prospects for continued viable collaborative enterprises. It is thus under the umbrella of the MBDF that mental and financial resources may be combined for the purpose of achieving viable and profitable economic cooperation. As a result of this profitable arrangement, the entire region will become more economically stable, and the prospects for peace and tranquility—as well as the seeds for equitable and fair future cooperative activities between Israel and Southern Lebanon—will be established.

■ The Problem

There exists today in Southern Lebanon a situation whose gravity and potential ramifications become more pronounced with the passage of time. These ramifications demand serious attention, consideration, and prompt but careful action.

Labor Problems in Southern Lebanon. The Southern Lebanese are in a difficult economic situation: the dire economic straits they are currently in leave them without the opportunity to achieve the dignity and prosperity that accompanies the attainment of economic strength. And as oil revenues plunge in the gulf states — sending scores of workers back to their countries each week — the plight of the Southern Lebanese becomes even more severe. Although exact numbers are elusive, an estimated 100,000 Shiites have already been sent back to Lebanon from Saudi Arabia and Kuwait, only to return to a homeland fraught with destruction and despair.

As the conditions of the Southern Lebanese worsen, an additional problem presents itself. The PLO, once firmly entrenched in the south, now eyes the region once again with the hopes of re-establishing itself for the "reconquest of Arab Palestine." Hezbollah and others also stalk the area with the real and frightening prospect of increasing their sphere of influence. The Southern Lebanese, with a Shiite majority, lack the strength to oppose the various terrorist organizations occupying their region. They lack the strength to forge their own society because they lack the economic growth necessary to employ their growing population. Put simply, the Southern Lebanese — economically depressed and devoid of opportunities — are becoming a more susceptible target for terrorism. Alleviating poverty in the area will alleviate the problem of terrorist organizations operating there.

Israel. For Israel, the situation in Southern Lebanon poses a particularly serious national security problem; Israel needs to end the tremendous security threat that the organizations working out of Southern Lebanon pose. For Israel to repeat the events of 1982, or to continue a full scale occupation of Southern Lebanon along the border, is inefficient and costly in terms of both manpower and resources. It is the long-term occupation of the Israeli "security" forces that will provoke the Shiites of that area into bitter enmity. Israel needs to explore the immediate steps that must be taken to alleviate this state of affairs, and to set in motion a process which will allow it to withdraw from the so-called "Security Zone," leaving the Shiites as the masters of their own region.

▪ The Solution

Out of this dire situation arises the hope of rebuilding relations between the Southern Lebanese and the Israelis. Both the Israelis and the Lebanese are seeking to create societies for themselves in which they can live in dignity, peace, freedom, and well-being. For the Southern Lebanese to create such a society, they must increase their economic opportunities. For the Israelis to create such a society, they must achieve peace and security along their borders, which, in turn, can be facilitated first by economic viability among the Southern Lebanese, and ultimately by economic cooperation across the two borders.

Under conditions of peace — and after a complete Israeli evacuation from the security zone (which, in light of current events, has been demonstrated to not be very secure) — economic cooperation would be the solution to the problems between Israel and Lebanon. Israel is a storehouse of technology and know-how in agricultural irrigation, foodstuffs processing, and textile manufacturing that is ripe for sale. Southern Lebanon is potentially rich in citrus and tobacco agricultural products, but the Lebanese can't sell them because they don't have access to major world markets. Israel has such access. It is clear that each of these nations possesses something the other desires, but because of the existing balance of terror, nothing is being done about it.

There are many benefits to economic cooperation for both sides. The Lebanese can be employed and their products sold world-wide, while Israeli technology and know-how are being sold in a new market (Southern Lebanon). On a larger scale, the Lebanese will obtain the dignity and security that accompanies economic growth and strength. With increased prosperity, they will be able to defend and protect themselves from outside invaders and terrorist predators. They will ultimately live in self sufficiency, brought about through economic growth. The Israelis, on the other hand, will obtain an increased measure of stability along their northern border. Through viable economic cooperation, both neighbors can coexist peacefully with each other while simultaneously enriching their people.

■ The Multinational Business Development Fund (MBDF)

This economic cooperation — by virtue of its nonpolitical, profitable nature — will also generate a climate attractive to new investors, whose financial resources will provide the catalyst for undertaking new ventures. These ventures will, in turn, cause further stability and growth for the region, making it attractive to scores of international and local investors. Such a cycle is self-perpetuating and beneficial to all concerned. These ventures will set the stage for further profitable cooperation between the two neighbors, thereby transforming a "balance of terror" to a "balance of prosperity."[1]

All of these goals can be reached through the Multinational Business Development Fund (MBDF). The MBDF is a non-political organization to be established in the United States — with an arm in Lebanon — by Americans and Lebanese concerned with enhancing the prospects for peace, prosperity, and the climate for moderation in Lebanon. The MBDF advocates an economic modality as a basis for resolving the crises in Lebanon and the elimination or reduction of terrorism. The MBDF advances the notion that economic development and the concomitant creation of "stakeholders" engaged in business enterprises — eventually co-owned by locals — is prerequisite for tranquility and regional security and stability. The creation of sound economic programs at the grass-roots (village and community) level and business-economic prosperity among the people of Southern Lebanon is axiomatic to long-term stability in Lebanon and along its borders. The MBDF hopes to ultimately unite Southern Lebanon — in an organic way — with regional and global centers of world commerce and finance, with the view that these economic linkages and transactions, coupled with viable indigenous business development, will lead to moderation in international relations — a view long advocated by Dr. Armand Hammer. Furthermore, the MBDF stands for Middle East regional security and economic cooperation with Lebanon — the south initially, and all of Lebanon eventually — playing a critical role in promoting these processes across Lebanon's borders.

One of the goals of the MBDF is to ultimately pass on participation stocks and shares in these ventures to workers, local managers and village cooperatives, thus making them effective co-owners and stakeholders. The shares can be acquired through direct labor contributions and other factor contributions by local entities in Southern Lebanon.

▪ The Structure of the MBDF

From the standpoint of the Southern Lebanese and their devastated economy, any economic arrangement will be an improvement on the current situation. From Israel's standpoint, any stability provided by an economic arrangement will be an improvement on the current situation. Yet in order for these ventures to succeed and benefit both parties, careful consideration must be given to their nature and structure. This paper discusses how these ventures should be implemented to achieve viable economic opportunities and stability for the Southern Lebanese, Israel, and the entire region. The cooperation scheme set forth by this proposal to facilitate this dynamic cooperation is the MBDF, and its triad, the International Production and Trading Structure.

An international production and trading system — or, simply put, a triad — is a complex arrangement whereby a project is not undertaken by a single firm, but rather through a "triadic" construct.[2] Each participating firm or entity supplies the necessary factors for which they have a competitive advantage in the value-added chain. These are (1) local inputs; (2) managerial services, technology, and market access; (3) transnational capital; and (4) impartial triad monitoring/management.

International Production and Trading Structure (Triad)

ARBITRATOR

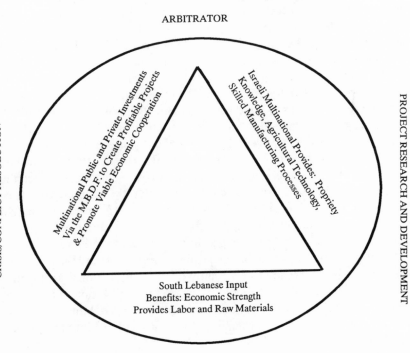

CRISIS/CONFLICT RESOLUTION

PROJECT RESEARCH AND DEVELOPMENT

INCREASE PROBABILITY OF SUCCESS

Local inputs in a triad refers to those elements supplied by the host community in which the project is being undertaken. The host may supply natural resources and/or labor. The representatives of the host may be the government itself, local developers, or other entities. In the ventures proposed here, local inputs (i.e., labor, agricultural products, etc.) will be provided by the Southern Lebanese.

Multinational entities participate in the triadic enterprise as *project managers and technical consultants*. These entities are not always direct financiers of projects, but provide services such as design/engineering, procurement, and training of management on a contractual basis. They may also provide *market access* to sell the output of a specific venture, either through established contracts or direct purchases.

International funding plays a major role in triadic enterprises. Funds are generated and allocated in the form of loans, and are tailor-made for the specific project. Once these projects become viable and profitable, the funds are paid back to the MBDF and the ownership shares are transferred from the fund to locals in Southern Lebanon. This will, over time, help locals at the grass-roots level to ultimately own their own businesses.

The triad would be overseen by the *Multinational Business Development Fund* (MBDF) — the group responsible for the success of the triad arrangement. The duties of this organization are: project selection, crisis/conflict management, the assurance of knowledge transfer, the assurance of a transfer of equity to locals over time, the creation of a low risk environment to attract public/private investment, and the definition and implementation of strategic policy so as to keep the projects profitable for all parties.

Synergy is often the result of the triadic arrangement, and the outcome of the venture is the creation of a jointly owned multinational arrangement which provides a cash flow, employment, and the utilization of technological skills. The shared goals of economic growth and stability, the genuine need for success, and the probability for continued viability are powerful conduits.

Southern Lebanese Inputs

In general, the South possesses the potential for low cost labor and low cost agricultural commodities, both of which sit idly due to the current situation. The MBDF plan is mutually advantageous for the farmers of Southern Lebanon as well as the laborers. The MBDF will set up local agri-business firms as well as agricultural warehouses, and will gather and buy the crops from the farmers of Southern Lebanon to upgrade, process, and resell in the world market. One party is selling their crop at competitive prices in the world market, and the other is employed. This will lead to stability and economic growth in the region, and the creation of stakeholders (in viable economic development) out of "gunholders."

Southern Lebanon's tremendous unemployed labor force is at the same time its most fruitful resource and its most pressing problem. For any arrangement to succeed, it must provide employment for a large number of people. This project would entail the construction of small manufacturing and distribution centers in Southern Lebanon along the border. After normalization of relations and peace among the two neighbors, labor and resources could move freely between them.

Tobacco and oranges are two of the most common crops in the South. Utilizing Israeli agricultural and irrigation technology, yields will increase. The crops will then be purchased by the small manufacturing outfits mentioned above, to be packaged and graded for export in the world market. The increased yield will reduce the cost of the raw material relative to the value-added costs, thereby increasing profit margins and making it a viable, profitable venture for both the Israelis and the Shiites.

Israeli Inputs

Israel is a very sophisticated agricultural producer. The Israeli advanced technology in irrigation techniques can boost crop yields in Southern Lebanon, thus creating economies of scale in raw goods production. Israeli multinationals can also provide "proprietary knowledge" to the project via services offered on a contractual or licensing basis. Managerial techniques, in the form of training local personnel, project coordination, and design/engineering may be provided on a contractual basis or on an equity basis.

As for textiles, many U.S. and Israeli ventures have been directly involved in the manufacture of textiles for export. One example is a direct investment held by "The Limited," a U.S. multinational corporation. These operations could be moved closer to the border so that the lower cost Lebanese labor can be utilized. By establishing transportation and communication networks in Southern Lebanon, and by providing processing and packaging facilities along the border, value may be added to semi-manufactured products by the Southern Lebanese. To further enhance the profitability of such an arrangement, Israel could take advantage of its status as an "export platform" — more specifically, their Free Trade arrangement with the U.S. — by providing value added to textiles and goods produced in Southern Lebanon and border plants for trade in the world market.

Financial Inputs

Initial revenues collected from the sources listed below would be used to create the funds credibility in order to produce the "seed money" needed to start this venture:

- U.S. government
- EEC national governments
- Multinational corporations
- U.S. philanthropic organizations (Jewish and others)
- Shiite Gulf and Western African groups

These funds must be sufficient to sustain the ventures until they are returning enough cash flows to operate independently, which could take up to a year or two.

Eventually, the MBDF will provide cash flow from their ongoing and profitable business ventures to finance other start-up businesses (operating similarly to the International Finance Corporation (IFC) of the World Bank). The IFC provides funds to entrepreneurs who undertake viable business ventures. In the early phase of the project, the IFC takes partial title to ownership. Once these enterprises become profitable and have sufficient cash flow, the IFC sells back its ownership shares to local entrepreneurs, thus allowing them to own and manage their own indigenous enterprises.

As projects are undertaken and returns begin to amass, government insurance agencies such as the U.S. Overseas Private Investment Corporation and other related agencies in the OECD countries will recognize Southern Lebanon as an area conducive to profitable investment. This recognition will allow private investors to invest in the fund while being insured against political risks in the region. Additional revenues can be raised at that point through bond sales and increasing the equity in the MBDF fund. It is thus necessary for the continued success of the MBDF that projects undertaken with fund money become self-sustaining, and thereby able to attract a stream of public and private funds.

MBDF Inputs

The MBDF is a nonpolitically-allied organization whose only mission is the success of the triad. The MBDF serves as an external entity that will, through its efforts, make the venture viable and profitable by insuring cooperation and the attainment of the mutual goals of all parties involved.

The MBDF will continually monitor the ever-changing international business environment so that the triad arrangement is flexible enough to change with world market conditions. It is the MBDF which will explore and re-search new projects and ventures. In addition, the MBDF will supply and train upper management to operate in the interests of the triad and the region in the long run, and not individual interests. This will help to secure long-term economic success and profitability.

Furthermore, an arrangement such as this one will not be without its problems, difficulties, and misunderstandings. It is the role of the MBDF to incorporate the appropriate monitoring systems to detect these problems in their early stage and solve them. The MBDF will see to it that agreements related to the venture are upheld, and will be as impartial as possible in its role as monitor.

The MBDF will also oversee the eventual transition of ownership to local entities in Southern Lebanon, generating positive effects similar to privatiza-tion and employee stock option plans. All the businesses created by the MBDF will, through a stock-ownership plan over a number of years, allow the transfer of ownership to co-workers and co-managers, thus creating stakeholders out of idle and unemployed workers in Southern Lebanon. As we have seen here in the United States and in Europe, participatory manage-ment and co-ownership plans lead to efficiency, improved understanding of corporate policies, priorities, and business options, and the dissipation of contempt felt in the past. These ideals can be transferable and enhanced through the Triad, and guaranteed by the MBDF. The eventual ownership of useful production capabilities will lead to the willingness of the Shiites to cooperate in this venture. It is through this vehicle that the Shiites will regain the dignity, stability, and economic strength which they covet and desire.

■ Reactions

From the onset, there will be groups consumed in their own interests who will openly oppose the plan, and attempt to manipulate and sabotage it.

The *PLO*, who already have a stronghold in Southern Lebanon, might be a belligerent force, and might oppose any attempt at economic cooperation which would benefit only the Southern Lebanese while not solving the Pales-tinian problem.

For similar reason *Iran* will assail any sort of Israeli-Shiite cooperative venture. Iran's radical *Hezbollah* advocates, wanting to spread their "reign of virtue," will view the moderate Lebanese Shiites as tainted and defiled. For the moderate Southern Lebanese, this consideration is not terribly sig-nificant. The moderate Shiites regard the notion of their Iranian counter-parts as radicalized and impractical. In addition, geography is on the side of the Shiites, as the reach of Iran's power into Southern Lebanon is extreme-ly limited.

Syria will openly oppose Israeli-Shiite cooperation, as they would want any venture to be initiated through Damascus rather than undertaken independently by the Southern Lebanese. Again, geography favors the Southern Lebanese, as Syria's influence beyond Sidon is tenuous.

Publicly, the *Maronites* in Beirut and the North will not favor this accord. However, their public disapproval will largely (if not completely) stem from pressure from Syria, the PLO, and other Arab states, coupled with a mildly egotistic desire to act as an intermediary between Israel and its people in the south. Maronite sentiments, however, will tacitly favor the venture because it will play into their aspirations for economic decentralization. Some might argue that this economic decentralization could lead to canonization of Lebanon, an outcome that we believe would work to the detriment of Lebanon and one which we strongly oppose. The success of this economic cooperation approach, and the resultant expansion and increase in economic activities, however, will actually lead to a decline in intercommunal conflict in Lebanon as a result of a partial reduction in economic scarcity, thus pulling the Lebanese together once again.

Finally, the *United States* will support and embrace this plan as it realizes that the prospects for mutual benefits and economic success in Southern Lebanon are far more preferable than the present situation and could reduce terrorism.

▪ Conclusion

The proposed joint economic cooperation presents brilliant opportunities for Israel and the Shiites of Southern Lebanon. It provides the means to explore and assess the economic needs of Lebanon's impoverished south. Once these needs are defined, ideas will be developed, projects researched, and sectors pinpointed in which resources may be used for the maximization of benefits for the entire region. The MBDF will provide the "seed resources" for the formation and inception of the venture, which, through its profitable nature, will ultimately lead to an abundant and consistent source of financing for all cooperative ventures. This proposal represents a meeting of the minds and the employment of capital for the inception of profitable economic cooperation between two nations, and the prospects of elevating and enriching all peoples concerned under a banner of new prosperity and dignity.

The above is predicated on the assumption that a complete and total Israeli withdrawal from the Security Zone in Southern Lebanon and a dismantling of the Lahad forces (the Southern Lebanese Army) must commence immediately, coupled with Israeli respect for Lebanese sovereignty. Placing U.N. forces in the Security Zone immediately could be a way out for all concerned. Otherwise, the longer the Israelis insist on keeping a foothold in Southern Lebanon—trampling on Lebanese sovereignty and infuriating Shiite sensibilities—the worse the prospect for tranquility, peace, and cooperation will become. The Israeli "Iron Fist" policy will only unleash rage, fanaticism, and despair, and will definitely reduce (if not completely eliminate) the chances for viable cooperation and a genuine and long-lasting peace between the two neighbors.

In addition to Israeli withdrawal from the Security Zone, the presence of intermediaries, under the auspices of groups such as the Armand Hammer project or a similar U.S.-European entity, is also a primary requirement.

Finally, the emphasis on an economic approach as a modality for peace and prosperity and towards resolving the conflict will afford the people of Southern Lebanon and the region decent housing, education, medical care, and opportunities for advancement. It will also allow people of goodwill to seek loftier goals and will weaken the influence of those who sow hatred and conflict. Economic cooperation, however, will not terminate the existing conflict if its fruits are not shared by the people at the grass-roots level— those who are directly affected. For no appeal can command the people's respect if its benefits accrue to only a few, while its pains are borne by many.

■ Notes

1. Ruth Arad, Seev Hirsch, and Alfred Tovias *The Economics of Peacemaking: Focus on the Egyptian-Israeli Situation*, Macmillan Press Ltd., London, 1983.

2. Riad A. Ajami, *Arab Response to the Multinationals*, New York: Praeger, 1979.

19

Key Findings of the Middle East Economic Cooperation Projects

Gideon Fishelson

These key findings are excerpts from various working papers and annual reports which have come out since 1982. A list of them is presented in Table 19.12.

The desirability of regional economic cooperation is not a new idea. Basic economic facts and observations long ago led to the conclusion that intra- and interregional economic cooperation would improve the economic well-being of those participating in the cooperation scheme. The four basic facts from which the improvement is derived are:

1) localized absolute scarcity of resources
2) uneven distribution of resources mainly in terms of relative proportions
3) locational differences in tastes and preferences
4) locational differences in technological know-how.

An overview of the world, as well as of each continent and regions within each continent reveals their division into national states each of which is bounded by political borders. These political boundaries tend to become also economic boundaries. This economic function is assigned to them artificially by the political process partly for the sake of the political power of the separate nations. The political borders either generate newly defined markets by splitting up what should have been one natural market or serve as obstacles to the free movements of goods, services, and factors of production among natural markets.

If the economic borders are perfectly sealed to all economic factors and goods and in all directions this amounts to self-sufficiency. However, the separation can be selective in terms of goods or factors or the partners with whom to exchange. Decisions regarding criteria for selection of trading partners may be economic but might also be, and are frequently, mainly political. The question that then arises is how do the various restrictions affect economic welfare?

The issue of how restrictions on economic interactions affect economic welfare is often not considered directly. Rather, it is replaced by other arguments in favor of the restrictions in spite of the unique advantages of economic cooperation. Frequently one can show the economic costs and the economic benefits of removing constraints and establishing cooperation and thus can prove that the net economic gains are positive. Such benefit-cost analyses are usually infeasible for noneconomic issues. Fortunately for the Middle East intra-regional economic cooperation projects whose research was financed by the Armand Hammer Fund, the results of benefit-costs analyses on noneconomic issues (i.e., social, political) can a priori be assumed to be positive. Hence, when the results from the economic studies are found to be favorable the conclusive evidence of the benefits of peace has been shown. Thus the obstacles to the start-up of cooperation cannot be explained on logical grounds.

As reported below, the projects related to Peace in the Middle East that have been researched all yielded benefit-cost analyses with positive results. Hence, the general conclusion is to move forward with these topics to the next stage, *a detailed* technical-economic study that could provide the blueprint for the actual implementation of the projects. Before presenting the topics studied in detail, I would like to return for a short while to the theoretical background for any regional cooperation.

From the 18th century modern economic theory has advocated inter-country exchange of goods and services. This theory was expanded in the 19th century with the Ricardian theory of comparative advantage. Since then the theories and arguments continue to flow (Hechsher, Ohlin, Schumpeter, Lerner, Samuelson, Johnson, Leinder, and many more). Their common subject was trade of goods and services. They hardly dealt with mobility of natural resources. This absence is not a reflection on their economic ingenuity; the reason is either the obviousness of the result, or, its perfect nonfeasibility. Since we examine real-life projects the implementation of which requires investments and resource use, the obvious has to be proven, and the notion of nonfeasibility wrestled with. Therefore, we have evaluated the feasibility of projects involving sharing of natural resources.

Another common characteristic of the trade theory studies is that of dealing in total net effects: "The total welfare will be improved." They do not examine intranational effects. Instead they use the compensation principle: "those that become better off can compensate those that become worse off and still be left with a positive residual." At this stage of our study the intranational effects have not been fully examined. In some cases (cooperation in the energy and fertilizers sectors) one can argue that there is no group or sector that would be adversely affected. However, the generalization of the argument "everybody benefits" to some sectors (e.g., water, agriculture, textiles) may not be appropriate or at least has as yet to be proven. Hence, our work is not yet complete and a careful analysis of intranational effects of the projects has to be done before implementation. It is worth recalling that sufficiently strong internal objections to a project can stop it even if its total net effect would be very positive.

The research about which I report has the following goals:

1) Identification of potential subjects for regional cooperation.

2) Outline of each subject, study of the framework in which it could occur and its evaluation in broad terms.

3) Identification of the singling out significance of each subject for the peace process in the Middle East.

Each of the projects that was analyzed has been shown to contribute to increased welfare in one of the following three ways:

1) Equalization of relative scarcity

2) Economies of scale

3) Economies of scope

The first category of topics involves sharing of relatively abundant natural resources (water, oil, gas, hydro power) and acquired experience and skill (agricultural technology, industrial experience).

The second category of topics has to do with the utilization of economies of scale in various production processes. The economies of scale would come about by generating a larger market for the product (cement, fertilizers). The economies of scale can also come about via increase in reliability (linking the electric system of the various countries).

The third aspect would be reached by offering a larger and more attractive basket of services to potential customers, e.g., tourism. The attractive natural resources to be used are already in the area; they just have to be packaged together in a way that would increase demand.

The projects that were investigated take a long-range view. They conform to national priorities without upsetting the internal social and economic balance. The projects that have already gone through the stage of initial investigation include:

a)	Water	f)	Cement
b)	Agriculture	g)	Textiles
c)	Energy	h)	Tourism
d)	Transportation	i)	Trade
e)	Fertilizers		

The first four projects are infrastructure projects. They would lay the grounds for private cooperation. Each one of these projects is briefly outlined and its interesting characteristics and research outcome described below.

Water

The details of several possible water projects that would be possible if there was peace are described in a separate report prepared by Elisha Kally. Water merits a separate investigation because it is the life-blood of economic activity in the arid/semiarid climate that characterizes the Middle East. The study's main conclusion is the economic and physical feasibility of supplying water to where it is critically needed, the West Bank and the Gaza Strip, from external sources such as the Nile, the Litani and the Yarmouk rivers. It is shown in the report that the most economic way to supply this water requires the cooperation of Israel via a multi-party exchange of water. The investment cost of these projects is only about half that of projects that would be possible if there was only partial or limited cooperation. The orders of magnitude are 350 and 640 million dollars respectively. The matrix of possible water transfer projects is presented in Table 19.1.

Agriculture

Agricultural cooperation has been studied in-depth only for cooperation between Egypt and Israel. Studies for cooperation among other pairs of economies (West Bank-Israel, Jordan-Israel) are still in process. The Egyptian-Israeli agricultural cooperation study is based upon the high degree of complementarity between the two sectors (apparent in differences in their agricultural outputs). The complementarity is due to the different natural

Table 19.1

Potential sources of water supply to the Gaza Strip and the West Bank (millions of m^3/year)

Source	Destination: Gaza	West Bank	Total
Nile	100	90	190
Yarmuk	-	80	80
Litani	-	80	80
Total	100	250	350

Source: Kalley, Elisha, *A Middle East Water Plan Under Peace,* Armand Hammer Fund for Economic Cooperation in the Middle East Under Peace, Tel Aviv, 1986.

conditions and constraints (climate, soil, water resources), differences in labor costs, availability of capital and extent of acquired knowledge, technology and experience of the two countries. Neither country is self-sufficient. It is important to mention that the agricultural cooperation has already started and that the main and perhaps almost exclusive beneficiary is and will be the Egyptian agricultural sector. In addition to the exchange of managerial experience and technological knowledge which can be shared, we constructed a long list of imports and exports of farm products, raw or processed, that can be traded by the two countries (See Table 19.2). All agricultural inputs traded, other than nitrogenous fertilizers, will be exported from Israel to Egypt. The main effect of these inputs will be to increase total output and the productivity of the traditional agricultural inputs in Egypt (land, labor and water). The agricultural cooperation report also recommends ventures in the agro-industries.

Energy

The energy cooperation project is regional in its scope. There is potential for both general and specific cooperative projects.

General cooperation would consist of integration of the power transmission grids of Egypt, Israel, Jordan and Lebanon. This integration would allow for taking advantage of the differences in peak demand periods and would increase the reliability of each of the domestic energy sectors without increasing their capacity. Specific diverse projects which could be carried out include:

(a) Purchases of surplus Egyptian natural gas by Israel. The gas is currently flared (wasted). It can be transferred via a pipeline for sale to Israel. This would entail lower investment costs than other potential gas export projects, bringing Egypt a higher profit from its natural gas. Table 19.3 summarized the conveyance costs to Israel for various alternatives. The most expensive of these is only about half the cost of gas liquefaction for exporting to Europe, the next best alternative use.

(b) Generating hydroelectric power from the Litani river in Lebanon. Today this potential energy source is not being used.

(c) A joint Israel-Jordan sea canal linking the Red Sea and the Dead Sea. This project would yield water resources, generate hydroelectric power and reduce water pollution to the Gulf of Aquba. A cost-benefit study yielded very promising results.

(d) An oil conveyance system from the Persian Gulf to the Mediterranean that would utilize most of an already existing pipeline – the Tapline. Considerable saving in investment and operation costs would be the major benefit.

Table 19.2

Imports and exports of farm products, raw or processed, and agricultural input commodities, Egypt and Israel, 1981, in US$ '000, and possible directions of trade

SITC Code	Product	Egypt Imports	Egypt Exports	Israel Imports	Israel Exports	Possible Directions of Trade
A.	Farm products, raw or processed					
11	Beverages	1,636	5,884	6,292	6,786	E>I,I>E
22	Oil seeds	20,319	5,974	170,474	15,024	E>I,I>E
262	Wool, animal hair	24,103	1,281	19,263	9,589	E>I,I>E
263.1	Raw cotton, excluding linters	--	457,091	30,890	121,833	E>I
421.3	Cottonseed oil	16,354	--	348	5,305	I>E
292.4	Vegetables used in pharmacy, etc.	2,754	6,231	6,038	--	E>I
292.5	Seeds for planting	5,276	1,184	5,182	7,153	I>E
011.4	Poultry, fresh, chilled or frozen	117,481	--	--	30,517	I>E
(013)	Meat, prepared, preserved	23,373	--	--	9,433	I>E
(023)	Butter	96,126	--	2,184	3,926	I>E
(025)	Eggs	12,372	--	2,994	3,080	I>E
042	Rice	--	42,608	18,805	--	E>I
054	Fresh & simply prepared vegetables	56,936	46,975	11,378	43,201	E>I,I>E
057	Fresh and dried fruits and nuts	40,797	53,111	12,857	317,698	E>I,I>E
058.9	Fruit and vegetable juice	373	9,543	18,228	115,275	E>I
062	Sugar, candy, excl. chocolates	674	--	3,661	4,500	E>I,I>E
075.2	Spices, excluding pepper	987	5,643	1,233	263	E>I

081.3	Oilcake and other residues	29,936	1,998	--	13,406	I>E
061.2	Refined sugar	244,314	18,874	106,640	--	E>I
061.5	Molasses	--	7,587	4,222	--	E>I

B. Agricultural Inputs

562.1	Chemical nitrogenous fertilizer	70,460	--	6,250	420	E>I
562.2	Chemical phosphatic fertilizer	25,415	184	--	40,349	I>E
561.9	Fertilizer, various	4,090	--	158	123,998	I>E
721.1	Cultivating machinery	4,662	--	1,739	8,272	I>E
712.9	Harvesting machinery	2,636	--	10,147	1,957	I>E
721.3	Dairy machinery	913	--	5,707	182	I>E
721.9	Agriculture machines, various	12,660	--	1,088	2,169	I>E
727	Food machinery, non-domestic	20,950	--	6,898	5,328	I>E

Source: Bahiri, Simcha, *Egyptian-Israeli Cooperation in Agricultural Development,* Armand Hammer Fund, 1986.

Table 19.3

Cost estimates for different sources and sizes of gas conveyance systems from Egypt to Israel

Sources of Gas and Distance	Annual Quantity 10⁶ tons FOE	Diameter of Pipeline, inches	Cost of Pipeline	Cost of Distribution System	Cost of Compression Stations	Miscellaneous Expenses and Interest during construction	Total Investment Costs	Returns of the Investment $/annual FOE	Operation Costs $/FOE	Total Cost of Conveyance $/FOE
			$ mill.	$ mill.	$ mill.	$ mill.	$ mill.			
Gulf 530 kms.	0.5	16	70	14	8	24	116	23.2	8.0	31.2
	1.0	20	92	21	14	32	159	15.9	5.9	21.8
	2.0	28	155	31	25	56	267	13.4	5.2	18.6
Delta 220 kms.	0.5	16	37	14	5	15	71	14.2	4.7	18.9
	1.0	20	50	21	9	22	102	10.2	3.4	13.7
	2.0	28	85	31	17	37	170	8.5	2.8	11.3

Source: Tal, Abraham, and Kally, Elisha, *A Gas Pipeline from Egypt to Israel*, Armand Hammer Fund, 1987.

Transportation

An adequate transportation infrastructure is a necessary precondition for any type of interregional cooperation, whether in trade, tourism, or economic and technological ventures. The reestablishment of the broken and inactive Middle Eastern transportation network would facilitate not only bilateral relations with Israel but also among the Arab countries. Transportation goals considered include a road that links Egypt with Jordan and continues from there North to Syria, and the construction of a deep water port at Gaza that would also serve Jordan and Iraq. Roads are essential for communication and trade as well as for cooperative ventures such as tourism. However, the study emphasizes the advantages of rail transportation. The cost advantages are obvious, perhaps 4 cents per ton/km vs. 12 cents per ton/km for 30 ton capacity trucks.

The Gaza port with the help of the road and rail links could service Jordan, Iraq, and possibly the Gulf States, as well as the West Bank and the Gaza Strip. Economic growth expected in the area, especially if there is peace, combined with the limited capacities and expansion possibilities of the Israeli Mediterranean ports and the need for another port in the south make the Gaza port very reasonable. The initial results of a cost benefit analysis of such a port is very promising with respect to Jordan and also Iraq (see Tables 19.4 and 19.5).

Fertilizers

The fertilizer industry is another potential Egyptian-Israeli cooperative venture which is derived from the complementarity of available resources. Israel lacks an adequate source of nitrogen to produce composite fertilizer products—NPK, since production of nitrogen compounds is energy intensive. At the same time, Egypt needs potash in order to create the NPK compound fertilizers. Furthermore, integrated projects in the fertilizer industry could benefit from economies of scale which would then provide the base for competitiveness in the international fertilizer market. Israel is already experienced in marketing fertilizer and has the network for their distribution. This marketing experience can be utilized efficiently to the advantage of both countries (see Tables 19.6 and 19.7).

Cement

The establishment of a cement plant south of El-Arish in the Sinai about fifty km. from the Israeli border would enable the export of surplus cement from Egypt to Israel. The advantages are: availability of local raw materials including energy, and the potential to take advantage of economies of scale.

Table 19.4

Comparative Costs of Shipping General Cargo from Geneva to Amman, Baghdad via Aqaba, Beirut or Gaza, per ton

(1)	*To Amman via Agaba*		
	a) Maritime transport -- 8 days at $1.50[1]		$12.00
	b) 0.15 probability of empty return voyage[2]		3.60
	c) Waiting time		3.00
	d) Suez Canal fees		7.50
	e) Overland transport Aqaba-Amman[3], $0.03x336 km.		10.10
		Total	36.20
(2)	*To Amman via Gaza*		
	a) Maritime transport -- 4 days at $1.50		6.00
	b) 0.15 probability of empty return voyage		0.60
	c) Waiting time		3.00
	d) Overland transport, Gaza-Amman, $0.03x200 km.		6.00
		Total	15.60
(3)	*To Baghdad via Basra*		
	a) Maritime transport -- 14 days at $1.50		21.00
	b) 0.8 probability of empty return voyage		10.50
	c) Waiting time		3.00
	d) Suez Canal fees		7.50
	e) Overland transport Basra-Baghdad - $0.03x400 km.		12.00
		Total	54.00
(4)	*To Baghdad via Aqaba*		
	a) Maritime transport -- 8 days at $1.50		12.00
	b) 0.5 probability of empty return voyage		3.60
	c) Waiting time		3.00
	d) Suez Canal fees		7.50
	e) Overland transport Aqaba-Baghdad - $0.03x1,200 km.		36.00
		Total	62.10
(5)	*To Baghdad via Gaza*		
	a) Maritime transport -- 4 days at $1.50		6.00
	b) 0.15 probability of empty return voyage		0.60
	c) Waiting time		3.00
	d) Overland transport Gaza-Baghdad - $0.03x1,070 km.		32.10
		Total	41.70

Table 19.4 (continued)

(6) *To Baghdad via Beirut*

a) Maritime transport -- 4 days at $1.50	6.00
b) 0.15 probability of empty return voyage	0.60
c) Waiting time	3.00
d) Overland transport Beirut-Baghdad - $0.03x950 km.	29.50
Total	38.10

[1]Data on cost of maritime transport were supplied by the Israel Maritime Institute.
[2]The charge for an empty return is 60 percent of the full freight charge.
[3]Estimates based on the rates of the Israel Transport Institute, adjusted to lower labor and fuel costs in the Arab states.

Source: Tal, Abraham, Silver, Hilary Wolpert, and Bahiri, Simcha, *Regional Cooperation in the Development of Transportation Infrastructure in the Middle East,* Armand Hammer Fund, 1988, Table 4.

Table 19.5
Costs of Shipping via Alternative Routes and Savings from Shipping via a Gaza Port

Transport Route	Cost, $ per ton	Savings via Gaza, $ per ton
Genova to Amman		
via Aqaba	36.20	20.30
via Gaza	15.50	-.-
Genova to Baghdad		
via Basra	54.00	12.30
via Aqaba	62.10	20.40
via Gaza	41.70	-.-
via Beirut	38.10	-3.60

Source: Tal, Abraham, Silver, Hilary Wolpert, and Bahiri, Simcha, *Regional Cooperation in the Development of Transportation Infrastructure in the Middle East,* Armand Hammer Fund, 1988, Table 5.

Table 19.6

Estimated Costs and Benefits in New Integrated Fertilizer Plants[1] (in percent of sales revenue)

Notation	Item	Israel	Egypt	Average
S	Sales Revenue	100	100	100
M	Materials, Purchases, Energy	51	45	48
VA	Value Added (S-M)	49	55	52
K_d	Depreciation (15 years)	8	8	8
H	Social Earning (VA-K_d)	41	47	44
K_{rp}	Repatriated Earnings & Profits n.e.s.[2]	7	13	10
NNVA	Net National Value Added (H-K_{rp})	34	34	34
L	Labor Costs	15	5	10
SS	Social Surplus (NNVA-L)[3]	19	29	24
P	Profit[4]	22	33	28
BT	Net Trade Balance[5]	62	62	62
NLVA	Non-Labor Value Added (SS+K_d+K_{rp})	34	50	42

[1]Actual data may differ considerably, depending on products and prices.
[2]Excluding depreciation.
[3]Social surplus includes unrepatriated profits and interest, rents, royalties, and taxes.
[4]Profits before tax are part of repatriated payments and social surplus. In Israel, 1980, these were about 20 percent.
[5]Equals exports less imports (direct, indirect, and repatriated payments). Lower Egyptian energy and materials imports offset by higher repatriated payments.

Source: Bahiri, Simcha, Egyptian-Israeli Cooperation in the Fertilizer Industry, The Armand Hammer Fund, 1986.

Table 19.7
National Costs and Benefits in Fertilizer Plants of 1 Million Tons Capacity
US$ millions per annum, 1980 prices*

Notation	Item	Israel	Egypt	Average
S	Sales Revenue	300	300	600
M	Materials & Purchases	147	165	312
VA	Value Added	24	24	48
K_d	Depreciation	153	135	288
H	Social Earnings	123	141	264
K_{rp}	Repatriated Payments & Profits	21	39	60
NNVA	Net National Value Added	102	102	204
L	Labor Costs	45	15	60
SS	Social Surplus	57	87	144
P	Profit (before tax)	66	99	165
BT	Net Trade Balance	186	186	372
I	Investment	330	330	660
I_n	National Investment (from domestic sources)	223	165	388
NE	Number of Employees	2,500	3,300	5,800

*See notes to Table 19.6.

Table 19.8
Summary of Comparative Cement Costs, Egypt and Israel US$ Per Ton,
1984 Prices

Item	Delivered Cost To/In Israel
Present average cost, existing Israeli plants	60
Average cost of a new plant located in Israel 600,000 ton capacity	45
Average cost of a new plant at El-Arish, 700,000 ton capacity, 500,000 for Israel (CIF)	38
Average cost of Israeli imports of foreign cement (CIF)	60

Item	Delivered Cost To/In Egypt
Present average cost, existing Egyptian plants	50
Average cost of a new plant at El-Arish, including production for Israel	33
Average cost of new plant at Ramlah (CIF)	55
Average cost of Egyptian imports of foreign cement (CIF)	60

Israel does not currently need this cement but if the construction industry reaches the activity level it achieved in the mid-70s then the available capacity of the cement plants in Israel will be insufficient. On economic grounds, given the economies of scale in cement production the best alternative source of cement supply to Israel is from Egypt (see Table 19.8).

Tourism

Possibilities for cooperation in the tourist industry in the Middle East are investigated in a forthcoming report. Nonpeace is the main reason why the Middle East lags behind the growth in world tourism; tourism is very sensitive to tensions and military incidents. The lack of peace also hinders multinational visits to the region which are a crucial prerequisite for further development of the tourist industry. If the infrastructure was good and border crossing was easy, tourists could visit Beirut, Jerusalem, Petra and Cairo, and neighboring attractions within a 14-day tour.

Peace is expected to increase multinational tourism. However, an increase in multinational tourism is expected to have two contradictory effects: 1) More tourists, 2) a shorter length of stay in each country. Fortunately, it is expected that the former would overweigh the latter. Israel might also face price competition from neighboring tourist industries.

It is argued that with peace and if recommendations for the basic needs of Western tourists are fulfilled, the number of tourists visiting the Middle East would more than double within a ten-year period.

Textiles and Clothing

A study we have recently completed, which is an update of a paper by Alfred Tovias, shows that since the textile and clothing industries of Egypt and Israel exhibit a wide range of complementarity, cooperation between them would improve the competitive position of both countries vis-a-vis third countries. The study further demonstrates that cooperation cannot be achieved instantaneously. It will require modifications in the existing institutional framework and trade agreements.

The benefits to be gained from cooperation in textiles stem from economies of scale and from the exchange of cotton yarn and fabrics (Egypt) for synthetics (Israel). Cooperation in clothing would utilize the Egyptian labor force for the labor-intensive operations such as sewing and Israel's access to the EEC and the U.S. markets. Egypt would also benefit from the Israeli knowledge of design, finishing dyeing and printing.

One Israeli company, Delta Ltd., already (1981) signed an agreement with an Egyptian company to establish in Egypt a plant that would employ 700 workers and produce annually a value of 24 million dollars. The project came to an end because of the Lebanon War in 1982. The potential profitability of this project for Delta and the hundreds of jobs it would have supplied in Egypt show the potential of this type of cooperation.

Bilateral Trade — Israel with Egypt, Jordan and Lebanon

Foreign trade is relatively large compared with the GNP in all four countries. All four countries also experience a trade deficit. In all four countries the major import items are industrial supplies and (except for Egypt) oil. Current major trading partners are European for imports and primarily European for exports (with Asia also representing a significant export market for Jordan and Lebanon).

Employing trade diversion and trade creation principles and recognizing the inherent advantage of border trade (almost no transfer costs) we estimated the potential volume of trade between Israel and her neighbors (adjusted for existing border trade and trade resistance). The trade diversion which could result from peace for each of the four countries is presented in Table 19.9. One should not dismiss the importance of new intraregional trade because its shares of total exports and total imports would not be large. The mere establishment of trade on the order of 1 billion dollars excluding oil is an important step when starting from a situation of no (overt) trade.

Conclusions

Below we summarize the benefits of peace with the presentation of a macroeconomic study of the Middle Eastern economies. Each of the detailed studies indicates the advantages of cooperation both to Israel and to each participating neighbor. One cannot at this stage determine who benefits more. This will also vary among projects. One thing is sure — the net benefit is positive. Even in the project from which Israel has the least to gain, textiles and clothing, a well-designed cooperative endeavor would be beneficial to the Israeli economy, although major adjustments would have to be made and the domestic clothing industry might suffer from Egyptian competition in certain products. The key results we have presented are based on very rough calculations. They are designed to be indicative. Now, if these are accepted and agreed upon by the relevant parties, then the green light can be given to creation of detailed studies and designs which can be followed by actual activities once the first signs of peace are observed.

Table 19.9
Adjusted trade diversion estimates

Country	Israel	Egypt	Jordan	Lebanon
Trade				
Export diversion ($M)	759.7	218.6 (752.6*)	9.8	8.8
Import diversion ($M)	237.2 (771.2*)	454.0	174.8	130.9
Export diversion as % of total exports	14.4	7.0 (24.1*)	1.3 1.3	2.2 2.2
Import diversion as % of total imports	3.0 (9.6*)	5.0	5.4	6.6

*including oil

Source: Raban, Yoel, *The Potential Trade Between Israel and Its Arab Neighbors,* 1987, Table 2.

Middle East Peace Scenarios

A simplified macro-economic model was employed to quantify the contribution of a peace settlement of the Arab-Israeli conflict. The method involves a comparison of two scenarios with respect to the economic growth, private consumption, civilian public consumption and trade deficit. The main reason for the economic changes would be the diversion of military expenditures to productive investments and nonmilitary public consumption. New economic opportunities are not taken into consideration. In spite of the pessimistic assumptions used, the results are impressive. The numbers below are increases in economic growth which are possible in the peaceful cooperation scenario beyond what would be expected if current trends (nonpeace) continue: 1-2 percent annual growth of GNP, 1-2 percent annual increase of private consumption and 2-3 percent of nonmilitary public expenditures.

These estimates of annual growth reflect improved economic welfare for all the countries to which the model was applied: the West Bank and Gaza, Israel, Egypt, Jordan, Lebanon and Syria (see Tables 19.10 and 19.11).

Table 19.10
Comparative Economic Indicators in the Aggressive Non-Cooperation Scenario - 1992

	Israel	WBG	Jordan	Lebanon	Egypt	Syria
Population Data						
1. Population (millions)	4.75	1.5	3.33	3.5	57.0	11.6
2. Population Growth, %	1.7	2.2	3.0	1.5	2.5	2.6
3. Employment (thousands)	1,600	290	620	830	16,500	3,030
Gross National Product and its Distribution, $ Millions						
4. Gross National Product	30,300	2,200	7,500	9,400	44,500	27,500
5. Private Consumption	18,900	1,650	5,100	6,770	28,930	18,150
6. Defense Expenditure	7,900	-.-	1,280	190	4,450	4,950
7. Civilian Government Expenditure	3,000	200	1,130	560	4,450	2,480
8. Investment	7,300	450	1,880	1,880	11,130	6,050
9. Total Resources	27,100	2,300	9,390	9,400	48,960	31,630
10. Import Surplus	6,800	100	1,890	-.-	4,460	4,130
11. Exports	14,000	600	3,000	6,000	13,500	5,000
12. Gross Civilian Product	22,400	2,200	6,220	9,210	40,050	22,550
13. Gross Domestic Savings	500	350	-10	1,880	6,670	1,920
Performance Indicators						
14. GNP Growth Rate, %	3.2	4.0	4.5	2.3	4.4	4.0
15. GNP per capita, $	6,380	1,470	2,250	2,690	780	2,370
16. GNP per Employed Person, $	18,940	7,590	12,100	11,320	2,700	9,080
17. Defense Expenditure per capita, $	1,660	-.-	380	50	80	430
18. Private Consumption per capita, $	3,980	1,100	1,530	1,930	510	1,560

Table 19.11
Comparative Economic Indicators in the Peaceful Cooperation Scenario - 1992

	Israel	WBG	Jordan	Lebanon	Egypt	Syria
Population Data						
1. Population (millions)	4.95	1.7	3.33	3.84	58.09	12.0
2. Population Growth, %	2.1	3.5	3.0	2.5	2.7	2.9
3. Employment (thousands)	1,700	310	620	1,060	17,200	3,150
Gross National Product and its Distribution, $ Millions						
4. Gross National Product	38,700	2,650	8,500	13,500	52,500	33,300
5. Private Consumption	22,400	1,850	5,610	9,720	32,460	21,310
6. Defense Expenditure	4,200	250	1,360	810	4,800	2,670
7. Civilian Government Expenditure	5,000	-.-	680	270	2,630	2,670
8. Investment	11,600	650	2,580	4,050	15,750	9,980
9. Total Resources	43,200	2,750	10,230	14,850	55,640	36,630
10. Import Surplus	4,500	100	1,730	1,350	3,140	3,340
11. Exports	18,000	850	4,000	7,000	14,850	6,000
12. Gross Civilian Product	33,700	500	7,820	13,230	49,870	30,630
13. Gross Domestic Savings	7,100	2,650	850	2,700	12,610	6,650
Performance Indicators						
14. GNP Growth Rate, %	5.8	6.0	6.0	6.0	6.1	6.0
15. GNP per capita, $	7,820	1,560	2,550	3,520	910	2,780
16. GNP per Employed Person, $	22,760	8,550	13,700	12,740	3,050	10,570
17. Defense Expenditure per capita, $	1,010	-.-	200	70	45	220
18. Private Consumption per capita, $	4,530	1,090	1,680	2,530	560	1,780

Table 19.12
Working papers and reports on which the study is based, *by author

1. Water - Elisha Kally
2. Agriculture - Elisha Kally
3. Energy - Elisha Kally, Abraham Tal
4. Transportation - Simcha Bahiri, Hilary Wolpert Silver, and Abraham Tal
5. Fertilizers - Simcha Bahiri
6. Cement - Simcha Bahiri
7. Textiles - Alfred Tovias and Hilary Wolpert
8. Tourism - Simcha Bahiri, Shelly Hecht
9. Trade - Yoel Raban
10. Peace Scenarios - Haim Ben Shahar, Simcha Bahiri

*Some are available as separate manuscripts from the Interdisciplinary Center for Technological Analysis and Forecasting.

Index

Agriculture
  and Mideast regional planning, 9, 58, 60,
    69, 71–72, 99, 176, 249–50, 340–41, 352–
    53(table)
  salt water, 329–30
  science and, 250
  and water, 6–7, 305, 330
Andean Group, 187, 192–95, 199, 207(nn
  7, 13)
Aqaba-Eilat canal/port project, 327–31
Arab countries
  economy, 5, 6(table)
  science and technology in, 244–51
  and tourism, 286–87, 287(Table 15.4), 288,
    296
  See also Arab League; Investment,
    economic cooperation; Middle East
Arab Israelis, 70–71, 90, 92
Arab League, 129, 130, 131–32
Arava, 268, 330
Argentina, 223, 229(fig.)
Armand Hammer Fund for Economic
  Cooperation in the Middle East, vii, 2,
  267, 268, 269–70, 348
Arms control, 103, 108–10, 111, 118(fig.),
  119(n7), 120(n12)
  future of, 105, 114–19
  and the superpowers, 105, 109, 110, 112,
    113, 116
Arms race, 15, 24, 34–35(table), 103, 105,
  106–8, 110–12, 114–15, 120(n10)
  economic burden of, 13, 16, 21(Table 1.5),
    25–26, 31, 53, 168–69
  See also Arms control; Defense

Balance of payments, 25, 39, 89, 201, 203
  oil effects on, 47–50, 198
  See also Trade
Bevan, Aneurin, 164–65
Brazil, 223, 228(fig.)

Camp David agreement, 3, 110, 111
  Arab League and, 130, 132
  an expanded, 115, 116, 119
Canada, 129, 132
Caribbean Community (CARICOM), 187
Cement, 355–60
Center for Strategic and International
  Studies (CSIS), 163, 170
Central American Common Market

(CACM), 187
Chile, 199, 207(nn 7, 13)
China, 214
Clothing industry, 10, 274, 276, 277–78,
  279, 360–61. See also Textiles
Communication, 11, 162, 253, 355
Construction industry
  and Arab employment, 62, 67, 70, 73, 74,
    75, 76(n10), 78(n24)
  and Egyptian-Israeli cooperation, 360
Coptics, 295–96

Debt
  Latin American foreign, 201–2, 203–5
  Mideast foreign, 161, 168–69, 175
  See also Foreign aid
Defense
  expenditures, 5, 13, 17–19, 20, 21–24,
    27(App. 1), 28(app.), 32, 39, 40–43, 44,
    47, 50–53, 85, 86(fig.), 87(table), 111
  Israeli objectives, 81, 83, 84, 85–87, 105,
    111, 112, 336
  See also Arms race

Economic cooperation
  in Latin America, 161–62, 181–82, 187–207
  and Mideast arms control, 116–19
  Mideast projects, 6–12, 250–51, 267–68,
    274–75, 276–80, 329, 335, 336–45, 349–
    62, 365(table). See also Water,
    Mideast regional management of
  prospects for, 4–6, 12, 96–100, 162, 234,
    235, 253, 280–82, 347
  risks of, 103–4, 141–42, 157–59, 280
  and technological investment, 209–10, 234,
    238
  theories on, 182–87, 200, 206–7, 271, 348–
    49
  See also Investment; Middle East Peace
    Development Fund; Protectionism
Economic growth
  and the arms race, 22–26
  labor and, 17, 59
  Mideast and, 6(table), 24(table), 362
  in occupied territories, 92
  Southern Lebanon and, 337, 341
  See also Economic cooperation
Economics
  and Mideast relations, 3–5, 12, 96–101,
    338, 347–48. See also Peace

and world peace, 167–68
See also Economic cooperation, theories on; Factor migration; Trade
Economic sanctions
  as foreign policy, 103, 123–26, 132–33, 139–40
  future use in Mideast, 133–40
  past use in Mideast, 126–33, 128(table), 140(n2)
Edmond de Rothschild Foundation, 169, 170
Education, 69, 96, 245, 246
Egypt
  and arms race, 107, 110, 112
  defense, 23, 24, 40–43, 54(n7), 86(fig.), 87(table), 112
  economy, 12, 16, 24, 40, 41–42(table), 133, 168, 232(fig.)
  and Gaza Strip, 79, 80, 84, 85, 87–88, 90
  and Israeli cooperative projects, 8, 9, 10, 276–80, 350–51, 352(table), 354(table), 355–61, 359(Table 19.8)
  and regional water management, 7, 304–7, 324
  and scientific research, 245–46
  and tourism, 283–301. See also Tourism
  trade, 361
  and the United States, 111, 127, 139. See also United States, and Egypt
  See also Middle East
Egyptian-Israeli peace treaty, 109, 110, 139, 163, 269, 283, 296
Egyptian Sinai project, 7, 305, 307, 311(map)
Emigration, 58. See also Labor, mobility
Employment
  and Aqaba-Eilat canal/port project, 330
  in Israel, Gaza Strip, and West Bank, 13–14, 56–59, 57(tables), 60–71, 71–73
  in Latin America, 203
  oil revenues and, 178
  skilled versus unskilled, 69–71, 74
  in Southern Lebanon, 336, 337, 341
  See also Labor
Energy, 7–9, 250, 329, 351
EUREKA, 241–42
European Economic Community, 1, 73, 181
  agreements with, 10, 278
  MBDF and, 342
  trade and, 208(n14), 264
  use of economic sanctions by, 137–38, 140(n9)
Exchange rates, 19–20, 26(nn 8, 9, 10), 40, 44

in Latin America, 190, 191, 192, 193, 194, 198, 200, 203, 205
Exports
  agricultural, 341
  labor, 18, 32, 40, 44–47. See also Labor, mobility
  manufacturing, 212(table), 214(table), 215, 219(table), 276, 341
  oil, 22–23, 40, 43. See also Oil
  See also Economic sanctions; Trade

Factor migration
  and economic cooperation, 142, 146–59
  for services, 260–62
Fertilizer industry, 9–10, 276, 277, 278–79, 355, 358(table), 359(Table 19.7)
Financial services, 205–6
Food, 248–49
Foreign aid, 29(app.)
  economic, 39, 40, 43, 44, 133–37
  and Mideast arms race, 15, 20, 23–26, 26(n11), 32, 38, 47, 50, 106, 108, 110
  and Mideast economic development, 161, 165–66, 168–69, 268
Foreign policy, 124–25. See also Economic sanctions
France, 127, 138, 223, 226(fig.)
Free Trade Area agreement, 10, 139, 341

Gafny, Arnon, 11, 163
Gaza Strip, 55
  economy, 94–96, 98–100
  employment, 60–71, 71–73, 76(nn 8, 10). See also Employment, in Israel, Gaza Strip, and West Bank; Wages
  future of, 98, 105, 111, 115, 116, 117–19
  labor force, 56–57, 57(tables), 58–59, 63(fig.), 65(fig.), 71–73, 90–95. See also Labor
  occupation of, 79, 80, 84–85, 88–90
  and travel to Egypt, 285–86, 287(Table 15.3)
  and water, 6, 7, 99, 303, 304, 307, 321–24, 350, 350(table)
  See also Egypt, and Gaza Strip
General Agreement on Tariffs and Trade (GATT), 189, 213, 254, 255, 259, 260–62
Germany, 213, 223, 227(fig.)
Ghor Valley
  canal, 307, 315, 316
  and water, 7, 307, 316
Global Infrastructure Fund (GIF), 243
Golan Heights, 84, 112, 116
Gulf Cooperation Council (GCC), 137

Hammer, Armand, 3
Hassan, Crown Prince, 245, 248, 249
Health, 95
Heckscher-Ohlin economic model, 142,
  146, 148, 149, 156
Hydroelectricity, 8, 317–20, 351

Immigration, 58, 70. See also Labor,
  mobility
Imports, 114
  food, 248
  labor, 32. See also Labor, mobility
  military, 17–18, 20, 31, 32, 34–35(Table
    2.2), 40, 43, 43–44, 47, 50. See also
    Arms race
  oil, 47–50. See also Oil
  See also Economic sanctions; Trade
Import substitution, 272
Industry
  changes in world, 210–234
  in Latin America, 188–89, 190–91, 192–95,
    199
  in Mideast, 58, 94–95, 95(table), 98–99,
    162, 176, 184–87, 223–34, 275–80. See
    also Clothing industry; Construction in-
    dustry
  and research, 238–40, 242
Infrastructure, 213, 243–44
  in Mideast, 11, 88, 95, 176, 246, 250, 324,
    325, 350, 355
International Centre for Desert Research
  (ICDR), 250
International Council of Scientific Unions
  (ICSU), 243
International Federation of Institutes for
  Advanced Study (IFIAS), 239–40, 242–
  43
International Monetary Fund (IMF), 117
Investment, 114
  and economic cooperation, 38, 40, 47, 142,
    161, 191, 192, 199, 274, 275, 278, 307,
    310, 312, 322, 337. See also Factor
    migration
  an international corporation for, 171, 172,
    177–78
  in occupied territories, 99
  potentials for, 6, 117, 240
  and risk insurance, 176–77, 342
  in technology, 209
  and trade in services, 260
  See also Middle East Peace Development
    Fund
Iran, 106, 343
Iraq, 106, 129, 136, 137, 329. See also

Middle East
Israel, 55
  and arms race, 86(fig.), 87(table), 107, 109,
    110–11, 116, 117–19
  economy, 5, 12, 16, 22, 24, 47–50, 51–
    52(table), 59, 133, 169, 361
  and Egyptian cooperative projects, 9, 10,
    276–80, 350–51, 355–61, 352–53(table),
    354(table), 359(Table 19.8)
  employment, 59–71, 77(n12). See also
    Employment, in Israel, Gaza Strip, and
    West Bank; Wages
  industry, 223, 231(fig.), 276–80
  labor force, 16–17, 56, 57(tables), 58, 74–
    75, 77(n17), 90–94
  as occupier, 79, 80, 83–90, 97–100. See
    also Gaza Strip; West Bank
  and regional water management, 7, 304,
    305, 307, 310–25, 328, 330, 350
  and Southern Lebanon, 336–37, 338, 341,
    344–45
  and tourism, 283–301. See also Tourism
  and the United States, 139. See also
    United States, and Israel
  See also Defense, Israeli objectives; Is-
    raeli-Arab conflict; Middle East
Israeli-Arab conflict
  economics and, 4, 16, 31, 362, 363(table)
  political elements, 269–70. See also
    Politics
  and water, 303, 321, 325, 327
  See also Arms race; Defense

Japan
  industry and, 223, 226(fig.)
  research and, 239, 242–43
  trade and, 213, 214
Jerusalem, 62, 76(n9), 79, 295–96
Joint Economic Middle East Peace Commission, 171–72
Jordan
  and arms race, 23, 24, 47, 86(fig.),
    87(table), 107, 111, 112
  economy, 16, 24, 44–47, 48–49(table), 133–
    36, 233(fig.), 361
  foreign aid to, 29(app.)
  labor force, 16–17
  scientific research in, 245
  water and, 6, 7, 307–17, 324, 328–30
  and West Bank, 79, 80, 83–84, 85, 87–88,
    89–90
  See also Middle East; United States, and
    Jordan

Kennen, George, 164
Keynes, John Maynard, 167–68
King, Alexander, 237

Labor
availability of, 5, 13, 16–17, 32–38, 56–59,
95(table), 268, 278, 340, 341, 360
industrial, 94–95
mobility, 18, 32, 40, 44–47, 55–56, 60–62,
67, 71–75, 89, 90–94, 117, 142, 195, 262.
See also Factor migration
scientific, 246
Latin America, 161–62, 187–207, 208(n14)
Latin American Free Trade Area
(LAFTA), 181, 187, 188–91, 207(nn 4,
5)
Latin American Integration Association
(LAIA), 187, 195–96, 207(n11)
Lebanon
and Israeli economic cooperation, 335–45
Maronites, 344
scientific research in, 246
trade and, 361
war in, 106, 178, 295
and water, 317–20, 324
See also Middle East
Libya
and arms, 106
and economic sanctions, 129, 138–39
See also Middle East
Litani River, 6, 7, 8, 317–20, 320(table),
321, 324, 351

Marshall, George C., 164, 166, 168
Marshall Plan, 164–65, 168
Marshall Plan for the Middle East. See
Middle East Peace Development Fund
Mexico, 223, 229(fig.)
Middle East, xii
arms and, 13, 15–26, 31–39, 50–53, 105–19
economic development, 5–11, 141, 159.
See also Economic cooperation,
Mideast projects; Infrastructure; Investment; Middle East Peace Development Fund
economy, 17(table), 19(Table 1.3),
27(App. 2), 33(table), 134(table), 249,
270, 335–37, 361–62, 363(table),
364(table). See also Agriculture;
Economic growth; Foreign aid; Trade;
Tourism
industry, 58, 94–95, 95(table), 98, 99, 162,
176, 184–87, 223–34, 275–80. See also
Industry

See also Economic sanctions; Politics
Middle East Peace Development Fund
(MEPDF), 11–12, 97, 117, 161, 163,
165–66, 167–79
Mubarak, Hosni, 12
Multinational Business Development
Fund (MBDF), 335, 337–45

Nasser, Gamal Abdel, 127, 132
Natural gas, 8, 351, 354(table)
Negev, 7, 249–50, 305, 307, 315
Nile River, 6, 7, 303, 304–7, 309(tables),
315, 321, 324
Nuclear weapons, 109, 110, 115, 120(n9)

Occupied territories. See Gaza Strip;
West Bank
Occupier-occupied relationship, 81–85
economics and, 14, 79–81, 85–88, 94–96,
97–101
and employment in Israel, 59–71, 90–94
and trade, 88–94
Oil
exporters, 33(table), 40, 43, 74, 129
importers, 47–50
and Iraqi pipeline, 329
and Latin America, 198–99, 207(n12)
and military spending, 13, 22–23, 31, 44,
50–53, 114
1973 embargo, 131–32
prices, 12, 22, 38, 50, 131
regional effects, 4, 7, 38–39, 112, 117, 129,
137, 178, 336
See also TAPLINE
OPEC, 31, 136
Organization for Economic Cooperation
and Development (OECD), 237–38

Palestine, 55, 79
Palestinians
and arms race, 107, 108, 111, 116
PLO, 336, 343, 344
role in Mideast of, 106, 112, 115, 324
Peace
and economic cooperation, 1, 5–6,
6(table), 12, 31, 96–101, 167–72, 176,
178, 270–73, 274–75, 280–81, 345, 348,
349, 360, 362, 364(table)
and economic sanctions, 137–38
planning for, 2–3, 267–68, 269–70, 282
and water management, 303, 304, 325, 327,
328, 329
See also Politics
Peres, Shimon, 11, 97, 163

PLO. See Palestinians
Political unrest
  occupied territories and, 92, 115
  recession and, 53, 117
  and religious extremism, 115, 163
  See also Terrorism
Politics
  and Arab-Israeli peace process, 4–5, 269–72, 274–75, 280–82
  and Israeli-Egyptian tourism, 295–96
  and Mideast water cooperation, 305, 310, 314(table), 321, 324–25
  relation to economics of, 347–48. See also Economics
  See also Economic sanctions; Israel-Arab conflict; Occupier-occupied relationship; Peace
Pollution, 329, 330, 351
Population
  Egyptian, 117
  and food production, 248–49
  growth and infrastructure, 213
  in Israel and occupied territories, 57(tables)
  See also Labor
Protectionism, 73, 100, 213
  and economic integration, 184–87, 194, 199, 201, 206, 208(n14)
  and free trade, 142, 146–49, 156, 158
  by occupiers, 89
  in services, 254–55, 259–60, 261, 263, 265
  See also Regulation

Qaddafi, Muammar, 138–39

Regulation, 258, 262–64, 275. See also Protectionism
Religious extremism. See Political unrest
Republic of Korea, 223, 228(fig.)
Rockefeller, David, 3, 12

Sadat, Anwar, 2, 3, 12, 294
Saudi Arabia
  and arms, 106
  economy, 36–37(table), 39, 233(fig.)
  regional economic influence of, 133, 136–37
  university research in, 244–45
  See also Middle East
Science, 237–48, 249–51. See also Technology
Sea of Galilee, 7, 310, 312, 315, 316–17, 320, 321, 324
Services

definition of, 255–58
  and developed countries, 211, 213
  and economic cooperation, 162, 253
  and trade, 254–255, 259–65, 265(n11)
Shiites, 343, 344–45
Simon, William, 3
Sinai, 84, 89, 110, 130
Sinai II accord, 130–31
Six Days War, 58–59
Social values, 247–48
Southeast Asia, 214
Soviet Union
  economy, 53, 223, 230(fig.)
  influence in Mideast of, 106, 112, 114, 136
  and Mideast arms race, 107–8, 113, 114. See also Arms control
  and Syria, 43, 108, 110, 111, 136
Standard of living, 95–96, 114, 117
Strategic Defense Initiative (SDI), 238, 239, 241
Suez Canal, 40, 127, 130, 330
Syria
  and arms race, 23, 24, 44, 107, 110, 112
  economy, 16, 24, 43–44, 45–46(table), 232(fig.)
  foreign aid to, 29(app.)
  and Saudi Arabia, 137
  on Shiite-Israeli cooperation, 344
  and Soviets, 111, 136. See also Soviet Union
  See also Middle East

Taba, 4
TAPLINE, 8–9, 351
Technology
  and culture, 247–48
  and economic development, 209–10, 234–35, 238
  global development of, 241–44
  and industrial change, 211, 213, 214, 215. See also Universities
  institutionalization of, 237–38
  Mideast regional cooperation in, 249–51, 341
  regional differences in, 94, 98, 100, 157, 240, 244, 247, 251
  transfers, 161, 162, 184–85, 240, 328
  See also Science
Tel Aviv University, 2, 6
Terrorism, 163
  and economic sanctions, 129, 137, 138–39
  effects on tourism, 301(n15)
  and Israeli-Palestinian relations, 111
  in Southern Lebanon, 336, 337, 344

Textiles, 10, 40, 274, 276, 277, 279, 341,
    360–61
Tourism
    Aqaba-Eilat and, 329, 330
    Egyptian-Israeli, 267, 283–301, 301(n15)
    in Mideast, 11, 38, 40, 47, 355, 360
Trade, 207(n6)
    international, 135(Table 6.3), 141–45,
        145(fig.), 156, 156(fig.), 158–59, 212–
        15, 218(table), 219, 219(table), 223–35,
        348
    in Latin America, 187–94, 195–96,
        197(table), 199–203, 205–6
    Mideast inter-country, 268, 270–75, 279–
        80, 281, 282(n3), 353–53(table), 355,
        361, 362(table)
    opportunities, 38, 47, 117, 330
    and regional planning, 10–11, 161, 162.
        See also Economic cooperation,
        theories on
    in services, 254–55, 259–65, 265(n11)
    and territorial occupation, 88–94, 99
    See also Economic sanctions; Factor
        migration
Transnational Corporations (TNCs), 239–
    40
Transportation
    and Aqaba-Eilat canal/port project, 330
    and economic cooperation, 11, 162, 253,
        265(n1), 355, 356–57(tables)
    Egyptian-Israeli, 284, 285(table),
        286(table), 293(table), 294(table)
Tripartite Declaration of 1950, 120(n12)
Two-Seas Project, 317, 318(map)

United Kingdom, 127, 213
United Nations
    North-South dialogue, 240
    science and technology programs, 238,
        239–40
    and Southern Lebanon, 345
    viability of, 240–41
United Nations 1947 Partition Plan, 79,
    81, 83
United States
    and economic sanctions, 123, 127–29, 130–
        31, 136, 137–39
    and Egypt, 26(n11), 40, 108, 111, 133, 166
    industry, 223, 227(fig.)

influence in Mideast of, 105, 106, 111–12,
    116–19
and Israel, 20, 50, 108, 111, 133, 166
and Jordan, 47, 133–36
and MBDF, 337, 342, 344
and Mideast arms race, 107–8, 113, 114.
    See also Arms control
research and, 238, 239, 241
trade and, 213, 254, 260–61, 262, 278, 341
Universities, 238–39, 244–47
Urbanization, 213

Vandenberg, Charles, 165, 166

Wages
    and economic integration, 195
    Jewish versus Arab, 61(table), 62, 68,
        76(n11), 90–92, 93(tables)
    See also Employment
Water
    Aqaba-Eilat canal/port project, 327–31
    Mideast regional management of, 4, 6–7,
        249–50, 267–68, 303–25, 327, 332–
        33(app.), 350, 350(table)
    in occupied territories, 99
West Bank, 55
    economy, 94–96, 98–100
    employment, 60–71, 71–73, 76(nn 8, 10).
        See also Employment, in Israel, Gaza
        Strip, and West Bank; Wages
    future of, 98, 105, 111, 112, 115, 116, 117–
        19
    labor force, 56–57, 57(tables), 58–59, 60,
        63(fig.), 65(fig.), 71–73, 90–95. See
        also Labor
    occupation and, 79, 80, 83–85, 88–90
    and travel to Egypt, 285–86, 287(Table
        15.3)
    and water, 6, 7, 99, 303, 307, 312, 316, 317,
        321–24, 350, 350(table)
    See also Jordan, and West Bank
Western Galilee and the Triangle, 79, 80,
    83
World Bank, 117, 173, 175
    IFC, 342

Yarmuk River, 303–4, 307–12, 315, 316,
    321, 324
Yemen, 127–29